BEFORE COPYRIGHT

THE FRENCH BOOK-PRIVILEGE SYSTEM
1498–1526

CAMBRIDGE STUDIES IN
PUBLISHING AND PRINTING HISTORY

BEFORE COPYRIGHT

THE FRENCH BOOK-PRIVILEGE SYSTEM
1498–1526

ELIZABETH ARMSTRONG

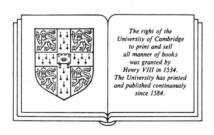

The right of the
University of Cambridge
to print and sell
all manner of books
was granted by
Henry VIII in 1534.
The University has printed
and published continuously
since 1584.

CAMBRIDGE UNIVERSITY PRESS

CAMBRIDGE

NEW YORK   PORT CHESTER

MELBOURNE   SYDNEY

Published by the Press Syndicate of the University of Cambridge
The Pitt Building, Trumpington Street, Cambridge CB1 1RP
40 West 20th Street, New York, NY 10011, USA
10 Stamford Road, Oakleigh, Melbourne 3166, Australia

First published 1990

Printed in Great Britain
at the University Press, Cambridge

British Library cataloguing in publication data
Armstrong, Elizabeth
Before copyright: the French book-privilege system
1498–1526. – (Cambridge studies in publishing and
printing history)
1. France. Publishing history
1. Title
070.5'0944

Library of Congress cataloguing in publication data
Armstrong, Elizabeth.
Before copyright: the French book-privilege system
1498–1526/Elizabeth Armstrong.
p.   cm.
Bibliography.
Includes index.
ISBN 0 521 37408 1
1. Book industries and trade – Law and legislation – France – History.
2. Printing industry – Law and legislation – France – History.
3. France – Charters, grants, privileges – History.
4. Book industries and trade – France – History – 16th century.
5. Printing – France – History – 16th century.
6. Bibliography – Early printed books – 16th century.
7. Incunabula – France – Bibliography.
1. Title.
KJV5973.A87 1990
070.5'0944 – dc19   89–7226   CIP

ISBN 0 521 37408 1

To John

CONTENTS

CONTENTS

ILLUSTRATIONS

Nos. 2, 5, 8 and 9 are photographed and reproduced by permission of the Bodleian Library, Nos. 3, 4 and 7 by permission of the British Library. No. 6 is made from a copy in the possession of the author.

PREFACE

My interest in sixteenth-century book-privileges, especially in France, goes back more than thirty years. Every instance that I met in my reading of French sixteenth-century literature, and in bibliographies and catalogues where they were mentioned, was noted. When the privileges in my files began to run into thousands, the question arose, what sort of book could result? The choice lay between a study of the subject throughout the century, which would be relatively superficial and leave many questions unanswered, and a more limited work, in which one reign or one period of years within the century would be thoroughly covered. The latter seemed to be more useful. And the first quarter of the century was the obvious choice. It was the crucial formative period in the development of book-privileges in France. It was the period when the system developed under the economic pressures which authors and publishers were experiencing, not under government legislation. It corresponded to a span of years of comparative peace and stability, ending with the defeat of Francis I at Pavia. And for the practical point of view it offered the possibility of something like completeness of treatment: the number of books being printed in France was large but not wholly unmanageable, whereas from 1530 onwards it increased enormously.

The sources used are listed in the Select bibliography, but a note on the method followed in tracing privileges may be of interest. For Paris-printed books, I worked through all the volumes of Philippe Renouard's *Imprimeurs parisiens*, the manuscripts of which are deposited in the Bibliothèque Nationale. This work contains a fully bibliographical description of every edition printed in Paris in the sixteenth century known to Renouard, including the mention of a privilege when there was one, though with no details of it. Only the sections on Josse Badius Ascensius and on Simon de Colines were published by the author. The Bibliothèque Nationale began to publish it in 1964, revising and adding to it where necessary, but the four volumes which have so far appeared have not progressed beyond the printer Blumenstock, with fascicules on Breyer, Brumen and Cavellat. This revision has added few editions not recorded by Renouard, but has provided some useful particulars. Brigitte Moreau's *Inventaire chronologique des éditions parisiennes du xvi͏ᵉ siècle*, of which the first volume, covering 1501 to 1510, came out in 1972, is now complete up to 1530. This constitutes a year-by-year survey of all Paris editions of which a copy or a record survives; it mentions the privilege when there is no other evidence for dating, and gives locations, which is invaluable for tracing the rarest books. For Lyon, I have used Baudrier's *Bibliographie lyonnaise*, which, with all its gaps and short-comings, gives details of, and even some complete texts of, privileges, and I have used also material available in the Bibliothèque Municipale at Lyon. For other places the *Répertoire biblio-graphique* of sixteenth-century French provincial printing has filled some gaps, and the better histories of printing in particular towns, such as La Bouralière on Poitiers, have been of great value. These authorities, and of course the registers of the Parlement of Paris, which are virtually the only surviving archival source, have made it possible to identify the books which obtained privileges in this period. I have made it my aim to examine at least one copy of every such extant book, to take all particulars, and to transcribe the privilege or summary of the privilege if printed in it. I have also examined a very large number of books on the off-chance that they might prove to contain a privilege.

A few books published 'Cum priuilegio' may have been missed, but it is probable that the present work takes into account something like 90 per cent of all surviving privileged books, and almost all the privileges of importance. The conclusions I have drawn are thus based not on random samples, but on a nearly complete survey. I hope the result will be of service to other scholars working on the sixteenth century.

ACKNOWLEDGEMENTS

In 1965 the Curators of the Bodleian Library awarded me the Gordon Duff Prize for an essay on 'Printers' and authors' privileges in France and the Low Countries in the sixteenth century'. This was a great encouragement to continue research in this field. I have also to thank the Board of the Faculty of Modern and Medieval Languages of Oxford University and Somerville College, Oxford, for several terms of sabbatical leave to pursue this work, and Somerville, in addition, for a research grant made to me in the term after my retirement.

I am glad to acknowledge the unfailing kindness of the archivists and staff of the Archives Nationales, Paris, over a number of years. I am grateful also to the authorities of the Archives Départementales of the Haute Garonne, Toulouse, and of the Gironde, Bordeaux, for giving me access to their records, though I was unsuccessful there in finding the originals of book-privileges granted by their respective Parlements. As most of my sources have proved to be in printed books, I have to thank particularly the librarians and staff of the Bodleian Library, the Cambridge University Library, the British Library; in Paris the Bibliothèque Nationale, the Mazarine Library, the Arsenal, Sainte-Geneviève, and the Faculté de Médecine; and in Poitiers the Bibliothèque Municipale. At the Bibliothèque Municipale of Lyon I received much assistance from Monsieur Henri-Jean Martin and from his successor Monsieur Guy Parguez, at Bordeaux from Monsieur Pierre Botineau, at Toulouse from Monsieur Christian Peligry, and at Niort from Monsieur Eric Surget.

Librarians who have courteously answered queries by post and sent xeroxes when required are Miss Jean Archibald, Assistant Librarian, Special Collections, Edinburgh University Library; Monsieur Nicolas Petit, *conservateur à la Réserve*, Sainte-Geneviève; Dr Xavier Lavagne, *conservateur en chef*, Bibliothèque Méjanes, Aix; and MM. and Mesdames Elizabeth Chopin, *Directeur*, Bibliothèque Municipale, Chaumont; François de Forbin, *conservateur des Fonds anciens*, Avignon; Valérie Neveu, *conservateur-adjoint*, Rouen; J. Pons, *conservateur en chef*, Albi; G. Tournouer, *conservateur en chef*, Lille, and Andrée Wuertz, *bibliothécaire-adjointe*, Troyes.

Dr Roger Highfield kindly allowed me to examine a book in the library of Merton College, Oxford, and Dr Miriam Griffin and Dr Elspeth Kennedy generously answered queries.

I am greatly indebted to Madame Jeanne Veyrin-Forrer, for putting at my disposal the precious manuscripts of Philippe Renouard in the Réserve of the Bibliothèque Nationale and her expert knowledge of sixteenth-century printers, and to Mademoiselle Brigitte Moreau, who by her published work and by her untiring helpfulness in finding answers to all my questions has provided essential elements in the present publication.

NOTE ON TRANSCRIPTION

In transcribing the original sources, including the titles of books, I have resolved all contractions and abbreviations. In dealing with sixteenth-century French, I have followed the practice of French scholars in transcribing historical and literary texts, as follows:

1   I and J, V and U, are distinguished in the modern way.
2   Cedilla and apostrophe are supplied.
3   Grave accents are supplied on après, près, dès, ès, où (meaning 'where'), çà, là and jà, and à (meaning 'at' or 'to').
4   Acute accents are supplied on the final syllable, for example in the past participle of first-conjugation verbs.
5   Capitals are supplied as modern usage requires them, e.g. all place-names, and surnames (family names) as well as Christian names (forenames).
6   Original punctuation is kept unless positively misleading.

The original spelling has been retained in all other respects, and words and letters omitted by mistake in the original have been supplied within the signs ⟨ ⟩.

NOTE ON PROPER NAMES

Any author who wrote in Latin in the sixteenth century might have at least three forms of his surname: the vernacular (itself often known in a variety of spellings and even of forms), a Latin one (formed either by adding a Latin termination or by translating the name into Latin), and a vernacular adaptation of the Latin. The authors of catalogues, being obliged to opt for one form, have in recent years chosen to standardise on the vernacular, and where this varies, on one particular form of it. I have tried to provide the vernacular form (when it is known) and the Latin form. But in the last resort I have chosen the name by which the author is best known to most readers.

SIGLA AND ABBREVIATIONS

CODE-NUMBERS OF PRIVILEGES IN REGISTER

CH	Royal chancery
PA	Parlements
PR	Prévôt of Paris and other royal officers
CP	Books printed 'Cum priuilegio'

ARCHIVES AND LIBRARIES

AN	Archives Nationales, Paris
Arsenal	Bibliothèque de l'Arsenal, Paris
BL	British Library (formerly British Museum), London
BM	Bibliothèque Municipale (of various French towns)
BN	Bibliothèque Nationale, Paris
Bodl.	Bodleian Library, Oxford
Cambridge UL	Cambridge University Library
Maz.	Bibliothèque Mazarine, Paris
Ste Geneviève	Bibliothèque Sainte Geneviève, Paris

PUBLICATIONS

GKW	Gesamtkatalog der Wiegendrücke
SATF	Société des Anciens Textes Français
SHF	Société de l'Histoire de France
STFM	Société des Textes Français Modernes
TLF	Textes Littéraires Français

OTHER

E.R.P.	Extrait des registres de Parlement
L.P.	Letters Patent
col.	colophon
comm.	commentary by
ed.	edited by

f.	folio (leaf)
n.s.	new style. Year beginning 1 January. (Used throughout this book.)
o.s.	old style. Year beginning at Easter, the French legal year-reckoning at this period. (Used in this book only when some ambiguity is to be avoided.)
pr.	printed by
s.d.	without date
s.l.	without place
tr.	translated by

1 · ORIGINS AND DEVELOPMENT OF BOOK-PRIVILEGES IN EUROPE

THE CONCEPT OF COPYRIGHT was unknown in the manuscript era, and was slow to develop even when printing with movable type had revolutionised the rate at which copies of a book could be produced. Once a book was published, it passed into the public domain. To seek to protect it, even for a short time, from unrestricted reprinting was to ask for an exception to be made in its favour. However, one concept was quite familiar and was to prove useful to authors and publishers asking for such protection. This was the right of a ruler to grant a 'privilege' or commercial monopoly, whether permanently or for a fixed period of time, within his jurisdiction, to the inventor or initiator of a new process, a new product or a new source of supply (such as mines) capable of exploitation for profit. This right can still be exercised by governments at the present day, and, in the guise of 'patents', such monopolies benefit the originators of articles as diverse as machines and medicines, the justification being to secure a fair return on the enterprise, ingenuity and financial outlay expended to perfect the article and put it on the market. The privileges to be studied in the present work were monopolies only in the most limited sense: they conferred on an author or publisher the exclusive rights in a new book or books for a very restricted period. But the monopoly concept had played a part in the evolution which led to the grant of book-privileges.[1]

It might be thought that the invention of printing was itself a technological feat worthy to be thus patented. In fact the Gutenberg-Fust partnership responsible for it made no such approach to the authorities. The partners evidently relied on keeping the exact process secret at least for long enough to get a useful start from possible competitors. Events proved this secrecy to be short-lived. But the firm, continued by Fust's son-in-law Peter Schoeffer and his sons, kept a leading position far into the sixteenth century. And Johann Schoeffer of Mainz, an eminent printer and type-cutter, in seeking a privilege in 1518 from the Emperor Maximilian I, made the plea (among others) that his grandfather was the inventor of printing. The Emperor, after checking this claim, granted the privilege. It was one of his last acts, and a fitting one, for he had been keenly interested in book-production both manuscript and

---

[1] For the Empire, this has been expertly studied by F. Lehne, 'Zur Rechtsgeschichte der kaiserlichen Druckprivilegien: ihre Bedeutung für die Geschichte des Urheberrechtes', *Mitteilungen des Österreichischen Instituts für Geschichtsforschung*, LIII (1939), pp. 323–409.

printed.[1] Innovations in type-design might also qualify for a privilege: Aldus Manutius obtained a privilege for his types from the Venetian government and from the Pope in 1502.[2]

A man who had no claim to have invented printing or even a new style of print might none the less be the first person to introduce printing to a country or city where it had hitherto not been practised. The first printer thus to appear on the scene sometimes secured from the authorities there the exclusive right to print in that place. A privilege of this kind was successfully sought by Johann de Spira in September 1469 from the government of Venice, threatening anyone else who tried to start a press there with fines and with the confiscation of his tools and his books. Printing had been brought in 1465 to the abbey of Subiaco, and transferred in 1467 to Rome, but it was still a relative novelty in Italy, and it is understandable that Venice grasped the opportunity of securing the services of a printer, who was well qualified and prepared to settle in the city. Even so, the councillors must have breathed a sigh of relief that Johann de Spira died very shortly after obtaining the privilege, for it soon became apparent that printers were coming to Venice in dozens, ideally placed as it was for trade, and it was indeed by the sixteenth century one of the greatest printing and publishing centres in Europe.[3] Between 1470 and 1480 the names of at least fifty printers practising in Venice are known. On the other hand in Spain the Catholic Kings granted a privilege (Seville, 25 December 1477) to Teodorico Aleman, probably Thierry Martens, *impresor de libros de molde* (printer) and bookseller, with many favours and exemptions for his trade, for the city and province of Murcia; this was evidently intended to encourage the supply of books and may have done so, but there is no evidence that any books were actually *printed* there as a result.[4]

GERMANY AND ITALY

But at an early stage it was realised also that a particular book might qualify for a privilege, at the request of author, publisher or printer. The earliest form

[1] *T. Livius Patauinus duobus libris auctus*, Mainz, 1518, fol. Bodl. Auct. L.1.10. Text of the Letters Patent printed on the verso of the title-page, dated Wels (in the Tyrol), 9 December 1518. The emperor died in January 1519. He had consulted reliable witnesses about the claim ('docti et moniti sumus fide dignorum testimonio'). For earlier grants by Maximilian for printed books, see below, pp. 14–15.

[2] Martin Lowry, *The world of Aldus Manutius* (Oxford, 1979), pp. 154–8. There is some discussion of privileges, chiefly in Italy, in Rudolph Hirsch, *Printing, selling and reading 1450–1550* (Wiesbaden, 1967), pp. 78–87.

[3] Rinaldo Fulin, 'Documenti per servire alla storia della tipografia veneziana', *Archivio Veneto*, XXIII (1882), pp. 86–8, and, for the text of Johann de Spira's grant, from the Notatorio del Collegio, Documenti, I, ibid., p. 99. See H. F. Brown, *The Venetian printing press 1469–1600* (London, 1891), and L. V. Gerulaitis, *Printing and publishing in fifteenth century Venice* (Chicago/London, 1976), p. 35.

[4] K. Haebler, *Early printers of Spain and Portugal* (London, Bibliographical Society, 1897), pp. 10–11.

of such a privilege dates from 1479. In that year Stephan Dold, Georg Reyser and Johann Beckenhub agreed with Rudolf von Scherenberg, bishop of Würzburg, to print for him the breviary of his diocese. This edition, when it appeared, bore the full text of a document dated Würzburg, 20 September 1479, by which the exclusive right to print the Würzburg breviary was conferred on these three printers with the authority of the bishop, dean and chapter.[1] This was a valuable monopoly, since the edition of the breviary thus authorised by their bishop would be required by all the clergy of his large diocese. The neighbouring diocese of Regensburg (Ratisbon) followed suit within a year. The bishop, Heinrich von Abendsberg, had 400 copies of the diocesan breviary printed at Würzburg, to be sold at three Rhenish guilders, and granted to the printers, by a privilege dated 13 June 1480, exclusive rights in the breviary within his diocese.[2] In each case, protection from competition, which might otherwise have been expected from the great printing centres, ensured a reasonable return for the outlay involved in printing these large and handsome books. In the sixteenth century too such episcopal privileges appear occasionally in Germany: thus the bishop of Strasbourg in 1511 granted a privilege for three years 'sub censuris ecclesiasticis' for an edition of the breviary which he had commissioned.[3]

In 1481, a six-year privilege was granted for a particular book by the duke of Milan. The book was the *Sforziad* of Johannes Simonetta, and the beneficiaries were the publishers, Antonius Zarottus and his partners. The work celebrated the Sforza family, and the duke recognised that the printing of it had been undertaken with his encouragement ('hortatu nostro'). The ducal Letters Patent accordingly forebade anyone else to print it in his dominions for six years or to import copies of it printed elsewhere, on pain of a fine of 200 ducats.[4] The size of the edition was to be 400 copies, and the period of six years requested and obtained by Zarottus was presumably the length of time he estimated it would take him to sell most of them. In 1484 the duke granted to Petro Justino da Tolentino the exclusive right to print the *Convivio* and other works of Francesco Filelfo, for five years, with a fine of 100 ducats for infringement. When it was brought to his attention that Zarottus and Simone de Magniago were printing this same work, he directed that they should not put their edition on sale until the privileged edition of Petro Justino had been sold.[5] The republic of Venice granted its first privilege for a particular book in 1486. It was a special case, being the history of the city itself, the *Rerum venetarum ab urbe condita opus* of Marcus Antonius Coccius Sabellicus. The Council, recognising its elegance and its historical accuracy,

[1] *Breuiarium herbipolense*, GKW 5356.   [2] *Breuiarium ratisponense*, GKW 5433.
[3] *Breuiarium argentinense*, Johann Pruess the Elder and his successors, Strasbourg, 1510–11, 8°. BL c.52.d.3.
[4] E. Motta, 'Di Filippo di Lavagna e di alcuni altri tipografi–editori milanesi', *Archivio Storico Lombardo*, ser. 3, x (1898), p. 67, Doc. xii (Archivio di Stato, Reg.duc.n.121, f. 57).
[5] Ibid. p. 51, Doc. i (Archivio di Stato, Missive, n. 160, f. 3).

granted the author permission to have it printed and prohibited anyone other than the printer of his choice from reprinting it in Venetian territory on pain of a fine of 500 ducats.[1] None of these Italian books, as printed, carries any indication that it was published under privilege. The privileges are known only from archival sources. The first person in Italy to hit on the idea of using the printed book itself to advertise the privilege seems to have been Bettin da Trezzo, in 1488, when his *Letilogia* was published in Milan by Zarottus. This displays a paraphrase by the author, in seventeen quatrains of Italian verse, of the Letters Patent he had obtained from the duke at Pavia on 10 March 1488, forbidding anyone to copy or sell the book within his dominions without the author's permission, on pain of a fine of 100 ducats.[2] The idea of the privilege was, however, gaining ground in the book-trade. On 22 August 1489 the publisher and printer of the *Orationes de sanctis* of Robertus Caracciolus obtained a privilege for the book from King Ferdinand of Naples, to run until they had sold out their edition of 2000 copies.[3] They none the less omitted to make any mention of the privilege in the book itself.

The next Milan privilege is of special interest because the ducal Letters Patent, preserved in the archives, incorporate verbatim the petition which had been submitted by the author, Donatus Bossius, for his *Cronaca* (16 February 1492).[4] In the petition, Bossius represented the time and labour he had expended in composing the book, and the injustice which would ensue if other people were free, as soon as it was in print, to reprint it and so rob him of the profit which he might otherwise expect. This argument was accepted by the duke, who added that the author was entitled to the fruits of his exertions in addition to the honour and glory which the publication would bring to him ('equum esse censemus ipsum preter scripti operis gloriam debitos etiam virtute sua ac annorum laboribus fructus percipere') and granted a privilege for ten years for the *Cronaca* whether in Latin or in Italian, within his dominions. We also learn from this document how closely the terms of the privilege, if granted, tended to follow those of the petition which had solicited it: much of the wording of the author's request is reproduced in the final grant, and details such as the length of time and the fine for infringement are exactly as proposed by the applicant.

Other examples of Milan privileges in the last years of the fifteenth century may be noted. The humanist Demetrio Chalcocondylas obtained privileges for scholarly works in 1493 and again in 1499.[5] Michael Fernus was granted

[1] Printed by R. Fulin, 'Primi privilegi di stampa in Venezia', *Archivio Veneto*, I (1871), p. 163 (Notatorio del Collegio 1481–89, pag. 115 t.°). The work was printed for Sabellicus by Andrea de' Torresani di Asola (Venice, 1487), fol.
[2] Motta, 'Di Filippo di Lavagna', pp. 70–2 (Doc. XIV).
[3] M. Fava and G. Bresciano, *La stampa a Napoli nel xv secolo* (Leipzig, 1911), I, no. XIX, pp. 192–3.
[4] Motta, 'Di Filippo di Lavagna', pp. 68–70 (Doc. XIII). (Archivio di Stato, Reg.duc.n.127, fol. 5 t.°.) The *Chronica bossiana* was published by Zarottus (Milan, 1492), fol. BL c.15.c.3.
[5] F. M. Valeri, *La corte di Ludovico il Moro* (Milan, 1923; Kraus reprint, 1970), IV, p. 112.

ten years for his edition of the works of Campanus, printed for him in Rome by Eucharius Silber. In this book the privilege is reproduced verbatim on the verso of the title-page.[1] The title-page was itself still something of a novelty in book-production, and this is one of the earliest examples – perhaps the earliest of all – of a practice which was to become common in the sixteenth century, and which anticipates however distantly the placing of the copyright notice in most books at the present day. Not content with printing the Letters Patent, granted at Vigevano on 26 March 1495, signed B. Chalcus, and sealed with the ducal seal on white wax, the beneficiary placed above it a warning notice headed INTERDICITUR, drawing the attention of possible interlopers to the penalties they would incur by infringing his privilege. The grounds for the grant were stated in the Letters Patent to be that Fernus had with great care and expense brought together the various works of Campanus 'from almost all over Italy', restored them to their pristine brilliance and arranged for them to be printed, but now feared lest the fruits of his labour and expenditure might be snatched by someone else ('ne ipsi fructus qui ex tanto labore atque impensa iure merito debent ab aliquo eripiantur'). The following year (1496) Joannes Vinzalius obtained a ten-year Milan privilege for a legal work, the *Consilia* of Franciscus Curtius.[2] Here only a summary of the grant is printed, at the end of the book, which takes the form of a particularly aggressive warning notice ('Ne in poenam non paruam imprudenter incurras, O Bibliopola auidissime...'). But it is stated in the book that Vinzalius had himself supplied the manuscript from which it was printed ('ex proprio exemplari') and had compiled the index, and these were probably the reasons for granting him the privilege. A privilege covering several different books was obtained a year later by Joannes Passiranus. It is printed in full in the edition of Sidonius Apollinaris, *Poema aureum* and *Epistole*, with commentary by Joannes Baptista Pius Bononiensis,[3] and in the edition of Fulgentius, *Enarrationes allegoricae fabularum* with a commentary by the same hand,[4] on the verso of the title-page, or what serves as a title-page. It was issued in Milan on 9 November 1497 under the ducal seal, and signed B. Chalcus. It was to run for five years, and constitutes a 'package' including Apicius, Nonius Marcellus, Festus Pompeius and an emended edition of Varro.

The king of France, Louis XII, when he had gained possession of Milan, began almost immediately to issue privileges as duke of Milan, following exactly the practice of his Sforza predecessor.[5] An edition of Plautus, with commentary by J. B. Pius, was published there in 1500 with a warning notice on the verso of the title-page that it was forbidden by royal letters for anyone

[1] 1495 fol. GKW 5939. BL IB 19006.
[2] Milan (U. Scinzenzeler), 1496, fol. GKW 7864. BL IC 26764.
[3] Milan (U. Scinzenzeler), 1498, fol. BL IB 26778 a.
[4] Milan (U. Scinzenzeler), 1498, fol. BL IB 26776.
[5] F. J. Norton, *Italian printers 1501–1520* (London; 1958), pp. xxvii–ix, first drew attention to these privileges.

to reprint the book, or import copies of it printed elsewhere in the duchy of Milan for five years ('Cautum est per literas regias ne quispiam audeat citra quinquennium hoc volumen imprimere aut alibi impressum in ditionem Mediolanensem importare sub poena quae in litteris publici sigilli continetur').[1] The edition of Sedulius and Prudentius by Janus Parrhasius published in 1501 provides the complete text of the Letters Patent granted to Parrhasius on 1 July 1501 for four years by the king-duke. It is clear that the editor in his petition had used the now familiar argument that an unauthorised reprint of his edition might defraud him of the fruits of his labours ('ne quis noua editione laboris eius quantuloscumque fructus interverteret...').[2] Louis XII and after him Francis I while in control of Milan continued to issue such privileges, or rather allowed them to be issued in their name by the Milanese chancery. One of the most interesting of the latter is the grant made to Andreas Calvus for his edition of Boccaccio's *Ameto* on 26 May 1520: Calvus must have argued that the existing printed editions of this text were so incorrect that 'it could hardly be believed that it was by so great an author' and that he himself had spared no trouble or expense to have it printed 'with that elegance and art with which the author left it written'.[3]

Venice began regularly granting privileges for particular books in 1492. The first, 3 January that year, went to Petrus Franciscus de Ravenna, a teacher of canon law at Padua University, who had devised a system of training the memory, which he embodied in a book entitled *Foenix*. He based his claim on the time and care he had spent in composing the book, and the risk that others might, once it was in print, reap the fruits of his labours ('ne alieni colligant fructus laborum et vigiliarum suarum'). Anyone in the Venetian state was accordingly forbidden to print the book, or sell copies of it printed elsewhere, on pain of confiscation of the books and a fine of twenty-five lire for each copy.[4] Three weeks later, Dr 'Joannes Dominicus Nigro' requested a privilege for two books 'both useful in the faculty of medicine'. He was not the author of them. But he had acquired manuscripts of them, and proposed to have them printed at his own expense. He feared lest others should reap the reward of the trouble and expense he had been at to secure and publish them. He obtained a privilege for ten years.[5] The printers and publishers were not slow to follow suit. Their demands became numerous, and excessive. By 1517 so many privileges had been granted, some of them for large groups or whole categories of books and for long periods, that it was paralysing the Venetian book-trade, and the Senate revoked all existing

[1] Milan (U. Scinzenzeler) 1500 fol. BL ɪʙ 26792.
[2] Milan (J. and C. Cotta, pr. G. Le Signerre) 1501 8⁰ BL 238.m.34.
[3] Milan (A. Minutianus) 1520 4⁰. BL 12470.ccc.8.
[4] Fulin, 'Documenti per servire alla storia della tipografia veneziana', p. 102 (Doc. 4).
[5] Ibid. pp. 102–3 (Doc. 5).

privileges not issued on its own authority. Henceforth privileges would be granted for new works only, and then only on a two-thirds majority vote.[1] There were on the other hand Italian states where privileges for books appear to have been given very infrequently. In Florence, for example, it was an unusual measure when Dante Popoleschi was granted by the republic a three-year privilege for his translation of Caesar's *Gallic War*, threatening a fine of 200 gold florins for infringement by anyone who should print it 'senza expressa licentia di decto Dante.'[2]

SPAIN, FRANCE, PORTUGAL, POLAND, SCOTLAND, SCANDINAVIA, ENGLAND

Isolated instances of book-privileges outside Germany or Italy began to appear in 1498. Dr Juliano Gutiérrez, physician to King Ferdinand and Queen Isabella, published his book on the treatment of gall-stones, *De la cura de la piedra*, on 4 April 1498, with a notice printed at the end stating that the Council had fixed the price of it at 75 *maravedís* and given a privilege that no one else should print or sell it.[3] It was also in 1498 that Dr Jacques Ponceau, *premier médecin* of Charles VIII of France, entrusted to the press of Johann Trechsel at Lyon a commentary on the *Canon* of Avicenna by Dr Jacques Despars or De Partibus, of which the printing was completed on 24 December 1498, and in which the terms of a royal privilege for five years are paraphrased by the author of the preface, Janus Lascaris.[4] In neither case was the grant followed by a rush of similar concessions. The next privilege in Spain is perhaps the three-year monopoly given in 1500 for an official publication, the *Ordenanzas reales sobre los paños*.[5] In France there is no trace of another until 1505.[6] In Portugal four books were printed 1501–4 which advertised a royal privilege. A *Glosa sobre las coplas de Jorge Manrique* (10 April 1501) prints the words 'con privilegio' on the title-page; a translation of Marco Polo (4 February 1502) bears the statement 'With the privilege of our lord the king that none should print this book nor sell it in all his realms and lordships without leave of Valentim Fernandes on pain of the penalties contained in the

---

[1] Ibid. p. 93.

[2] The text of the privilege, 30 October 1518, in the name of the *Priori di Liberta & Gonfaloniere di Iustitia del popolo Fiorentino*, signed 'Ego Iacobus Ser Michaellis de Duccis de Pistorio Notarius dictorum dominorum de Mandato', is printed facing the last page of the text (f. Q 6ʳ) of the book. Florence, Io. Stephano di Carlo da Pavia, 1518, 4°. BL 293.f.27. Cf. Norton, *Italian printers*, p. xxix.

[3] Toledo (Peter Hagenbach for Melchior de Gurizzo), 1498, fol. The summary of the privilege is on f. 86, the last leaf, which is missing in some copies: it is reproduced by K. Haebler, *Bibliografía ibérica del siglo xv* (The Hague/Leipzig, 1903), p. 147.

[4] CH 1498, 1.

[5] Haebler, *Bibliografía ibérica*, I, n° 501. Seville (Stanislaus Polonus), 1500, fol. The summary of the privilege is printed on the title-page, after the royal arms.

[6] PR 1505, 1. See below, p. 49.

grant of his privilege, the price 110 *reais*'; an official publication, the *Regimento dos oficiais das cidades, vilas e lugares deste reino* (29 March 1504), begins the colophon with the words 'Com autoridade e previlegio del rey nosso senhor...'.[1] A *Cathecismo pequeno* by Diogo Ortiz de Villegas, bishop of Ceuta (20 July 1504) prints on the title-page, which bears the bishop's arms, the words 'Emprimido com privilegio del Rey nosso senhor.'[2] There appear to be no other Portuguese privileges until 1534.

The first fully documented book-privilege granted by a lay authority in northern Europe is that given by King Alexander of Poland at Cracow on 30 September 1505 to Johann Haller.[3] By the terms of this grant, Haller, who had printed in Cracow since the previous year, obtained a monopoly not of all printing there but in any of the works which he printed. Thus no printer or bookseller, native or alien, might import into Poland or sell within the kingdom any book which Haller had printed, and any copies put on sale in contravention of this privilege were to be confiscated for the benefit of Haller. Protected from the fear of foreign competition, he undertook to print the laws of the kingdom, *Commune inclyti Poloniae Regni priuilegium*, for Chancellor Lasky (27 January 1506), – the privilege is mentioned in the colophon – and as a further inducement to do so he was granted immunity from taxation.[4] When the king died and was succeeded by his younger brother, the more famous Sigismund I, Haller obtained a confirmation of his privilege.[5]

But the ecclesiastical authorities in Poland also found it useful to support Haller. Joannes Konarski, bishop of Cracow, finding many of the breviaries in use in his diocese to be defective, had a revised text prepared, and entrusted it to Haller to print, directing all his clergy to purchase Haller's edition.[6] And in due course he also granted a privilege for six years to Haller for the Cracow Missal, adding to the penalties for infringement decreed by the king that of excommunication (27 October 1509).[7] A similar privilege granted by the bishop of Poznań to Haller led to a lawsuit between Haller and Casper Tilycz alias Cristek, a citizen and merchant of Poznań, who had imported service-books printed elsewhere; a settlement reached in the bishop's court eventually obliged Caspar to make over to Haller the copies he had in stock both in Poznań and in Wroclaw on conditions to be agreed between them, and Casper was threatened with a fine of 1000 florins plus excommunication if he were to

[1] All printed at Lisbon by Valentim Fernandes. See Jorge Peixoto, 'Os privilégios de impressão dos livros em Portugal no século XVI', *Gutenberg-Jahrbuch* (1969), pp. 265–72.
[2] This item printed at Lisbon by Valentim Fernandes in partnership with João Pedro Bonhomini de Cremona. Described, with illustration of title-page, in A. Rosenthal Ltd, Catalogue 75, pp. 74–5 (no. 1152A).
[3] J. Ptaśnik (ed.) *Monumenta poloniae typographica xv et xvi saeculorum*, Vol. I, *Cracovia impressorum xv et xvi saeculorum* (Leopoli, Sumptibus Instituti Ossoliniani, 1922), Part [II], no. 105 (pp. 46–7), quoting Matr.Regni Pol.21, f. 293.
[4] Ibid. no. 108 (p. 48), quoting Matr.Regni Pol.21, f. 361 v°.   [5] Ibid. n. 112.
[6] Ibid. no. 117 (p. 53).
[7] Ibid. no. 125.

repeat the offence (12 September 1515).[1] In a fresh edition of the Cracow Missal printed that year, and dedicated to Bishop Joannes Konarski (1 February 1516), Haller took the opportunity of addressing prospective pirates aggressively:

> To booksellers: It is not without great cost that these Missals have issued from our press into the light of day. Therefore if any man induced by greed or avarice, or motivated by the frenzy of envy, presume to print them or put on sale copies printed elsewhere, let him be warned, lest he incur the penalties of the privilege granted to us by the King's Majesty.[2]

He had in fact perhaps more printing work on his hands than he could manage: he and Jodocus Decius got a special 6-year privilege on 25 April 1516 for Cracow Breviaries and *Cursus* which were to be printed for them *in France*.[3] And an agreement between Haller and three other printers was officially recorded on 10 June 1517 under the heading *Concordia librariorum*.[4]

Haller had occupied a position not unlike that of the King's Printers later in France – such royal printers undertaking much official printing mainly at their own expense but being recompensed by the exclusive right within the realm in any books they should be the first to print. But Haller never seems to have been called Printer to the King. And a transition was taking place to the system, perhaps fairer, of granting privileges for individual books: thus Decius obtained on 19 August 1519 a six-year privilege for the *Cronica Polonorum* of Mathia de Myechow.[5]

In Scotland, James IV granted permission on 15 September 1507 to Walter Chepman and Andrew Myllar to set up a printing press in Edinburgh, with a privilege which prohibited the import from elsewhere of the books they printed.[6] This measure seems to have been aimed at securing the presence of a printing press, 'at our instance and request, for our plesour, the honour and proffit of our realme and liegis', somewhat as in the case of the grant by the king of Poland two years before, but it particularly mentioned the production of 'mess bukes efter our awin scottis use' and the most ambitious undertaking of the new press was in fact an edition of the breviary according to the use of Aberdeen in 1510. By the time it came out, Chepman's name only appeared in it, and the press thereafter came to an end of its short life – not, however, before Chepman had successfully prosecuted before the Privy Council (14 January 1510) certain merchants of Edinburgh who had infringed the privilege by importing service-books of the Sarum use.[7]

In Scandinavia the earliest privileges were those issued on ecclesiastical

[1] Ibid. no. 182 (pp. 74–5).
[2] Th. Wierzbowski, *Polonica xv ac xvi saeculorum* (Warsaw, 1889), no. 2076.
[3] Ptaśnik, *Monumenta*, no 194.   [4] Ibid. no. 203   [5] Ibid. no. 216.
[6] *Registrum secreti sigilli regum scotorum. The Register of the Privy Seal of Scotland, I (A.D. 1488–1529)*, ed. M. Livingstone, H. M. Register Office (Edinburgh, 1908), no. 1546, pp. 223–4.
[7] R. Dickson and J. P. Edmond, *Annals of Scottish printing* (Cambridge, 1890), pp. 7–8.

authority. In 1510 the *Psalterium upsalense* was printed by Paul Grijs at Uppsala in the house of the archdeacon Ravaldus, Jacobus Ulvsson being archbishop of Uppsala and primate of the kingdom of Sweden, 'Cum priuilegiis'.[1] In 1514 a fine folio missal for the use of Lund was printed at Paris by Wolfgang Hopyl, an internationally known specialist in the production of liturgical books: the printing was supervised by one of the Lund clergy, Cristiernus Petrus, and appeared 'with privilege of the most reverend lord in Christ Birgerus by the grace of God archbishop of Lund'.[2] A *Canon* of Roskilde in Denmark was printed by Poul Raeff at Nyborg in 1522, displaying the arms of Bishop Lage Urne, and the words 'Cum priuilegio'.[3] An edition of Murmellius, *De latina constructione* and Despauterius, *Rudimenta*, edited by Chr. Therkelsen, had been printed at Copenhagen by Poul Raeff in 1519, with the words 'cum priuilegio' at the end,[4] I do not know on whose authority – ecclesiastical (possible, for an educational book) or royal (presumably Christian II). Otherwise privileges hardly appear until after the Reformation, when they are associated with authorised Protestant forms of service and translations of the Bible or parts of it.[5]

William Caxton, who introduced printing into England in 1476, transferring his press from Bruges to Westminster, sought no privilege, though he enjoyed the support of the Yorkist dynasty and of Yorkist lords. His business prospered without the need being felt for protection against competitors on his own well-chosen ground. The earliest English book-privilege is displayed in a book dated 15 May 1518, a commentary on Aristotle's *Ethics* by John Dedecus or Dedicus. This was published at Oxford by John Scolar. The privilege, for seven years, was granted by the chancellor of the university, who was William Warham, archbishop of Canterbury, and until 1515 chancellor of England. Its scope was confined to the University of Oxford and its precincts.[6] As the work was evidently in demand in academic circles in England, the benefits of the privilege, if limited, may have been very material. The book perhaps attracted the attention of Richard Pynson, the King's Printer. At all events, Pynson advertised his edition, dated 13 November 1518, of Cuthbert Tunstall's oration on the proposed marriage between Princess Mary, daughter of

[1] Isak Collijn, *Sveriges bibliografi intill år 1600*, Vol. 1, *1478–1530* (Uppsala, 1934–8), pp. 202–9.
[2] L. Nielsen, *Dansk bibliografi 1482–1550* (Copenhagen, 1919), no. 181. Miss Elizabeth Knowles kindly brought it to my attention that it was about 1514 that the archdiocese of Uppsala became independent of the domination of Lund, as it was in 1514 that Gustav Trolle, member of a powerful Swedish house, became archbishop of Uppsala. The printing of the Lund Missal may have been a measure taken by the Archbishop of Lund to assert and publicise his authority.
[3] Ibid. no.38. [4] Ibid. no. 190. [5] Ibid. no. 52, 196, 269 etc.
[6] The privilege is printed on the last page (f. N 4ᵛ), after the end of the text and the colophon. It reads (contractions resolved): 'Cum privilegio. Vetitum est per edictum sub sigillo cancellariatus ne quis in septennio hoc insigne opus imprimat vel aliorum ductu impensis venditet in universitate Oxonie: aut infra precinctum eiusdem: sub pena amissionis omnium librorum et quinque librarum sterlingarum pro singulis sic venditis ubiubi impressi fuerint preter penam pretaxatam in decreto.' Oxford, 1518, 4°. Bodl. Arch.A.e.76 (STC 6458).

Henry VIII, and the Dauphin of France, 'cum priuilegio a rege indulto, ne quis hanc orationem intra biennium in regno Angliae imprimat, aut alibi impressam et importatam in eodem regno Angliae vendat'.[1] This seems to be the first English royal privilege.

THE PAPACY

Privileges were naturally valid only within the jurisdiction of the authority which granted them. The area within which a privilege was effective, even in principle, might thus be relatively small. At first sight therefore it may seem strange that a privilege should be sought at all from the duke of Milan or from the king of England when printers throughout the rest of Europe were free to reprint the books which it purported to protect. In some cases clearly the greatest danger from unauthorised reprints came from printers in the same state, in the same town or even in the same street. Works of great local interest, such as the history of Venice by Sabellicus, or the chronicle of Milan by Bossius, would be most in demand in the place itself and accordingly offer the greatest temptation to printers there. Even if printers outside that area were free to reprint the book, booksellers within the area were not free to put such an edition on sale. Pynson's privilege for Tunstall's *Oratio* did not stop Froben from reprinting it almost at once in Basle[2] and selling it where he wished on the continent, but Pynson could prosecute anyone attempting to import Froben's edition into England. In the intensely competitive book-trade of Italy, where between 1500 and 1520 there were sixty-five presses in Venice and twenty-one both in Rome and Milan, for instance, a privilege was of real significance which banned any other edition throughout the whole duchy of Milan, a wealthy, populous and largely industrialised territory including towns like Brescia, Pavia and Cremona. Still, the author and publisher of a book of general interest might have their eye on possible profits to be made further afield. Printing in the first twenty years of the sixteenth century was going on in forty-nine different places in Italy.[3]

A prudent and far-sighted author might attempt to prevent his new book from being pirated in these circumstances by extending his privilege coverage beyond the state in which he or his publisher resided. A notable example here is that of Ariosto, with his completed *magnum opus*, the *Orlando Furioso*, ready to be printed by Mazocco at Ferrara in 1516, and destined – as he and his printer probably guessed – to enjoy tremendous success. In a determined attempt to forestall the pirates, and to keep control himself over the printing and sales of

---

[1] The summary of the privilege is printed at the end (f.B 6ʳ), incorporated in the colophon. London, 1518, 4°. Bodl. 4°. т.20(1) Th. Seld. (STC 24320).
[2] Tunstall, *In laudem matrimonii oratio* (Basle, 1519), 4°. For Pynson's privilege, see above, pp. 10–11.
[3] Norton, *Italian printers, passim*.

the book, he obtained a privilege from Pope Leo X (dated 27 March 1516, and signed by Jacobus Sadoletus), forbidding anyone to print or sell the work without the author's command and concession, on pain of excommunication and of a fine of 100 ducats and confiscation of the offending copies. In the terms of this papal indult we see two considerations being given equal weight: that the books should be issued *correct* by the author's care and diligence, and that the profit, if any, should be enjoyed by him rather than by others. Not only this, but he secured a privilege from the king of France (perhaps including the duchy of Milan) and from the republic of Venice, 'and from other potentates'.[1] No doubt the latter included the duke of Ferrara, but his privilege by itself would have been little help to Ariosto, whereas for piracy of his book to be illegal in the papal states and in the dominions of Milan and Venice gave him protection (at least in theory) from a very large number of potential competitors. Four years later, the edition of Boccaccio's *Ameto* by Andreas Calvus, already mentioned,[2] carries not only the privilege of Francis I as duke of Milan, but also that of the Pope, dated 1 June 1520, granted for 5 years with a fine of 1000 ducats.[3] In 1521 an Italian translation of Juan de Flores, *Historia de Isabella e Aurelio*, 'a spece di Andrea Calvo', states at the end of the colophon that it was published with grace and privilege of the Pope and of the most christian king,[4] no doubt the same privilege as for the *Ameto*.

Papal book-privileges seem to have been granted occasionally from the time of Sixtus IV. Antonius Zarottus of Milan published *Regulae* of St Jerome and St Augustine 'Ex patris patruum maximi Sixti Quarti priuilegio'.[5] Julius II gave privileges for *Medecina Plinii* (1 July 1509) and for Thomas de Vio Cajetanus, *Auctoritas Papae et Concilii* (19 November 1511), both to Roman publishers.[6] Leo X gave them more frequently, often visibly with the intention of favouring scholars. They were not limited to books published in Rome or in the papal states. They extended to Florence,[7] to Ferrara,[8] to Asti,[9] to

---

[1] 'Congratia e privilegio' on the title-page; on f. a 2, the text of the papal indult, addressed to Ariosto, followed by the statement about the other privileges, details of which are not given. BL G.11061. Cf. below, p. 62, n. 2.

[2] See above, p. 6.   [3] On verso of title-page, facing the Francis I privilege.

[4] BL 837.f.30. Reproduced in Giulia Bologna, *Le cinquecentine della Biblioteca Trivulziana*, vol. I, *Le edizioni milanesi* (Milan, 1965), no. 188, Tavola 4.

[5] Caterina Santoro, *Libri illustrati milanesi del rinascimento* (Milan, 1956), no. 33.

[6] Norton, *Italian printers*, pp. xvii–xviii.

[7] To Philippus de Giuntis & Sons of Florence, ten years, 15 February 1516, for the translation of Dioscorides by Marcellus Virgilius, 'secretarius florentinus'. *De medica materia*, 1518, fol. Bodl.D.1.2.Med., privilege printed at the end.

[8] To Ariosto for *Orlando Furioso*, Rome, 27 March 1516, for the author's lifetime. See above, n. 1.

[9] To Alberto Bruno for his *De statutis feminas et cognatorum lineam a successionibus excludentibus*, Rome, 2 April 1518. G. Vernazza di Freney, *Dizionario dei tipografi in Piemonte* (Turin, 1859), p. 85.

Nuremberg[1] and to Geneva.[2]

Papal privileges were expensive. When Michael Hummelberg, in Rome, set about obtaining a five-year privilege from Leo X for Froben's edition of the works of St Jerome, prepared by Erasmus, he was told by Roman booksellers whom he consulted that it would cost about thirty gold pieces. Submitting the request to the Pope through a series of highly placed and benevolently disposed intermediaries, he eventually secured the privilege for six ducats. 'No one, believe me,' he wrote to Froben, enclosing the document and requesting repayment, 'could have obtained it for so little.'[3]

To my knowledge, there exists as yet no general and systematic study of papal book-privileges in this period. For this reason, I have ventured to give some examples of their scope and geographical distribution. In principle, they were indeed universal. But Josse Badius was to reprint Cajetanus, *Psalmi Dauidici*, 1532, fol., knowing that the Italian first edition had a ten-year papal privilege which was still valid, having obtained from doctors of Paris University advice to the effect that this privilege applied only to the papal states within which the Pope was temporal sovereign.[4] A Milan publisher, who infringed a ten-year papal privilege of 1515 and was prosecuted for it by the privilege-holder, managed with some specious excuses and no doubt with some expense to secure a pardon and permission to sell his edition, but took care to print in it the documents in the case.[5]

THE EMPIRE AND THE LOW COUNTRIES

A possibility in privilege coverage, first thought of by the German humanist and poet Conrad Celtes, was a grant by the Holy Roman Emperor. In 1501 Celtes published the first edition of the works of Hroswitha, the manuscript of which he had discovered. It was printed at Nuremberg for him, or rather for the 'sodolitas' or consortium which he had organised. In the preface Celtes paraphrased an imperial privilege which forbade anyone to print 'this and the other printed copies' in any of the imperial cities for the next ten years on pain

[1] To Hans Koberger for Franciscus Irenicus, *Germania*, 1518, fol. Bodl.E.1.22.Art. The privilege, for five years, 14 January 1518, is printed on the verso of the title-page.
[2] To Jacques Vivian, for Pierre Michault, *Le doctrinal de Court*, 1522, 4°. BN Rés.Ye 858. Privilege, for three years, date not given, printed on verso of title-page.
[3] A. Horawitz, *Analecten zur Geschichte des Humanismus in Schwaben, 1512–1518*, Vienna, 1877, p. 217, no. xxxviii (30 August 1516). The fee paid by Koberger for the privilege referred to above, n. 1, was in fact thirty florins.
[4] Ph. Renouard, *Bibliographie des impressions et des oeuvres de Josse Badius Ascensius* (1908), III, 354–5.
[5] Tacitus, *Libri quinque nouiter inuenti cum reliquis operibus* (Rome, S. Guilleretus, 1515), fol. This being the first edition of the first six books of Tacitus' *Annales*, the editor, P. Beroaldus, obtained the privilege. It was copied at Milan by A. Minutianus, 1517, 4°.

of certain fines.[1] This remained an isolated case for several years. Grants by the emperor were neither sought nor given except for books of considerable importance. In principle they were far-reaching: they prohibited unauthorised reprints in the imperial cities, among which were some of the most active printing centres in Europe. The first such privilege of which the text is known was for a treatise on obstetrics by a well-known doctor of the time, Eucharius Rösslin, which he called the 'rose-garden of pregnant women and of midwives' (*Der schwangern Frauen und Hebammen Rosengarten*). This was a practical book intended for people who were not doctors, and is accordingly written in the vernacular. There is however nothing homely about the book. It is well printed, and illustrated with two fine woodcuts, a frontispiece showing the author presenting his book to the duchess of Brunswick, attended by her ladies, and a picture of a great lady in childbirth assisted by a midwife and by a lady in waiting who is supporting her. There is also a series of stylised diagrams showing the different positions that babies – including twins – can occupy in the uterus. For this work, Dr Rösslin obtained from the Emperor Maximilian a six-year privilege (Cologne, 24 September 1512) in which copying the book during that time was forbidden throughout his dominions, likewise the import of copies printed elsewhere, on pain of a fine of ten gold marks. The book was printed by Martin Flach at Strasbourg, with the privilege, which is in German, set out in full at the beginning.[2] Flach reprinted it in 1522, omitting the privilege, which had of course by then expired. In Latin, Dutch, English and French translations the book was still being printed in the second half of the century.

Another important privilege granted in much the same terms under the imperial seal, this time in Latin, was made at the request of the imperial secretary Jacobus Spiegel to Matthias Schurer, printer of Strasbourg, for the first edition of the chronicle of Otto of Freising, edited by Cuspinianus,[3] and for other works which he should be the first in Germany to print (Vienna, 6 May 1514). This was the publication of a notable historical source and a great work of scholarship, printed with due splendour, the title-page depicting Maximilian enthroned, with his arms and those of his territories. An expression of *policy* is first found in the imperial privilege granted to the Vienna publisher Leonardus Alantse for the poem *De bello norico* dedicated by its author Riccardus Bartholinus to the emperor. In a long preamble, Maximilian expressed his concern at the wrong continually being done to men of learning and their publishers by unscrupulous printers who cynically profited by their labours, and his determination to prevent this happening at

[1] Bodl. fol. Θ 446. Allusion to privilege on f. a2ᵛ ('dato etiam a cesareo senatu priuilegio ne quis hanc et alia exemplaria impressa in decem annis post me et sodales meos in liberis et imperialibus urbibus imprimere auderet: sub certa et debita mulcta').

[2] BN Rés.Te 121. l. Privilege on f. A2.   [3] BL c.75.d.4(1). Privilege on f. AA2.

least to works which, like this one, were printed by his command (Innsbruck, 1 January 1515).[1]

Although this and other privileges were granted by Maximilian, application for privileges from the emperor was not a common practice. For one thing they usually cost a great deal. Froben obtained an imperial five-year privilege for the edition of St Jerome, in addition to the papal privilege already mentioned, and a four-year privilege for the New Testament, also edited by Erasmus.[2] Prompted no doubt by Froben, Erasmus wrote on 28 January 1523 to Willibald Pirckheimer asking him to obtain a two-year privilege to cover any work which Froben should be the first person to print, if possible in time to apply to his forthcoming *Paraphrasis* on St John's Gospel, dedicated to the emperor.[3] Pirckheimer was able to secure the desired privilege 'gratis and without payment, which is very rare with us'. Reporting this good news to Erasmus on 17 February 1523, Pirckheimer advised him to write to thank the councillor Varnbüler who had personally drawn up the privilege, and to see that Froben sent him a complimentary copy of the book, 'for such a document, especially a general one, could not have been obtained under twenty gold pieces.'[4] The benevolence of Varnbüler in helping to obtain an imperial privilege is also acknowledged in the preface addressed to him by another Basle printer, Andreas Cratander, in his edition of Cicero, 1528, but it does not appear that it was granted free of charge.[5] Under the emperor Charles V forty-one privileges are recorded in the imperial chancery for the period 1522–56, though many more than this are known from their appearance in books.[6]

There are however some instructive records to consider from territories in the Low Countries, some of which claimed independence from the Empire, notably the registers of the use of the seal of the duchy of Brabant. Brabant was one of the lands united under the rule of the Valois dukes of Burgundy which the Archduke Charles, destined to become the Emperor Charles V, inherited through his grandmother Mary of Burgundy, the first wife of Maximilian I. It included a number of towns where printing was practised from an early date: Brussels, Antwerp and Louvain in particular. No privileges for this area are known earlier than 1512. Imperial privileges, valid in provinces which were part of the Empire, such as Holland, did not apply here. According to Willem Vorsterman of Antwerp, who had been printing for several years when in 1514 he first applied for a privilege, it had been the custom and usage in Brabant, when a printer printed something new, for the

---

[1] Bodl.Buchanan e.22. Privilege on f. 2 of the prelims.
[2] Erasmus, *Opus Epistolarum*, ed. P. S. Allen, Vol. v, Ep. 1341, line 10, p. 202.
[3] Ibid. Ep. 1341.   [4] Ibid., Ep. 1344.
[5] K. Schottenloher, *Die Widmungsvorrede im Buch des 16ten Jahrhunderts* (Münster, 1953), p. 199.
[6] K. Schottenloher, 'Die Druckprivilegien des 16ten Jahrhunderts', *Gutenberg-Jahrbuch* (1933), pp. 89–111.

other printers to refrain from reprinting it for three years.[1] This 'gentlemen's agreement' had already by then broken down.

The first privilege application to the Council of the duchy, made by another Antwerp printer, Claes de Greve, in 1512, was prompted in the first instance by a dispute with an unscrupulous competitor in the same town. It is very circumstantial. Claes had a potential best-seller to print, the Almanac for the coming year by Dr Jasper Laet. Almanacs were always in demand: they provided a reliable calendar, phases of the moon, etc. as well as astrological predictions about weather and events.[2] Laet's were particularly popular at this time. And as Claes began to print, with the approach of the New Year, Henrik Bosbas and his associates managed to get hold of an advance copy: working secretly, 'with four or five presses and fifteen or sixteen workmen', over Christmas time, which was anyway illegal, they were able to put Laet's Almanac on sale more quickly and cheaply than Claes. Claes had had the law of Bosbas in Antwerp, and secured a certain sum by way of compensation, but Bosbas was unrepentant and openly threatened to pirate his copies again. And so Claes presented a petition to 'the emperor and the prince', that is, to Maximilian in his capacity as guardian of his grandson Charles, who was not yet of age, and to Charles himself as 'prince', duke of Brabant. In this petition, Claes set out at length the story of the injustices done and threatened by Bosbas, and invoked the practice of other places where the authorities already provided protection against unfair reprinting: in Paris, in Venice, in Lyon and elsewhere, printers received privileges whereby the profit on their new publications was safe-guarded for a set period, and he asked for a privilege of ten years in any work which he should be the first person in the duchy to print. This petition came before the Council of Brabant in Brussels and was granted in the terms requested (except that *six* years and not *ten* were given). Claes paid the standard fee for the use of the seal of Brabant, 12s 6d, and was evidently well satisfied with the effect of the privilege, for he paid the same sum to have it renewed in 1519.

As the payments for use of the seal on this and similar documents issued by the Council of Brabant were carefully recorded, with the petitions, and the record happens to be extant, we can trace the development of book-privileges here with some precision. Claes de Greve's original application was followed

---

[1] P. Verheyden, 'Drukkersoctrooien in de 16e eeuw,' *Tijdschrift voor Boek- en Bibliotheekswesen*, VIII (1910), p. 204.

[2] For example, Erhard Ratdolt, who published a number of calendars and almanacs, actually paid qualified astronomers to draw them up or revise them (e.g. Johannes Mueller). Cf. Symon de Phares, *Recueil des plus célèbres astrologues*, ed. E. Wickersheimer (Paris, 1929), pp. 263–4, 267. John Dorne, a Dutch bookseller in Oxford whose day-book has been preserved for 1520, sold about forty books described as Almanacs or Prognostications, one of them definitely by Jasper Laet, between 19 January and the end of the month. F. Madan, *Daybook of John Dorne*, in *Collectanea*, I, ed. C. R. L. Fletcher, Oxford Historical Society (Oxford, 1885), pp. 78–82, item 155, pronosticon jasper.

by that of Thomas vander Noot (30 January 1512), who planned to reintroduce the art of printing into his native city of Brussels. Vander Noot's petition, embodied in the privilege, represented the great benefits to education and scholarship resulting from a good supply of books and the advantages which printing could offer in this respect. More particularly he argued that his printing programme included 'several new works and books in diverse languages which he has acquired with great expense and trouble both from the authors who composed them and since then have looked over, inspected and corrected them, and otherwise.' The Council gave him, in response to this plea, a three-year privilege in any books etc. which he should be the first in Brabant to print,[1] and he renewed this, without waiting for the expiry of the privilege, on 23 April 1513.[2]

There followed Willem Vorsterman (13 September 1514), Jan van Doesborch (18 September 1515), and Michael van Hoochstraten (18 February 1516), all of Antwerp; Doen Peters (23 December 1516) of Amsterdam – he evidently hoped to sell his books in Brabant as well as Holland – Laureynse Haeyen (21 November 1517) of 'sHertogenbosch, Thierry Martens (8 February 1519) of Louvain, and Jan Thibault (14 March 1519) of Antwerp.[3] These were personal privileges, protecting any work which the applicants claimed to be new in Brabant. Although the privilege might be seen as a licence to print in these cases as well as a commercial monopoly in the particular books in question, there is no record of any control being exercised over the choice of publication, until the grant to Jan van Doesborch in 1515. On that occasion the printer was directed to show the books he intended to publish beforehand to the priest of the church of Our Lady (now the cathedral) and to the magistrates at Antwerp, and the same principle was applied to Michael van Hoochstraten.[4] No such condition was however regularly made before 1519 when alarm at the effects of the Reformation were beginning to be felt. The grants to Doen Peters and to Laureys Hayen had no censorship element in them: the latter indeed included quite different conditions – that the works to be covered by the privilege should be new and that they should be correctly and legibly printed.[5] The individual books with any pretentions to being new, at least in Brabant, which these printers brought out during the years covered by their grants, bear (normally on the title-page) the advertisement 'Cum gratia et priuilegio', without further details.

The series of privileges given under the seal of the duchy does not exhaust the grants made during these years for Brabant. A legal work by Lambertus de Ramponibus was printed at Ghent, in Flanders, 13 September 1513, by Simon Cock and Jodocus Petrus de Hallis, both described as 'having their

---

[1] Verheyden, 'Drukkersoctrooien', p. 209, no. 2. Vander Noot's rather high-flown rhetoric included a reference to 'dame clergie' ('Lady Learning'); this allegorical figure puzzled Verheyden, who thought the scribe must have misread 'par l'art d'impression'.
[2] Ibid. no. 3.   [3] Ibid. nos. 4–11 (pp. 210–11).   [4] Ibid. pp. 203–5.   [5] Ibid. no. 8.

origins in Brabant'. This was issued with privilege of the Archduke Charles, duke of Burgundy, Brabant etc., forbidding anyone to print it or to sell copies printed elsewhere, for the next three years in Brabant and the lands depending on Brabant, on pain of confiscation of their books and other penalties contained in the privilege.[1] It seems possible that this privilege was issued at Ghent, and hence escaped registration at Brussels. The printers' concern was clearly to protect their interests in Brabant and probably especially against competitors in Antwerp: Simon Cock afterwards in fact transferred his business to Antwerp.

When Thierry Martens applied for a privilege from the Council of Brabant on 8 February 1519, he had been displaying since 1515 on some of his books a four-year privilege remarkable for being granted jointly by the Archduke Charles (the future Emperor Charles V) and by his grandfather the Emperor Maximilian I. This forbade copying of the book or books in question for four years in all their dominions.[2] Maximilian's authority extended to the hereditary Habsburg lands and to the whole of the empire, and that of Charles to all the lands of the Burgundian Netherlands, including Brabant which claimed independence from the empire. The privilege thus protected Martens's publications, at least in principle, over a wide area and against a large number of possible competitors. It was quite a reasonable provision, in view of the long and eminent career which Martens had conducted first in Alost, then in Antwerp and finally in Louvain. It seems possible that his application to the Council of Brabant was prompted by the news of the death of Maximilian at Wels on 12 January 1519, which was known within a few days at Louvain and at Brussels. The validity of the Maximilian-and-Charles privilege might be considered to have expired with the emperor's death. A four-year privilege from the Council of Brabant, which he received promptly and unconditionally, was at least an interim measure to protect his interests.

While the Council of Brabant continued to issue privileges, the Councils of Holland and of Flanders did likewise. The Privy Council also sometimes took a hand. It was consulted, and so was the Regent, Margaret of Austria, before the first privilege was granted to Willem Vorsterman.[3] It granted a four-year privilege (Brussels, 9 October 1517), to a printer of Leiden, in Holland, Jan Corneliszoen or Zeversoen, for the Chronicle of Holland, Zealand and Friesland, newly compiled by C. Aurelius (the 'Divisiekronieck').[4] This was printed in full at the end of the book. An up to date chron-

---

[1] BL 5051.a.23. Privilege-summary at end of text, on f. lix^r.
[2] At least two examples in 1515: W. Nijhoff and M. E. Kronenberg, *Nederlandsche Bibliographie van 1500 tot 1540* (The Hague, 1923–42), nos. 9, 45; and one in 1516, ibid. no. 15, Charles in the latter being entitled king of Spain.
[3] Verheyden, 'Drukkersoctrooien', pp. 205–7.
[4] *Die cronycke van Hollandt, Zeelandt en Vrieslant*, 1517, fol. Nijhoff and Kronenberg, *Nederlandsche Bibliographie*, nos. 613, 614. I have used the copy in the Koninklijke Bibliotheek at The Hague.

icle of one of the provinces or cities always tended to be a best-seller, and the printer, whose petition is partly paraphrased in the grant itself, naturally emphasised that this one had never been printed before and that it would be costly and troublesome to produce. What was said in a book like this might, however, also have political implications. The government of the Low Countries was therefore interested in promoting it, if it was acceptable, and the printer gained something like official authorisation, which could not fail to help the sales of the book. In fact, the only condition made in the grant is that the book should be printed within four years from the date of the privilege – a sensible provision which other privilege-giving bodies might have followed to prevent unreasonable staking out of claims for the future. In a later book of the same kind, the *Compendium chronicorum Flandriae* of Jacobus Meyerus (Nuremberg, 1538), Charles as emperor but also as count of Flanders appears as the giver of a substantial privilege to the author in recognition of his long and careful historical researches (three years; the author had requested six). This privilege, given by the emperor and his Council (Brussels, 19 February 1536), and signed by the secretary de Langhe, was however given only after the book had first been given to the Council of Flanders to inspect, and on condition that, on their advice, certain corrections and changes should be made and the mention of certain privileges of towns etc. should be omitted.[1]

Had Charles V been as personally interested as his grandfather Maximilian in promoting literary works and their publication, he might have imposed some measure of uniformity on the operation of the privilege-system within his vast dominions, even allowing for each of his territories being separately administered. As it was, privileges continued to be given separately by him in his different capacities, and sometimes in different terms for the same book. As emperor, as duke of Brabant or count of Flanders, as king of Spain, or indeed as king of Castile as distinct from king of Aragon, the rights he granted did not necessarily bear any relation to each other.[2]

Within the empire, princes were free to grant privileges, which were valid within their own territory. It does not appear that they often did so. The Electors of Saxony, beginning with Johann Friedrich in 1533, gave a small

Privilege on f. 436ᵛ, signed 'By den Coninc in sinen hogen Rade. Hanneton onderteykent'. The king was not in fact personally present as he had sailed on 8 September 1517 for Spain to claim the succession there. Hanneton, who signed the grant, was the Audiencier.
[1] Bodl. 4°. m.69.Art. Privilege printed on verso of title-page and the facing page. Meyerus even gave details of the authenticated copy of the original which he possessed: 'Collation en faicte à l'original et trouvé et accordé par moy. Edinghē.'
[2] E.g. the grants for the Spanish translation of *Le chevalier délibéré*, Antwerp, 8 December 1552: Brabant, ten years; Castile, twelve years; Aragon, fifteen years. J. Peeters-Fontainas, 'Les éditions espagnoles du *Chevalier délibéré* d'Olivier de La Marche', *De Gulden Passer* (1960), pp. 178–92. The judicial separation of the kingdoms, in this respect, was to lead to widespread 'piratical' printing, especially by Aragonese printers. D. W. Cruickshank, 'Some aspects of Spanish book-production in the Golden Age', *The Library*, Fifth Series, xxxi (March 1976), p. 4, n. 14.

number of privileges.[1] In the first quarter of the sixteenth century the only instance I have noticed is a privilege granted by Duke Antoine II of Lorraine in 1518 to a priest, Pierre Jacobi, who had set up a printing press at Saint-Nicolas-du-Port, then the most important commercial centre in the duchy. It was for a Latin poem narrating the victory won in 1477 at the battle of Nancy by the duke's father René II. The author, Pierre de Blarru, died in 1510 without having seen it published, but it was eventually printed as a fine book, with a woodcut of Duke René on the title-page and the complete text of the privilege on the verso, under the ducal arms, for two years (4 September 1518, renewed for five years on 21 February 1519 because printing had been delayed).[2] The privilege advertised the duke's authorisation and approval, which may have encouraged his loyal subjects to buy the book. The printer in fact had no competitors to fear within the duchy, and had no protection against those outside it. When Nicolas Volcyr de Sérouville prepared his illustrated account of the suppression of the peasants' revolt in 1525 by Duke Antoine, he went to Paris to have it printed and obtained a privilege from the Prévôt of Paris (PR 1527, 1).[3]

[1] Hans Volz, 'Wittenberger Bibeldruckprivilegien des 16ten und beginnenden 17ten Jahrhunderts', *Gutenberg-Jahrbuch* (1955), pp. 133–9.
[2] Petrus de Blarrorivo, *Liber Nanceidos*, 1518 fol. BN Rés.g.yc 7, 8, 9.
[3] See below, p. 117.

2 · PRIVILEGE-GRANTING
AUTHORITIES IN FRANCE

THE KINGDOM OF FRANCE, in the first quarter of the sixteenth century, was a favourable territory in which to try out the privilege-system. By then it was, like Italy, a country in which the book-trade was highly developed, both in the production of printed books and in the marketing of them. Unlike Italy, it was a single state, with a formidable centralised administration which effectively controlled the whole land. England was indeed as centralised as France, but still had only a small native printing industry mainly serving local needs; a high proportion of the printed books required in the country was imported from abroad.[1] The French government did not need, as did that for instance of Scotland or of Poland, to offer privileges to induce printers to come and work in its cities. The natural play of economic forces had by 1500 brought printers in abundance to Paris, Lyon, Rouen and other centres in France.

By the early sixteenth century a very large number of firms in France, great and small, were making their living out of the manufacture or sale of printed books, and a highly competitive situation was building up, especially in the hunt for copy. Here as elsewhere there was probably a body of opinion among respectable printers and publishers which recognised the prior right of the first publisher, and regarded it as unethical to reprint until he had had a reasonable chance to sell his edition. But if reprinting was unethical it was not illegal. It was clearly a temptation to unscrupulous rivals to make cheap copies at once of a publication brought out with trouble and expense by the original publisher. Authors or editors who had their works printed at their own expense, or at least had some financial stake in their publication, were equally threatened in their interests.

Printing in France began in 1470 and expanded over the ensuing thirty-five years without any publisher or author feeling the need to obtain a privilege, except for an isolated instance in 1498 (CH 1498, 1). But in 1505 an enterprising popular poet and impresario who was his own publisher, Pierre Gringore, sought a privilege for his newest work (PR 1505, 1). By 1507 a leading Paris publisher, Antoine Vérard, had secured from Louis XII a grant, of which the full text is not extant, but which evidently covered for three years any book which he should be the first person to publish (CH 1507, 1).

[1] Elizabeth Armstrong, 'English purchases of printed books from the Continent 1465–1526', *English Historical Review*, XCIV (1979), 268–90.

Vérard had been in business since 1485 and had brought out a couple of hundred editions, many of them first editions of French medieval texts, finely printed and illustrated. He had supplied books to members of the royal family in France and in England. He clearly thought the time had come to seek protection, and avail himself of his connections with the French court. He was followed by Guillaume Eustace, bookseller to the king since about 1497 (CH 1508, 2), who obtained rights for two years in any new book he should publish, though apparently only in certain categories. The quest for legal protection gathered momentum. Privileges had proved of limited value in countries which were politically fragmented, rendering a privilege granted in one state valueless in another. In France, where the authority of the king was everywhere exercised and enforced, experienced people like Vérard saw that they might prove to be more effectual.

Not surprisingly, then, almost all the known applications for privileges in France were directed to the state, whether to the royal chancery, the Parlements or to officers of the Crown. The very few traces of privileges granted by bishops, universities or religious orders will be discussed in Part Two of this chapter.

PART ONE: ROYAL

THE ROYAL CHANCERY

The issue of privileges

The royal chancery is known to have issued 106 Letters Patent conferring book-privileges during this period. Of these the earliest may possibly have been granted by Charles VIII (CH 1498, 1), though Louis XII had succeeded him by the time the book in question was published. Louis XII granted twenty-five between 1507 and 1514, and Francis I granted eighty-one between 1515 and 1526. The full text of the Letters Patent is extant for sixty of them. None of the original documents survives, but the majority of the beneficiaries had their privilege printed *in extenso* in the books to which it related. The remainder are known from paraphrases, summaries or extracts printed in the books, or, in a few cases, from a bare mention 'Cum priuilegio regis' on the title-page.

The largest number of these grants made in any one year was six under Louis XII (1514) and twelve under Francis I (1519). The number of *books* published under these privileges was larger than the number of grants. The three-year grant to Antoine Vérard (CH 1507, 1), which is known only from the summaries of it which he printed, evidently protected any book which he should be the first person to publish, and he invoked it in at least nineteen of his books, between 1508 and 1512. This personal privilege was followed by a

Plate 1   Printer's mark of Guillaume Eustace in *Sotise à huit personnaiges* (1508)

similar grant to Guillaume Eustace, bookseller to the king, for two years (CH 1508, 2), also known only from summaries, which seems likewise to have applied to new books, but perhaps only within certain categories. Eustace mentioned it in sixteen of his books, and had a special printer's mark made for use in some of these (see Plate 1). On other occasions he applied for an ordinary privilege as other publishers did (CH 1514, 3; 1517, 2; 1521, 1) and not only to the royal chancery but to the Parlement of Paris (PA 1510, 4; 1512, 5; 1512, 9). To beneficiaries other than Vérard and Eustace no such personal privileges were given, but a considerable number of Letters Patent were issued which included two or more books in a single privilege, a few even for a veritable 'package' of anything up to eight books (e.g. CH 1512, 1). Thus over 150 books may have appeared during this period under grants from the royal chancery.

All these privileges were granted in response to a petition. The initiative came from the authors and the publishers. But the king and his chancery were not unprepared for the demand when it came. The chancery was constantly dealing with applications for royal favours, such as petitions for naturalisation, and could readily adapt its forms to a new kind of concession. And for book-privileges there were already precedents. Not only was there the one fifteenth-century French grant which had already been made (CH 1498, 1). There was the example of the chancery of the duchy of Milan, which was taken over by Louis XII as soon as Ludovico Sforza had fled from the city (2 September 1499). The ducal chancery continued to function, separately from the chancery of France, though under French rule duties there were shared between French and Milanese officials.[1] One of the latter, the secretary who signed as B. Calcus, had served under the Sforza dukes and actually put his name to at least three of the book-privileges granted by Ludovico.[2] Not surprisingly the king-duke was soon being petitioned by his Italian subjects for privileges on the same lines as those granted by his Sforza predecessor. And on 1 July 1501 Janus Parrhasius obtained a four-year privilege for his edition of Sedulius and Prudentius, signed 'Per Regem ducem Mediolani, Ad relationem Consilii, Iulius',[3] an edition which was duly printed by Guillelmus Le Signerre and published that year. This was apparently the first of such privileges, but it was followed by others. And if such business was mainly dealt with by the Italian secretaries in the Milan chancery, their French colleagues working daily alongside them had plenty of opportunity to hear of privileges being granted to authors and publishers and to see them being embodied in official documents. Among these French secretaries there were

---

[1] L. G. Pélissier, Les sources milanaises de l'histoire de Louis XII: Trois registres de lettres ducales de Louis XII aux Archives de Milan (1892), pp. 4–5.

[2] For the Convivio of Filelfo, 10 November 1483, for the works of Campanus, 26 March 1495, and for Fulgentius and other books, 9 November 1497.

[3] Milan, 1501, 8°. The Letters Patent are printed on f. p 6ᵛ. BN Rés.pYc 1739.

indeed two who are later to be found signing book-privileges in the royal chancery in France: Pierre Garbot, who signed a grant to Guillaume Eustace in 1514 (CH 1514; 3), and Robert Gedoyn, afterwards the *secrétaire des finances*, who signed a grant at Blois in November 1512 (CII 1512, 4) and subsequently several others (CH 1518, 5; 1519, 4; 1519, 6).[1]

Continuity can also be shown between the privilege-system in Milan and in France in the case of authors. Giovanni Francesco Conti, called Quinziano Stoa, was crowned poet laureate by Louis XII in Milan in 1509, and his neo-Latin poem *Orpheos* (BN Rés.myc 706) came out in 1510 at Milan under the king's privilege applying to the whole of the duchy, which is summarised at the end of the text. But Stoa followed the king to France, and by 1514 he was publishing a new poem, in praise of Paris, *Cleopolis*, together with a reprint of *Orpheos*, issued by Jean de Gourmont, with a privilege obtained from the Parlement of Paris (PA 1514, 8), and dedicated to the chancellor of France Antoine Duprat. The Milan connection may well have stimulated privilege-consciousness among French authors frequenting the royal court, though it did not create it. Eloi d'Amerval (CH 1508, 1), Nicole Bohier (CH 1509, 1) and Jean Lemaire de Belges (CH 1509, 2) had already obtained royal privileges before Louis XII's conquest of the duchy.

The first applicant – or the first successful applicant – to Louis XII in the sixteenth century for a particular book was Eloi d'Amerval, author of the *Livre de la deablerie*, who was choir-master of Sainte-Croix of Orleans, that is, of the cathedral. Although little is known of him at the present day, he might easily have been known personally to the king, who had been duke of Orleans before his accession, or at least to members of the royal court. The *Deablerie* was his only work, a satire on contemporary society, which perhaps developed from organising plays (to be performed by the choir school) of the irreverent kind which was allowed at certain seasons of the year. Evidently he set store by it, and was going to reap the sole benefit from it for as long as he could. The work did in fact have a certain success, for his publisher Michel Le Noir reprinted in a different format some years later, and Alain Lotrian, who only set up in business in 1525, thought it worthwhile to issue another edition of it.[2] In the mean time, Eloi chose a moment when the court and the chancery were at Blois, not far from Orleans, and duly obtained his privilege (CH 1508, 1). Le Noir for his part may have been induced to give the prominence that he did to the privilege, or even have suggested it to Eloi, because he had himself lost a lawsuit four years before to an author whose book he had published without permission.[3]

All Letters Patent issued by the royal chancery went out in the king's name

---

[1] For the activity of Garbot in the Milan chancery there is evidence starting with a document signed by him in Milan on 26 October 1499 (Pélissier, *Les sources milanaises*, p. 5); for that of Gedoyn, a document signed by him in Milan on 12 July 1501 (ibid. p. 16).

[2] BL 85.e.21 and 85.e.20.   [3] See below, p. 36.

and in principle they emanated from him. It may indeed be assumed that the very first requests for privileges from authors and publishers entailed a decision by the king in person. It was a favour of a new kind. If granted, details would have to be settled, such as the length of time for which the monopoly should be allowed to run, which could thereafter serve as precedents. Subsequently the king's part in the grant of most privileges was probably nominal. An occasion like the formal presentation of a hitherto unpublished work to the king or queen by the author may sometimes have given an opportunity for a privilege to be requested and for verbal assent to be given. The request would then be passed to one of the secretaries in attendance, to be dealt with in the chancery. A highly developed administration existed, under the direction of the chancellor, for giving effect to grants of this kind. Letters Patent were authenticated by the royal seal and by the signature of a royal secretary or other authorised signatory in the chancery. The king's signature was not required on them, as it was required on *Lettres Closes* addressed to individuals. All, however, needed an act of authorisation or *jussio* from an official empowered to make a decision. When any matter of principle was involved, which could not be settled by looking up precedents, reference would be made to the chancellor, or, in turn, by the chancellor to the Council or to the king himself. Almost daily consultation between the king and the chancellor existed for much of the time, and any question for the king's decision could easily be submitted to him.

The grant of a privilege from the royal chancery was an exercise of the royal prerogative, and in principle a personal favour: there could be uncertainty whether a privilege granted by one king was valid under his successor. Galliot Du Pré obtained a grant for three years on 6 May 1514 for *Le grant coustumier de France* from Louis XII (CH 1514, 1(2)). He had not yet published the book when the king died at the end of that year. With very good legal advice at his disposal – he had a shop in the *palais* and specialised in law-books – he judged it prudent to seek confirmation of the privilege from the new king. This he duly received, in the form of Letters Patent issued anew, to which the old privilege 'soubz nostre contreseel' was attached. The king recognised that the applicant 'feared now lest, because the Letters are not obtained from us, they may be invalid, unless he has our express Letters' ('ledit exposant doubte à present qu'au moyen que lesdites lettres ne sont de nous obtenues elle<s> luy soient de nul effect sans avoir sur ce noz lettres expresses', CH 1515, 3). Galliot was no doubt particularly anxious that his papers should be in order since *Le grant coustumier* was a publication of national importance. But similar doubts were still current some years later. Pierre Attaignant obtained a prorogation of his privilege from Henry II on his accession in 1547, without waiting for the expiry of his six-year privilege which Francis I had last renewed in 1543.[1] And the poet Ronsard, enjoying a 'perpetual' privilege for his works, granted to him by Henry II on 23 February 1559, hastened to apply afresh to Francis II on his accession, fearing that someone might claim that the privilege had automatically lapsed on the death of the sovereign who had given it ('creignant qu'on voulsist pretendre le Privilege à lui octroyé par nostre dict feu Seigneur et pere estre expiré par son deces').[2]

Seen from the point of view of the chancery, let alone from that of the king in whose name all Letters Patent were issued from it, grants of book-privileges formed a very small proportion of its activities and concerned very small favours. In the course of fifteen days, 15–30 June 1517, and that during a period when the chancery was moving from place to place and therefore not operating at full strength, it issued 117 Letters, of which twenty-four were *lettres simples*, the category to which book-privileges belonged: only one of these was a book-privilege (CH 1517, 5). In the 1530s, when the extant records are more complete, it can be seen more clearly what a veritable torrent of Letters regularly poured out from the chancery. In the second half of 1535, for instance, a total of 1,687 Letters is recorded, 1,085 of them *lettres simples*. It has been estimated that, if the chancellor held his regular audience for the use of the seal twice a week, he must have sealed some fifty-five to fifty-seven Letters at each session, not counting the few for which the fee was waived.[3]

Book-privileges cost the Crown nothing to give. There were other favours which involved some sacrifice: ennoblement of a commoner meant that he and his family were henceforth exempt from ordinary taxation, naturalisation of a foreigner meant that his possessions if he died in France could no longer be claimed as *aubaine*, and so on. There was no such disadvantage in giving a short-term monopoly to an author or publisher for a particular new book. Similarly, as far as the chancellor and his staff were concerned, they had nothing to lose by facilitating the grant of book-privileges. Indeed the reverse was true. Unlike present-day civil servants, every operation that went through their hands tended to bring them not only work but personal profit. The official fees for drawing up the document and for the use of the seal provided the funds from which they were paid, and a proportion of the fee might even be payable direct to them, e.g. 1s out of a 6s fee to the notary concerned.[4] Secretaries and clerks could also expect some perquisites. Few transactions of this kind went through in the sixteenth century without some customary gift to an official. At Brussels on 20 January 1534 Roger Hang-ouart, acting on behalf of the city of Lille, paid 56s for a one-year imperial privilege for the *Coutumes* of the city which had been recently drawn up, before

---

[1] Daniel Heartz, *Pierre Attaignant, royal printer of music* (University of California Press, 1969), pp. 174, 184, 188.
[2] Pierre de Ronsard, *Œuvres complètes*, ed. P. Laumonier (STFM), Vol. x, p. 169.
[3] H. Michaud, *La Grande Chancellerie et les écritures royales au XVIᵉ siècle* (1967), p. 340.
[4] Ibid. p. 336, n. 1.

proceeding to Antwerp to have them printed: he also paid 12s – a gratuity of about 21 per cent of the official fee – to the clerk.[1] No one concerned, therefore, had any reason to refuse a book-privilege from the chancery to an applicant who was prepared to pay for it, as long as the applicant could make out a reasonable case for it. Why then did applicants in France go, even more often than to the chancery, to the lawcourts, and quite frequently to the Prévôt of Paris?

Sometimes it is possible to discern reasons why a petitioner elected to apply to an authority other than the royal chancery. An applicant wishing to publish in print the *style* of a particular lawcourt would naturally apply to the court concerned, for its consent and for a privilege. The prospective publisher of a newly codified or newly revised *Coutume* would in most cases go to the Parlement. If on the contrary he was venturing on copy which would be obviously unwelcome to the Parlement, such as the text of the Concordat of Francis I and the papacy, or a royal *Ordonnance* which the Parlement had objected to registering, he would have a motive for preferring to go to the chancery.

Otherwise, all the royal authorities were evidently equally willing to entertain requests for privileges for any kind of publication and from any kind of applicant. Considerations of opportunity, convenience and cost seem usually to have dictated the choice of authority to approach. More authors are to be found among successful applicants for privileges from the chancery, perhaps simply because they were in a better position to attend the royal court or have useful connections with it. If publishers seem to show a preference for the Parlement or another of the lawcourts, the explanation is probably to be sought here too in most cases in purely practical circumstances.

Movements of the royal chancery: a problem for applicants

An applicant for a privilege from the chancery would, if the royal court was in residence at Paris, have no further to go than would be necessary if he were applying to the Parlement or to the Prévôt. Considerations of state or pleasure, war or diplomacy, however, often took the king of France at this period for weeks or even months at a time to other places. And with the king, or closely following him, moved not only his household but the entire centre of government, the diplomatic corps, the secretaries of state, and the chancery.

The problems created by this itinerant habit were serious but not insuperable for the applicant while Louis XII was king. He never resided for long in

---

[1] *Catalogue de la Bibliothèque de la ville de Lille: Jurisprudence* (Lille, 1870), p. 262, quoting the *Compte de la ville pour un an fini le 31 octobre 1534*, ff. vij^{xx}xij^v and vij^{xx}iiij^{r-v}: *Coustumes & usaiges de la ville ... de Lille*, Martin Lempereur (Antwerp) for Michel Willem (Lille), 1534, 4°. BN F.Rés.1062. The privilege signed 'Par Lempereur en son conseil & signé M. Stric', is printed on ff. A ii^{r-v}. The practice of the French royal chancery was very similar.

his capital city. But, by the time applications for book-privileges to the chancery became frequent, he could usually be found at one of the royal residences in the Loire valley, particularly at Blois, and on occasion his business took him to Lyon and other major cities [1] Thus the whereabouts of his chancery at any particular time could at least be ascertained with some certainty. Applicants naturally preferred to wait, if they waited at all, until they could do their business with the chancery on the spot. The king was at Lyon in August 1511. No Paris applicants sought him out there. On the other hand Jacques de Bouys, bookseller of the university of Orleans, found it convenient to get a privilege there (CH 1511, 3) for his edition of Jacobus de Belviso, *Consuetudines et usus feudorum*, edited by Nicolas Beraldus, since he was in any case having the book printed in Lyon by Jacques Sacon. And the Lyon bookseller Jean Robion was presumably delighted to get a privilege on the spot, without having to pay for a journey to Paris, for Antonius de Petrutia, *Tractatus de viribus iuramenti*, which he and Jean de Clauso were having printed by Jean de Vingle (25 August 1511) and published that year on 11 November (CH 1511, 2). Apart from these, all the Louis XII book-privileges of which details are known were granted either at Paris or at Blois.

The physical difficulties a privilege-seeker might have to overcome to attend the royal court and chancery became much more formidable in 1515 after the accession of Francis I, who travelled extensively in his kingdom, not to mention campaigning abroad. Though these habits made the king familiar with and to his people in many parts of France, they caused frequent hardships for men whose business took them or kept them at court, as we know in particular from the bitter complaints of the *corps diplomatique*, as recorded by the Venetian ambassadors.[2] Had these peregrinations followed a regular pattern, at least in peace-time, authors and publishers would have had some idea when to expect the chancery in Paris or in Lyon, or wherever it might be. As it was, though the king spent (according to a reliable calculation) on average one day in every eleven in Paris during the whole of his reign,[3] the reality was between long absences and long periods of residence, both equally unpredictable.

There was always in the *palais*, with the Parlement of Paris, a 'chancellerie', which was permanent, but in the absence of the chancellor and the great seal it was not able to transact more than routine business,[4] and there is only one

---

[1] F. Maillard, 'Itinéraire de Louis XII (1498–1515)', *Bulletin philologique et historique de Comité des Travaux historiques et scientifiques* (1979), pp. 171–206.

[2] E.g. 'Relation de Marin Giustiniano', in *Relations des ambassadeurs vénitiens sur les affaires de France*, ed. N. Tommaseo (1838), pp. 96–109.

[3] Houdart, *Les châteaux royaux de Saint-Germain*, Vol. 1, p. 246 (quoted by L. Hautecoeur, *Histoire de l'architecture classique en France*, nouvelle édition, Vol. 1, pt. 1, 1963, p. 228, n. 2). Cf. the *Itinéraire* printed in the *Catalogue des Actes de François Ier* (Académie des Sciénces Morales), Vol. VIII, pp. 412–533.

[4] Michaud, *La grande chancellerie*, p. 331.

possible case of this 'petite chancellerie' issuing privileges for books (PA 1512, 9).[1]

Francis I was indeed in Paris when the first book-privileges of his reign were granted. It was there that the chancery issued a privilege to Galliot Du Pré on 20 January 1515 for *L'hystoire du sainct greaal* (CH 1515, 1) and to Dr Jean Falcon of Lyon on 19 February for *Les notables declaratifs sur le Guidon* (CH 1515, 1A) published in due course by Constantin Fradin at Lyon. Another Paris publisher followed suit, Antoine Bonnemère (CH 1515, 2), and Galliot Du Pré soon afterwards obtained confirmation of a Louis XII privilege (CH 1515, 3, cf. CH 1514, 1(2)). And on 26 April Geofroy de Marnef, with Simon Vincent of Lyon, were granted a privilege by the chancery for the treatise *De seditiosis*, by Nicole Bohier, a royal *conseiller* (CH 1515, 4). But the king himself left Paris on 24 April. He was already planning an invasion of Italy to recover the duchy of Milan. By 12 July he was in Lyon, where he was to spend three weeks completing his preparations. It was accordingly to Lyon that Jean Petit of Paris had to go, or send his representative, to seek out the royal chancery when he needed a privilege to protect an important 'package' of new publications (CH 1515, 5). Thenceforth Paris applicants evidently resigned themselves to doing without privileges from the royal chancery until the king's return from Italy.

For a provincial privilege-seeker, on the other hand, the direction taken by the king's itinerary might prove a windfall. At the end of July, Francis left Lyon to join his army which had been assembling at Grenoble, the capital of the Dauphiné. Hearing of this, an enterprising bookseller at Valence, who had a new book ready for publication by a renowned local jurist and historian, Aymar du Rivail, rode or sent to Grenoble in time to secure a privilege for it from the king-dauphin on 8 August 1515, just before Francis left for Italy with the chancellor (CH 1515, 6). Back in Lyon, members of the king's Council and some of the staff of the chancery were still there in sufficient strength to deal with an application by Nicole Bohier on behalf of the Lyon publisher Simon Vincent, for a three-year privilege (CH 1515, 7), granted on 16 August 'Par le roy, à la relation du conseil'. This was a grant to which the agreement of the chancellor might have already been given or could be assumed. The beneficiary was the same Nicole Bohier whose treatise *De seditiosis* had received a privilege earlier that year (CH 1515, 4). He was a learned lawyer, a trusted servant of the Crown and a member of the king's Council. The books in question were all sponsored by Bohier: an edition by Jean Thierry of the *Quaestiones* on civil law by Pierre de Belleperche, a former chancellor of France (d. 1308); the *Commentaria* on the *coutumes* of the duchy of Burgundy by Barthélemy de Chasseneuz, doctor of law, King's Advocate in the *bailliage* of Autun, afterwards President of the Parlement of Toulouse; and another legal

---

[1] Cf. below, p. 70.

work, the *Tractatus* and *Singularia* of Guido Papa, edited by Jean Thierry. The chancery evidently issued a privilege a few days later, at Lyon, on 21 August (CH 1515, 8) to Pierre Balet of Lyon for an edition of Jacobus de Belviso, *Practica iudiciaria in criminalibus.*

The king had appointed his mother, Louise of Savoy, as Regent of France in his absence on 15 July 1515. She and the queen, who was expecting her first child, took up residence at Amboise, and the government was carried on from there. She was provided with the *petit sceau*, entrusted to the safe keeping of Mondot de La Marthonnye, which sufficed to authenticate Letters Patent while the chancellor with the Great Seal was away. Members of the staff of the chancery who did not accompany the king and the chancellor to Italy re-grouped round her. Some members of the Council and some of the royal secretaries were with her. If Amboise was a fair distance to go, for applicants from Paris or Lyon, specially to seek a privilege, it was relatively convenient for Guillaume Bouchet of Poitiers in quest of a privilege for Malleret, *De electionibus*, which he obtained at Amboise on 19 September (CH 1515, 9): the journey to Paris would have been nearly three times as far.

There were on the other hand successful applications at places along the route followed by the king on his return journey. In addition to the opportunities offered by the court's stay at Lyon in March–May 1516 to Lyon applicants (e.g. CH 1516, 5), the king's brief visit to Crémieu (Isère) was marked by the grant of a privilege to Hugues Descousu, 'docteur en tous droitz' on 19 May (CH 1516, 1). As the king, after leaving Lyon, journeyed home by easy stages, he reached the little town of Issoire (Puy-de-Dôme). There, on 20 July 1516, advantage was taken of the presence, however brief, of the royal chancery by Vincent Cigauld, 'juge ordinaire de la ville et conté de Brivadoys', who had to come only the relatively short ride from Brive (Corrèze) to obtain a privilege for his legal works, which he too was planning to have printed at Lyon (CH 1516, 2).

· By that autumn, the court and the chancery were back in Paris, and the grant of privileges there resumed. But in the summer of 1517 the king went on a progress through Picardy and Normandy, culminating in a state entry into Rouen on 2 August 1517. And it was while the court was still at Rouen that Michel Le Noir of Paris obtained his important 'package' privilege for four books (CH 1517, 6). More often it was the Rouen applicants who had to journey to Paris. Such was the case of Simon Gruel when he sought a privilege for a pioneer work on French rhetoric by the Rouen author Pierre Le Fèvre (or Fabri) three years later (CH 1520, 6).

The provincial author or publisher who came in quest for a privilege to the chancery when it was in Paris might at least be able to combine this operation with other business. And indeed a Paris applicant might be able to combine a visit to the chancery at Rouen or Lyon, for instance, with other business. On occasion, he might be prepared to make a special journey still further afield in search of a privilege. In the first half of 1518, when the royal court was in the Loire valley, privileges were obtained by Enguilbert de Marnef (CH 1518, 1) and by the scholar Vincent Doesmier (CH 1518, 3) at Amboise and by Jean Petit (CH 1518, 4) at Angers. A particularly long absence from Paris on the part of the king, from 13 October 1520 to 9 December 1521, is reflected in the small number of privileges issued by the chancery during this period.

Dr Gabriel de Tarregua of Bordeaux received a grant for his medical works on 10 November 1520 at Amboise (CH 1520, 10), and he or his representative may have been glad not to have to journey further in winter to find the royal court and the chancery. Jean Petit of Paris, or his agent, on the other hand, had to track them down as they were setting out for Burgundy when he secured a privilege on 2 April 1521 at Sancerre (Cher) (CH 1521, 3). Journeys of this kind were quite beyond the means of most authors and publishers, involving much expense in travel and an absence of days or even weeks from their profession or their business. Even Saint-Germain-en-Laye, where the royal court often settled for fairly long periods, and which is by modern standards within easy reach of Paris, was rarely sought out by applicants: Regnault Chaudière applied there twice within a few weeks in 1519 (CH 1519, 4 and CH 1519, 5) and Enguilbert de Marnef once three years later (CH 1522, 6). Two authors, Nicole Bohier (CH 1519, 5) and Jean d'Ivry (CH 1519, 7) pursued the court a little further down the Seine when it was at Carrières (Seine-et-Oise).

The residence of the royal court and the chancery in Paris in the winter of 1521–2 is marked by several applications by Paris publishers (CH 1521, 4; 1521, 5; 1522, 1), but by April both were in Lyon: there in June advantage was taken of the presence of each by a Lyon publisher to obtain a privilege (CH 1522, 3) and by the mathematician Oronce Finé (CH 1522, 4). In July Jacques de Mortières of Châlons-sur-Saône got a grant for his translation of a work by Mantuanus (CH 1522, 5). No doubt he also had the opportunity of presenting it personally to Marguerite, duchess of Alençon, the king's sister, to whom it is dedicated, as she was in Lyon then with the court.

There is a particularly long gap in the last part of the period here under consideration, after the grant of privileges in the spring of 1523 at Paris, on 23 March (CH 1523, 2) and on 2 April (CH 1523, 3). No further privileges are known to have been issued by the chancery in 1523. Only one is known with certainty for 1524, the grant obtained at Avignon on 23 September by Geofroy Tory (CH 1524, 2), though two other books published that year advertise a royal privilege, which may have been granted earlier (CH 1524, 1, and CH 1524, 3). None at all is known for 1525 until October–November when there are four (CH 1525, 1, 2, 3 and 4), and, after that, none until July 1526 (CH 1526, 1).

This disruption can be explained at least to a large extent by the events of the reign. The king was only very briefly in Paris in the summer of 1523 (22–4

July) before going to Lyon to await news of his forces in Italy. On learning of the treason of the Constable, the duc de Bourbon, he went to Blois, where he spent the winter, a severe winter which must have discouraged petitioners from Paris or Lyon from seeking out the royal chancery there. After a short visit to Paris in March 1524 to urge on the trial of Bourbon, he returned to Blois. On 12 July 1524 he left on the expedition to Italy which was to end in the disastrous battle of Pavia (24 February 1525), at which he was defeated and taken prisoner. His mother Louise of Savoy was Regent and set up her headquarters at the monastery of Saint-Just close to Lyon. The chancellor Duprat with the Great Seal, members of the Council, and senior secretaries of state were with her. Here they received news of the battle of Pavia and here they waited for the latest news in the negotiations for the king's release. And here the chancery gave three book-privileges, two to Lyon publishers and one to a Paris author, while far away in Rennes the chancery of the duchy of Brittany issued to its *huissier* a privilege in the king's name for the *style*, recently authorised by the Regent, to be used in the Breton courts (CH 1525, 3).[1]

On the king's return from imprisonment in Spain, the news that he had set foot on French soil was sent from Bayonne by Jean de Selve on Sunday 18 March and was received in Paris late on Wednesday 21 March.[2] Such was the speed which could be achieved by experienced official messengers with fresh horses held ready at every stage of the journey, regardless of expense. Conditions for the ordinary traveller were very different. And the familiar difficulties reasserted themselves for privilege-seekers, as the king took his time about coming back to his capital, and soon left it again. Galliot Du Pré or his representative in July found the chancery at Amboise (CH 1526, 1) and Geofroy Tory in September at Chenonceaux (CH 1526, 2).

In contrast to the vagaries of the royal chancery, the lawcourts functioned predictably and regularly, if not always expeditiously, and had a permanent home. The Parlement of Paris, for instance, occupied buildings of the *palais*, on the Ile de la Cité, in the heart of Paris.

Parlement: origins of Parlement privilege-giving

From 1507 to 1526 inclusive, at least 112 privileges for printed books were issued on the authority of the sovereign courts. The Parlement of Paris contributed 102 of these. The remainder was made up by the Parlement of Toulouse (7), the Parlement of Rouen (2), the Cour des Aides in Paris (1) and the Grands Jours of the duchy of Berry (1). The Parlement of Paris occasionally granted privileges covering two or more books: thus the total

---

[1] See below, p. 92.

[2] *Captivité du roi François 1er*, ed. A. Champollion-Figeac (1847), pp. 518–19, 522–3.

number of *books* known to have been published under these privileges appears to be 127. The number of *grants* had reached ten per year by 1512. Thereafter there was no tendency to increase. There were, however, fluctuations. The grave circumstances in France in 1523–4 are reflected in a drop to one in 1523, followed by a leap to fourteen in 1524, falling back to nine in 1525 and three in 1526. Normally the annual number of grants varied from three to ten.

Many of these grants are known only from the printed books themselves, in which a transcript is provided of the certified copy of the court's decision. Only forty-four of the 102 grants made by the Parlement of Paris have been found recorded in the registers of the Parlement. On the other hand the registers record a couple of grants for items which have not survived or perhaps were never published (e.g. PA 1524, 6A), and they can sometimes prove that the Parlement was the authority for the privilege where the book itself bears only the words 'Cum priuilegio' (e.g. PA 1512, 7). The absence of an entry in the registers is not in itself remarkable. It is by no means unheard of for a judgement of the Parlement, even concerning an important lawsuit, and even when the registers were very well kept, to be unrecorded in the surviving volumes of the registers.[1] Such a high proportion of omissions as that occurring in the case of the book-privileges can however hardly be an accident. Either some of the *conseillers* thought the grant of such a privilege of enough consequence to be entered in the main register, while others did not, or else the applicant himself chose whether or not to ask for permanent registration of his privilege, which was after all a short-term concession never valid for more than four years at most, no doubt paying an extra fee accordingly if he opted for registration. In the seventeenth century, when the Parlement no longer had the right to grant privileges on its own authority, it was still often called upon by beneficiaries to *register* privileges obtained from the royal chancery.[2] This procedure was not universal or compulsory, and it was an extra expense, but it was adopted by privilege-holders who thought their grants especially likely to be contested. Such considerations may well, in the earlier period, have influenced authors and publishers who had obtained privileges from the Parlement itself, in deciding whether or not to ask for the grant to be incorporated in the registers in their final and permanent form.

For a lawcourt to grant book-privileges at all was most unusual in the context of the privilege-system as it had been growing up in the rest of Europe. How then had the French Parlement come to give them?

The Parlement of Paris was the highest court of appeal for the kingdom of France. Its duty of checking and registering all royal edicts and ordinances

---

[1] E.g. *English suits before the Parlement of Paris 1420–1436*, ed. C. T. Allmand and C. A. J. Armstrong, Camden Fourth Series, XXVI (Royal Historical Society, 1982), p. 25, n. 17.

[2] H.-J. Martin, *Livre, pouvoirs et société à Paris au xviiᵉ siècle*, Publications du Centre de recherches d'Histoire et de Philologie de la ivᵉ Section de l'Ecole Pratique des Hautes Etudes, Paris: VI, Histoire et civilisation du livre, 3 (Geneva), 1969, I, p. 448.

even enabled it to exercise a certain political function, by querying the validity of legislation of which it disapproved, though its powers did not develop on the same lines as those of the English Parliament. Within the Paris area, the city itself and the surrounding Parisis, it functioned also as a court of first instance. In this capacity it was however expensive and many litigants preferred the alternative of the court of the Prévôt of Paris. Within this area too the Parlement had also for a long time acted as a body which ensured the supply of food and fuel to the capital, regulated the prices of essential commodities, and took part in keeping order among trades and crafts. It had thus become natural for residents in Paris, particularly artisans and merchants, to look to the Parlement for justice even in relatively minor matters. Hitherto, the book-trade had lain outside its jurisdiction: in the manuscript era, this was controlled by the university, through its *librarii jurati* who controlled the copying of books and the selling and hiring of them. Printing changed this situation. It was a new craft, without restrictions or regulations. Anyone could set up a press. Anyone could finance or sell printed books. Understandably, then, cases involving printed books had begun to come before the Parlement before the end of the fifteenth century. On 8 January 1486, an *arrêt* of the Parlement allowed Vincent Commin, bookseller of Paris, to put on sale in Sens or elsewhere the breviaries and missals of the archdiocese of Sens (which then included Paris) which he had printed, notwithstanding the opposition of the archbishop of Sens.[1] Another *arrêt*, of 7 September 1503, authorised Macé Panthoul, bookseller at Troyes, to put on sale an edition of the synodal statutes of that diocese, the sale of which had been suspended by the king's officers owing to incorrect wording found in them, on condition that he made the required corrections.[2]

The Parlement had also begun to appreciate the usefulness of printing for its own purposes, namely for circulating large numbers of correct copies of laws and regulations. On 30 August 1499 it paid the Paris printers Gervais Coignart and Jean Bonhomme the sum of twelve *livres parisis* for 100 bound copies of certain *ordonnances* supplied by them to the king's *procureur général* to be sent out to royal officers throughout the kingdom. The following 6 March it paid Coignart forty *livres parisis* for 200 copies of other *ordonnances*, for the *procureur général* to send out, duly signed and sealed to authenticate them, 'aux juges et officiers des provinces de ce royaume.'[3] In 1504 an author brought a case in the Parlement against a bookseller for causing a work of his to be printed without his permission. The author, Dr Guillaume Cop, a well-known member of the Paris Faculty of Medicine, regularly prepared almanacs for the coming year. Such publications always sold well, especially when the name of

---

[1] Reprinted in A. Claudin, *Histoire de l'imprimerie en France*, II (1901), p. 508, n. 1.
[2] L. Morin, *Histoire corporative des artisans du livre à Troyes* (1900) (Extrait des *Mémoires de la Société académique de l'Aube*, 1899–1900, vols. 63–4), p. 276, Pièces justificatives 1.
[3] AN x 1 A 1504, f. 402ʳ, and x 1 A 1505, f. 78ᵛ.

a scientist of repute was attached to them, and could be a considerable source of profit.[1] A Paris bookseller, Jean Boissier, had contrived to secure a copy of Guillaume Cop's almanac and to have it printed and sold. Apparently he continued to deal in it even when Cop had obtained an *arrêt* from the Parlement forbidding him to sell any copies which Cop himself had not signed, and so authenticated. A further petition to the Parlement from Cop resulted in Boissier being summoned before the court and forbidden on pain of imprisonment and fine to sell any of Cop's 'armenatz' which had not been signed by the author (5 March 1504).[2] This meant that Cop could withhold his signature and therefore stop the sale of unauthorised copies. We are here, it seems, close to the familiar formula 'None genuine without this signature'. Cop may indeed have thought of his signature on an almanac upon which the public relied for correct information on phases of the moon, hours of day-light etc., as being like a signature on a medical prescription, that is, a guarantee of professional authority. The Parlement itself was familiar with the idea of authenticating by signature every copy of an official printed publication, as we have seen, and it was to require such a signature when it first gave privileges to *greffiers* for printed editions of the *Coutumes*. But Cop's method of protecting his literary property was not, to my knowledge, copied by any other author, during this period, and, however effective, it did not constitute a privilege.

By May 1504 the Parlement was dealing with a lawsuit between the author and royal publicist André de La Vigne and the university printer and bookseller Michel Le Noir, who was printing a work which La Vigne petitioned the Parlement to stop, on 30 April 1504. At the first hearing, on 11 May 1504, the court gave La Vigne two weeks to prepare his case, and allowed Le Noir, according to *his* petition, to complete the printing, with the proviso that no copies of his edition should yet be put on sale. The court's judgement went against Le Noir. On 3 June 1504 it decided that neither he nor any other bookseller or printer of Paris were to print or sell the two works in question, *Le vergier de honneur* and *Les regnars traversans*, until 1 April of the following year, on pain of confiscation of the edition and of a fine. Le Noir was in addition condemned to paying the costs of the case.[3] There are details about this case which are perplexing. *Le vergier de honneur* was certainly by André de La Vigne, but *Les regnars traversans* was neither by him nor, as Michel Le Noir (following Antoine Vérard) claimed when his edition finally appeared, by Sebastian Brant,[4] but by Jean Bouchet of Poitiers.

[1] Cf. above, p. 16.

[2] 'La court a fait defenses audit Boissier à peine de prison et d'amende arbitraire de ne vendre aucuns armenatz faits par ledit Le Cop sinon qu'il les ait prealablement signez.' AN x 1 A 1509, f. 94^r.

[3] AN x 1 A 1509, f. 171^r, 3 June 1504. For the earlier hearing, see f. 154^r.

[4] *Les regnars traversans* was first published, under the name of Sebastien Brand, by Vérard, among books undated but published 1500–3. J. Macfarlane, *Antoine Vérard* (1900), p. 74, no. 149. Le

The first application, or at least the first successful application, to the Parlement of Paris, for a privilege came three years later, in June 1507. A Paris bookseller, Eustace de Brie, whose shop was a few streets away from the Parlement, at the sign of the *Sabot*, behind the church of St Mary Magdalene, found himself that summer with two highly topical and highly saleable items, which he could not hope to publish in the ordinary way without the risk of them being immediately copied by competitors. It is probably no accident that one of these items, *La louenge des roys de France*, was by André de La Vigne, who had good reason to know the dangers of unauthorised printers getting hold of his works. The other, too, was a work which he may have been instrumental in producing, as secretary to the queen and a regular writer on behalf of royal policies: *La chronique de Gennes*, an anonymous account of the king's conquest of Genoa. As this includes the royal *ordonnance* issued at Genoa and dated 10 May 1507, it was almost an official publication, as well as being undisguised propaganda for the king. There could be no question at that moment of seeking a privilege from the royal chancery. Indeed the chancery had not then granted any book-privileges except the one obtained nearly ten years before for Johannes Trechsel (CH 1498, 1) and possibly the personal privilege obtained by Antoine Vérard which seems to have been granted before the beginning of 1508 (CH 1507, 1). So, perhaps in consultation with La Vigne, Eustace de Brie went to the Parlement with a *requête*. And he duly received a privilege, for one year, dated 17 June 1507, given jointly by the Parlement and the king's *procureur général* in the Parlement, the terms of which he summarised in the colophon of both books (PA 1507, 1).

The Parlement was creating a precedent, and it was significant that it issued its first book-privilege in association with the *procureur du roi*. It was granting a favour of a new kind, of a kind which it might be thought only the king himself could grant. And the favour was for books of which the content closely concerned the king. Since the fourteenth century the Parlement had been asserting its status as the king's supreme court to do justice in his name and to preserve the royal prerogative against any encroachment. It was therefore the established practice of the Parlement to consult the *procureur du roi* in any case brought before it which might directly or indirectly, practically or theoretically, affect the interests of the Crown, before the court proceeded to adjudicate on a petition requiring the approval of the Parlement. If the Parlement judged in the petitioner's favour, he could then obtain from it, on payment, *lettres royaux* or an *arrêt*, which represented the formal dispensation of royal justice. Consultation with the *procureur du roi* thus naturally followed the first petition for a book-privilege. Small as the grant of a short-term monopoly for two small books might seem, it could not be allowed to serve as a precedent without the most careful consideration. The procedure of issuing the privilege

---

Noir's edition, dated 21 May 1504 (BN yh 61 Rés.), shows signs of a change of plan after *Les regnars traversans* and it does not include *Le vergier de honneur.*

jointly with the *procureur du roi* was not followed again. The point had been settled, in principle. But the Parlement was to be found throughout this period consulting him on any special occasion when the case under consideration seemed to call for it, e.g. 'ouy sur ce le procureur general du roy' (PA 1525, 8, cf. PA 1526, 2). The Cour des Aides when granting a privilege, its only one during this time, did likewise (PA 1517, 4). The *procureur du roi* attached to the Parlement of Toulouse was similarly consulted, on at least one occasion, about the grant of a book privilege: 'Oye la responce et dire du procureur du roy' (PA 1517, 3). The *procureur du roi* who participated in the first grant of a book-privilege by the Parlement of Paris, Guillaume Roger, had then only just assumed his functions, his predecessor Jean Burdelot having died in office in March 1507. He held the position until 1523, so he may have contributed to a certain consistency of policy towards the granting of privileges. He may also have helped to ensure some uniformity of practice, in the early stages, between the Parlement and the *prévôté* of Paris. He had *ex officio* to preside over the *prévôté* if the office of Prévôt fell vacant, and this happened twice, once on the death in September 1509 of Jacques d'Estouteville, who had been Prévôt since 1479, and again on the death of Jacques de Coligny in May 1512, the second term extending until March 1513 when Gabriel d'Allegre was appointed Prévôt.[1]

The precedent thus established by the grant to Eustace de Brie did not unloose a flood of applications for book-privileges to the Parlement. There was however an application the following spring. It concerned a translation into French of the Pragmatic Sanction with a treatise on the plurality of benefices by Guillaume Pérault. The beneficiary was Martin Alexandre 'and his partners' ('pour Martin Alixandre et ses consors'), and the term allowed was again one year, the colophon giving the date 12 April 1508 (PA 1508, 1).

Parlement of Paris, Grands Jours, Cour des Aides

Signs of development in the Parlement privilege system appeared in 1509. Four privileges were granted. Two of these were obtained by leading University booksellers. These two are the first Parlement privileges of which the complete text is known. In each case an authenticated *Extraict des registres de Parlement* is printed prominently in the book itself, an example which was destined to be followed by most though not quite all subsequent holders of such privileges. The first was an edition of a work attributed to St Bruno, an *Expositio* on the Epistles of St Paul, printed and published by Berthold Rembolt, a much-respected printer who had originally come to Paris to work with Ulrich Gering, the proto-typographer of France (PA 1509, 1). The second was a new work by the Scottish scholastic philosopher John Mair or

---

[1] See below, p. 52.

Major, published by Poncet le Preux, who was about to become one of the *libraires jurés* of the University, and Jean Granjon, who already was one (PA 1509, 3).

Rembolt, who was himself a university graduate, had evidently represented in his application or *requête* that the editing of the *Expositio* had been commissioned by the university itself from certain doctors of theology. It may be conjectured that the initiative had come from St Bruno's own order, the Carthusians. At any rate the importance of the publication and the high standing of its sponsors and of its publisher satisfied the Parliament, and it became the first of many purely scholarly books to obtain a privilege in France. The privilege itself ran as follows (see Plate 2):

¶ Extraict des registres de Parlement.

¶ Veue par la court la requeste à elle baillee par maistre Berthole Rembolt maistre libraire de l'université de Paris. Par laquelle / et pour les causes contenues en icelle il requeroit inhibicions et defenses estre faictes à tous libraires et imprimeurs tant de ceste ville de Paris que d'ailleurs: de ne imprimer ou faire imprimer jusques à six ans le livre composé par ung nommé maistre Bruno premier prieur de l'ordre chartreuse sur les epistres de sainct Paul: veu et corrigé par plusieurs docteurs en theologie à ce commis par ladicte université: et par icelluy Rembolt fait imprimer. Veuz aussi aucuns arrestz de ladicte court donnez en pareil cas / Et tout consideré ladicte court a ordonné et ordonne inhibicions et defenses estre faictes à tous libraires et imprimeurs et aultres quelzconques de ne imprimer ou faire imprimer de huy jusques à trois ans ledict livre et exposicion des epistres saint Paul / sur peine de confiscacion desditz livres et d'amende arbitraire. Faict en parlement / le .xij. jour de Janvier l'an Mil cinq cens huit.

Collacion est faicte.
Robert.

The words 'veuz aussi aucuns arrestz de ladicte court donnez en pareil cas' show that precedents were already building up. The form of the grant made to Poncet Le Preux and Jean Granjon for Mair's *Quartus sententiarum* four months later (PA 1509, 3) is in fact almost identical. Two other book-privileges in 1509 extended the scope of the system in a direction much more closely connected with the Parlement's own operations: the publication of the *Coutumes*, the customary law which governed most of northern France, which it was one of the great tasks of the monarchy and of the Parlement in the fifteenth and sixteenth century to revise and codify, province by province. To print them was to bring them within the reach of all who needed them: magistrates, advocates, royal officers, administrators of institutions and religious orders, landowners and private citizens.

A moment came when the printing of the *Coutumes* was recognised as a possible source of profit. It occurred to the *greffier* or head clerk of the *bailliage* of Chartres, where an inquiry had recently been held by the Parlement commissioners to revise the *Coutume*, to ask the Parlement as a suitable perquisite, in view of the extra work he had been obliged to undertake while on duty during these proceedings, for the exclusive right at least for a limited

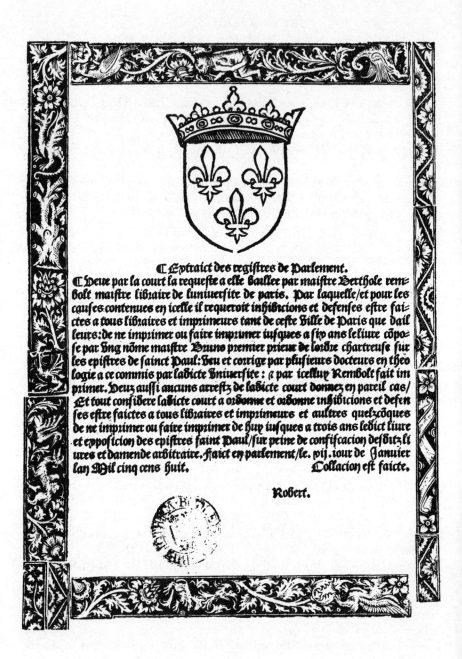

Plate 2   Parlement privilege for St Bruno's *Expositio* on the Pauline Epistles (1509)
(*reduced*)

Defenfe dela court.

¶ Et aladicte court pmis ꝗ donne cõge a maiſtre Jehã Dabert licēcie en loir greffier de la feneſchaucee dãiou de faire ipzimer icelles couſtumes enſēble les bēdze ꝗ diſtri buer p luy ou autruy p luy ꝫ mis ꝗ dicelles pzēdze le pzoufit ꝗ emolumēt ſe aucū y peut auoir Et oultre a fait celle court ſhibitiõ ꝗ defēſes ſur certaines et grãdes peines au roy a appliꝗr a to⁹ ꝗ chacuns impzimeurs libzaires et autres gens de quelque eſtat quilz foient de non impzimer ou faire im- pzimer / bendze / diſtribuer ou achater leſ- dictes couſtumes / ſi a ce faire par icelluy Dabert ne ſont cõmis ꝗ de luy en ce faiſãt aduouez / et foiēt icelles fignees dudit da- bert. Et ce iuſques a deur ans ꝑchains be nãs entiers et reuoluz commēcãs le rriii. iour de mars Lan Mil cinq cens et neuf.

Plate 3   Parlement privilege for the *Coutumes* of Anjou granted to Jean Dabert, *greffier* of Anjou, with his signature and paraphe. (1510)

period in the publication and sale of the *Coutume*. This was granted, no doubt the more readily because the Parlement thus ensured that there would be an adequate supply of printed copies without being itself put to any expense. The signature of the *greffier*, Michel La Troyne, on each copy, was sufficient proof to the general public that the publication was officially approved (PA 1509, 2).

A similar grant soon afterwards in the same circumstances to the *greffier* of the *sénéchaussée* of Maine, Martin Le Saige, for the *Coutume* of Maine (PA 1509, 4) expressly stipulates that each copy should be signed by him. And the following year a grant for the *Coutume* of Anjou to Jean Dabert, *greffier* of the *sénéchaussée* of Anjou, entitling him to take any profit therefrom if there was any profit to be had ('et d'icelles prendre le proufit et emolument se aucun y peut avoir') prohibited the sale of any copies not bearing his signature – which indeed appears on surviving copies of the original edition (PA 1510, 1). The privilege granted only a few months later to the *greffiers* of the *bailliage* of Orleans, on the other hand (PA 1510, 2), made no condition that each copy should be authenticated by their signature, and the condition lapsed finally when the Parlement began to grant privileges for *Coutumes* to applicants like Jean Petit (PA 1511, 1, and PA 1511, 4), who had no connection with the legal process of codifying the *Coutumes*.

By 1510 some of the grants of book-privileges are recorded in the registers of the Parlement. Among these is a grant to Jean Petit and Michel Le Noir (PA 1510, 3) for the first edition of *Le parement des dames de honneur* by Olivier de La Marche. For this we possess the text of the privilege as written out in the registers of the court and also the authenticated copy as printed in the book itself. All such instances prove the accuracy of the printed version, which normally differs from the original only in minute points of spelling.

The decision of Jean Petit to go in for privileges consolidated the system as a regular feature of book-trade business, for he was the wealthiest and the most prolific of all the Paris publishers of his time. And although he was to obtain seven grants from the chancery, including some for a 'package' of several books,[1] he went twice as often to the Parlement (fourteen as against seven).

Of the more specialised sovereign courts in Paris none had any reason to grant book-privileges, in the ordinary course of events. However the Cour des Aides gave a privilege for the *Ordonnances royaulx sur le faict des tailles, aydes et gabelles*, issued by the king at Montereul on 30 June 1517. The experienced Galliot Du Pré lost little time in finding his way to the court to seek a privilege for them. The Cour des Aides, to which such a proposal was new, consulted the *procureur général du Roy*. It then gave Galliot the privilege, for one year as he had requested, and he printed the *Extraict des registres de la court des aydes*, as signed by the *greffier*, Brinon, on the verso of the title-page (exactly as he was

---

[1] See below, pp. 131–6.

accustomed to do with privileges obtained from the Parlement), dated 27 July (PA 1517, 4).

When the number of lawsuits appeared to require it, the Parlement could send commissioners chosen from its own conseillers to a provincial capital to hold *Grands Jours*, or Great Sessions, assisted by local officials and magistrates. One of these courts was set up in 1518 at Bourges, the capital of the duchy of Berry, just three years after Francis I, on his accession, had endowed his only sister Marguerite with the duchy. And an enterprising Bourges bookseller, Pierre de Sartières, immediately submitted a petition for a privilege to print the document setting up the court, *La chartre de l'erection des grans jours de Berry*, with the *Stille* and certain Ordonnances of the *bailli* (PA 1518, 5). This was duly granted by the court itself, in the name of the duchess ('Avec privilege de ma Dame') and with her arms and the arms of France displayed in the book. Otherwise the pattern of the privileges given by the parent court, the Parlement of Paris, is followed exactly, as can be seen in the 'Extraict des registres de la court des grans jours de Berry' dated 12 July 1518 and signed by the *greffier*, Vaucheron, printed on the verso of the title-page. Sartières only sought, and only obtained, a privilege preventing other editions within the duchy itself ('ne les imprimer ne vendre ou Pays et Duchié de Berry'), but this was virtually the only area within which there would be customers for the book. But he sought a privilege for four years and only obtained two: the *Grands Jours*, like the Parlement itself, was reluctant to give long monopolies. The *Grands Jours* of Poitiers was to grant a three-year privilege on 26 October 1531 to Jacques Bouchet and Etienne de Marnef, booksellers of Poitiers, for Jean Bouchet, *Les correctes et additionnées Annalles d'Acquitaine*,[1] at the request of the author, himself a Poitiers lawyer and man of letters. He had recently brought his very popular *Annalles* up to date, that is, to 1531, after several reprints: the first edition had come out in 1524 under a privilege granted by the Parlement of Paris (PA 1524, 15).

The Parlement of Paris abstained consistently, one might almost say studiously, from using the word 'privilege' in referring to the grants it gave to authors and publishers. Possibly it regarded the term as associated with the personal exercise of the king's prerogative. It referred to the concession as a 'delay' or respite (PA 1513, 2) or as 'lesdictes deffences' (PA 1515, 4; PA 1516, 7). It did not, however, prevent the beneficiaries from describing their Parlement grants as privileges: the *greffiers* of the *prévôté* at the Châtelet caused the words 'Avec le privilege de messieurs de Parlement' to be printed on the title-page of *Les coustumes generalles de la prevosté et vicomté de Paris*, for which the Parlement had given them two years (PA 1513, 2), and they of all people were the least likely to be guilty of a legal inexactitude. The Parlement

---

[1] The privilege is printed on the verso of the title, headed 'Extraict des Registres des Grans Jours' and signed Dutillet. BN Rés. Lk¹ 25.c. Cf. also A. de La Bouralière, *L'imprimerie et la librairie à Poitiers pendant le xvi* siècle* (1900), pp. 86–7.

of Toulouse actually directed that the words 'Cum priuilegio' should be printed on a book for which it gave a privilege (PA 1517, 3).

The right of the Parlement to grant privileges was removed by Charles IX in 1566, when it became a legal requirement that all new books should have both licence and privilege from the chancery. However, when Paris was under the control of the *Ligue* from 1585 to 1594, and no access to the royal chancery was possible, the Parlement was applied to by Paris publishers for privileges and duly dispensed some.[1] The function which it had exercised for some sixty years in helping to keep order within the book-trade had not been wholly forgotten.

Provincial Parlements

That a privilege granted by the Parlement of Paris applied throughout France was understood, though rarely stated. On one occasion at least, none the less, in response to a petition by Constantin Fradin of Lyon, who had perhaps decided or been advised by his lawyer to ask for an explicit declaration to this effect, the Parlement made a grant 'defendant à tous aultres imprimeurs et librayres *du royaume de France et des terres appartenantes à ycelluy* ne imprimer ne faire imprimer, vendre ne faire vendre ledit livre jusques au terme de deux ans...' (italics mine) (PA 1520, 6).

The jurisdiction of the Parlement of Paris indeed extended over the whole of France. Certain territories, however, over which the Crown had obtained control only when the historic kingdom of France was already in existence, possessed their own Parlements. The most senior of these was the Parlement of Toulouse (Languedoc), created by Philip IV in 1303, followed by the Parlement of Grenoble (Dauphiné), the Parlement of Bordeaux (Guyenne), the Parlement of Dijon (Burgundy), the Parlement of Rouen (Normandy), and the Parlement of Aix (Provence). Some of these provincial Parlements issued book-privileges. The number is small, but significant.

Toulouse was not only a provincial capital. It was the seat of a university, with busy faculties of law and medicine, an important ecclesiastical centre with many religious houses, and a focal point on the trade route between Lyon and Spain. There was accordingly a considerable local book-trade, both before and after the introduction of printing. Sooner or later an author or publisher in Languedoc was likely to think of applying for a privilege to his own Parlement: the Parlements had regular communication with each other, but for a private individual in Toulouse the 709 kilometres between him and Paris was a serious inducement to seeking protection from piracy nearer home. It seems highly probable that a public oration delivered in Cahors University, published at Toulouse in 1509 by Jean Faure (PA 1509, 5),

---

[1] Denis Pallier, *Recherches sur l'imprimerie à Paris pendant la Ligue 1585–1594* (Geneva, 1976), *passim*.

received its privilege from the Parlement of Toulouse, especially as the orator, Marc de Rorgues, professor both of canon and civil law, a *conseiller*, was also vicar general of the bishop of Cahors, and responding to the conferment of an honorary degree in law from the University of Cahors.

In 1512 Jean de Clauso of Toulouse obtained a privilege from the Toulouse Parlement for *Les Ordonnances royaulx* (PA 1512, 6). For these *Ordonnances*, published on 27 April 1512, the Paris Parlement had given a privilege on 12 May 1512 to Jean Petit (PA 1512, 4), but the Toulouse Parlement, on receiving them for registration, was perfectly entitled to give a separate privilege within its own jurisdiction. It may be safely assumed also that *De Tholosanorum gestis*, an almost official account of the history and institutions of Toulouse, by Nicole Bertrand, published at Toulouse in 1515 'Cum gratia amplissimoque Priuilegio' (PA 1515, 5), had a privilege from the Parlement of Toulouse, of which Bertrand was a senior *conseiller*. The enlarged French edition of Bertrand's work, *Les gestes des Tholosains*, which came out two years later, indeed boasts a privilege from the Toulouse Parlement, displayed in full (PA 1517, 3). Although Bertrand's book, in both the Latin and the French version, might easily have qualified for a privilege from the Parlement of Paris or for that matter from the royal chancery, it is understandable that his publishers contented themselves with a privilege granted by the Parlement of Toulouse. This, after all, meant that no bookseller could legally deal in any other edition for the stipulated period within the Parlement's jurisdiction, that is to say, the whole of Languedoc, including not only Toulouse itself but towns as important as (for instance) Nîmes. Was not this precisely the area in which the book would necessarily be of the greatest interest? Would any publisher outside this area, if he could not lawfully sell any of his edition here, bother to reprint the book at all? So might the argument well have gone, and the long and costly journey to the Parlement of Paris, or to seek out the royal court and the chancery, had no longer to be contemplated.

Nor was it only works of mainly or purely Languedoc interest which received privileges from the Parlement of Toulouse. That Parlement granted, also in 1517, a privilege to a prominent Toulouse doctor, Etienne Chenu, for his *Regimen castitatis conseruatiuum*, followed by an anti-semitic tract, *Liber arboris Judaice* (PA 1517, 5). The grant is printed in the book itself, as an 'Extraict des registres de Parlement', certified by Michaelis, the Toulouse *greffier*, in exactly the same way as grants by the Paris Parlement are reproduced in the books concerned. More directly concerned with the work of the Parlement was *Les articles et confirmations des privileges du pais de Languedoc*; as soon as this had been approved and confirmed by the Parlement, Mathieu Du Monde of Toulouse obtained a grant for it from two of the *conseillers* (PA 1522, 7). The following year Antoine Le Blanc had a privilege for the *coutume* of Toulouse (PA 1523, 2). The *conseiller* who granted it was careful to have the text checked first by the *cappitols* of the city. And when Le Blanc received his corrected copy back, with 'permission, faculté et licence', and a five-year privilege, it was on condition that he show the book when printed (or perhaps rather in proof) to the authorities for it to be checked before putting it on sale. The privilege was granted on 1 April 1523 (n.s.) and the book complete with 'Cum priuilegio' and the arms of Toulouse on the title-page was finished on 23 June: it is dated 1522, no doubt because Le Blanc had begun to print it before Easter, as soon as he had the privilege, therefore within 1522 (o.s.).

The Parlement of Toulouse was to continue granting privileges after the period here being studied, mainly it seems for books of special use or interest within its own jurisdiction. Thus a commentary on the *Adagia* of Erasmus by Joannes Maurus, a schoolmaster at Montauban, was published with a three-year privilege granted by the Parlement and signed by the *conseiller* Jacques Rivirie, on 2 March 1527, to Maître Gilbert Grosset, 'Librayre de la Ville et Cité de Montalban'. The little book was dedicated to Sanche Hebrard, another *conseiller* of the Parlement (PA 1527, 1).

There is documentary evidence, as has been seen, for the Parlement of Toulouse giving privileges for books, from 1512 onwards. There is on the other hand no sign of a Toulouse publisher having obtained a privilege from the royal chancery or from the Parlement of Paris. Louis XII granted a privilege at Lyon on 25 August 1511 for a book of which the publishers were Jean Robion of Lyon and Jean de Clauso of Toulouse, but the beneficiary was Jean Robion (CH 1511, 2). A strong presumption therefore exists that the few Toulouse publications which appeared 'Cum priuilegio', without any further particulars, were privileged by the Parlement of Toulouse and I have ventured so to classify them in the Register.

An isolated case occurs in 1521 of a Toulouse publication being privileged by the Prévôt of Paris. This was the *Aurea summa de fuga vitiorum*, edited by the Toulouse Dominican Jean Vignier or Vignerius, dedicated to Jean de Basilhac, bishop-elect of Carcassonne, and a member of the Parlement of Toulouse, and published by two Toulouse booksellers, Anthoine Maurin and Gaston Recolene. For some reason, the publishers employed a Paris press to print it, that of Jean (II) Du Pré. It seems likely that Jean Du Pré, who by this time had experience himself of obtaining privileges, was commissioned by the publishers to obtain one on their behalf (PR 1521, 2).

The Parlement of Rouen, designated as such in 1515 but formerly the Echiquier of the duchy of Normandy and still generally known under that title in the early sixteenth century, likewise presided over an area within which book-production and the book-trade were important. Rouen itself was a thriving centre of printing, especially the printing of liturgical books, and exported extensively to England and other foreign countries. Caen had a flourishing university, and did some printing and publishing as well as bookselling. The Rouen Parlement does not, however, seem to have been called upon frequently for book-privileges in the period up to 1526, and gave them only for publications in which the court itself was actively concerned. Its own *Ordonnances contre la peste* and other regulations were published by Martin Morin on 12 September 1513 with the following privilege printed on the title-page:

¶ Lesquelles ordonnances ont esté baillees et commandees imprimer et vendre à maistre Martin Morin demourant devant Saint Lo. le .xii. jour de septembre l'an mil cinq cens et traize. Et deffend ladicte court à tous autres imprimeurs et libraires eulx ingerer imprimer ou faire imprimer lesdictes ordonnances ne d'en vendre ou acheter que celles imprimees par ledict Morin. Le tout jusques au premier jour de mars prochain venant. (PA 1513, 3)

In 1516 it granted a privilege to Jean Richard for an edition of its own 'stille et ordre de proceder' (PA 1516, 3), to be published in partnership with Michel Angier of Caen, as an appendage to *Le grand coustumier de Normandie*. This exactly follows the pattern of the Paris Parlement privileges, the *Extraict des registres de Parlement* being printed at the end of the *Stille* to which it refers, with the authenticating signature of the *greffier*. A grant was also made in 1519 to Thomas Du Four, for ordinances recently published by the Parlement regulating within its jurisdiction the arrangements for controlling plague, prostitution and vagrancy (PA 1519, 3).

The Parlement of Bordeaux is not known to have issued a book-privilege until 1527. When it did, on 4 September that year, the subject of the privilege was the *Coutume* of the city and province within its jurisdiction.[1] The city, important as it was, did not at this period function as an active printing and publishing centre like Toulouse or Rouen. Dr Gabriel de Tarregua preferred to seek the protection of a privilege from the royal chancery for his medical writings in 1520, even at the cost of a journey to the court, which was then at Amboise (CH 1520, 10). He would have been in a strong position to obtain one from the Parlement of Bordeaux had he applied to it: his treatise on the treatment of plague had been printed at Bordeaux the previous year at public and civic request.[2] Eighteen years later the Parlement of Bordeaux was sufficiently confident of its privilege-giving powers within its own area to grant a three-year privilege to François Morpain, a printer of the city, who had requested it to forbid 'tous les imprimeurs libraires de ce Ressort de imprimer ou faire imprimer ledit Tracté, à tous marchans de n'en vendre d'autre impression dans troys ans, à peine de mil livres tournois': the book in

---

[1] See below, pp. 198–9.
[2] *Tracté contre la peste ... composé à la requeste de messigneurs les maire et soubsmaire et jurés de Bourdeaulx* (Bordeaux, Gaspard Philippe, 1519), 4°. Cf. A. Claudin, *Les origines et les débuts de l'imprimerie à Bordeaux* (1897), pp. 13–14.

question was *Linguae vasconum primitiae*, by Bernard Dechepart, *curé* of Saint-Michel-le-Vieux, the first text ever to be printed in the Basque language.[1]

Other Parlements are to be found occasionally granting book-privileges during the following thirty years after 1526, but the publications concerned are all, it appears, directly connected with the work of the courts and the administration of justice within the Parlement's jurisdiction. Thus the Parlement of Brittany, sitting at Nantes on 7 September 1535, granted Thomas Mestrard, bookseller of Rennes, a two-year privilege in its own *constitutions* and *ordonnances*: this confirmed a grant made to Mestrard at the previous session of the Parlement, held at Rennes, which he had been unable to use because he had not succeeded in securing copies of the texts in time.[2] Again on 30 September 1539, at Nantes, the Parlement gave Mestrard, in partnership with Philippe Bourgoignon, a three-year privilege for the royal *constitutions et ordonnances*, published by the Parlement, and on 1 October 1540 at Rennes gave Mestrard a two-year privilege in its own *constitutions et ordonnances* existing or to be determined during the current session.[3] Even the short-lived Parlement of Chambéry, set up during the French rule in Savoy, granted a privilege, for five years, for its own *Stile et reiglement sur le Faict de la Justice* (8 August 1553), valid within its own *ressort*, at the request of Pierre de Portonariis, a printer of Lyon.[4]

THE PRÉVÔT OF PARIS AND ROYAL OFFICERS IN THE PROVINCES

The routine administration of justice and the keeping of the peace under the king was the responsibility of officers called Baillis, or, in some provinces, Sénéchaux, whose jurisdiction covered a wide area. These officers, often men of rank and importance, who might also be royal councillors, each had a Lieutenant, usually possessing high legal qualifications, and a staff of *greffiers* and financial officials, as well as having at their disposal forces which today would be called police. The court of each such officer had its own notaries and advocates, and a *procureur du roi*. Within each *bailliage* or *sénéchaussée* each main town or district had a Prévôt. The Prévôt of Paris was himself so important that he was more than the equivalent of a Bailli or Sénéchal in the provinces and took precedence over them all. His court was held in the Châtelet, a stronghold of which the only vestige to survive at the present day is the Tour Saint-Jacques, but which in the sixteenth century dominated the right bank of the Seine, opposite the Parlement on the Ile de la Cité. The policing of Paris

[1] 1545, 4°. BN Rés. Y° 1. The extract from the registers of the Parlement of Bordeaux, dated the last day of April 1545, signed 'Collation est faicte, De Pontac', is printed at the end (f. G4ʳ).

[2] G. Lepreux, *Gallia typographica*, série départementale, Vol. IV, *Province de Bretagne* (1913), *Documenta*, no. 947 (pp. 2–3).

[3] Ibid. *Documenta*, nos. 949 (pp. 5–6) and 952 (pp. 8–9).

[4] F. Mugnier, *Marc-Claude de Buttet, poète savoisien* (1896), pp. 95–6.

was in his hands. He had both a *Lieutenant Civil* and a *Lieutenant Criminel*. In addition he had special responsibilities for the University of Paris.

Authors, publishers and printers who feared unfair competition, particularly from unscrupulous rivals in their own neighbourhood, might well think of resorting to one of these officers. Here they could expect if not instant justice at least relatively expeditious and effective justice in their own locality. The most powerful officer of them all, the Prévôt of Paris, directly controlled the city which was the largest centre of book-production and bookselling in the kingdom.

Seventy privileges are known to have been granted on such authority, one of these certainly by the lieutenant of the Bailli of Rouen (PR 1514, 5), but most of them by the Prévôt of Paris. Under Louis XII, these royal officers also gave at least four *congés*, which conferred official approval without apparently expressly forbidding other editions (e.g. PR 1509, 4*).[1] On one early occasion, a request for a privilege, which had been submitted in the first instance to the Parlement of Paris, was referred by the Parlement to the Prévôt ('De par le prevost de Paris en ensuyvant la requeste presentée en la court de Parlement de par Maistre Jehan Divry', PR 1508, 1). This procedure, not unusual in itself, is exceptional in the case of book-privileges. It is in fact the earliest case on which the Prévôt is named as the source of a privilege. Privileges given on the authority of the Prévôt are however referred to from 1505 onwards in formulae such as 'par l'ordonnance de justice'. The earliest of these was advertised by the poet and publicist Pierre Gringore in his *Les folles entreprises* (PR 1505, 1) as follows:

¶ Il est dit par l'ordonnance de justice que l'acteur de ce dict livre nommé Pierre Gringoire a privilege de le vendre et distribuer du jourdhuy jusques à ung an / sans que autre le puisse faire imprimer ne vendre fors ceulx à qui il en ballera et distribuera / et ce sur peine de confiscation des livres et d'amende arbitraire. Imprimé à Paris par Maistre Pierre Le Dru imprimeur pour icelluy Gringoire le .xxiii. jour de decembre. L'an mil cinq cens et cinq.

Certainly in 1514 short-term privileges were being granted on the authority of the Prévôt of Paris for printed accounts of current events. On 15 August that year Louis XII concluded the Peace of Saint-Germain-en-Laye with Henry VIII of England. The following day the official announcement of the treaty by Normandy Herald took place in the Prévôt's court at the Châtelet. There were present the Prévôt himself and his lieutenants, several of the *examinateurs* of the court, and the *greffier* or clerk of the court, Almaury, who signed the record. The next day, 17 August, a privilege and licence was granted to Guillaume Sanxon, 'libraire', to have the text of the treaty printed, forbidding all other booksellers and printers of the city to print it for the

---

[1] See below, pp. 112–13. These *congés* are included in the Register (PR) under the date to which they belong, for the sake of completeness, but are marked with an asterisk to distinguish them from the grants which are expressly privileges.

following eight days (PR 1514, 2). The privilege bears two signatures, that of G. Maillart, the Prévôt's *Lieutenant criminel*, and that of Almaury the *greffier*. The ensuing marriage between Louis XII and Henry VIII's sister Mary (afterwards duchess of Suffolk) was celebrated on 9 October 1514 on the princess's arrival in French territory at Abbeville. A description of this event was sent to Paris by an anonymous guest at the Abbeville festivities, and an eight-day privilege for the exclusive right to have it printed and sold was granted on 25 October to Guillaume Mart, 'libraire', issued under the signet of the Prévôt and signed by Almaury (PR 1514, 3).[1]

The first privilege issued by the Prévôt of Paris of which the full text is available (PR 1514, 2) is headed 'De par le prevost de Paris ou son lieutenant criminel'. I know of no other case during this period in which the *Lieutenant Criminel* was involved in the grant of a privilege. The *Lieutenant Criminel* Jean Morin was to grant a one-year privilege (the applicant had requested three years) on 27 February 1536 (n.s.) for a French translation of Eucharius Rösslin, *De partu hominis* (originally published in German in 1513), in response to a *requête* from Jean Foucher (BN te [121] 3). This was certainly an unusual procedure.

In the provinces also important officers of the Crown occasionally issued book-privileges on their own authority, at the request of a local author, bookseller or printer. The first fully documented example is that of the Lieutenant General of the Bailli of Rouen, who granted a privilege on 24 November 1514 to Martin Morin for one year for a theological work by Pierre Fabri, *Le defensore de la concepcion de la glorieuse vierge Marie*, author and printer both being resident in Rouen (PR 1514, 5).

Other provincial officers were already familiar with the granting of book-privileges through having been required by the beneficiaries of royal privileges to proceed to an *entérinement* or registration of the Letters Patent ensuring that the court of the Bailli or Sénéchal would be already appraised of the privilege-holder's rights in the event of a case being brought there for infringement of the monopoly. The Lieutenant General of the *sénéchaussée* of Lyon[2] had been thus required by the famous author Jean Lemaire de Belges to register the Letters Patent granted to him by Louis XII at Lyon on 30 January 1509 for *Les illustrations de Gaule*. He also issued his own *Lettres d'atache*

---

[1] Neither Guillaume Sanxon nor Guillaume Mart are otherwise known as booksellers. It may have been by a misunderstanding that they are so designated. They may have been simply people well placed, by personal connections with the Prévôt or a member of his staff, to secure a grant for these highly saleable pamphlets. Anyone, at this period, could sell or finance printed books, and that included people in other professions. A Jehan Sanxon was lieutenant of the Bailli of Touraine at Châtillon-sur-Indre in 1507 (*Gallia regia*, ed. G. Dupont-Ferrier (1924–61), VI, p. 23) and published a commentary on the *Consuetudines* of Touraine in 1523. A Jean Sanson, *docteur en droit*, became a *conseiller* of the Parlement in 1533 (E. Maugis, *Histoire du Parlement de Paris*, III (1916), p. 174). Guillaume may have been a member of this family.

[2] Claude le Charron, *docteur ès droiz*. *Gallia regia*, III, pp. 595–6.

50

to accompany the royal privilege, adding certain details which were within his competence to determine, notably a fine of 500 livres tournois for infringement of the privilege, dated 20 August 1509 (CH 1509, 2).

I have found no certain instance of a book-privilege being granted on the authority of the Sénéchal of Lyon until twenty-three years after the period here under review. On 25 January 1549 a privilege was granted for the handsomely illustrated souvenir programme of Henry II's state entry into Lyon in September 1548,[1] to be printed by Guillaume Roville or Rouillé, which the city had subsidised to the tune of twelve *écus d'or soleil*. The *Lieutenant*, Du Peyrat, 'ouy sur ce les Conseilliers et Eschevins de la ville de Lyon', not only conferred the exclusive right for two years in this official account of the festivities, both the edition in French and the edition in Italian, but forebade the sale of any other accounts (several of which had already appeared in Paris) on the grounds that they were inaccurate. However, twenty books printed and published at Lyon from 1507 to 1525 bear the simple formula 'Cum priuilegio', without any further details, and it is at least possible that some of these refer to privileges granted by the Sénéchal. Although there are cases of Lyon publishers going to the Parlement of Paris for privileges, the journey was long enough to deter many would-be applicants from doing so.

It was possible also for a provincial Bailli or Sénéchal to give his permission and authority for the publication of a book, as we have seen the Prévôt of Paris do. De Marnef printed *Le stille des auditoires de messieurs le bailly de Berry et le prevost de Bourges* (completed 16 January 1512) at Paris 'par l'auctorité, congié et licence de monseigneur le bailly de Berry ou son lieutenant' (PR 1512, 1).[2] This was not a privilege, in the sense of forbidding the printing or sale of any edition except De Marnef's. It was, however, the official guide to the procedure in the court of the Bailli of the royal duchy of Berry and in that of his subordinate the Prévôt of the city of Bourges, so that lawyers and property-owners had good reason to wish to possess the edition approved by the Bailli himself in preference to any other. The Lieutenant General of the Sénéchal of Anjou, with the 'gens tenans le siège presidial' of Angers, were on the other hand to give a real privilege, an exclusive right for three years for the printing of the *Stille et Reiglement* of his own court, to Angers publisher-printer Pierre Jounot, on 24 December 1563.[3]

Only in the case of the Prévôt of Paris did a system of privilege-granting develop which really rivalled or complemented the activity of the Parlement. This development can be traced from 1516, when for the first time the Prévôt's

---

[1] *La magnificence de la superbe entrée de la cité de Lyon faicte au roy Henry deuxiesme* (Lyon, G. Rouillé, 1549), 4°. BL 811.g.33. A summary of the privilege is printed on the verso of the title-page. See also V. L. Saulnier, *Maurice Scève*, I (1948), p. 340.

[2] The Bailli at this date was Pierre du Puy, chevalier, seigneur de Vatan, by 1514 *conseiller et chambellan du roi*: his Lieutenant General was Maître Jehan Fradet. *Gallia regia*, I, pp. 379, 382.

[3] L'abbé Pasquier and V. Dauphin, *Imprimeurs et libraires de l'Anjou* (Angers, 1932), p. 162.

privilege was printed in full in the books concerned. Clément Longis obtained an order from the Lieutenant General of the Prévôt, Ruzé, for two years, for *La vie et les miracles de Saint Eusice*, on 19 September 1516 (PR 1516, 1), and from then onwards a privilege was issued by the Prévôt or one of his officials every month or two for most of the period, though never as frequently as by the Parlement. The system continued for at least twenty-five years after 1526. A late example is the four-year privilege dated 3 October 1550 and signed P. Seguier, granted to Arnoul L'Angelier and Gilles Corrozet for the second and enlarged edition of Joachim Du Bellay's *L'Olive*.[1]

The practice of the Prévôt differed little from that of the Parlement. The terms of years asked for in the *requête* were sometimes not granted in full, suggesting that here also serious consideration was given to the duration of the privilege. Privileges were most commonly given for one, two or three years, exceptionally for four (e.g. PR 1521, 2). Usually the same penalties were specified as those favoured by the Parlement: confiscation of unauthorised copies, and a fine. The *procureur du roi* in the Prévôt's court at the Châtelet was consulted if the proposed publication seemed to concern the interests of the Crown ('Ouy sur ce les gens du roy', PR 1516, 1; 'Et ouys sur ce les gens du roy', PR 1521, 4).

It may be supposed that the *Prévôté*, as an alternative to the Parlement, offered to certain authors and publishers in Paris a facility of which they availed themselves for personal reasons: that they had other business to transact at the *Prévôté*, that they knew the Prévôt, the Lieutenant or one of the clerks who might expedite the granting of their application, or that the fees were not quite so high. It was resorted to from an early date, but until 1515 exclusively for ephemeral publications. From 1516 to 1526 there was a marked expansion in the number and importance of the book-privileges obtained from it.

It can hardly be coincidence that these years correspond to the period when the Prévôt was Gabriel, baron d'Allegre, seigneur de Saint-Just, *conseiller et chambellan du roi*. Some active interest on his part in the grant of book-privileges is indeed suggested by the fact that he personally signed ten of the privileges issued by the *Prévôté* during his term of office,[2] of those which are known in sufficient detail to give the name of the signatory (the others are signed either by his Lieutenant Louis Ruzé, by the *greffier* Almaury or by one of the clerks J. de Calais, J. Corbie and I. Lormier). Allegre, as well as his Lieutenant Ruzé who signed the privilege, is thanked by the publisher Toussaint Denys in some Latin verses in the *Compendium parisiensis universitatis*

[1] Reprinted in Du Bellay, *Œuvres poétiques*, ed. H. Chamard, STFM (1908), Vol. I, p. 3.

[2] PR 1516, 5; 1517, 2; 1518, 1; 1518, 2; 1518, 3; 1519, 1; 1520, 3; 1520, 12; 1525, 2; 1526, 1. Under his successor Jean de La Barre, comte d'Etampes, the first book-privileges issued by the *Prévôté* were signed Moifait; La Barre himself signed the grant of 11 March 1530 to Nicole Volcyr de Serouville for *La chronicque abregée* printed by Nicolas Couteau for Didier Maheu (BL 9315.aaa.7.)

(PR 1517, 1) for granting the privilege, which is dated 2 March 1516 – that is, 1517 n.s. ('Presentem cuius trutinauit lima libellum / Ne quis eum prohibens bibliopola premat / Quam bene iussisti faciens rata vota precantis / Possit ut expensas sic releuare graues.')

The participation of the *Lieutenant Civil*, Louis Rusé or Ruzé, in the granting of privileges by the Prévôt is attested not only by complete grants authenticated by his signature (e.g. PR 1516, 1; 1517, 1; 1520, 4; 1523, 3; 1525, 1) but by many references to his authority in the Latin summaries of privileges favoured particularly by Badius. The latter often attempts to weave into the summary some flattery of the *Lieutenant Civil*, e.g. 'suffragio literarum bonarum doctissimi et dulcissimi praesidii L. Ruzei' (PR 1520, 10), and on at least one occasion the book is actually dedicated to him (PR 1519, 3). Ruzé was indeed a man of some learning, to the point of receiving letters in Greek from Budé, and he may have given some impetus to the fashion among academic publishers like Badius, and among literary men, for resorting for privileges to the Prévôt.

That change of fashion is signalled in 1516 by requests submitted to the Prévôt by two authors resident in Paris, very different from each other but both of some standing and both making their first application for a privilege. One was Guillaume Michel de Tours, who obtained a grant for his pious allegorical fantasy *La forest de conscience* (PR 1516, 2). The other was Dr de Celaya, a Spanish member of the Faculty of Theology, who sought protection for philosophical works, which appear to be his current courses of lectures: he went for a privilege for three of these works in succession, the first two within a month of each other (PR 1516, 3 and PR 1516, 4), the third six months later (PR 1517, 3). For his next works, Celaya left it to his publisher, Hémon Le Fèvre, to apply for a privilege, and Le Fèvre went to the Parlement (PA 1517, 9), perhaps because a group of three different books was involved. On the other hand, when Guillaume Michel de Tours entrusted Hémon Le Fèvre as his publisher with the task of obtaining a privilege for his next allegory, *Le siècle doré*, in 1522, Le Fèvre went to the Prévôt (PR 1522, 1).

From 1516 too some notable *libraires jurés* of the University of Paris favoured the Prévôt as a dispenser of privileges. Jean de La Garde, for instance, had five grants from the Prévôt as against two from the chancery and two from the Parlement. Among others were Josse Badius, Galliot Du Pré, François Regnault, Pierre Le Brodeur, Toussaint Denys, Jacques Nyverd, Damien Higman, Gilles de Gourmont and Conrad Resch. All these are to be found on other occasions applying to the chancery or to the Parlement of Paris. Jean Petit, however, seems to have obtained only one privilege from the Prévôt in the years up to 1526, and Bonnemere, Chaudière, Chevallon, Gerlier, Granjon, Gromors, Kerver, Le Noir and Roce appear *never* to have obtained privileges from this source.

The variety of authorities from which it was possible to obtain valid book-privileges in France might be expected to lead to instances of conflicting grants. The amount of consultation which went on all the time is known however to have been considerable, and was adequate to prevent this, during the period under study here.

A clash between a privilege granted for the local *Coutume* by the Parlement of Bordeaux, and a privilege for the same work granted by the royal chancery, in 1527, to different beneficiaries, was the fault of the *greffier* of the Parlement of Bordeaux, who obtained the second privilege for himself.[1] Later there was to be a more serious clash. In 1549, Galliot Du Pré obtained a five-year grant from the Parlement of Paris for Jean Du Tillet's *Chronique des roys de France*, which he published in 1550. The following year, Martin Le Mesgissier of Rouen not only had it printed, in defiance of Galliot's privilege, but obtained a two-year privilege for it from the Parlement of Rouen.[2] Galliot had to obtain Letters Patent from the royal chancery, which he finally did on 15 June 1552, granting him a six-year privilege in the book, establishing his prior right. The Rouen publishers had claimed, according to the Letters Patent, that they were not subject to the Parlement of Paris ('aucuns Libraires de nostre ville de Rouen, en contemnant la permission de nostredicte Cour de parlement, auroyent fait imprimer ledict abregé, disans lesdicts Imprimeurs & Libraires n'estre subjects à nostredicte Cour de parlement de Paris').[3]

Occasionally during the period up to 1526 publishers advertised the possession of a privilege from two different French authorities. Guillaume Eustace printed a Parlement grant dated 13 August 1510 in his edition of a legal work (PA 1510, 4), for two years, and then added, 'Pour plus amples defenses et inhibitions', a summary of a royal privilege dated Blois, 13 August (no year-date), signed Des Landes, which may well be his 'personal' privilege (CH 1508, 2). The opinion here implied, that two privileges afforded 'plus amples defenses', is not, to my knowledge, expressed elsewhere. Sometimes a double grant is probably the result of the applicant or his representatives having set in motion two separate petitions, hoping one at least would succeed: such apparently is the two-year Parlement privilege (PA 1512, 1) obtained by Jean Petit for the Lent sermons of Jean Raulin, a book which he managed to have included in the 'package' three-year privilege obtained from the royal chancery at Blois seven days later (CH 1512, 1; see below, p. 131–2), resulting in the unusual formula 'Cum gratia et priuilcgio regis et curie parlementi'. Yves Gallois on the other hand printed a romance 'Cum

---

[1] See below, pp. 198–9.

[2] *La chronique des roys de France* (Rouen, M. Le Mesgissier, 1551), 8°. BL 1059.a.1(2). The title has the words 'Avec privilege', and the Rouen privilege, 18 April 1551, is printed on the verso.

[3] Du Pré's first edition of *La chronique des roys de France* is 1550, 8°. BL 1058.b.13. His second edition (1552–3, 8°. BL 9200.bb.24) contains, as does the first, the Parlement of Paris grant of 9 July 1549, printed on the verso of the title, and in addition the Letters Patent of Henry II (Paris, 15 June 1552), on the following pages.

priuillegio supreme curie et prepositi parisiensis in triennium' (PA 1518, 2). The privilege of this was summarised in words beginning, 'Il est permis par messeigneurs de parlement et de par monseigneur le prevost de Paris'. This could be, on the face of it, a privilege given jointly by the Parlement and the Prévôt. It seems more probable that Gallois, for reasons best known to himself, obtained two separate privileges. It was probably, however, the atmosphere of crisis and uncertainty in Paris at the time which drove Galliot Du Pré to obtain a privilege from the Parlement on 7 September 1524 for his important work on the Councils of the Church (PA 1524, 13). He already held a valid privilege for it, issued by the chancery on 25 August 1520 to run for three years from the date of completion, and had taken it for *entérinement* by the Prévôt (CH 1520, 3). The Parlement was then to Parisians the highest authority visibly functioning.

PART TWO: ACADEMIC AND ECCLESIASTICAL

We have seen instances of privileges granted on the sole authority of bishops and universities.[1] Were any such grants made in France? There was no bishop in France who exercised temporal sovereignty over the whole or part of his diocese. And in the period here being considered there are no certain examples of privileges issued entirely on French episcopal authority. It was not unknown in France for prelates to devote themselves to editing a correct text of the breviary or missal of their diocese for their clergy and to have it printed at their expense. An early example is the Vienne breviary printed by Johann Neumeister at Lyons in 1490 for Angelo Cato, then archbishop of Vienne.[2] Evidently the existence of an authorised edition would be a deterrent to other publishers, but no penalties against reprinting were threatened. In fact only a handful of the huge number of liturgical books produced in France at this time claim a privilege at all. Antoine Vérard claimed a privilege for his Book of Hours published 14 July 1508,[3] on the strength of his newly acquired personal privilege, but not for any later ones. A breviary of the diocese of Saint-Pol-de-Léon, in Brittany, came out in 1516 'cum priuilegio' (*CP* 1516, 6), and a Poitiers Missal was published 'cum priuilegio' in 1525 (*CP* 1525, 3). These could possibly have been privileges granted by a bishop. There are however certainly cases where a privilege for a service-book was granted by the king, and these begin in 1522, when Jacques Mareschal dit Roland took advantage of the presence of the royal court and the chancery in Lyon that summer to secure a privilege (CH 1522, 3) for an edition of the missal of Clermont and of Saint-Flour as well as for *Ordonnances royaulx*.[4] A bishop's

---

[1] See above, pp. 3, 8–10.   [2] GKW no. 5507.

[3] CH 1507, 1 (no. 5), and Macfarlane, *Antoine Vérard*, no. 240.

[4] Baudrier, *Bibliographie lyonnaise*, xi, pp. 421–3, questioned the genuineness of the privilege, mainly because he doubted whether Mareschal could have waited until 1525 to use a privilege granted in 1522, but there are many instances of such delays. See also Antoine Vernière, *Note sur le premier livre connu imprimé à Clermont en 1523* (Brioude, 1882).

privilege was not in itself a sufficient protection, from the commercial point of view. That at least was the declared opinion of Jean Petit, as recorded just after the end of the period here studied, in 1527. In that year Petit was the chief promoter of a magnificent missal for the use of Evreaux, embodying a revision by the bishop or his staff and published by his order, displaying on the title-page the words 'Cum priuilegio Regis et eiusdem diocesis episcopi ne quispiam usque ad quadrennium eiusmodi imprimat vel imprimi faciat' (CH 1527, 2). On the verso appear, printed in full, Letters Patent granted to Petit for this edition, given at Paris on 7 November 1527. In them, the recapitulation of Petit's *requête* to the chancery runs as follows,

De la partie de nostre amé Jehan Petit libraire juré en l'université de Paris Nous a esté exposé que puis nagueres Nostre amé et feal conseiller l'evesque d'Evreux par luy ou ses officiers et commis a fait corrigier et amender et reduire au vray us et coustume de son église les messels pour dire le divin service selon l'église cathédrale dudit Evreux. Lesquels messels audict usaige d'Evreux ainsi corrigés et amendés il a bailliés audict exposant pour les imprimer en luy donnant permission de ce faire, et que aultre que ledit exposant ne les puisse faire ou imprimer selon ladite coppie. *Mais ledite exposant ne les ose imprimer ne faire les frais qu'il y conviendra faire, s'il n'a de nous permission de les imprimer, et previllege que aultre que luy ne les puisse imprimer ledit temps de six ans / sur ladite coppie.* Affin que ledit exposant se puisse aucunement rembourcer desdits frais, mises et impenses humblement requerant sur ce icelluy privillege. (italics mine)

The royal chancery responded with a privilege, but for four years from the date of the grant, not the six years which Petit said he had been given by the bishop. The same year Petit was the principal publisher of an equally grand missal for the use of Rouen, *Missale rothomagense*, completed on 8 October 1527. This has only 'Cum priuilegio regis' on the title-page, but the privilege, printed on the verso, refers to Petit having first received the revised copy from the archbishop of Rouen with permission 'et previllege que aultre que ledict exposant ne les puisse faire ou imprimer selon ladicte coppie de sept ans advenir', and it continues, exactly as in the Evreux missal just described, 'Mais ledit exposant ne les oze imprimer' etc. The royal privilege must indeed have been granted by the same Letters Patent as that of the Evreux missal, for both are for four years, both are dated Paris, 7 November 1527 and they are signed by the same secretary. No doubt the six-year privilege of the bishop of Evreux, and the seven-year privilege of the archbishop of Rouen (Georges II d'Amboise) were recommendations which weighed heavily with the royal chancery in considering Petit's request, yet four years was in itself a substantial privilege and exceptional for a service-book, and it was not prepared to extend the duration to the full term of years which episcopal authority proposed.

Not only the royal chancery but the sovereign courts were by then applied to by publishers who desired an exception to be made to the unwritten rule that liturgical books did not qualify for privileges. The same year as the

Evreux missal, Jean Petit and Louis Bouvet sought a privilege from the Parlement of Rouen for the antiphoners of Rouen diocese, 'never before having been printed'. Their request was opposed before the Parlement by a Rouen bookseller called Pierre Lignant.[1] Petit and Bouvet claimed that they had been asked to publish the antiphoners 'par plusieurs gens d'église', and the Parlement sought the advice of Messire Guillaume Dyeul, 'l'un des chappelains de l'Eglise N.D. de Rouen, scavant et expert en tel cas', as well as that of the 'gens du roy', before finding in favour of Petit and Bouvet. These are the only references in the case to ecclesiastical authority (PA 1527, 3).

Such later instances as have come to light again illustrate the principle that an episcopal privilege for the service-books of a diocese, when granted at all, was regarded by publishers as insufficient when unsupported by a lay authority. The cardinal archbishop of Lyon, in 1542, gave a privilege for five years for a new *Liber Sacerdotalis*, issued on his authority, a very handsome book with much music. But the publisher also obtained royal Letters Patent, which conferred a privilege for two years.[2]

The revised synodal *Constitutiones* of the archdiocese of Bordeaux were printed at Bordeaux by Jean Guyart in 1524 'cum priuilegio' (*CP* 1524, 1), without any particulars of the privilege being given. It may have been granted by the Parlement of Bordeaux. On the other hand it may have been given by the archbishop, who was Jean de Foix, a great personage, son of Jean, count of Candale and of Catherine, daughter of Gaston IV, count of Foix, and who was archbishop from 1501 until his death in 1529.[3] A privilege given by him would have covered the whole ecclesiastical province of Deuxième Aquitaine, which extended far beyond the jurisdiction of the Parlement of Bordeaux as far north as Poitiers. The *Ordinationes synodales* of the diocese of Orleans on the other hand were undoubtedly published under a privilege given by the Parlement of Paris (PA 1525, 6).

A bishop might be regarded as entitled to issue a privilege for the *style* of his own court, by analogy with lay courts which had authorised and protected a particular edition of their *style*. The first case when this principle was undoubtedly asserted did not come until 1534, and it concerned the *Statutorum liber* of the episcopal court of the diocese of Albi. Here the bishop is stated to have revised the text, and a legal document signed by the archdeacon, as the bishop's vicar general, and the apostolic *protonotarius*, granted the exclusive right to print and sell the book within the diocese for three years to Jean

---

[1] See also below, pp. 197–8.

[2] *Liber sacerdotalis* (Lyon, Joannes Grototus for Corneille de Sept-granges, 1542), 4°. BM Lyon Rés. 311452 and 316981. Summaries of both privileges on verso of title-page, printed on a strip of paper pasted in.

[3] *Gallia christiana*, Vol. II (1720), pp. 846–47, which does not however mention ordinances published in his name for clergy of his archdiocese.

Richard, bookseller of Albi, who had it printed at Toulouse.[1] Little wonder that Jean Richard thought this privilege adequate, without resort to chancery or Parlement: the bishop of Albi had been, since 1528, no less a person than Antoine Du Prat, the chancellor of France. Already in 1529, the *style* of the archiepiscopal court of Bourges had been published with 'Cum priuilegio' on the title-page, and the arms of the archbishop, François de Tournon, prominently displayed, the book to be sold at the Sign of the Lily in Bourges.[2] Tournon was a powerful person, and it is just possible that he may not only have authorised the publication but granted the privilege, within his jurisdiction.

The word 'privilege' itself could be used by an ecclesiastical authority almost as the equivalent of an imprimatur. Thus Denis Roce published in 1511 a 'golden treasury' of poetry, the *Aerarium aureum poetarum*, by Jacobus Gaudensis, O.P., edited by Guillaume Cheron of the College of Montaigu in Paris University, which prints an 'Epistola cum priuilegio' on the verso of the title-page. This proves to be a letter to the author by Henricus Zelen, the Official of the diocese of Cologne, commending the work and incorporating a licence to publish it (1511, 4°. Maz. 18822).

As regards privileges granted by universities, there are two instances of a privilege given by the University of Paris, one additional to a normal privilege, one standing alone.

In 1512 Josse Badius published a book, 'Cum priuilegio' printed on the title-page, which gave on the last printed page, after the colophon, the following statement:

Cautumque est et districte prohibitum auctoritate regia *et dictae uniuersitatis* ne quis praesumat praesentem libellum denuo imprimere sub poena arbitraria. (italics mine)

The book in question was the treatise *Auctoritas papae et concilii* of Thomas de Vio, Cardinal Cajetanus, published the previous year in Rome by Marcello Silber, and sent from the second synod of Pisa to the University of Paris to be examined ('A sacrosancta generali synodo Pisana secunda ad almam uniuersitatem parisiensem missus'). That the University of Paris was indeed involved in the publication of the book by Badius is clear from the argument which broke out on the subject between the university and its Faculty of Theology in 1516, after the conclusion of the Concordat between Francis I and the Pope: the faculty then wished Badius to hand over all copies of the book, for a fee of 20 *écus*, until a new refutation of it had been published, while the university wished him to sell them.[3] It is an isolated case of the university's

---

[1] *Spiritualis curia Albiensis statutorum liber*, Albi (Jean Richard) [1534], 4°. Desbarreaux-Bernard (le dr.), *Establissement de l'imprimerie dans la province de Languedoc* (Toulouse, 1876), pp. 218–22.

[2] *Stilus ecclesiasticae iurisdictionis archiepiscopalis biturensis* (1529), 8°, printed for an unnamed Bourges bookseller by Simon de Colines. Ph. Renouard, *Bibliographie des éditions de S. de Colines, 1520–1546* (1894), pp. 143–4.

[3] See P. Renouard, *Imprimeurs parisiens*, Vol. II, no. 203 (p. 101).

authority being invoked in addition to 'royal authority' – the latter meaning, I
think, a privilege issued by the Prévôt of Paris or by his Lieutenant Louis
Ruzé, whose help in obtaining privileges is acknowledged more than once by
Badius (e.g. PR 1519, 2). What the terms were of the university privilege,
Badius does not say.

There is, however, one later occasion when Badius published a book for the
University of Paris in which a privilege given by the university itself stands
alone. The word 'privilege' is in fact avoided by Badius, who uses on the
title-page the formula 'sub cautione ad calcem explicanda', and by the form of
privilege itself printed at the end, which refers to 'hanc cautionem', but the
intended effect was identical with that of a privilege issued on royal authority,
namely, to prohibit the printing and sale of any other edition for a fixed
period, in this case for two years. The intervention of the university was not, as
in the case of the 1518 privilege granted by the Chancellor of Oxford
University, in favour of a work of scholarship by one of its members.[1] It was to
secure the publication of the *Determinatio* of the Faculty of Theology, dated 15
April 1521, condemning propositions culled from the *De captiuitate Babylonica*
and other works of Martin Luther.[2] Badius was enjoined, upon his oath as a
libraire juré of the university, to print sedulously the *Definitio*, from the
authenticated copy given him. Other printers were forbidden to print it, or to
sell copies printed elsewhere, for two years, without express permission. To
enforce this prohibition, the university brought into play all the sanctions it
had at its disposal to threaten printers and book-sellers who might disregard
its orders: any official of the university (such as a *libraire juré*) who contravened
the order would be deprived of his office, and any other person who did so
would be debarred from ever being appointed to such an office, as well as
incurring the extreme displeasure of the university:

Prohibemusque caeteris omnibus tam iuratis quam non iuratis sub poena amittendi
officii, si quod a nobis habent, & sub praeiudicio nunquam habendi, si nullum habent,
& summae indignationis uniuersitatis, ne biennio proximo sine nostra authoritate
imprimant, aut alibi impressam vendant.

The order is signed by Jean Le Coincte, Rector of the university: not so great a
position as the title denotes at the present day, since the Rector was elected
annually from among teaching members of the Faculty of Arts, but one which
gave him sufficient authority to issue such an order.[3] The 'cautio' is preceded
by an attestation that the book is correctly printed from the official copy of the

[1] See above, p. 10.
[2] *Determinatio theologicae Facultatis Parisiensis super doctrina lutheriana hactenus per eam visa*, s.d. 4°
(ff. 16). I have used the copy in the Bodleian Library, c.2.10(5) Linc. Cf. Ph. Renouard, *Badius*,
Vol. II, pp. 402–3, and *Imprimeurs parisiens*, Vol. II, no. 495 (p. 207).
[3] Le Coincte was to become a doctor of Theology in 1526 and a canon of Amiens in 1529. J. K.
Farge, *Biographical register of Paris doctors of theology 1500–1536* (Toronto, 1980), no. 276
(pp. 252–3).

Determinatio supplied by the Faculty of Theology from its registers ('Ad quorum exemplar de mandato nostro praesentes fuisse fideliter impressas testamur'). I have found no other example of a privilege issued solely on the authority of Paris University. The object of it was certainly exceptional.

It might be expected that religious orders would authorise a particular edition or publisher when printing liturgical or other books for the use of the order, and discourage the circulation of others. In practice it seems that this was rarely done, at least explicitly. An exception must however be recognised in the case of the Carthusians. For many years the order had laboured to produce an edition of the works of its founder, St Bruno, and by 1524 this project was completed. The veteran Paris university printer Josse Badius Ascensius received the manuscript, sent to him by the Prior of the order, Gulielmus Bibaucius or Bibaut,[1] from the Grande Chartreuse, and printed it in a handsome folio volume in 1524, including a *Life* of St Bruno with illustrations. On the title-page Badius placed the words 'sub gratia & priuilegio post vitam explicandis', and indeed immediately after the Life of the saint there appear two separate privileges, one (summarised in Latin, following Badius' usual practice) granted by Louis Ruzé the *Lieutenant Civil* of the Prévôt of Paris, for four years, the other granted by the Prior of the order. The latter, perhaps also a summary of a longer document, reads:

Cauit etiam Reuerendissimus Carthusiæ magnæ prior ordinis pater generalis, ne dicto quadrennio durante, quispiam Religiosorum suorum aliubi curet imprimenda, aut impressa coemat, Sub solita Religiosis poena.

G. Prior Carthusiæ

(PR 1524, 2)

Badius, usually very sparing in his allusions to privileges, gave equal weight to both these. What advantages did he see in the second? It did not enable him, as did that of the *Lieutenant Civil*, to sue in the French courts any competitor who reprinted his edition, or sold within the kingdom of France copies of it printed abroad. But it was valid for all members of the Carthusian order throughout Europe. And they must have been the most obvious customers for the works of St Bruno. If *they* were forbidden by the Prior to reproduce or to purchase any other edition for four years, a publisher in Venice or Basle or Nuremberg might well decide against reprinting it until Badius' privilege had expired. With this example in mind, we may surmise that the 'Cum priuilegio' in Thielman Kerver's reprint of the *Breuiarium Cartusiense* in 1522 (*CP* 1522, 4) may likewise reflect the official approbation of the order.

A book required by all members of a particular religious order was an item of commercial interest in the book-trade. For one particular religious house to have its own breviary printed was on the other hand a luxury. And the

---

[1] There are traces of connection between Badius and Bibaut as early as 1498, when Bibaut was Provincial of the order in Holland. A. Renaudet, *Préréforme et humanisme ... à Paris pendant les premières guerres d'Italie (1494–1517)* (1916), p. 382, n. 8.

production by Thielman Kerver in 1518 of a beautiful little breviary for the nuns of Fontevrault (CH 1518, 7), each part concluding with the words 'Cum priuilegio' printed in red, is indeed exceptional. The convent was the most famous in France, a royal foundation of which the king was Visitor, the members ladies from the noblest families in the land, and the abbess by long tradition a member of the royal family (at this time Renée of Bourbon-Vendôme). An edition of 200 copies would probably suffice to supply all the nuns for the time being, and demand after that would be limited to replacement of copies mislaid or worn out – not negligible for a book in daily use, but still small. Surviving copies show how much these breviaries were prized by their owners, and how carefully older nuns handed them on to younger ones of whom they were fond by gift or bequest. A reprint was not needed until 1526, when it was supplied by Kerver's widow, again with a privilege. The abbess could no doubt have forbidden the use of any other breviary within the community. This would constitute a privilege, though of a very limited kind. She could also have intervened effectively to support Kerver's request for a privilege from the king, as a mark of favour to Kerver for undertaking the printing and publishing of it. And I think the privilege must emanate from the royal chancery. In practice it can have brought Kerver little commercial gain, but it was a recognition of his high standing as a printer of service-books. That any authority, outside the abbey, other than the royal chancery would have ventured to grant a privilege for the breviary of Fontevrault is unthinkable.

Very occasionally, under Francis I, books were published which advertise possession of a papal privilege as well as a royal one. Two editions, both printed in Lyon, both no doubt saleable in Italy, have this feature. The first was a medical text, declaring that it was published 'Cum priuilegio Pontificis maximi Leonis decimi & Francisci christianissimi Francorum regis' (CH 1515, 10). The second is a pretty pocket edition of the Latin poems of Mantuanus, 'Cum gratia et priuilegio apostolico et victoriosissimi Francisci Francorum regis' (CH 1516, 5). The text of a papal privilege granted to the author, Johannes Eck, is printed as well as the royal Letters Patent in De primatu Petri (CH 1521, 4). This was relevant to the subject of the book, for the privilege recognised Eck as the champion of the papacy against Luther.

These appear to be the only French examples in this period of a 'multiple' privilege, that is, a privilege obtained from an authority outside the country of origin of the book as well as within it. Just outside the frontiers of the kingdom, in papal territory, at Avignon, a local bookseller, Jean de Channey, published the treatise De peste by Gian Francesco Riva di San Nazzaro, with a privilege dated 12 September 1522 issued by the Cardinal Legate of Avignon, threatening offenders with a fine of 100 gold pieces, confiscation of their copies and excommunication. The book was promptly reprinted (17 December

1522) by Vincent de Portonariis at Lyon. Jean de Channey immediately heard of this and appointed a *procureur* 'pour poursuivre tous ceux qui en violation de son privilege détiendraient ou colporteraient le susdit traité' (5 January 1523).[1] But privileges given on papal authority alone were considered to be of doubtful validity in France.[2]

[1] Archives de Vaucluse, Notaires (fonds Pons) no. 2082, f. 6ᵛ, cited by P. Pansier, *Histoire du livre à Avignon*, 3 vols. (Avignon, 1922), II, pp. 71 and 82.

[2] Cf. above, p. 13. Later, foreign publishers with an eye to the French market, e.g. those of Basle, sometimes took the precaution of obtaining privileges from the King of France. See also Albert Labarre, 'Editions et privilèges d'André Wechel à Francfort et à Hanau 1582–1627', *Gutenberg-Jahrbuch*, 1970, pp. 238–50.

3 · SEEKING AND GRANTING PRIVILEGES: FORMS, CONDITIONS AND PROCEDURES

T HE FIRST STEP towards obtaining a privilege was for the applicant to draw up a *requête* or petition. Though the concession being sought related to new circumstances, the presentation of the *requête* followed a time-honoured form. Whatever the authority applied to, the applicant began 'Supplie humblement...', referring to himself in the third person, and proceeded to set out the favour he desired and his reasons for requesting it. Initially at least, the petitioner would probably seek the help of a lawyer in drafting the petition. Frequent privilege-seekers like Jean Petit or Galliot Du Pré soon had previous applications which they had only to look up and copy. The submission of the *requête* was probably effected through the intermediary of a *procureur*.

THE ROYAL CHANCERY: LETTERS PATENT

If the petition was submitted to the royal chancery, it was addressed to the king himself. In due course the Letters Patent, if granted, were likewise written as from the king ('Louis par la grace de Dieu etc.'), to the royal officials, notifying them of his decision to accede to the applicant's request, and instructing them to enforce, if so required by the applicant, the measures taken in his favour.

All Letters Patent had to be authenticated by the secretary who had drawn them up, and most printers who displayed the text of their privilege or a careful summary of it were particular to include the name of the secretary who had signed it and the form he had used to record his authority for so doing. In those of which the complete text is printed, three formulae are commonly found throughout the period: 'Par le Roy à la relation du Conseil' (twenty-one examples), 'Par le Roy à vostre relation' (twenty examples), and simply 'Par le Roy' (sixteen examples). The first meant that the grant had been authorised by the King's Council. The second invoked the authority of the chancellor, the words 'yours' and 'you' being used because the document would be submitted to him for approval and for the imposition of the seal. The third, which seems to have been signed mainly by very senior officials, had been prepared in the absence of direct instructions from the Council or the chancellor, in the light of the secretary's knowledge of practice and precedents. In four cases one of the *maîtres des requêtes* is named as having been present when the grant was approved: Maître Pierre de La Vernade (CH 1513, 3 and CH 1514, 1, the latter recording that 'others' were present also), and Maître Jean Hurault 'and others' (CH 1514, 4 and CH 1519, 4, the 1514 privilege also bearing the words 'par le conseil'). Very occasionally the presence at the grant is recorded of some great person unconnected with the routine administration. This was clearly someone who supported the application and wished to show his interest and approval. The bishop of Paris, Etienne Poncher, was present ('praesente et annuente'), and others, at the grant of the privilege for the works of Henry of Ghent (CH 1518, 5). The king's confessor, the Dominican Guillaume Petit or Parvy, then bishop of Troyes, was present, 'and others', at the grant of a privilege for a group of five or more works which included the first edition of Claude de Seyssel, *La grant monarchie de France* (CH 1519, 6).

Fourteen royal secretaries signed book-privileges once only in the period up to 1526 inclusive: Breton, Barthélemy, Guernadon, Hillaire, Juvyneau, de La Chenaye, Mareschal, Morelet, Portier, de Rillac, de Sanzay (or Sauzay), Thiboust, Thurin and de Veignolles; and six signed twice only: Bucelly, Garbot, Longuet, Maillart, de Neufville and Saugeon. The nine who account for all the other known signatures are Deslandes (eleven), Bordel and Hervoet (six each), Guiot (five), de Moulins and Gedoyn (four each), Geuffroy, Robertet and Ruzé (three each). The prominence of François des Landes probably does not denote any particular interest on his part in book-privileges: he had been received into the college of secretaries between 1504 and 1507 and was very active in the chancery throughout the period.[1] Who actually signed the document for presentation to the chancellor depended on the circumstances in the chancery at that moment and who was available. In some cases it was an important official. Nicolas de Neufville was the *audiencier*. Robert Gedoyn was *secrétaire des finances*. 'Robertet' must be either Florimund Robertet, the most important secretary of all at the time, or his cousin Jean Robertet, *secrétaire et trésorier de France*.

Once empowered to proceed with the grant of the privilege, or able to proceed in virtue of powers delegated to him, the secretary drafted the text of the Letters Patent. He would have in front of him the written petition from the author or publisher. This was easily adapted to form the basis of the preamble. He would also have notes of any instructions given to him by the Council or by the chancellor. And he would look up specimens of the forms which had been used in similar circumstances, to serve as models. Having established the text, he would make, or direct a clerk to make, a fair copy of the Letters Patent, and sign it himself when it was completed and checked.

---

[1] Michaud, *La grande chancellerie*, p. 116. For Deslandes, and for other secretaries above-mentioned whose careers, like his, had begun under Louis XII, see A. Lapeyre and R. Scheurer, *Les notaires et secrétaires du roi sous les règnes de Louis XI, Charles VIII et Louis XII, 1461–1515*, Collection de documents inédits sur l'histoire de France, série in-4° (Paris, 1978).

The drawing up of the draft, and the transcription, would each take about an hour. The document, with other letters for which that secretary was responsible, would then be brought to the next audience to be sealed. At the audience, the chancellor sat in state at a table, with the Great Seal in front of him. The documents were brought to him one by one, and, if approved, were duly sealed by the *chauffe-cire*. *Lettres simples* like book privileges, conferring a grant of limited duration, were sealed in yellow wax on a single tape or thread. Very careful privilege-holders sometimes mentioned this when printing the Letters Patent,[1] though it was standard practice. The document, once sealed, was taken to the next meeting held by the *audiencier*, which was a purely financial meeting, at which the fee due on each document was determined and recorded in the accounts. The recipient could than pay the fee, and claim his Letters Patent.

The chancellor presiding at the sealing of documents is depicted in a bas-relief on the monument which Chancellor Duprat ordered for himself to be erected in the cathedral of Sens, now in the Palais Synodal.[2] This shows, in a slightly stylised manner, the ceremony as it would have taken place with the maximum solemnity, in Paris or at one of the great royal residences like Amboise. About twenty people are present as well as the chancellor: officials, guards, petitioners and other onlookers. The bustle of coming and going must have been considerable, remote from the rooms occupied by the king in a large palace but more insistent when the accommodation available was more restricted. Thus there are traces, at some royal *châteaux* where Francis I made relatively long stays, of a special building having been provided for the chancery outside the walls. At Loches (Indre-et-Loire) *La Chancellerie* can still be seen in the street leading up to the castle gates,[3] the present building dating partly from 1534 and partly from 1551. There is also a small house known as *La Chancellerie* in the grounds of Chenonceaux, the *château* of which Francis gained possession in 1524 from Thomas Bohier, and which was later to be enlarged and transformed for Diane de Poitiers by Philibert de Lorme: it was at Chenonceaux that Geofroy Tory obtained his privilege in 1526 for *Champfleury* (CH 1526, 2). The chancery was none the less quite prepared to do business in much less convenient surroundings than these. When the king was travelling, the staff would often have to unpack their belongings and their records, their stocks of paper and parchment and ink and sealing wax and tools in some makeshift room. There they assembled what tables and chairs they could, hung the chancellor's official tapestry with its fleurs de lys, posted the guards, and opened up. If the chancellor himself received the best available accommodation after the king, his office must often have functioned

---

[1] CH 1516, 2; 1517, 3; 1518, 1; 1520, 8; 1520, 10; 1524, 2; 1525, 3; 1526, 2.

[2] Photograph in C. Terrasse, *François Iᵉʳ, Le roi et le règne*, I (1945), p. 176 (planche VIII).

[3] Photograph in L. Hautecoeur, *Histoire de l'architecture classique en France, nouvelle édition* (1965), I, ii, p. 320 (Fig. 101).

in very cramped quarters. It was in circumstances like these, rather than in the pomp displayed in Du Prat's monument, that Vincent Cigauld is likely to have obtained his privilege at Issoire (CH 1516, 2) or Jean Petit at Sancerre (CH 1521, 3).

So eager were some applicants to seize an opportunity of securing a privilege from the royal chancery that they might seek it for a book which they could not have ready until several months later – quite a serious matter if the concession ran from the date of the grant itself (e.g. CH 1514, 1 (1)) – or hold up a book, which had been completed and dated some time before, until they could publish it under royal Letters Patent.

Most publishers who sought privileges were content to receive the grant in their own name, or, in the case of a shared enterprise, their own name plus that of a partner. Some, however, took the precaution of having their partner or partners included unnamed, knowing probably that the book would be published in association with another firm but not having yet completed the arrangements. Jean Petit's summary of his privilege for the *Chronica cronicarum* begins with the words, 'Le roy nostre sire a donné privilege quatre ans à Jehan Petit, libraire juré de l'université de Paris (et à ses compaignons) pour ceste presente Carte' (CH 1521, 3): the book was published five months later in partnership with François Regnault. An earlier privilege obtained by Petit, for a whole 'package' or programme of books all eventually published by partnerships which were headed by Petit, must have contained a similar provision.[1]

Occasionally the exclusive right to sell the books, for the period covered by the privilege, is expressly stated to cover the publisher's factors and agents. Symon Gruel had the sole right to print and sell a book 'ou faire vendre et adenerer tant par luy que ses facteurs entremetteurs' (CH 1520, 6). Michel Le Noir 'et ses commys' are included in an earlier privilege (CH 1513, 3).

Exceptionally, Francis I granted after his return in 1527 a book-privilege in the form of *Lettres Closes* (CH 1527, 1) addressed direct to the beneficiary, Jacques Colin,[2] for editing and arranging for the printing of various translations by the late Claude de Seyssel of Greek historians, for four years. It was however primarily a *commission* to Jacques Colin to do this, preceded by a preamble declaring the king's interest in promoting learning: the privilege was an additional encouragement and partial reward ('affin que vous et vosditz commis soiez plus soigneulx et ententifz à la conduicte dudict euvre et aucunement rembourcé et recompensé des fraiz et vaccacions que vous y conviendra faire'). There are clear reasons for this unusual procedure.

---

[1] See below, pp. 131–4.

[2] On Colin see V. L. Bourrilly, *Jacques Colin, abbé de Saint-Ambroise* (Paris, 1905), and H. Michaud, *La grande chancellerie*, p. 181. On one occasion an author obtained a privilege in the form of *Lettres closes* addressed 'Au prevost de Paris ou son lieutenant', beginning 'Supplie humblement nostre bien aymé Le Moyne sans froc...' in favour of Pasquier Le Moyne, the king's *portier*, for *L'ardant miroir de grace*, Paris, 3 August 1519 (CH 1519, 9).

Jacques Colin was not only one of the royal secretaries but also a favoured member of the royal household, in which he held the position of *valet de chambre, aumônier et lecteur du roi*, and was entrusted with various diplomatic missions. He was also a man of letters and translator in his own right, author (among other works) of the first French version of Castiglione's *The Courtier*. Moreover, the works of Seyssel were lying in manuscript in the royal libary since they had been presented to the king. This unusual grant did not create a precedent.

The Letters Patent by which Louis XII and Francis I granted book-privileges were most commonly addressed to the Prévôt of Paris in the first instance and then to all the other royal magistrates and officers. Thus the first privilege granted to an author by Louis XII begins, 'Loys par la grace de dieu Roy de France au prevost de Paris et à tous noz aultres justiciers ou à leurs lieuxtenans salut et dilection' (CH 1508, 1). Sometimes however the applicant, or his legal adviser, had one or more of the provincial Sénéchaux or Baillis expressly included, as well as the Prévôt of Paris, in this opening sentence. The officer most frequently mentioned in this way is the Sénéchal of Lyon, e.g. 'Aux prevost de Paris, seneschal de Lyon, et à tous noz aultres justiciers et officiers ...' (CH 1514, 4). In the event of the privilege being infringed, it was in the local court that the privilege-holder would have to prosecute the offender: in the case of an alleged pirating in Lyon, the action would be brought in the court of the Sénéchal of Lyon, whether the plaintiff was in Lyon or elsewhere in France. If the Letters Patent were addressed specifically to the Sénéchal, it would probably make the action easier to bring, especially if the privilege-holder had taken the precaution of having the Letters Patent registered in the Sénéchal's court immediately on obtaining them. The variations in the form of address thus reflect the applicant's estimate of the quarter from which possible infringements of his privilege were most likely to come. Normally the Prévôt of Paris, is named first, not only because he took precedence over all the other royal officers, but because Paris was the most important city in the French book-trade. If the Sénéchal of Lyon follows, it is occasionally in company with others: in one privilege the Bailli of Berry is mentioned (CH 1515, 4), in another the Sénéchal of Poitou (CH 1515, 9), the latter privilege being to an applicant from Poitiers. In special circumstances the provincial official may even be addressed first. The privilege given to Jean Lemaire de Belges (CH 1509, 2), granted by Louis XII at Lyon for a book printed at Lyon and immediately registered by Lemaire with the Sénéchal's court, begins, 'Aux Senechal de Lyon, Bailly de Mascon, Prevost de Paris et à tous noz autres justiciers ...' (cf. CH 1511, 3; CH 1515, 7). The privilege obtained by Jean Lode, a schoolmaster of Orleans, is addressed to the Bailli of Orleans, the Prévôt of Paris, and the Sénéchal of Lyon, in that order (CH 1513, 2): 'Aux bayllif d'Orleans, prevost de Paris, seneschal de Lion, et à tous nos aultres justiciers ...'.

Exceptionally, the Letters Patent conferring a royal privilege might be addressed to a provincial Parlement or even to the Parlement of Paris, before going on to mention the Prévôt of Paris and other officers. A privilege granted by Louis XII at Lyon (CH 1511, 2) to Jean Robion for Antonius de Petrutia's *Tractatus de viribus juramenti* was addressed to the Echiquier or Parlement of Rouen, 'les gens tenans nostre court de l'eschiquier à Rouen, prevost de Paris, seneschal de Lyon ...'. It is clear from the text of the privilege that Jean Robion, who was operating in Lyon, especially feared for some reason that this book might be pirated in Normandy, that is, at Rouen or Caen, for the grant is expressly stated to apply 'tant en nostre royaulme, duché de Normandie, que aultres terres et seigneuries estans en nostre obeyssance.'

A privilege granted in 1515 in Grenoble by Francis I as king-dauphin (he had as yet no son to hold the title of dauphin) to a bookseller of Valence, within the jurisdiction of the Parlement of Grenoble (CH 1515, 6) was addressed 'A nos aimés et feaulx les gouverneur ou son lieutenant et gens tenans nostre court de Parlement du Dauphiné séant à Grenoble' and then to the Prévôt of Paris, the Sénéchal of Lyon and the other officers or their lieutenants. The privilege granted to Vincent Doesmier for Jacques Almain's *Aurea opuscula* (CH 1518, 3) was addressed to the Parlement of Paris, 'à nos amés et feaulx conseilliers les gens tenant nostre court de Parlement' and then 'aux prevost de Paris, Seneschal de Lyon, Baillis de Rouen et de Caen, et à tous nos justiciers ...'. The nature of the book may partly explain this. Almain had been a champion of the conciliar movement and of Gallican liberties against the papacy. This was a controversial political issue, on which the king and the Parlement disagreed. As for the reference to Rouen and Caen, the printers there might be keen to reprint the work since Almain had been a well-known professor of Caen University.

The Letters Patent issued by the royal chancery to a successful applicant were his direct evidence that he had received such a grant. It was therefore in his interests to preserve the document with the greatest care. It would no doubt be kept in the chest or box where he put away title-deeds to property, copies of wills and inventories, evidence of *rentes* he possessed, and contracts. A privilege-holder who decided against printing the document *in extenso* in the book or books concerned might print a statement expressing his readiness to show it if required.[1] Normally it would be brought out only for the compositor to set up from it the text of the Letters Patent as they were to be printed.

There were, however, cases when the holder, even when intending to publish the full text, brought it to be *entériné*, that is, confirmed and registered, in the court of the royal official who administered his area. Evidence that this formality had been accomplished might then be obtained, in the form of *lettres d'attache* issued under the seal of the *prévôté* or *sénéchaussée*. Eight such cases are

---

[1] See below, pp. 158–9.

recorded with the printed text of the privilege. The first two are *lettres d'attache* from the Lieutenant General of Lyon (the office of Sénéchal of Lyon being vacant), one to Jean Lemaire de Belges (CH 1509, 2) and the other to Nicole Bohier (CH 1512, 3). The rest date from the years 1514–21 inclusive and were given by the Prévôt of Paris. Of the latter, two were obtained by Guillaume Eustace, two by Jean de La Garde, one by Jean Petit and one by Conrad Resch. A privilege for two years granted on 26 August 1514 to Eustace (CH 1514, 3) covered a French translation of Livy, the *Grans croniques de France*, and *Le grant coustumier de Sens*: in each book Eustace had the Letters Patent printed followed by the words 'Et a l'enterinement desdictes lettres signé Almaury', Almaury being an authorised signatory of the *prévôté*. Seven years later Eustace secured a privilege, again for two years, for a French translation of the letters of St Jerome and a devotional work by Guillaume Alexis (CH 1521, 1); in the St Jerome he displayed his Letters Patent and also the full text of letters from the *prévôté* recording the *entérinement*.[1] This seems to have been the only occasion when the terms of the *entérinement* were printed in full by a Paris privilege-holder. Jean de La Garde, in his edition of the *Coutumes générales* of France (CH 1517, 3), gave however the following careful particulars immediately after the text of the royal privilege itself,

Lesdictes lettres de privillege enterinees par monseigneur le prevost de Paris ainsi qu'il appert par ses lettres dattees du vendredi .xx. jour de mars Mil cinq cens et seize signé Corbie et seellee [*sic*] en cire verte.

The signature is that of one of the clerks at the Châtelet who regularly signed official documents. The sealing in green wax, in the royal chancery a sign of importance, may reflect the official or semi-official character of the publication. The date shows that, in favourable circumstances, the royal chancery being in residence in Paris and the applicant a Paris publisher, *entérinement* could follow the grant of the privilege with little delay, in this case on 20 March following the grant made on 9 March.

Even so, it would not have been worth going to the trouble and extra expense of *entérinement* for a privilege of very short duration. But the holders of privileges for two years and upwards from the royal chancery in some cases evidently thought it worth doing. Did all those who did so advertise in the book concerned that they had carried out this formality? It is improbable. And in the absence of the relevant archives of the *prévôté* of Paris for the period up to 1526 there is no means of knowing.

PARLEMENT: ARRÊTS

Like the chancery, the Parlement of Paris entertained applications for book-privileges among many other matters, most of them of far greater moment.

[1] See below, p. 116.

But, unlike the chancery, the Parlement did not issue the privilege, if granted, in the form of an imposing sealed document. The successful applicant could obtain an authenticated transcript of the judgement of the court, an 'extrait des registres de Parlement'. This was written out on a strip of parchment and signed by an authorised official of the court, with the words 'Collation est faicte'. The signature is usually that of the *greffier*, normally the *greffier civil* (e.g. Du Tillet) but occasionally the *greffier criminel* (e.g. Robert) who could act for him if he was not available. The signature, unlike that of the royal secretary upon Letters Patent, was not an essential of the grant, but only an attestation that the transcript was a true copy of the judgement of the court which had conferred the grant. The privilege-holder, having paid for this transcript, in most cases had it printed carefully in the book to which it referred.

There was one exception. Once in 1512 the Parlement issued a privilege in the form of Letters Patent, as from the king, in Latin (PA 1512, 8). This was exceptional in its form, but not in its scope, for it was the standard two-year grant. And the form was probably chosen in view of the contents of the books to be covered by the privilege. These were: a corrected edition of the Style of the court, as formulated by the famous fourteenth-century advocate Guillaume de Brueil or De Brolio; an *Ordinatio* of the court on thirteen particular points of the Style; a set of *Ordonnances* for the guidance of litigants; and a translation into Latin of the classic French legal farce *Pathelin*. This *priuilegium regale* in the name of Louis XII 'in parlamento nostro' 6 September 1512, granted to Guillaume Eustace, was signed by Maître Antoine Robert, who was both one of the royal secretaries and the *greffier criminel* of the Parlement. In the case of the Style, at least, Robert was himself the author of the revised edition, and had given it to Eustace with the authority of the court, as Eustace makes clear in his colophon, while also accepting the cost of publishing it.[1] It guaranteed that this publication, and the two like it, would be printed carefully, as befitted texts so vital to all who had business in the courts, without expense to the court. That the arrangement was some special bargain negotiated on behalf of the court by Robert is clear.

Books were usually submitted, with the application, when the printing of them had just been completed or was ready to be completed within a short time, perhaps in proof. A sample of the books for which we have both the date of completion and the date of the Paris Parlement privilege, taken in a typical year (1516), gives the result shown in the table.

---

[1] 'Impressus Parisius procurante et auctore nobili viro Magistro Anthonio Robert notario et secretario Regio ac graphario criminali supreme curie parlamenti ipsius impensis honesti viri Guillermi Eustace uniuersitatis Parisiensis librarii iurati ... Quod quidem opus dictus grapharius corrigendum et prefato Eustace imprimendum ipsius supreme curie nutu tradere curauit.' *Stilus parlamenti* (PA 1512, 9(1)), f. J 1ᵛ.

	Date of Privilege	Date of completion of printing
PA 1516, 1	5 January	18 January
PA 1516, 2	16 January	13 January
PA 1516, 4	10 March	27 March
PA 1516, 5	10 March	27 March
PA 1516, 8	23 September	25 October
PA 1516, 9	24 October	24 October

The Parlement then, if it saw fit, obtained a report on the book from a commissioner appointed for the purpose – not necessarily one of the members of the *Conseil* – and occasionally from a specialist called in to give his opinion on it.[1] It then scrutinised the duration of the privilege requested by the applicant, sometimes agreeing it, more often reducing it (e.g. from three years to two).[2]

Applications for privileges were frequently granted by the Parlement for a shorter period than had been requested.[3] Were they ever refused altogether? Such cases would normally leave no trace in the surviving records: an application considered frivolous would not go further than a first hearing in the Chambre des Requêtes. There happens to be one instance, however, where it *is* known that an application was refused. The application in question was from Nicolas de La Barre, and it was for *two* items: one was the Papal Bull canonising Saint Francis of Paola, the other was 'ung petit livre intitulé *De Inuentoribus Rerum*' (PA 1520, 1). The Parlement granted a privilege for the Papal Bull, but ignored the second item, nor has any publication by La Barre of it been found.[4]

ROYAL OFFICERS: LETTERS PATENT, ORDERS ETC.

Privileges issued by the Prévôt of Paris could take at least three forms.

There are Letters Patent, there are orders 'De par le prevost de Paris', and there are *requêtes* as presented by the applicant with the Prévôt's written consent below.

Letters Patent issued in the Prévôt's name, given under the seal of the *prévôté*, and bearing the signature of the Prévôt himself or of an authorised signatory, are printed in full in eight books,[5] and are explicitly referred to in six others. They must necessarily have been the most expensive.

Orders 'De par le prevost de Paris' are very common. These, when issued by one of his subordinates, were usually given under his signet, to judge by those which the beneficiary printed in full. Those signed by Gabriel d'Allegre in person when he was Prévôt do not mention sealing, as if the Prévôt's signature was sufficient authentication in itself, and in two cases in 1520 he

---

[1] See below, pp. 106–7.   [2] See below, p. 121.   [3] See below, pp. 120–1.
[4] See below, p. 93.
[5] PR 1516, 2; 1520, 5; 1521, 4; 1522, 3; 1523, 1; 1523, 5; 1525, 3; 1526, 2.

indeed says expressly 'soubz nostre seing manuel' (PR 1520, 3, and PR 1520, 11).

The practice of printing a *summary* only of the privilege was however common. The following example illustrates this practice:

Il est permis de par monseigneur le lieutenant civil à Toussains Denis libraire demourant à Paris de vendre et distribuer ce present livre. Et defend à tous marchans libraires imprimeurs et aultres de ne imprimer ne vendre par trois ans à venir aultres que ceulx dudit Toussains sur amende de dix livres *comme plus amplement est contenu audit privilege* donné le .ii. iour de mars l'an Mil cinq centz et seze. Ainsi signé   Ruzé. (PR 1517, 1)

The words which I have italicised show that a more elaborate form of privilege lay behind the form which the beneficiary chose to print.

If the form in which book-privileges were issued by the Prévôt seem, on the available evidence, to be unstandardised, this may be partly due to a clientele whose needs varied from full Letters Patent, on the same lines as those given by the chancery, to the simplest authenticated statement that an exclusive right had been duly conferred if only for a matter of weeks or even days.

We possess six specimens of the sort of *requête* which was submitted to the Prévôt by publishers. In these six instances, the privilege was issued to and printed by the recipient in the form described above, that is, the Prévôt or one of his authorised representatives wrote the permission and privilege across the bottom of the *requête*, adding the date and his signature. Publishers who received and advertised their privilege in this form were François Regnault (PR 1517, 7), Hémon Le Fèvre (PR 1520, 3 and PR 1522, 1), Pierre Le Brodeur (PR 1520, 12 and PR 1525, 1) and Gilles de Gourmont (PR 1523, 3). They had the whole transaction prominently displayed in the books concerned, their *requête* in its entirety followed by the Prévôt's reply. Possibly this form of grant was more expeditious than the Letters Patent. It was certainly cheaper, since it involved less clerical work at the Prévôt's office. There was, however, nothing perfunctory about it. Book-privileges in this form were sometimes given even in the papal chancery.[1] The earliest known to have been issued by the Prévôt of Paris includes the written consent of the king's *procureur* in the court, signed Bouchier, as well as the Prévôt's privilege given under his signet and signed Corbie (PR 1517, 7). I give it here in full as a specimen:

A monseigneur le prevost de Paris ou son lieutenant.

Supplie humblement Françoys Regnault libraire juré / en l'université de Paris Comme ledict suppliant puis naguieres ayt faict commencer à imprimer le grant voyage de Jherusalem qui est ung beau livre auquel il a faict adjouster plusieurs entreprinses guerres / et batailles faictes en la terre saincte par les Roys et princes

---

[1] E.g. Guillaume Peraldus, *Sermones*, Avignon, 1519, 8° (BN Rés.D.46868) printed the text of the petition to the Pope by the publisher Jean de Chenney, followed by the words, 'Concessum ut peti.in presentia D. N. pape. J°. Casertañ. Datum Rome apud Sanctum Petrum pridie kal. Octob4. Anno septimo', i.e. 30 September 1519.

chrestiens: comme Charlemaigne Sainct Loys / Godeffroy de Boullion / et autres princes / qu'il a faict extraire de Vincent historial et aultres croniques pour tousjours inciter les princes crestiens à vertu et chevalerie et à soy exerciter aulx armes mesmes contre les adversaires de nostre foy / en quoy faisant ledict suppliant a beaucop frayé du sien. Et doubte que quelque autre imprimeur ou librairie les vuellle cy apres Incontinent qu'il aura achevé les reimprimer ce qui seroit l'empecher de retirer ses frayz et mises et le frustrer de son labeur s'il n'avoit de vous quelque deffense. Ce considerer et en ensuyvant plusieurs autres voz ordonnances en pareil cas. Il vous plaise de vostre benigne grace ordonner deffence(s) estre faites à tous autres libraires: et imprimeurs de non imprimer ou faire imprimer ledict livre ainsi par ledict suppliant imprimer [*sic* for imprimé] d'ycy à troys ans affin que ledict suppliant puisse soy remborcer de ses fraiz. Et vous ferez bien.

> Consentio pro rege à la permission: Et
> deffence à tous autres jusques à ung an.
> Ainsi signé Bouchier:
> De par le provost de Paris.

Pour consideration du contenu en ceste requeste et veu le consentement du procureur du roy nostre sire ou chastelet de Paris cy dessus escript. Il est permis au suppliant de imprimer ou faire imprimer le livre intitulé le grant voyage de Jherusalem mencionné en ceste requeste. Et est deffendu à tous imprimeurs de ne imprimer ne faire imprimer ledict livre d'hui jusques à ung an. Sur peine de confiscation desdictz livres et d'amende arbitraire.

Faict soubz nostre signet le quatriesme jour de septembre l'an mil cinque cens dixsept.

> Ainsi signé Corbie.

(cf. plate 7 for another example.)

CONDITIONS: INSTANCES OF PRICE-CONTROL

Among the conditions which could be attached to the grant of a book-privilege was the imposition of a maximum price, or the stipulation that a reasonable price should be charged.

The privileges issued by the French royal chancery never during this period fixed the price of a book as did those granted, for instance, by the kings of Spain and of Portugal.[1] At most, and then just after the period, the beneficiary was said to be allowed to sell his book 'à juste prix' (CH 1528, 2).

Alone among the privilege-granting authorities in France, the Parlement of Paris sometimes laid down a maximum price which the beneficiary might legally charge for the book in question. It also (particularly in 1524–6) sometimes made it a condition that the book should be sold at a reasonable price ('à prix raisonnable', e.g. PA 1524, 7). It had long concerned itself with regulating the price of essential commodities in the Paris area, and it was natural that sooner or later it should make such a stipulation. The grant of a monopoly, even for only two or three years, must not seem to encourage profiteering. The Parlement, however, made no such stipulation in its earliest

---

[1] See above, pp. 7–8.

grants (e.g. PA 1509, 1) and it never had a consistent policy about price regulation in them. I have noticed fourteen examples of imposing a maximum price, and five of them are in 1516. Possibly some of the *conseillers* attached more importance to price control than others.

The maximum price, when specified, is expressed in terms of the *livre tournois* (l.t.) or of the *livre parisis* (l.p.). These pounds were made up of 20 *solidi* or *sous*, each of these worth 12 *denarii* or *deniers*. The *livre tournois* was worth sixteen *sous parisis*, while the *livre parisis* was traditionally twenty-five *sous tournois*.

The question first arose when the *greffiers* of Orleans petitioned for a privilege to have the *Coutumes* of the *bailliage* of Orleans printed (PA 1510, 2). They themselves proposed that the court should determine a reasonable price. It was decided that each copy should be sold at five s.t. ('pourveu qu'ils ne les pourront vendre que V s.ts. piece'). Subsequently the Parlement standardised on a maximum price of three s.t. unbound and four s.t. bound for the *Coutumes* of Auvergne (PA 1511, 1), Chaumont (PA 1511, 4), Paris (PA 1513, 2), Vitry (PA 1516, 1), and Troyes (PA 1516, 7). In the case of the *Coutume* of Paris, the Parlement thought the matter of sufficient importance to depute two *conseillers* to examine the printed copies, and only on receiving their report and recommendation ten days later did the court fix the price. We see from this case too that anyone disregarding the maximum price was liable to confiscation of the books and an *amende arbitraire* – the same penalty as threatened anyone infringing the privilege. No mention is made of a maximum price in the grant given for the *Coutume* of Bourbonnais (PA 1522, 6), but the *Coutume* of Blois was to be sold 'à prix raisonnable' (PA 1524, 11). It is evident that a great many people *had* to buy these *Coutumes*, and the temptation to overcharge was very real. The same sort of preoccupation no doubt explains the trouble that the Parlement took over the synodal statutes of Orleans, which the clergy of the diocese would have to buy. Chevallon's *requête* was granted, to be allowed to sell them, with privilege, but only 'oy le rapport de certains commissaires commis à visiter ledit livre et s'enquerre du pris auquel il devrait estre vendu', as a result of which the price was fixed at a maximum of twelve d.p. (PA 1525, 6). The certified copy of the privilege which Chevallon obtained, and which he printed, did not include these particulars, but they are known from the entry in the register of the Parlement.

The earliest non-official work to be assigned a maximum price was Olivier de La Marche, *Le parement des dames de honneur* (PA 1510, 3). This was to be sold at not more than three s.t. More substantial publications, which obviously cost more to print, were allowed a higher maximum price. A work of scholastic philosophy could be charged at six s.t. (PA 1514, 2), a legal commentary at eight s.t. (PA 1514, 3), a critical edition of Quintilian with commentary at sixteen s.t. (PA 1516, 2). Other maximum prices, fixed in terms of *livres parisis*, are two s.p. for a slim volume of Latin verse (PA 1514, 5), four s.p. for a guide book to Italy with a map (PA 1515, 4), eight s.p. for a chronicle of Savoy (PA 1516, 4), fourteen s.p. for Aristotle's *Phisica* with a new translation (PA 1518, 7), the latter price being explicitly for copies 'en blanc', that is, in sheets, books only being on sale ready bound which like the *Coutumes* were in constant demand. The highest price fixed during this period in *livres parisis* is twenty s.p. for Guillaume Fillastre on the Golden Fleece (PA 1516, 5) and the lowest is twelve d.p. for the synodal statutes of Orleans (PA 1525, 6). The Prévôt of Paris never at this period set a maximum price. He did however occasionally make it a condition that the publisher should sell it at a reasonable price: 'pourveu que icelluy Du Pré mette ledict livre à juste prix' (PR 1520, 5); 'pourveu que ledit Aubry vende ledit livre à pris raisonnable et non excessif' (PR 1521, 4; PR 1523, 5).

Just after the end of the period here studied, the provincial Parlements show some signs of wishing to regulate the price of the books for which they gave privileges. The Parlement of Toulouse used the expression 'le vendre et adenerer à prix competent et raisonnable' (PA 1527, 1). The Echiquier of Rouen, and adjudicating in a case of conflicting *requêtes* for a privilege in the antiphoner of the diocese of Rouen, which must have been a costly book to produce, with music, for use in the choir, was to fix a maximum price of four l.t. for a copy on paper and twenty-two l.t. for a copy on parchment: 'Pourveu qu'ilz ne les pourroient vendre c'est assavoir ceulx imprimez en parchemin au dessus de vingt deux livres tournois et ceulx imprimez en papier au dessus de quatre livres tournois piece' (PA 1527, 3).

The stipulation that the privileged book should be sold at a reasonable price was not accompanied by the threat of any specific penalty for disregarding it, as was the condition that a named maximum price should not be exceeded. But it may have enabled members of the trade and of the public to lodge a complaint if they thought the beneficiary or his agents were charging an exorbitant amount for it.

PERSONAL APPROACHES

An expedient which occurred very naturally to certain authors seeking a privilege from the royal chancery, especially lawyers and royal officials, was to offer the dedication of the book in question to the chancellor. If the chancellor accepted the dedication, he might be expected to look favourably on the request for privilege. Thus Louis XII's chancellor Jean de Ganay received the dedication of the *Coutume* of Bourges edited and provided with a commentary by Nicole Bohier (CH 1509, 1 (2)), which was included in a privilege issued to Bohier by the chancery at Lyon on 1 June 1509, and of the *Tractatus* on the powers of the king's council by Jean Montaigne (CH 1512, 3), granted a privilege at Blois on 3 June 1512. Jean de Ganay had been first president of the Parlement of Paris before his elevation to the chancellorship in January 1508, and his brother Germain, later bishop of Orleans, was a *conseiller clerc* in the Parlement of Paris. And so it is not hard to see how Josse Badius, dedicating to Germain de Ganay his edition of Valerius Maximus, came to thank him for having facilitated the grant of a royal privilege (the first, in fact, which Badius obtained), in the words, 'quoniam tuo faustissimo suffragio regia maiestas sic respexit ut privilegio et gratia in fronte praefixis eam dignata sit' (CH 1510, 1). And for that matter it may have smoothed the way for Jean Petit, in obtaining a privilege from the Parlement for the treatise *Militaris disciplina enchiridion*, by Jean Surgetus, *in legibus licentiatus*, that the author had dedicated it to Jean de Ganay (PA 1512, 2).

The death of Jean de Ganay in June 1512 left the great office of chancellor vacant, and Louis XII did not fill it, contenting himself with appointing Etienne Poncher, bishop of Paris, *garde des sceaux*. At least one privilege was given during that interregnum for a book which was dedicated to Poncher, and the author of it, Jean Randin, a canon lawyer, describes himself as formerly the confessor and chaplain of Jean de Ganay when he was chancellor, and now *promotor* and advocate in the bishop's court. Randin did not, however, seek a privilege from the royal chancery, to which his association with the late chancellor and with the present *garde des sceaux* would have given him ready access. He and his publisher, the Paris bookseller Jacques Guillotoys, applied instead to the Parlement (PA 1512, 10). This was probably for the simple reason that it was more convenient, as, in December 1512, when they wanted the privilege, Louis XII was at Blois.

At the accession of Francis I, in January 1515, a new chancellor was at once appointed. This was Antoine Du Prat, the first president of the Parlement. Du Prat had already received the dedication of the poem *Cleopolis*, in praise of Paris, by Quinziano Stoa, which was granted a privilege by the Parlement (PA 1514, 8), as well as complimentary verses and a dedication in the *Coustumes d'Auvergne* (PA 1511, 1) in the codification of which he had taken a leading part. Nicole Bohier, quick off the mark as usual, dedicated his *De seditiosis* to the new chancellor, and his publishers were given a royal privilege for it by 26 April 1515 (CH 1515, 4). Dedications or complimentary verses to Du Prat are to be found in a number of books enjoying privileges issued by the royal chancery (CH 1516, 2; 1518, 6 (2); 1519, 5 (1); 1519, 6; 1523, 1; 1524, 1; 1525, 3), in at least one issued by the Parlement (PA 1522, 3), and in several published 'Cum privilegio' with no other details (*CP* 1514, 4; 1517, 1; 1525, 1). On other occasions, a book bearing a privilege from the Parlement proves to be dedicated to one of the *conseillers*. Among these are the *Regule* of Socinus edited by B. de Fossombrone, for which Galliot Du Pré obtained a privilege (PA 1513, 1); the dedication, by Jean Gerlier, an advocate at the Châtelet, son of Durand Gerlier the publisher, is addressed to Arnald L'Huillier, who had been his tutor in law, and who was a *conseiller*. A later example is provided by the *Epitomata* of Laziardus, or Le Jars, which Hémon Le Fèvre (joint publisher of the book with Jean Kerver) dedicated to Nicolas de Bèze, archdeacon of Etampes, one of the *conseillers clercs* in the Parlement of Paris, and incidentally uncle of Théodore de Bèze the future Reformer (PA 1521, 3). A *conseiller* who had thus accepted the dedication of a book could no doubt be counted on to expedite the grant of a privilege for it in the court.

An applicant who had no connections of his own with the world of the chancery might be able to call upon the help of a friend or patron who had such connections. Such a motive might for instance underlie the dedication of a translation by Jean Lode, an Orleans schoolmaster, to Pierre Berruyer, who occupied the position at Orleans of King's Advocate (CH 1513, 2). Any connection with the royal court might be pressed into service. Thus the author Jean Bouchet was to ask Madame de Monstereuil-Bonnyn (Anne Gouffier), who was *gouvernante* to the king's daughters, to put in a good word for him with the royal secretary Villandry, to whom he had sent an application for a privilege,[1] for *Le jugement poetic de l'honneur fémenin*, which appeared in 1538.

Personal records by beneficiaries of the granting of privileges to them are inevitably very rare. Jean Lemaire de Belges wrote to Barangier on 15 July 1509 from Bourg-en-Bresse: 'Au surplus je m'en voy bien bref à Lyon, tant pour faire imprimer les Singularitez de Madame, dont monsieur le Chancelier me baille privilege.'[2] The Letters Patent being dated Lyon, 30 July, it appears that Lemaire had received a personal assurance from the chancellor, presumably by letter, that the privilege would be granted. An expression of thanks to the *conseillers* who had granted him his privilege (PA 1522, 7), by the Toulouse publisher Mathieu de Monde, took the form of a *rondeau* printed at the end of the book, addressed personally to them by name, in which, if the verse is deplorably flabby, the sentiment is heartfelt:

Graces à messeigneurs les conseillers H. Reynier & S. Raynier pour le privilleige par eulx octroyé

> S'il est ainsi, que les Atheniens,
> Medes persans, grecs, macedoniens
> Ayent establi loix decrets et edicts
> Allencontre de ces ingrats mauldits,
> Raison le veult et les droits anciens:
> Tels meschans sont plus inhumains que chiens
> Et indignes d'estre appellés chrestiens,
> De toutes gens reprouvés et hais,
>   S'il est ainsi.
> Pourtant esse que le corps et les biens
> Sont tout à vous, et dès cy je me tiens
> Vostre humble serf, priant qu'en paradis
> Vous soit rendu, faisant fin à mes dicts:
> Ingratitude ne vallut oncques riens,
>   S'il est ainsi.

---

[1] Bouchet, *Epistres morales et familieres* (1545), fol. Epist. 96, f. 75.
[2] Jacques Abelard, *Les illustrations de Gaule et singularitez de Troye: Etude des éditions. Genèse de l'oeuvre* (Geneva, 1976), p. 223.

4 · GROUNDS FOR SEEKING AND GRANTING PRIVILEGES

DURING THE PERIOD 1505 to 1526 inclusive, the printing presses of Paris alone produced at least 7,719 editions.[1] Of these, the proportion known to have been covered by privileges is about $5\frac{1}{4}$ per cent. It is unlikely that the proportion of privileged books is any higher, or even as high, for any provincial centre in France. The proportion is not large, and most books undoubtedly came out to take their chance in the public domain.

What were the considerations, then, which decided authors or publishers to seek privileges, and the authorities to grant them? In the absence of any formal statement of policy on the part of the authorities, we turn to the arguments advanced by successful applicants.

The grounds on which applicants made their plea for a privilege are known from various sources, although no autograph original of a *requête* dating from the first quarter of the sixteenth century is extant. The Letters Patent issued by the chancery, of which the text is known for sixty, and by the *prévôté* of Paris, of which the text is known for eight, recapitulate in the preamble the terms in which the successful petitioner had presented his case. This was standard form in all such grants. Although the outline of the form is standardised, and had been so for generations, the arguments used in these applications for privileges are not. The object of the petition was something new, and authors and publishers differed considerably, or their legal advisers did, in their estimate of what arguments would weigh most with the authority to which they were applying. The text of the Letters Patent therefore repays very close study. In addition to this indirect evidence, there are six *requêtes* by publishers to the *prévôté* of Paris which were reprinted verbatim by the beneficiaries with the Prévôt's favourable reply,[2] and one *requête* to the Parlement of Toulouse which is preserved entire within the privilege itself and printed in the book (PA 1517, 3).

Grants of privileges by the Parlement of Paris are uninformative in this respect. The court never gave the reasons for its decisions in the registers, and it is only very rarely that there are traces of the arguments which the petitioner had used.

---

[1] Statistics obtained from Brigitte Moreau, *Inventaire chronologique des éditions parisiennes du xvie siècle*, 3 vols. (1972–85), I, pp. 141–390; II, pp. 57–630; and III, pp. 49–319.

[2] For this form of privilege, see above, pp. 72–3.

FAIR RETURN FOR EXPENDITURE OF TIME, SKILL AND MONEY, AND OTHER ARGUMENTS

Authors

To deal first with applications made by authors, the following extract from the Letters Patent granted by Louis XII to Eloi d'Amerval (CH 1508, 1), the earliest French privilege obtained by an author of which the full text is known, probably reflects what Eloi had said in his *requête*:

He has made and composed a fine book treating of sundry merry, diverting and profitable matters concerning the way of life of each estate of society, which book is entitled *Eloi's Show of Devils*, in making and composing the which book the said petitioner has thereon employed and spent a great deal of time and expended a large portion of his substance. For this reason, both to communicate the said book to those who shall desire to see it and to profit by it, and also to recover and retrieve part of what it has cost him to make it and compose it, he would gladly have the said book printed, he only and no one else, until such time as it shall please us, if it were our pleasure to give him leave and licence to do so and to impart to him in this matter our grace and liberality.[1]

The economic considerations which Eloi had evidently put forward were to remain uppermost in most requests for privileges, whether by authors or publishers. The interests of both are represented in the next privilege sought by an author (CH 1509, 1), that of the lawyer Nicole Bohier. For Bohier, planning to publish a whole group or 'package' of works composed or edited by himself, sought a grant in favour of a particular publisher, Simon Vincent of Lyon, with whom he was in fact to work for many years in a harmonious symbiosis. He began indeed by emphasising the expenditure of his own time and labour on the works, as Eloi had done ('il s'est aplicqué et employé temps à faire, diter et rediger par escript certains livres') and his eagerness to have them printed so that, in the words of the Letters Patent, 'son dit ouvraige soyt communiqué tant à noz subgetz que à aultres qui auront vouloyr et desir de iceulx veoyr et visiter'. He then reported the misgivings of his prospective publisher on the subject of possible unauthorised reprints:

ledit Symon Vincent libraire dessusdit a dit et remonstré audit Boyer nostredit conseillier que pour ce que incontinent apres que il auroit faict imprimer lesdis livres ausquels comme dict est conviendra mettre et employer le sien: aulcuns aultres

---

[1] Il a fait et composé ung beau livre le quel traicte de plusieurs plaisantes recreatives et profitables matieres touchant la maniere de vivre en chascun estat. Leque<l> livre est intitulé la deablerie de eloy. En faisant et composant lequelt [*sic*] livre ledit suppliant y a employé et vaqué grande espace de temps frayé et despendu grant partie de sa substance. A ceste cause tant à fin de communiquer le dit livre à ceulx qui auront desir de le veoir et d'y prouffiter que pour recouvrer et retirer partie de ce qu'il luy a cousté à faire et composer il feroit voulentiers imprimer ledit livre luy seul et non autre jusques à tel temps qu'il nous plaira. Si nostre plaisir estoit luy donner congé et licence de ce faire. Et nostre grace et liberalité sur ce luy impartir.

libraries pourroyent semblablement: iceulx reimprimer: ledit Symon Vincent ne pourroyt recouvrer ne soy satisfaire de ses ditz fraiz et mises.[1]

And in response the Letters Patent duly noted the expenditure of Bohier's time upon the composition of the books ('pour consideration qu'il a prins et employez son temps à faire, diter, rediger et construire lesdicts livres') and also recognised that Vincent should be enabled to recover his expenses ('desirans à ceste cause qu'il se puisse rembourcer desdictz fraiz, mises et impenses').

The petition of Jean Lemaire de Belges for the first book of *Les illustrations de Gaule et singularitez de Troye* (CH 1509, 2) on the other hand, was to ensure a fair return for his own labours and expenses ('à ce que ledit exposant puisse estre recompensé de ses paines, salaires, labeurs, coustz et mises qu'il a faictes à compiler iceulx livres'). Lemaire, who was a man of fame and wealth, had indeed clearly paid for the printing himself: the formula 'Imprimé ... pour maistre Jan Lemaire Indiciaire et historiographe de la Royne' in Book I indicates this, and in the *Traictié intitulé de la difference des scismes* of 1511 the printer says, 'Pour maistre Jan le Maire Indiciaire et historiographe. Expensis propriis.' The outlay of which Lemaire spoke must also have included the expenditure of his time and skill, the purchase of books, possibly the employment of a secretary, and so forth. The Letters Patent obtained by Guillaume Michel de Tours from the Prévôt of Paris for *La forest de conscience* (PR 1516, 2) refer specifically to the author having borne the cost of printing ('En composant lequel livre ledit Guillaume Michel dict avoir employé beaucoup de son temps et frayé de grans deniers pour le papier, façon et impression'). The privilege granted by the Parlement of Toulouse to Etienne Chenu refers only in general terms to the arguments he had used in his petition (PA 1517, 5), but there is a formal declaration printed in his book that he had both corrected it and paid for the printing ('correctum est autem hoc opus ... per me ipsum Stephanum Chanuti huius operis authorem, et sumptu proprio caracteribus impressoriis redactum' (f. J 2^v)), and it seems unlikely that he would have failed to include this in his *requête*. Pierre Gringore had even had illustrations specially made for *Les fantasies de mère Sotte*, twenty-eight of them in fact, and this fact figured prominently in his Letters Patent:

il s'est applicqué à ditter et composer ung livre intitulé les fantasies de mere sotte où il a vacqué par long temps / et tant en ce faisant que aussi à faire pourtraire et tailler plusieurs hystoires pour la decoration dudit livre conformes aux matieres contenues en icelluy (CH 1516, 3)

A privilege granted to Dr Jean Falcon for *Les notables sur le Guidon* (CH 1515, 1A) recalls his main point as having been his fear that, once published, his book might be printed by any merchant or bookseller who wished to do so,

---

[1] In quoting from the printed text of Bohier's privilege I have corrected the following misprints: 'Vnicent' for *Vincent*, 'se' for *ses*, and 'employer' for *employez* or *employé*.

which would be to his 'tres grant prejudice et dommaige'. The grant was made however expressly that he might be recompensed for 'ses peines, salaires, labeurs, coustz et mises', the same wording as that used to Lemaire de Belges. Hugues Descousu, a lawyer, sought like Nicole Bohier a privilege in favour of a particular publisher of Lyon with whom he proposed to deal, in this case Pierre Balet: he urged both the labour of preparing his work and the expense involved ('auquel il a prins grant cure et sollicitude tant ès compositions que corrections ... avec plusieurs grans fraitz et coustements', CH 1516, 1). Vincent Cigauld, another lawyer and a royal official, emphasised the time and labour he had lavished on his books ('en laquelle euvre il a vacqué et travaillé par plusieurs et diverses journées en grant labeur'), but also his fears that, if unprotected, they could be reprinted by others so that he derived no profit from them ('tellement que ne luy vint à nul prouffit', CH 1516, 2). Authors of translations put forward similar arguments. Jacques de Mortières, seeking a privilege (CH 1522, 5) for his French version of the *Parthenice* of Mantuanus, asked 'que ledit exposant puisse aulcunement estre satisfait des frays et missions qu'il a faitz à ladicte translation'. Gringore, with a verse translation into French of the Hours of Our Lady to protect (CH 1525, 2), feared lest 'les aultres libraires et imprimeurs les vousissent semblablement imprimer et faire imprimer et par ce moyen le frustrer de ses peines, mises et labeurs'.

So persistent throughout the period are the references made by authors to the expectation of profit, if duly protected by a privilege, that the question must be asked how they hoped to make this profit. Some, as has been seen, undoubtedly financed the edition themselves, and would receive the proceeds from sales of the book, minus any commission which they might owe a bookseller for handling it. Such authors must however have been a minority of those who obtained privileges. It is possible that others, without being in a position to pay the whole cost, had some financial stake in the enterprise. After the Edict of Villers-Cotterêts (1539), when formal contracts before a notary were required for many transactions which had hitherto been made verbally or by simple signed agreement, there is documentary evidence of participation by authors in the financing of their books. Thus on 18 November 1546, François Baudouin, an advocate in the Parlement and a prolific writer on civil law, entered into a contract of this kind with the Paris printer-publisher Jean Loys, former manager of the press of Josse Badius: he obtained a receipt from Loys for the sum of ten *écus d'or soleil* for a share in the printing of his *Prolegomena*, 280 copies of which were to be sold for his benefit, and for a further sum of 468 *livres tournois* representing a half-share in the edition of 1,300 copies of his Commentaries on the Institutes, the proceeds of 650 copies to be sold for his benefit, so that he would receive exactly half the proceeds of the copies sold.[1] Such arrangements may have been practised before 1526.

[1] E. Coyecque, *Recueil des actes notariés relatifs à l'histoire de Paris et de ses environs au xvie siècle*, 2 vols. (1905–23), II, no. 4093.

It was not necessary, however, for the author to prove that he or his publisher was going to lose financially if he failed to obtain a privilege. Expenditure of time and professional skill on the composition of a book was accepted as an adequate reason for considering the grant of a privilege. Three orders given in succession by the Prévôt of Paris in 1516–17 show this clearly. Juan de Celaya, a Spanish scholastic philosopher in the University of Paris, made a formal affirmation each time in the court of the Prévôt that he was the author of the book, that he had composed it at his own expense, and in doing so toiled a great time ('et en ce faisant vacqué par longue espace de temps', PR 1516, 3 and 4; PR 1517, 3). This statement no doubt distinguished Celaya's position from that of a writer commissioned by a patron or publisher to work for a fee, or directed by an employer whom he served as a secretary, or indeed by a religious house which might have assigned to one of its members the composition of such a commentary as one of his duties. It was accepted by the Prévôt as sufficient grounds for the grant of a privilege to the author.

It might be expected that authors would argue the originality or usefulness of their productions. They rarely did so. Eloi d'Amerval called his *Deablerie* 'un beau livre' and gave a few words of description of its scope. Jean Lode went a little further in describing the poems and translations for which he sought a privilege (CH 1513, 2) 'tous utiles livres et moult prouffitables chascun en son espece', and in declaring that he wished to publish them 'tant pour le prouffit et utilitate [sic] de la chose publicque que aussi pour estre premié et sallarié de partie de ses peines labeur et vacations qu'il a prinses en la composition correction et traduction desditz livres'. Few authors had the assurance to claim, as did Gringore (CH 1516, 3), that they aimed not only at recovering their expenses but at public entertainment ('tant pour recouvrer partie de ses mises et vacations que pour donner plaisir et recreation aux lysans et escoutans': the word 'escoutans' indicates that the author expected a popular success, for the practice of reading aloud, mainly cultivated at the present day for children or for people who are ill or blind, is well attested both in literature and in pictures in the sixteenth century, one person reading to a circle of listeners of whom some might be working with their hands meanwhile and some of whom might indeed be illiterate).

The argument of Jean Lode, on the other hand, was taken up by several authors or editors of more serious works. Nicole Bohier edited three legal works for which he obtained a privilege in favour of Simon Vincent (CH 1515, 7), 'pour le bien, prouffit et utilité de la chose publique', though he did not fail to point out also the time and trouble that he, and others working for him, had taken to prepare these books for publication, and the expense that Simon Vincent would incur in having them printed. Similarly, applying for a privilege four years later for Petrus de Ancharano's commentaries on the Decretals, Bohier claimed that he wished to print them 'pour l'utilité de nostre royaulme et chose publicque', having obtained the text 'à grant peine et labeur' (CH 1519, 5). Vincent Doesmier, editing the posthumous *Aurea opuscula* of Jacques Almain, with the help of his own notes on Almain's lectures, invoked 'le bien et utilité de la chose publicque, mesmement des escoliers et estudians en ladicto univcroité de Paris et aultres universités de nostre royaulme' (CH 1518, 3). Gabriel de Tarregua represented that his *Summae* of various medical subjects was 'fort utille et profitable à la chose publique et pour le gouvernement des cors humains', but the grant also recognised the usual argument, that he did not wish 'ses labeurs et vaccations, fraiz, mises et despens luy demourer illusoires' (CH 1520, 9). No other French medical writer who obtained a privilege during this period thought of mentioning the value of his work to science or humanity, to judge from the terms of the grants.

Authors, and doctors not least among them, must have been aware of the risk of garbled unauthorised versions of their works appearing in print, by which their professional, personal or literary reputation might be damaged. This consideration is slow to find expression in their applications for privileges, though it may underlie the argument (for instance) of Jean Falcon as to the 'tres grant prejudice et dommaige' which would result from anyone being free to reprint his book, as well as financial loss. An attempt was made unsuccessfully in 1525 by Robert Messier, head of the Franciscan Order in France, to obtain from the Parlement of Paris a privilege which would have vested in Claude Chevallon for life the exclusive right to publish Messier's works. All other booksellers and printers were to be forbidden to print them, 'à cause des grandes faultes et abus qui se y pourroient faire'. Messier was a popular preacher, and he may have feared that printers less responsible and less orthodox than Chevallon might, intentionally or otherwise, introduce errors into the text which might distort the sense of what he had said. He may have been concerned too that his style should not be disfigured by the printer's errors, for it consisted of a lively but unpredictable mixture of French and Latin. The Parlement in any case ignored this request. What it gave him was a two-year privilege for the particular volume which he had laid before it on this occasion, his sermons on the Gospels and Epistles for Lent (PA 1525, 1). Nicolas Volcyr de Sérouville was to obtain a privilege just after the end of the period here studied (PR 1527, 1) from the *prévôté* for his account of *La victoire obtenue contre les seduyctz et abusez lutheriens par Anthoine, duc de Calabre*. He had a strong case for a privilege, on many grounds, but he particularly stressed the 'scandal' that might be caused to him by unauthorised reprints 'pour les faultes et incorrections que lesditz imprimeurs y pourroient commetre en son absence'. It is not clear whether he was mainly concerned lest printers' errors should make what he had written look offensive or lest they should render his style absurd or obscure. By 1554 it was being stated in royal grants that wrong was done to an author by unauthorised and incorrect printing of his works, and that he was naturally the best person to supervise the printing.[1] Such ideas may have been in the mind of some authors and of some officials before 1526, but they are not expressed in any privilege.

Publishers

Publishers who sought privilege naturally tended to put forward economic arguments in support of their request: that they had incurred or planned to incur great expense in securing and printing a new item on which they could not hope to make a fair profit unless other French members of the book-trade were restrained from reprinting it or selling copies printed elsewhere, until the first edition had been given a reasonable time to sell.

Sometimes however the difficulty and cost of acquiring the manuscript is particularly stressed. Thus Antoine Bonnemère represented that he had taken great trouble to secure the copy of a romance of Judas Maccabeus by Charles de Saint-Gelais ('qu'il a prins grant peine de recouvrer') (CH 1514, 4). Regnauld Chaudière proposed to publish *La grant monarchie de France* of Claude de Scyssel and other works of the same author, 'desquelz livres il a recouvert le double à grant peine et difficulté' (CH 1519, 6(1)). These were living authors. The cost here might include paying the author a fee (or giving his secretary a present), or promising some free copies of the book, in return for buying or borrowing a manuscript of his work. As far as Seyssel is concerned, the only existing manuscript of *La monarchie de France* (the epithet 'grant' seems to have been an addition made by the publisher) is the fine copy presented to Francis I by the author in 1515 (BN MS FF 5212). What Chaudière printed from was either a rather poor transcript of this or possibly a working copy kept by the author: it was certainly a less good text than the presentation copy, quite apart from inaccuracies contributed by the printer.[2] Still, it was something of a triumph to have tracked down a copy at all. Old, and retired to his native Savoy, as archbishop of Turin, Seyssel seems to have cared little about having his book printed.[3]

To acquire a hitherto unpublished work by a famous author of the past might also genuinely involve considerable effort and expense. Colleges and religious houses might be pleased to lend MSS of scholarly works from their

---

[1] E.g. Ronsard, *Œuvres complètes*, STFM, ed. P. Laumonier, VI (1930), 3–6 (privilege Fontainebleau, 4 January 1554 n.s.). Also in grants to less famous authors, e.g. Guillaume Aubert, *L'histoire des guerres* (1559), 4° (privilege Bar-le-Duc, 30 September 1559).

[2] Claude de Seyssel, *La monarchie de France et deux autres fragments politiques*, ed. Jacques Poujol (1961), 'Notice: Histoire du texte', pp. 91–3.

[3] Ibid., pp. 17–18.

libraries, perhaps with a promise of some free copies:[1] contacts with publishers, especially with the university publishers in Paris, were close. But it was in the collections of princely and noble houses, or in private hands in the families of lawyers and civil servants, in their town houses or their *châteaux*, that finds could still be made of interesting *vernacular* texts from the past. To obtain information, to make the necessary contacts, to get leave to borrow or transcribe an irreplaceable family heirloom, might be costly. We can believe Galliot Du Pré when he says, in asking for a privilege which covered among other things *Le temple Jehan Boccacce* of Chastellain: 'Et aussi que à grande difficulté ledict suppliant a recouvert la coppie dudict livre' (CH 1517, 1 (2)). How did François Regnault (PA 1516, 5) obtain the text of Guillaume Fillastre's, *Le livre de la Toison d'Or*, of which the only copies were manuscripts made for knights of the Order of the Golden Fleece? Was it a coincidence that 1516 was the year when Francis I was elected a knight of the Order at the chapter held in Brussels?

In the case of learned works already fairly well known, a publisher sometimes represented that his edition had been prepared by specialists of high standing, to whom he had been at the additional expense of paying a fee or at least their expenses. Thus Pierre Balet of Lyon said in opening his application that he had caused certain great scholars and men of experience ('aulcungs grans clers et gens de experience'), at much expense, to revise and correct the *Practica judiciaria in criminalibus* of Jacobus de Belviso. (CH 1515, 8). The expense of commissioning translation into French of works already in circulation, whether learned or otherwise, is an argument met with more frequently. Durand Gerlier, for instance, in a privilege granted for this and other books (CH 1519, 2), is said to have caused the Georgics of Virgil to be translated, copied, corrected, collated and moralised (by Guillaume Michel of Tours) 'à grans fraictz et despens'.

It was not, however, only from Latin, or even from Italian or Spanish, that publishers commissioned translations. Certain romances written in Old French or even Early Middle French were unearthed by publishers which they judged still capable of pleasing readers but which, owing to the great changes which had taken place in the language, required to be modernised if they were to be read with enjoyment by amateurs of chivalric adventure under Louis XII or Francis I. Thus Michel Le Noir discovered *Huon de Bordeaux*, which he caused to be transcribed and translated from old and ancient language into good style and current French ('il a fait escripre et translater de vieil et ancien langaige en bon stille et commun françoys') or, as the title-page says, 'Nouvellement

---

[1] Henricus Bebelius wrote to Michael Hummelberg on 23 January 1513 that he could not provide Hummelberg with a copy of his recent book because, of the ten free copies which he had received from the publisher, he had been obliged to give all to various abbots and colleges under existing agreements ('Ego enim nullum habeo, nam decem accepi dono, quae ex composito quibusdam abbatibus et collegiis debebam'). A. Horawitz, *Analecten zur Geschichte des Humanismus in Schwaben 1512–1518* (Vienna, 1877), p. 25.

Oys par la grace de dieu Roy de france au pre/
uost de paris/ et a tous noz aultres Justiciers et officiers ou a leurs lieuptes
tenans et a chascun deulx sicomme a luy appartiendra salut· De la partie de nostre bien ay/
me Michel le noir lung des vingtquatre libraires iurez en Luniuersite de paris Nous a este
exposé que puis naguerres il a fait escripre et translater de vieil et ancien langaige a bon stille
et commun francoys vng beau liure intitule huon de Bordeaulx· Lequel en son temps fut vng
vaillant cheualier qui fist beaucoup de vaillances ainsi quil est contenu oudict liure· Lequel
ledit suppliant a fait corriger et mettre en bonne forme a le feroit voulentiers imprimer affin
quil fust communicque et manifeste a tout chascun/ a q en lisant icelluy plusie²s princes che/
ualiers escuyers et aultres gens de bien se pourront grandement recreer a veoir de lexercice
des armes et de la guerre et aultres faitz vertueulx/ mais ledit suppliant ne le feroit faire im/
primer sans noz conge licence et permission· et q de nostre grace a liberalite luy octroyons gra/
ce et preuillege que aultre que luy ne le puisse faire imprimer plustost que de deux ans a comp/
ter du iour et dacte que ledit liure sera acheue de imprimer/ affin q̃ il puisse recouurer ses fraitz
et mises/ pource est il que nous ces choses considerees inclinans liberallement a la supplica/
cion et requeste dudict suppliant et en faueur daulcuns noz seruiteurs speciaulx qui pource
ont requis et supplie a pour luy suppliant· Pour ces causes a autres a ce nous mouuans auos
donne permis et octroye donnons permetons et octroyons de nostre grace especial par ces pre
sentes/ conge licence et permission quil puisse et luy soit loysible et permis imprimer ledit li/
ure dessus declaire sans ce que aultre imprimeur que luy le puisse imprimer iusques a deux
ans entiers a compter comme dit est dessus. Si vous mandons a commandons a a chascun
de vous sicomme a luy appartiendra que en faisant iouyr ledit suppliant de noz presens con
ge grace permission/ octroy et de tout le contenu en ces presentes vous faictes ou faictes fai/
re inhibicion et deffence de par nous sur grans peines a noz a appliquer a tous imprimeurs
et libraires tant de nostre ville de paris que daillieurs quilz ne imprimét ou facent imprimer
ledit liure durant ledit temps sans le vouloir et consentement dudit supplyant/ a ce sur peine
de confiscacion de ce quil seroit trouue en leur possession desditz liures· Car tel est nostre plai
sir non obstant quelzconques lettres a ce contraires mandons a commandons a tous noz iu
sticiers/ officiers/ et subgetz a vous en ce faisant soit obey· Donne a paris le neufuiesme iour
de iuing· Lan de grace mil cinq cens et,treize·Et de nostre regne le seiziesme·

    C Par le roy Maistre pierre de la Vernade maistre des reque/
stes ordinaires present·   Signe.

               J·Morelet·

Plate 4   Chancery privilege for the romance *Huon de Bordeaux* (1513)
(*reduced*)

redigé en bon françoys ...'. That he had to pay someone who could understand the original to carry out this task was a valid additional argument (CH 1513, 3; see Plate 4).

Sometimes publishers sought to strengthen their case in applying for a privilege by pointing out that the book in question was dedicated to some noble or princely personage or undertaken at the bidding of such a person. Alain Bouchard had prepared the *Grandes cronicques de Bretaigne* with the encouragement of Queen Anne, duchess of Brittany, and would have dedicated it to her but for her untimely death, as he says in his preface. His publisher, Galliot Du Pré, had clearly made play with this circumstance in his application, for Louis XII's privilege (CH 1514, 1 (1)) calls the chronicle 'ung livre des histoires de Bretaigne de tous les princes qui ont esté jusques au temps du Duc Francoys de Bretaigne dernierement faictz à l'honneur et louenge de feue nostre treschere et tresamee compaigne la royne que dieu absoulle'. Antoine Bonnemère had claimed in his request for the romance of Judas Maccabeus, already mentioned (CH 1514, 4), that he pursued a deliberate policy of publishing books written in praise of the king and the royal family, the work being dedicated by its author to the duke of Valois, the future Francis I, called by Louis XII his 'son' as heir presumptive ('chacun jour se applique et emploie à faire imprimer ou imprimer plusieurs beaulx livres tant en nostre louenge que des nostres, et mesmement ... la saincte hystoire des Machabées translate de latin en françois à la louenge de nostre trescher et tresamé ilz le duc de Vaillois'). Galliot Du Pré, applying to the Prévôt for the *Summaire ou Epitome* of Budé's *De Asse*, refers to the book having been 'présenté au roy nostre sire' (PR 1523, 1) but otherwise this approach seems to have lost favour after the reign of Louis XII.

Assertions that the book in question will be useful to the public, or to a particular section of it, on the other hand, become more common, beginning with the claim of Michel Le Noir (CH 1513, 3) that he wished to print *Huon de Bordeaux* 'affin ... qu'en lisant icelluy plusieurs princes chevaliers escuyers et aultres gens de bien se pourront recreer et veoir de l'exercice des armes et de la guerre et aultres faits vertueulx'. The aim of entertaining and inspiring nobles and gentlemen to deeds of valour is expressed in very similar terms in the privilege obtained by Galliot Du Pré for the herald Montjoie's account of the *pas d'armes* held to mark the entry into Paris of the new queen, Mary, daughter of Henry VII of England:

qui est la louenge et honneur de nostre royaulme de nostre chier fils et de tous nos princes chevaliers gentils hommes affin quen ce voyant et lisant ils se puissent exciter aux armes pour acquerir les honneur et gloire militaire ensemble fouyr et eviter oysiveté (CH 1514, 5)

It also figures in François Regnault's privilege from the Prévôt for *Le grant voyage de Jerusalem* (PR 1517, 7). Jean Granjon, applying to the Parlement for a privilege in two works of scholastic philosophy, emphasised on the other hand their usefulness to the academic world – 'au profit et utilité des estudians' (PA 1514, 9). The concept was extended by the Poitiers bookseller Guillaume Bouchet, in seeking a privilege from the chancery for Etienne Malleret's *De electionibus*, which he called 'grandement proufitable à tous gens de lectres et au bien publique' (CH 1515, 9). The subject of the book was undeniably a national issue, the king's control over elections to all important church benefices, which was about to be consecrated by his Concordat with the Pope. Highly relevant also was the claim of the Paris publisher Jean de La Garde, that his plan of printing the *Coustumes generalles* of the kingdom was, in the words of the Letters Patent, for 'le bien, prouffit et utilité de noz subjectz et de la chose publique' (CH 1517, 3).

Soon this kind of phrase was being used of a wider range of publications. Granting Galliot Du Pré's petition for books which included the treatise of Francesco Patrizi (Patricius), *De regno et regis institutione*, Francis I's chancery accepted that 'lesdictz livres sont utilles à nous et à la chose publicque' (CH 1519, 3). Such developments could become known quite quickly throughout France, since most beneficiaries printed the full text of their Letters Patent prominently in the book concerned, where it could easily be studied by authors and publishers who were interested in using the system. Antoine Le Blanc, a bookseller of Toulouse, whose *requête* is preserved in its entirety, as submitted to the Toulouse Parlement (PA 1517, 3) urged 'le grant bien, profit et utilité de la chose publicque' and 'l'augmentation de la foy crestienne' in putting forward *Les gestes des Tholosains*, not to mention 'l'honneur du Roy, l'exaltation et sublimité de sa préeminence et de son auctorité' and the benefit of 'plusieurs gens de bien tant nobles, bourgeoys que marchans' who desired to be able to read the book in French, as well as the great expenditure of time, trouble and money involved in having it printed.

Some applicants to the Parlement of Paris also followed suit, if without the *méridional* rhetoric employed by Le Blanc. The grant to Jean de Gourmont for two books by Guy de Fontenaye describes them as 'de nouvel imprimés par ledit Gourmont pour le bien et utilité de la chose publicque, à grans fraiz, mises et despens' (PA 1517, 2); the grant to Claude Chevallon for a 'package' of several works, by the popular preacher Guillaume Pepin and others, recalls a claim that each of these books was printed 'au profit, bien et utilité de la chose publicque, et à grans frais, mises et despens' (PA 1519, 4). There was an increasing tendency to dwell on this consideration, and to extend its use. Conrad Resch seems for instance to be stretching the point somewhat further in invoking 'le bien, profit et utilité de la chose publique' to get a royal privilege for the *Tractatus noticiarum* of the theologian Gervase Waim (CH 1519, 1) and later for Eck's treatise against Luther *De primatu Petri* (CH 1521, 3). A Rouen publisher, Simon Gruel, claimed that he wished to produce *Le grant et vray art de pleine rhétorique* of Pierre Fabri 'pour le bien, proffit et utilité de la chose publique' (CH 1520, 6), and Simon de Colines referred to'le prouffit et utilité de la chose publicque' in applying for the *Promptuarium* of Jean de Montholon, a two-volume dictionary of canon and civil law (CH 1520, 7).

More daringly Galliot Du Pré, applying to the Prévôt of Paris for a privilege in a French translation of Erasmus' *Praise of Folly*, asserted 'que pour l'utilité de la chose publicque il avoit fait imprimer lesdictes louenges de folie' (PR 1520, 5, see Plate 5). Hémon Le Fèvre applied to the Prévôt eighteen months later for Guillaume Michel's *Le siècle doré*, 'lequel il feroit voluntiers imprimer pour l'utillité de la chose publicque et pour recouvrer ses frais' (PR 1522, 1): this, though a work of fiction, at least related a vision of society transformed, through the application of Christian principles by all its members, into an ideal state. The use of such formulae, replacing the older tradition of invoking connections wtih the royal family or the nobility, suggests a growing realisation that the publication of good books hitherto not printed was a matter where the public interest was concerned. However, applicants were clearly not *expected* to prove merit or usefulness in the book concerned: most privileges show no sign of such an argument having been used.

The literary excellence or entertainment value of the book is invoked even more rarely. Hémon Le Fèvre said of the romance *Gérard de Nevers* that 'ledit livre et hystoire en icelluy contenue est fort plaisante' (PR 1520, 3); and Galliot Du Pré of *Ysaïe le Triste* that it was 'pour la recreation des gentils hommes et jeunes gens qui appetent à lire ung livre de la table ronde' (PR 1522, 3).

Jean de La Garde successfully applied for a royal privilege (CH 1520, 8) for *Le violier des histoires rommaines moralisées*, of which he had commissioned the translation into French from the *Gesta Romanorum*, 'pour le proufit, utilité de plusieurs personnes,' so that readers who did not know Latin could find much recreation in it ('à veoir laquelle translation plusieurs personnes non latins pourroient prendre grande recreacion'), but the expense of having the translation made 'par homme expert et litteré' and the cost of printing it constitute the main argument. François Regnault contrived to combine all these arguments in his application for *Le rozier historial* (CH 1523, 2): beginning with the great cost and outlay involved in printing it, he went on to recall that it had been written for Louis XI ('jadis composé à la requeste du feu roy Loys xiᵉ que dieu absoulle') and to claim that it was 'un beau livre, tresutille et plaisant à lire, et ouquel les lisans pourront prouffiter et apprendre'.

Bernard Aubry at about the same period presented his case to the Prévôt of Paris for a work by the famous logician Johannes Dullaert, with additions by Johannes Drabbe, very comprehensively:

il avoit vacqué par longue espace de temps employé et despendu grans deniers. Lequel livre n'avait esté au par avant ce imprimé. Et pour ce que ledict livre est utile et proffitable pour donner recreation servir et aux enfans escoliers estudians et les

¶ Erasme Roterodame

De la declamation des louenges de follie/faicte fa=
cessieur et profitable pour congnoistre ses erreurs
et abuz du monde.

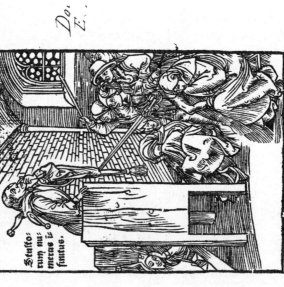

Stulto=
rum nu=
merus ē
finitus.

On les vend a paris par Galliot du pre Mar=
chant Libraire/demeurant sur le pont nostre dame
a lenseigne de la Galiee/Et en sa grād salle du pa=
lais au tiers pillier.

☞ Auec priuilege ☜

Le priuilege

Tous ceulx qui

ces presentes lettres verront Ga=
briel Daron seigneur Dalege/
sainct iust/meillau/toxet faict di=
re (puisso) Conseiller chambel=
lan du Roy nostre sire/ et garde de
la preuoste de paris salut. Scauoir faisons que deue
la requeste a nous faicte par Galliot du pre marchant
Libraire demourant a Paris/ Disant que grans frais
il auoit fait imprimer vng liure intitule Erasme des
louenges de folie/ lequel nauoit encores au parauant
este imprime. Et neatmoins doubte iceulluy du que
autres Libraires ou Imprimeurs se souffissent im=
primer ou faire imprimer vng liure pour le frustre de sa peine qz
a eu a icelluy liure recouurer qui seroit au grant pre=
iudice (z dōmaige dudict du pre/ au moien dequoy no)
auroit acquis attendu que pour futile te de la chose pu=
blique il auoit fait imprimer lesdictes louenges de fo
lie (z pour ce faire il auoit emploie gros deniers/ sup=
plios souffissōs permettre de publier et vēdre lesdictes sou
enges. et Deffenses estre faictes a tous aultres Libraires
et imprimeurs de ne les vēdre ou imprimer iusques a
trois ans sur peine de confiscation desdictz liures (z da
mende arbitraire. Ce considere et Eu de nous ledit sie
ure Auons permis et permettons audit du pre de pu=
blier et vēdre ledit liure intitule Erasme des louen

enhorter de bien en mieulx pour les faitz contenuz en iceluy livre ...' (PR 1521, 4, cf. PR 1523, 5)

No application is known which fails to give prominence to the economic argument: the enterprise and outlay of the applicant will not obtain a reasonable reward unless he is given a fair chance to sell his edition before it can be reprinted in France or cheap reprints from abroad can be put on sale.

Other applicants

Not all privilege-seekers were authors or *libraires*. One category of privilege-holders exists which comes under the heading neither of 'authors' nor of 'publishers', though their grounds for seeking the privilege had more affinity with that of authors. These were the *greffiers* who obtained privileges for the *Coutumes* of the jurisdiction within which they exercised their office. It was their responsibility to see that the text, as finally determined by the commissioners, was correctly recorded and transcribed for eventual approval by the king and registration by the Parlement. The *greffiers* asked the Parlement for a privilege 'pour les récompenser de leurs peines' as those of Orleans said (PA 1510, 2). When applying to the royal chancery, it was sometimes thought appropriate to elaborate on the usefulness of the project. Thus Pierre Marchant, *greffier* of Poitou, in 1517, did not claim that his plan to finance a printed edition of the revised *coutume* was new, but that more copies were badly needed: 'And it has already been copied several times, but, because the said copies are not enough to supply everyone who wishes to possess the said Coustumier, and also because writing it out is laborious, the said suppliant would like to have it printed and would bear the expense of the said printing, if it was agreeable to us also that none but he should print it for a time.'[1]

A different kind of initiative, in which the community itself ensured that the local *Coutume* should be available in print, is exemplified by the action of the *échevins, manans et habitans* of Blois in 1524. They themselves obtained a privilege for it (PA 1524, 11) and employed a Paris firm to print it. They may have come to some arrangements with their printers, who were also booksellers, to assist with marketing copies of the book in Paris, but they were clearly themselves the publishers. The colophon states that the *Coutumes* were 'imprimées à Paris par Anthoine et Nicolas les Couteaulx, imprimeurs oudit Paris, pour messeigneurs les eschevins de ladicte ville de Bloys. Et furent achevées le .xxiiiie. jour de Septembre L'an mil cinc cens .xxiii.' The

---

[1] Et ja a esté coppié plusieurs fois, mais par ce que lesdictes copies ne sont suffisantes à fournir à chascun qui appète avoir ledit Coustumier aussi que l'escripture d'icelluy est onéreuse ledit suppliant le feroit voulentiers imprimer et feroit les frais de ladicte impression s'il nous plaisoit aussi que autre que luy ne le fist imprimer pour quelque temps (CH 1517, 5).

dedication shows that the plan had powerful backing. It was addressed to the queen, who is said to have taken a keen interest in the work of the commission which drew up the *Coutume*, by one of the two commissioners appointed to preside over it, Jean Prévost, himself a native of Blois. As a *conseiller* of the Parlement, Prévost was in a position to facilitate the grant of a privilege. It was issued on the usual grounds of enabling the sponsors of the publication to recover their expenses. But the dedication emphasises the theme of public usefulness, and this may have featured among the arguments put forward by the applicants.

It might be expected that not only the *greffier* but some other official of one of the courts competent to grant privileges would, on occasion, himself obtain a privilege for some new item for publication which had come into his hands. The only such case seems to be that of Jean Baudouyn, *huissier* of the Council and chancery of the duchy of Brittany. Letters Patent were issued to him on the authority of the Council in the chancery of Brittany in the name of the king, who was then in captivity in Spain, and who is described as the usufructuary and administrator of the duchy for his eldest son, his wife Queen Claude the heiress of Brittany having died the previous year. The privilege (CH 1525, 3) was for the *statutz, ordonnances et édit* drawn up to regulate the *style* or procedure of the Breton courts, which had been approved by Louise of Savoy as Regent at Condrieu in September, and the Letters Patent were given at Rennes on 25 October 1525. Baudouyn did not have the sort of claim to an interest in this copy that the local *greffiers* could plead for the *Coutumes* of their area; he would not have been directly concerned in drawing up the official text. But he was an important official whose duties would include enforcement of the regulations, such as summoning persons required to appear before the Council. And he had an additional qualification: he was himself a printer. This is not only mentioned in the Letters Patent ('ses experiences oudict art de imprimerie') but attested by an edition printed by him dated Rennes, 21 May 1524, the *Liber Marbodi*,[1] produced in association with a well-known bookseller and publisher of Rennes, Jean Macé, for the bishop of Rennes. As the only printer in Rennes at that time, Baudouyn was indeed an obvious choice, though he is not known for certain to have printed anything afterwards, no doubt finding his work as *huissier* hard to combine with even part-time operation of a press and a good deal more lucrative.

THE CRITERION OF NEWNESS

All French authorities concerned with granting book-privileges normally restricted them to texts which were being published for the first time. If the

---

[1] I.e. Works of Marbode, bishop of Rennes 1096–1123. 1524, 8°. BN Rés.pᵧᴄ 1533. Cf. Lepreux, *Gallia Typographica*, IV, pp. 19–24.

books had been printed but were by then out of print, if they were being printed for the first time in translation, if they contained a substantial addition or improvement to an existing publication, they might qualify: not otherwise. Whether the rightness of this principle was self-evident to the authorities at the time is uncertain. No discussion of the subject is recorded. Possibly it was clarified by specific applications being received and, after consideration, or after opposition from other publishers, being refused. Thus a thrusting applicant might have tried about 1508 to secure a privilege in some established favourite like the *Roman de la Rose*, or the Chronicles of Froissart, or the farce of *Maître Pathelin*. Such an application, if made (for instance) to the Parlement of Paris, would probably have been contested by other members of the book-trade as soon as it reached the first hearing, if not indeed queried by the magistrates themselves. All these texts had been printed freely already, and only gross favouritism could have removed them from the common stock to assign them exclusively to a particular firm. On the other hand a newly *modernised* version of the *Roman de la Rose* won a privilege (PR 1526, 2), a *translation into Latin* of *Pathelin* was privileged (PA 1512, 9 (4)), and much later Denis Sauvage was to obtain a privilege for his pioneer critical edition of Froissart. Again, someone might have tried to obtain a privilege for any of the works of Erasmus, a European best-seller, giving him the exclusive French rights in it. In practice, among the many French publishers who printed and reprinted works of Erasmus in the period up to 1526 the only one who appears to have obtained a privilege was Conrad Resch, for the seven-part commentary on the Lord's Prayer (PA 1524, 1) of which his was the first edition to appear after its original publication shortly before at Basle, and for the *Paraphrasis in euangelium Matthei* (CH 1523, 4). Galliot Du Pré indeed obtained a privilege for the *Praise of Folly*, but that was for the first translation into French, which Galliot had commissioned (PR 1520, 5).

It so happens that a best-seller hardly less famous than the most celebrated works of Erasmus is known to have been turned down by the Parlement of Paris when it was proposed for a privilege. Nicolas de La Barre applied on 12 May 1520 for a grant for the Papal Bull canonising Saint Francis of Paola, 'et ung petit livre intitulé de Inuentoribus Rerum' (PA 1520, 1). This can hardly be anything else than Polydore Vergil's *De inuentoribus rerum*, which had been first published at Venice in 1499. For twenty years this had been reprinted both in Italy and in France.[1] One may charitably suppose that La Barre was unaware of this. Evidently the Parlement was not. It gave the privilege for the Papal Bull only, ignoring the request for *De inuentoribus rerum* to be included. The first translation into French, on the other hand, obtained a privilege (PR 1520, 12).

If on the other hand a book *had* been printed before, but some years before,

[1] Denys Hay, *Polydore Vergil: renaissance historian and man of letters* (Oxford, 1952), Chapter III. Polydore added three books – VI–VIII – to the text in 1521, but La Barre cannot have had this additional material in his hands in Paris in May 1520.

and abroad, so that it was virtually unobtainable in France, the authorities occasionally allowed a privilege for it. The first edition of *Le livre de roi Modus*[1] was printed at Chambéry, outside the kingdom of France, in 1486. It was written between 1354 and 1377; thirty-two manuscripts survive, showing that it was very popular, especially the sections on hunting and falconry. It had not been reprinted since. Jean Jehannot sought and obtained a privilege for it (CP 1521, 5). In his dedication to Charles, duc de Vendôme, he explained that he had corrected and modernised the text, and had printed it, instead of in folio (as the first edition had been) in a small format more handy for sportsmen wishing to take it with them ('et icelluy fait imprimer en petit vollume pour plus plaisamment porter aux champs').

In the few cases of a book having been printed earlier, in Italy, the argument that it was out of print, and unobtainable in France at least, also probably weighed. Badius published an edition of Plutarch's *Lives* in Latin translation in 1514, with Jean Petit. It was not new. Badius pointed out candidly in the title that he was following the edition of Pylades Brixianus (Giovanni Boccardo of Brescia) printed by Jacobus Britannicus at Brescia in 1499. It is possible that a complete collection of the *Lives* had not been printed before in France. It is possible that good Italian editions were themselves out of print. Badius' edition (CH 1514, 6 (1)) was itself reprinted in Italy within two years.[2] Arguments of this kind probably lie behind the formula to be found in a Toulouse book of 1519, 'Cis Alpes caracteribus calchographariis antehac nusquam redactus' – never printed before on this side of the Alps (PA 1519, 5), and of 1520, 'numquam antea citra Alpes notulis divulgata stanneis' (PA 1520, 4). These were law-books by Italian scholars, no doubt needed in the law faculty and difficult to obtain.

Exceptionally, Guillaume Eustace obtained a privilege for two books which had been printed already in France, the French translation of Livy and the *Grans croniques de France* (CH 1514, 3, (1 and 2)). Twenty years or so before, he said, the late Antoine Vérard had published them, each in three volumes,[3] and the books were in demand, so that they were now out of print ('tellement que pour le present ne s'en treuve aucuns à vendre'), and he planned to supply this need by reprinting them. But in view of the cost of printing them – they were each three folio volumes – he was afraid to do so without a privilege. The royal chancery accepted his argument. But it seems to have been the only case of its kind.

It is indeed clear from a study of the books published under privilege during this period (see below, Chapter 8) that nearly all had some claim to be new.

[1] Modern critical edition by G. Tilander, SATF, 2 vols (1932). R. Bossuat, *Manuel bibliographique de la littérature française du moyen âge* (Melun, 1951), nos. 5533–46.
[2] Ed. G. Vercellanus after J. Badius, pr. M. Sessam and P. de Ravanis (Venice, 1516), fol. VL 10604.k.6.
[3] The *grans croniques de France* had been printed for Vérard in 1493. The Livy translation had appeared in 1487, not in Vérard's name.

To what extent was this made explicit by the grants or the beneficiaries in the books themselves? It was superfluous to state that newly revised *coutumes*, newly issued *ordonnances*, newly concluded treaties, or accounts of events which had only just happened, were being printed for the first time. Similarly, an author with a new work to publish had no reason to emphasise that it had not been printed before. The publisher, if it was he who applied for the privilege, naturally said simply that it was 'ung livre nommé l'istoire du droit civil composé nouvellement par maistre Aymar Rivail' (CH 1515, 6) or 'ung livre nouvellement composé ... intitulé Sermones quadragesimales reverendi patris Bonifacii' (PA 1517, 1), 'un petit traicté intitulé la discipline d'amour divine nouvellement composé à Paris' (CH 1519, 6 (2)), 'ung livre d'arismethique & geometrie novellement composé par maistre Estienne de La Roche' (PA 1520, 2 (1)), and so on.

An author seeking a privilege for works which were only in part composed by him, including translations or editions of texts by others, was on the other hand careful to make clear that *none* of them had been printed before. Jean Lode represented the 'peines, labeur et vacations qu'il a prinses en la composition, correction et traduction desditz livres tant latins que vulgaires, qui jamais ne furent imprimez' (CH 1513, 2). Nicole Bohier acting as editor of legal texts from the past was equally punctilious: 'attendu que lesdictes questions de Bella Pertica ne furent onques imprimées' (CH 1515, 7 (1)); 'les quels livres ne furent jamais imprimés' (CH 1519, 5).

Publishers who were proposing a book which was not new, in the sense of being newly composed, but which was being printed for the first time, varied somewhat in their practice, to judge from the recapitulation of their petitions embodied in Letters Patent from the chancery. Often there is such a rigmarole about the great difficulty and cost of securing the copy at all, or in having it translated, or specially edited, that the *inédit* character of the work is self-evident. But two privileges granted on the same day to different publishers by Louis XII's chancery when he was at Lyon expressly take account of the fact that the books in question had not been printed before: 'Et attendu que, comme dit est, il n'a encore jamais esté imprimé (CH 1511, 2, and CH 1511, 3). From then on, formulae like 'Lequel livre ne fut jamais imprimé (CH 1515, 9), 'Bons et prouffitables livres qui oncques ne furent imprimez' (CH 1519, 2) and 'Qui ne fut jamais imprimé' (CH 1520, 1) are fairly common with publishers who applied to the royal chancery, in cases where it is not immediately obvious that the book was a first edition. In some cases the wording makes it clear, though it is not expressly stated, e.g. the French translation of Egidio Colonna's *Liber de regimine principum* (CH 1517, 2) 'lequel ledict suppliant, affin qu'il ne demourast occulte, le feroit voulentiers imprimer'. The few Letters Patent issued by the Prévôt of Paris show the same feature. Thus Galliot Du Pré presenting the first French translation of the

Praise of Folly described it as 'ung livre intitulé Erasme des louenges de folie, lequel n'auroit encores au paravant esté imprimé' (PR 1520, 5), and Bernard Aubry, proposing a work of Johannes Dullaert, said of it 'lequel n'avoit esté au par avant ce imprimé (PR 1521, 4). The form in which Parlement privileges were normally recorded gives no indication of this or any other argument that had been used by the applicant, but in one of the earliest grants to be given by court for a learned work the book is described as 'Ung livre intitulé Dionysius Cisterciensis Sur les quatre livre <s> de sentance <s>, lequel ne fust jamais imprimé que maintenant par luy [Poncet Le Preux]' (PA 1511, 2). And where, which was usually the case, the 'Extraict des registres de Parlement' which the publisher had printed in the book made no mention of the fact that the work was being printed for the first time, he sometimes made this clear on the title-page: thus the title may be followed by a formula such as 'nunquam antehac impressus' (PA 1518, 1).

Where the publisher decided not to print or summarise the privilege at all, but to put only 'Cum priuilegio regio' or 'Cum priuilegio' on the title-page, he might think it prudent to advertise that his book was a first edition by including a mention on the title-page or in the colophon. The *Speculum morale* of Johannes Vitalis, or Vidal Du Four, bore only the words 'Cum regio priuilegio' on the title-page, with no other details (CH 1513, 5), but the publisher specified that the *Speculum* was 'hucusque non impressum'. Berthold Rembolt described the collection of St Gregory's writings on the New Testament as 'nunquam antea typis excusum' (*CP* 1516, 1), and in the same year Jean Granjon advertised John Mair's *Insolubilia* as *nunquam prius impressa* (*CP* 1516, 3), while among later examples we find François Regnault publishing the *Sermones quadragesimales* of Clerée as 'alias nusquam impressi' (*CP* 1520, 18).

The circumstances in which the Parlement was prepared to consider granting a privilege for a work which had been printed before are illustrated by a grant obtained on 21 April 1514 by Galliot Du Pré (PA 1514, 4). This concerned the treatise *De beneficio* or *Tractatus beneficialis* of Jean de Selve, doctor of civil and canon law, and himself a *conseiller* of the Parlement, a book which became something of a standard work, still reprinted in the seventeenth century. Galliot du Pré's application was for a *reprint* of the book (which had been published first in 1504). The reprint was however to be a revised edition and to include a new feature, namely an index or repertory, which would of course make the book more useful to those who wished to consult it but involve time and expense to compile. It was also to eliminate a number of inaccuracies which had marred the first edition. ('Lequel, reveu et corrigé, ledit Galliot a fait reimprimer et y adjouster une table ou repertoire, pource que la premiere impression estoit sans table et y avoit plusieurs faultes et incorrections.') The Parlement granted this application, though for two years only and not for three as Galliot had requested – a scaling down of the favour sought which was in line with the court's usual practice and not a sign of misgiving. Jean de Selve was a future president of the Parlement; even in 1514 he was already a person of some influence. His colleagues would no doubt lend a sympathetic ear to a plea from his publisher for this privilege. They would not wholly depart from their usual principles. And their reasons for making even this concession are carefully recorded.

The Parlement granted a two-year privilege on 7 September 1518 to the printer-publisher Henry Estienne for Aristotle's *Phisica* in Latin, 'puis nagueres corrigé, augmenté et translaté à plus part de grec en latin par maistres Jaques Fabri et Francois Wateble' (PA 1518, 7). The Greek text of all Aristotle's surviving works had been printed by Aldus Manutius at Venice 1495–8, but most scientists and philosophers still naturally relied on translations into Latin; the latter (both medieval and humanist) were already in print long since. François Wateblé or Vatablus, the future Royal Professor of Hebrew and also a scholar in Greek, in association with Jacques Lefèvre and using the printing skill of Henry Estienne, had however produced an edition with considerable claims to originality. In the first place the standard medieval Latin version, the 'antique tralatio', was carefully revised by reference to the Greek text and corrected where it seemed to be corrupt. This was then printed in parallel columns with a *modern* Latin translation, the first three books in the version of Argyropylus (1460), but the remainder in a new version by Vatablus himself. These particulars, given by Vatablus in his dedication to Guillaume Briçonnet, who (he said) had suggested the plan 'ante paucolos annos', amplify the grounds on which the Parlement could be persuaded to judge that there was a sufficient element of new work in the publication to justify a privilege. Estienne could not have prevented competitors from continuing to publish Latin versions of the *Physics* already in circulation, but he could establish a title to the Vatablus translation specially made for this edition and for the way it was presented side by side with the 'antiqua tralatio', possibly also for the emendations made by Vatablus to the 'antiqua tralatio'.

In 1512 Jean Petit, with Poncet le Preux, published the *Summa in questionibus Armenorum* of Richard FitzRalph, archbishop of Armagh, a work inspired by the discussions which FitzRalph had had in Rome in 1349 with envoys of the Armenian church, followed by a group of FitzRalph's sermons preached in London in 1356–7. This material had never been printed before ('nusquam antea impressioni demandata' as the editor, Jean Le Sueur, correctly stated in his dedication). There was, however, a single sermon of FitzRalph which *had* been printed before. This was the so-called *Defensorium curatorum*, or defence of the secular clergy against the mendicant orders, which FitzRalph preached on 8 November 1357 before Innocent VI and the full consistory in Rome. Of this Le Sueur says, in a note at the end of the sermons, that he had omitted it because it was already in print ('unum tamen omisi quia est impressus et vocatur deffensorium curatorum'). It had indeed been printed in France at least four times by 1500, three times by itself and then with a reply to it (which had not been printed before) by R. Chonoe, the latter edition prepared by Josse Badius Ascensius and printed by Trechsel at Lyon in 1496. All these may well have been out of print by 1512, but though not themselves privileged, they disqualified the text from being included in a collection of FitzRalph's sermons published under privilege. Whether Le Sueur, or Jean Petit, decided to exclude it on these grounds from Petit's application for a privilege, or whether its inclusion was refused by someone in the chancellor's office who looked through the list of proposed works submitted by Petit, there is no means of telling. But the decision to exclude it, from a collection of works by FitzRalph in which it would have been very appropriate, is not easily accounted for in any other way.

Where a marked improvement could be claimed by the applicant in the completeness and correctness of the text, even when most of the text at least was already in print, a privilege might be granted. Thus in 1526 Galliot du Pré published an attempt at a collected edition of the works of Alain Chartier. Chartier was one of the most respected authors of the early fifteenth century. His works circulated in a large number of manuscripts, and some of them had already been printed well before 1500. The nearest approach to a hitherto unpublished text included by Galliot was *Le débat du gras et du maigre*, otherwise known as *Le débat des deux fortunés d'amours*, of which he said on the title-page 'qui n'auroit encores esté imprimé': it had in fact been printed before, but only in an anthology called the *Jardin de Plaisance* in 1501,[1] which he might possibly have missed. Galliot's preamble admitted candidly that most of the book had long since been in print, but maintained that hitherto the available editions were incorrect and mutilated in many places ('Et si on disoit d'aventure que le livre a esté par longtemps devant ceste moderne saison veu et regardé, je le concede. Toutesfois il estoit mal correct et tronqué en divers lieux...') Accordingly the Prévôt's privilege (PR 1526, 2(2)) made clear that other printers could continue to reprint the traditional text, but *not* Galliot's corrected text ('ledit livre ainsi corrigé comme dit est, sur la coppie dudit suppliant').

Most privileges were granted by the authorities on the simple principle of ensuring a fair return for expenditure of time, money and skill. A distinct intention of promoting literature and learning is slow to find expression, before 1527, even in royal Letters Patent. Concern for public utility is voiced occasionally: 'Pour le bien et utilité de la chose publique laquelle desirons de tout en tout estre bien observée et gardée en bonne politique et justice comme protecteurs d'icelle', in a law-book written with the convenience of the royal officers in mind (CH 1511, 2): 'desirans subvenir à noz subjectz selon l'exigence des cas, et le bien, prouffit et utilité des noz subjectz et de la chose

---

[1] *The poetical works of Alain Chartier*, ed. J. C. Laidlaw (Cambridge, 1974), p. 155.

publique estre observez et entretenuz' (CH 1517, 3) in the *Coutumes generalles*, which was virtually an official publication. There are none of the grandiloquent phrases which begin to appear in Francis I's Letters Patent after his return from Madrid, e g 'Pourquoy nous ces choses considerés, desirans de tout nostre povoir faire florir les bonnes lettres en nostre royaulme et mettre en evidance...', to be read in the privilege for René Bertaut's *Le livre doré de Marc Aurèle* (1531 4°). The privilege granted to Enguilbert de Marnef for *Le grant routtier* of Pierre Garcie dit Ferrande (CH 1520, 4) has the phrase 'Pourquoy nous ces choses considerees, et qui desirons que tous bons livres qui ne furent jamais imprimez soient manifestes...' This is the nearest approach to such a statement before 1527.

5 · GRANT OF PRIVILEGE AND PERMISSION TO PRINT

THE SUBMISSION OF A NEW BOOK to the royal chancery, to the Parlement or to a royal official to obtain a privilege was throughout this period a voluntary act, initiated by the applicant for his own advantage. It did not form part of any organised system of licensing.

Much later, in 1566, Charles IX decreed by Article 78 of the Edict of Moulins that no new book should be published 'sans notre congé et permission et lettres de privilege expediées sous notre grand scel.'[1] From 1566 onwards, until the end of the Ancien Régime, the separate identity of the privilege, as a commercial concession, was merged in that of a licence to print.

No such connection with the granting of privileges was made by Francis I when he ordered on 18 March 1521 that any new works should be examined and approved by representatives of the University of Paris, and in particular that any concerning the Christian faith or the interpretation of Holy Scripture should be passed as orthodox by the Faculty of Theology before being put on sale.[2] In principle, henceforth no such book could be published at all in France without having received the approval of the Faculty, whether it was to be published under privilege or not.

What element of permission or licence had there been hitherto in the grant of a privilege, and did the requirement of March 1521 change it in any way?

THE ROYAL CHANCERY

There is no direct evidence that books were censored or scrutinised before being granted a privilege in the royal chancery. The chancellor probably looked through them, or deputed one of his staff to do so, to check that they contained nothing objectionable, as his was the final responsibility for the correctness of all Letters Patent. Some of the early privileges were sought by authors so well known to the royal court, or recommended by persons of such high standing in it, that there can have been no problem. The first author to obtain a privilege from Louis XII for a particular book, Eloi d'Amerval, was

---

[1] F. A. Isambert, *Recueil général des anciennes lois françaises*, XIV, 1re partie, p. 210.
[2] Charles Jourdain, *Index chronologicus chartarum pertinentium ad historiam universitatis Parisiensis* (1892), no. 1594, p. 326. Royal Order in Parlement repeating the provision, 4 November 1521, ibid., no. 1597, p. 327.

in this category (CH 1508, 1). As choirmaster of Orleans cathedral he may well have been known personally to the king, and his application had the backing of powerful friends though these are not named ('en faveur mesmement d'aucuns noz especiaulx serviteurs qui pour ce nous ont supplié et requis').[1] He had secured (as he tells his readers in the course of a versified colophon at the end of the book, *Le livre de la deablerie*) the written approval of two Paris doctors of theology, Guillaume de Quercu and Pierre Charpentier. He can hardly have made this up. They were both well-known characters. Guillaume de Quercu, or Du Chesne, was actually to be deputed by the Faculty to act as one of its censors when the censorship of new books concerning religion became compulsory.[2] Whether this written approval was submitted with d'Amerval's *requête* to the chancery, or played any part in the decision to grant him a privilege, is not known. Certainly it is not mentioned in the Letters Patent. From the tone of d'Amerval's verses one might rather infer that it was invoked as an added recommendation, like a testimonial or an extract from a favourable review:

> Il est vray, ainsi que j'entens,
> Que deux maistres tresreverends,
> Fort renommez en grant clergie
> Et docteurs en theologie
> De Paris la noble cité,
> Tenus, il est bien verité,
> Deux fermes pillers de la foy,
> Scientifique<s>, je le croy,
> Et dignes d'en porter l'escu,
> Maistre Guillaume de Quercu
> Et maistre Pierre Charpentier,
> Ce livre icy tout entier
> Ont visité deligemment
> Et postillé semblablement.
> C'est la Deablerie d'Eloy,
> Et l'ont trouvée de bon aloy
> Et approuvé il ont ainsi,
> Fidel et catholique aussi.
> Et chascun d'eulx par son beau signe
> Testifient que il est digne
> D'estre imprimé honnestement,
> Car maint y a enseignement.

To produce this evidence of orthodoxy seems at any rate to have been the author's own idea. Possibly it was mainly an advertisement. Possibly it was a precaution, his satire on contemporary society being fairly wide-ranging.

Two important privileges granted by Louis XII's chancery the following year went to authors who must have been eminently *persona grata* to the king.

[1] Cf. 'et en faveur d'aulcuns noz serviteurs speciaulx qui pource ont requis et supplié à ycelluy suppliant' in the privilege for *Huon de Bordeaux* (CH 1513, 3).
[2] See below, pp. 110–11.

The first was Nicole Bohier or Boyer, licentiate in canon and civil law, who was a member of the Grand Conseil (CH 1509, 1). The second was to Jean Lemaire de Belges, the most famous French-language author of the period, who was about to enter the service of the queen of France as her historiographer (CH 1509, 2). The privilege obtained by the Paris publisher Jean Petit for a group of scholarly books, notably sources for the history of France (CH 1512, 1), could have been readily given in consideration of the active part taken in promoting the series by Guillaume Petit, bishop of Senlis, the king's confessor and Inquisitor of France: a magnificent copy of one of them, presented to the king, is extant in the Bibliothèque Nationale (BN Vélins 272–5) with Guillaume Petit's inscription recording that he had caused it and other volumes to be printed. About such applications there can have been little heart-searching in the chancery.

Nevertheless the majority of Letters Patent of which we possess the complete text reflect applications which sought *permission* in some form or other. It is true that, while petitions for royal privileges tended to begin by asking for permission to print a particular book, the emphasis is often on permission to be the *only* person to print it for a space of time, e.g. 'Il feroit voulentiers imprimer ledit livre, luy seul et non autre, jusques à tel temps qu'il nous plaira, si nostre plaisir estoit luy donner congé et licence de ce faire' (CH 1508, 1); 'nous a humblement requis permettre audit Vincent que luy seul et non aultre puisse imprimer et reimprimer lesdictz livres' (CH 1509, 1); 'luy permettre que luy seul et non aultre puisse imprimer ou reimprimer ledit euvre jusques à tel temps qu'il nous plaira' (CH 1514, 4). Doubt or fear whether the new work should be published at all without royal permission is however frequently expressed by applicants, e.g. '[Mais] il doubte qu'il ne peust ou osast ce faire sans noz congé et licence' (CH 1509, 2); 'ne l'oseroit faire imprimer sans noz congé, licence et permission' (CH 1513, 3); 'il doubte qu'il ne peult ou osast faire imprimer sans nostre congié ou licence ... une translation par luy faicte' (CH 1522, 5); 'il n'oseroit ce faire sans noz congé et vouloir et aussi pour doubte que, apres qu'il les auroit faict imprimer, aucuns libraires voulsissent faire le semblable' (CH 1519, 5). Many applicants did not explicitly ask for permission: they preferred to set out their case and then request the royal protection and grace, e.g. 'Il doubte perdre les grans fraiz et mises qu'il convient à les faire parachever se quelque autre les faisoit semblablement imprimer s'il n'avoit sur ce noz lettres et provisions à ce necessaires' (CH 1514, 3); 'il doubte que après que yceluy livre sera publié que aucun marchant ou libraire le vousist faire imprimer, qui serait à son tresgrant prejudice et dommaige, si par nous ne luy estoit sur ce pourveu de remede convenable' (CH 1515, 1); 'il doubte que apres qu'il les aura faict imprimer aultres les voulsissent semblablement imprimer ... nous humblement requerant sur ce luy pourveoir et impartir nostre grace' (CH 1516, 2), 'requerant sur ce nostre provision' (CH 1517,

3), 'nous humblement requerant sur ce luy impartir nostre grace' (CH 1520, 7). In response to such petitions, when granted, the Crown used terms in use since the reign of Charles V, like *permission, congé* and *licence*, but usually in close conjunction with the intention of permitting the applicant to be the only person entitled to publish the book or books in question for a fixed period, e.g. 'donnons, permettons et ottroyons de nostre grace especial par ces presentes, congé et licence et permission qu'il puisse et luy loyse, luy seul et non aultre, faire imprimer ledit livre' (CH 1508, 1); 'A iceluy avons permis et octroyé ... de nostre especialle plaine puissance et auctorité royalle que le livre dessusdit imprimé il puisse faire vendre et adenerer ... sans que pendant ledit temps aucun marchant ou librayre autreque celuy ou ceulx qui auront charge dudit suppliant <puisse> le faire ou faire faire imprimer pendant ledit temps' (CH 1515, 1); 'octroions et permettons de grace especiale par ces presentes, que durant le temps de trois ans prochains venans il puisse seul faire imprimer ... sans que durant ledit temps aultre quelconque se puisse entremettre de imprimer lesdictes euvres' (CH 1516, 2); 'permettons et octroyons que luy seul puisse imprimer, vendre ne adenerer en nostre royaulme, pays et seigneurie ledit livre' (CH 1520, 7).

Occasionally the petitions to be allowed to publish the book, and to be given the sole rights in it for a space of time, are presented as two separate issues. Galliot Du Pré in a petition of 1519 asked first 'que luy voulsissions iceulx livres permectre imprimer et vendre en nostre pays, royaulme et ailleurs', then represented the high cost of printing them and asked for other editions to be prohibited for four years; the grant accordingly first gave him permission to print and sell the books as often as should seem good to him, and then proceeded to forbid other editions to be printed or sold for four years (CH 1519, 3). All royal grants imply permission and approval, but none was sought except with the intention of also obtaining a privilege. It is the more curious that the term 'privilege' itself, though understood and freely used in the book-trade as a commercial term, and familiar to all lawyers, is late making an appearance in the Letters Patent. The earliest use of it seems to be in response to Durant Gerlier's petition for printing the Concordat and other works: 'Se il nous plaisoit luy permettre et octroyer privilege et grace', which speaks of 'noz presens grace, otroy et privillege' (CH 1519, 2); the next known example, four years later, speaks of 'lettres de privillege et provision' (CH 1523, 1).

Did the legal requirement introduced in 1521, that no new work concerning religion should be published without first having been passed by the Faculty of Theology, have any visible effect on the 'permission' element in grants issued by the royal chancery? Did the Letters Patent thereafter record having seen evidence of such approval, or make the privilege conditional upon such approval being obtained? As far as can be judged from the grants for religious books made by the chancery from 1521 to 1527, this was not the case.

Presumably the chancery assumed that applicants knew the law and that they would make it their business to obtain the required certificate of orthodoxy from the Faculty before putting the book on sale. Only one of these grants mentions having seen an *advis* of the Faculty (CH 1523, 5). The applicant in this instance was a foreigner.

Could securing a privilege from the chancery enable the beneficiary then to disregard a negative reply from the Faculty? There is nothing to suggest that he would have been immune from prosecution had he published the offending book in these circumstances. A 'conflict of powers' has indeed been postulated in the case of the *Heures de nostre dame translatees en Francoys et mises en rihtme*, by Pierre Gringore alias Mère Sotte, for which the author obtained a privilege 10 October 1525 from the chancery, then at Lyon (CH 1525, 2).[1] How could this privilege have been granted, when the Faculty of Theology had decided some time before against allowing the book to be printed? Was not this an attempt to have the Faculty's decision overridden or circumvented, by securing royal Letters Patent in the author's favour? Certainly no one knew the privilege system better than Gringore. His had been the first privilege ever granted to a French author, twenty years before (PR 1505, 1), and, as a trusted publicist of the Crown, he had been granted several in the intervening years. But a manoeuvre on his part to play off one authority against another is unlikely. He was by this time the Vaudement Herald to Antoine, duke of Lorraine, and his translation was dedicated to the duchess, Renée de Bourbon. And it was the duke, a pillar of orthodoxy, like all his family, who had submitted the translation to the Faculty of Theology in Paris, possibly as a precaution against a work of this kind, which might be open to criticism as it stood being published by an important official in his service and with a dedication to his wife. At the duke's request, the Faculty appointed two of its members, François de Combles and Nicolas Ensche, to examine the work on 24 July 1523.[2] Following their report, the Faculty made its decision, in the context of a heated debate on the question of allowing French translations of the Bible. There had never been any question of preventing Books of Hours from circulating in the vernacular, though a verse translation might give rise to some licence. Gringore's personal orthodoxy was never queried. The theo-

[1] F. M. Higman, *Censorship and the Sorbonne: a bibliographical study of books in French censured by the Faculty of Theology of the university of Paris 1520–1551*, Travaux d'humanisme et Renaissance, 172 (Geneva, 1979), p. 79. I think the suspicions here expressed about the form of the privilege are groundless. The chancery was perfectly competent to issue such a grant in the king's name while his mother was acting as Regent (see above, p. 33), and the clauses beginning 'Et en cas de debat...' do not imply that trouble was expected but are legal formulae found in many chancery privileges, e.g. that for *L'hystoire du sainct greaal* (CH 1515, 1; see below, pp. 33 and 142).

[2] Farge, *Biographical Register of Paris doctors of Theology 1500–1536*, pp. 106 and 156. Cf. the same author's *Orthodoxy and Reform in early reformation France: the Faculty of Theology of Paris, 1500–1543* (Leiden, 1985), pp. 178–9.

logian's objections to his *Heures*, as submitted to them in manuscript, may not have been insuperable, nor Gringore unduly unwilling to satisfy them before having his work printed. Indeed his readiness to comply with the directions of the theologians is expressed in the manuscript verses added to the vellum copy presented to the duchess of Lorraine:

> Mais ay monstré les differends passaiges
> A doctes clers, prudens lettrez et saiges,
> Mieulx entendans le spirituel scens
> Que je ne fais ...
> Suyvant tousjours la seure oppinion
> Des gens lectrez à leur discretion.[1]

If the *Heures* were published later openly by Jean Petit, a prominent and prudent *libraire juré* of Paris University, with a privilege from the royal chancery; if the title-page stated that they were translated and versified by the command of the duchess; if the work was reprinted with additional *Chants royaulx*, under a further royal privilege (CH 1527, 3); if the work never appeared in any of the lists of books condemned by the Faculty – one possible explanation is evidently that the offending material was deleted or amended to take account of the Faculty's censures.

THE PARLEMENT OF PARIS

As for the Parlement, the earliest privilege of which we have the complete text makes no mention of receiving or granting a request for *permission* to print and publish the book in question:

The court having seen the petition presented to it by Master Berthold Rembolt, master bookseller of the university of Paris, by which, and for the reasons therein contained, he requested that it should be forbidden and made unlawful for all booksellers and printers both of this city of Paris and elsewhere to print or cause to be printed, for six years, the book composed by one Master Bruno, first Prior of the Carthusian Order, on the Epistles of St Paul, examined and corrected by several doctors of theology appointed for the purpose by the said university, and printed to the order of the said Rembolt: having seen also certain judgements of the said court given in like cases, and all things considered: the said court has ordered and orders it to be forbidden and made unlawful for all booksellers and printers, and others however they may be, to print or cause to be printed from this day for three years the said book and exposition of the Epistles of St Paul, on pain of confiscation of the said books and of a fine at the discretion of the court. Enacted in Parlement the twelfth day of January the year one thousand five hundred and eight. (PA 1509, 1; see Plate 2)

A form of request of this kind, asking for others to be forbidden to print or sell the book, was frequently used until the 1520s, and the Parlement continued to grant requests so worded without any mention of permission.

[1] Louis Karl, 'Les Heures de Nostre Dame par Pierre Gringore,' *Revue du Seizième Siècle*, XVIII (1931), pp. 352–5.

Other applicants evidently preferred to begin their petition by asking the court's *leave* to publish the book, and follow this up by asking that others should be prevented from doing so. When granting a request presented in this form the Parlement usually, though not invariably, gave its leave and said so explicitly.

Among the earliest requests for Parlement privileges were those submitted by *greffiers* for the *Coutumes* of their district. The text of the *Coutumes* was so eminently the business of the Parlement itself that it was natural for the *greffiers* to begin by asking for leave to have it printed (e.g. 'ils requeroient ... que, pour les recompenser de leurs peines, leur feust permis icelles Coustumes faire imprimer à leur proufict', PA 1510, 2) and then seek the exclusive rights in it. Some other applicants followed suit. Jean Petit sought permission as well as privilege for Raulin's sermons ('il requeroit permission luy estre faicte de exposer et mettre en vente ung livre intitulé *Opus sermonum*') and the Parlement gave it ('Et tout consideré la court a permis et permet audit Petit libraire mettre et exposer en vente ledit livre', PA 1512, 1). However, there are throughout the period Parlement privileges in which no reference whatever is made either to permission having been sought or to permission having been granted:[1] these are indeed more numerous than those where permission is mentioned. There are even cases where the applicant began by asking permission and where the court in its reply made no reference to this but simply granted the request for a privilege (PA 1515, 1).

Whether or not the *arrêt* mentioned expressly the seeking or giving of permission, the Parlement often recorded that it had taken steps to satisfy itself about the contents of the book before reaching its decision. Frequently it appointed commissioners to 'visit' or inspect the copy submitted by the applicant and to report on it. An early example uses the words 'oy le rapport des commissaires deputez par la court à visiter ledict livre' (PA 1510, 3). A common formula was 'Oy le rapport de certain commissaire commis á veoir et visiter ledict livre' (e.g. PA 1512, 1). Such a commissioner might be a member of the court itself: thus, 'Oy le rapport de certain conseiller d'icelle court' (PA 1512, 9). More often the task was probably delegated to a member of a court like the *Chambre des Enquêtes*. Sometimes a specialist opinion was sought. Thus before granting a privilege for *Le mirouer de penitence* the Parlement consulted the Penitentiary of the diocese of Paris, recording that it had heard the report of 'Maistre Jehan Bricot, docteur en theologie, et Penitencier de Paris, auquel ledit livre a esté par ordonnance de ladite court communiqué' (PA 1512, 3). For a commentary on the *Sentences* by Guillermus de Rubione, the Parlement heard the report of its own commissioner and also of certain theologians which it had summoned with him to give their opinion, 'ouy le raport de certain commissaire commis à veoir et visiter ledit livre, appelés avec luy aucuns Theologiens, et ouy leur raport' (PA 1518, 3). For the first

---

[1] E.g. PA 1512, 9; 1514, 1; 1514, 5; 1514, 9; 1514, 10; 1515, 2; 1516, 8; 1517, 1; 1517, 2; 1517, 6; 1517, 7; 1518, 1; 1518, 3; 1519, 3; 1520, 1.

edition of the works of Dionysius Cisterciensis, the publisher submitted a notarially witnessed attestation made in the court of the Prévôt by the editor, Jean Masières, that the work he had edited contained nothing other than 'bonne doctrine et digne de promulgation et profitable à tous estudians en Theologie' (PA 1511, 2). Jean Masières was himself a Paris doctor of theology, and *proviseur* of the Cistercian college of St Bernard in the University of Paris. This did not exempt the book from being referred by the Parlement to a commissioner of its own choice before the privilege was granted ('Et oy le rapport de certain commissaire deputé par la court en ceste partie, et tout consideré'). The Parlement counted a number of *conseillers clercs* among its own members. Although most of these clerics were specialists in law rather than in theology, some of them were quite competent to give an opinion on the religious books submitted to the Parlement with an application for a privilege.

In some cases a report was required, not because it was desired to see that there was nothing objectionable in the contents of the book, but because there was doubt as to whether it qualified for a privilege or for how long. This was probably the point at issue when a commentary on Aristotle's *Praedicamenta* was submitted to a representative of the court 'together with certain persons of the University of Paris' ('oy le rapport de certain commissaire commis a visiter ledit livre avec aucuns de l'université de Paris'). Professional philosophers were probably called in, to determine whether the commentary was an original contribution to the subject or not (PA 1514, 2). Another instance is probably the *Octo libri physicorum* of John Mair, though this did not require the assistance of outside experts: ('Veu par la court ladicte requeste et oy le rapport de certain commissaire d'icelle court') (PA 1526, 3).

In other cases the grant of the privilege went through without any such examination. Sometimes the identity of the author is sufficient explanation of this immunity. If Jean Petit obtained a privilege for the *Fragmenta* of Jacques Cappel without any mention being made of 'visiting' the book, it was no doubt because Cappel was *avocat du roi* in the court (PA 1517, 8). Occasionally the proposed publication was vouched for by some other authority. Thus Nicolas de La Barre was granted a privilege for the Bull of Canonisation of St Francis of Paola 'veu par la court ladite requeste, le vidimus de ladite ville [de Paris], et tout consideré', which must refer to a certificate from the City of Paris, presumably from the Prévôt des Marchands (PA 1520, 1).

It is at first sight surprising, on the other hand, to find among the books which the court agreed to privilege without doing more than seeing the book ('Veu aussi ledit livre et tout consideré'), the first edition of the *Mémoires* of Philippe de Commynes (PA 1524, 3), to be published by Galliot Du Pré. Commynes had suffered imprisonment for his part in the 'Guerre folle', and though the accession of Louis XII (whose part, as duke of Orleans, he had taken) allowed him to end his days in peace, he had no desire by then to stir up trouble by publishing his memoirs. When he died in 1511, it was well known

107

that he had been writing them, and a few copies circulated among his friends and relatives. A proposal to print them, even without the part relating to the most recent events, the reign of Charles VIII, of which Galliot had evidently been unable to get a copy, could hardly fail only fourteen years later to arouse some apprehension in certain circles. People who had read them in manuscript must have noticed that Commynes, disillusioned with what he had gained by deserting the duke of Burgundy, was in places critical of the French monarchy. Did the Parlement, which had condemned him in 1489 to ten years of relegation, or banishment to his own estates, really make such a perfunctory examination of his book as could be made in court while business was in progress, before allowing the privilege which would inevitably be read as giving it official approval? A recollection recorded by François Beaucaire de Peguillon (1514–91), bishop of Metz, provides a possible clue to an explanation. In his *Rerum gallicarum commentarii ab anno christi 1461 ad annum 1580*, Beaucaire discussed some of the omissions and inaccuracies to be found in the printed text of Commynes. A trustworthy person once told him that it was Jean de Selve, then president of the Parlement of Paris, who handed over the work of Commynes to the printer. Selve first revised and corrected the text, or rather, in the view of Beaucaire's informant, seriously mutilated it in several places, in his ignorance of history, as the informant knew from having seen the work complete in manuscript.[1] If it was indeed the president of the court who gave Galliot the copy, after himself revising it, there would clearly be no necessity to appoint someone to report on it. And if the president indeed made cuts in the text, or alterations, it might have been out of policy rather than ignorance. In fact, the most obviously politically sensitive passages in Commynes do not seem to have been tampered with in Galliot's edition, e.g. the remarks about Louis XI and the Parlement itself. The book, issued with the title 'Cronique et hystoire faicte et composée par feu Messire Philippe de Commines, chevalier, seigneur d'Argenton, contenans les choses advenues durant le regne du roy Loys xie', was completed on 26 April 1524: by 7 September 1524 Galliot had already brought out a second edition in which there is greater completeness and accuracy, whether through access to a better copy or through a change of policy on the part of the editor is not known. It was to be another publisher, Enguilbert de Marnef, in 1528, who secured the second part of the work, covering the reign of Charles VIII, with a privilege from the Parlement dated 3 August 1528. Galliot none the less lived to publish the pioneer critical edition of the whole of Commynes' work by Denis Sauvage – the first to give the book the title *Mémoires* – with a privilege for six years granted by Henry II at Paris on 13 July 1552.

[1] Quoted, from the *Rerum gallicarum commentarii* (published posthumously at Lyon in 1625), by Bernard de Mandrot in his edition of the *Mémoires* (1901), Vol. 1, introduction, pp. xc–xci. The standard edition of the complete *Mémoires* of Commynes is that of Joseph Calmette, in the series Les Classiques de l'Histoire de France au moyen âge (1924).

To print unwittingly material which was objectionable to the State was not the only danger that a privilege-seeker might fear from the contents of a book he wished to publish. To print what was objectionable to a powerful family or individual was another.

As at the present day, the memoirs or autobiographies of men who had played an important part in public life might arouse the interest of the reading public, but might contain matter liable to prove personally or politically embarrassing to people still alive or to the families of people mentioned in them. The *Mémoires* of Olivier de La Marche were still unpublished in 1504, two years after his death, when Charles de Lalaing received information that La Marche had included his father, Josse de Lalaing, among the nobles who supported the rebels of Ghent in 1482 in their refusal to release the young Philip of Austria and in their opposition to his father Maximilian. Philip, now sovereign in the Low Countries, agreed to Charles' request that a committee should investigate the text of the *Mémoires*, of which La Marche's widow was made to produce her copy. As a result, order went forth that the offending passage mentioning Josse de Lalaing was to be excised, and that anyone possessing the original or copies was to see that it was cut out. It does not, in fact, occur in any surviving manuscript of the *Mémoires*, nor in the printed editions, beginning with that of Denis Sauvage (Lyon, 1562), and the incident is known only from the Chronicles of Molinet, not published until the nineteenth century.[1] The possessor of a manuscript of this kind when approached by a publisher, or the publisher offered copy of this nature, might well feel more secure against possible complaints if the publication was to appear protected by a privilege. When Jean Petit sought a privilege for the first time from the Parlement of Paris it was for a late work of Olivier de La Marche, *Le parement et triumphe des dames de honneur* (PA 1510, 3). Certainly he may have anticipated that it would be eagerly read, and therefore particularly at risk from unauthorised reprints. But there may have been other reasons. La Marche was known as having been a devoted servant of the house of Burgundy. No work by him had yet been printed under his own name in France, though *Le chevalier délibéré* had been published as an anonymous work by Vérard and others. And *Le parement* celebrated a number of recently deceased great ladies, Marie de Bourgogne among them, whose relatives might take exception to what was said about them being published. To obtain a privilege from the Parlement for the publication might be in some measure regarded as a safeguard, obliging the Parlement itself to accept responsibility for the contents of the book being inoffensive. Some light on this aspect of the Parlement's privilege grants is thrown by an incident several years later.

In 1522 the archbishop of Sens, Etienne Poncher, and his nephew François

[1] *Mémoires d'Olivier de la Marche*, ed. H. Beaune and J. D'Arbaumont, SHF (1888), IV, Notice bibliographique, pp. cvii–viii and III, 264–6. *Chroniques de Jean Molinet*, ed. G. Doutrepont and O. Jodogne, Académie Royale de Belgique, 3 vols. (Brussels, 1935–7), II, pp. 546–8.

Poncher, who had succeeded him as bishop of Paris, took exception to the Preamble of a book on the seven penitential psalms, which they regarded as a personal attack on themselves. The author, Geoffroy Boussard, was an old and respected theologian in the College of Navarre, a former chancellor of the church and University of Paris, and the present Dean of the Faculty of Theology. In the Preamble, which took the form of a prayer to Christ, Boussard denounced certain abuses rife in the church, among them the plurality of benefices, of which the Ponchers were undeniably a glaring example. Poncher's expostulations to the Faculty, which had evidently passed the book as orthodox, had little result,[1] and he transferred his attack to the Parlement, which had granted the publisher, Jean Olivier, a privilege for it (PA 1522, 4). The Parlement sent for Olivier forthwith and questioned him as to who had given him the Preamble and whether it had been added *after* the grant of the privilege. Eventually the Ponchers won their case in the Parlement against Boussard,[2] and the Parlement was clearly anxious to claim that, in granting a privilege for the book as a whole, it had not given its approval to the offending Preamble. Had Boussard or his publisher really slipped the Preamble in afterwards, whether deliberately or out of careless-ness?[3] Or was the Parlement saving its face, in maintaining that it had not included the Preamble in the privilege, having possibly assumed in reality that something written by the Dean of the Faculty required no serious scrutiny or that criticisms of the plurality of benefices were fair comment? . . .

Up to 1521, the Parlement treated applications for books on religion no differently from those on any other subject. As has been seen, it had most of the books submitted to it examined by a person of its own choice, and this might on occasion call for the advice of a theologian. Henceforth the task of determining whether a religious book was orthodox or not was the responsi-bility of the Faculty of Theology or its representatives. An *imprimatur* from the Faculty did not, however, in itself entitle the applicant to be granted a privilege, or constitute a condition for being granted one. The first publisher known to have printed his *visa* from the Faculty of Theology verbatim in the book concerned, as well as his Parlement privilege, was Claude Chevallon, bringing out the fourteenth-century *Reductorium morale* of Pierre Bersuire (PA 1522, 3). It is evident from the terms of the *visa* that his first move was to obtain the privilege from the Parlement in the usual way. Only then did he submit the book to the Faculty, showing them the *requête* which he had made to the Parlement and the reply of the Parlement. The Faculty appointed two of its members, Noël Beda and Guillaume de Quercu, to act as censors, and

---

[1] J.-A. Clerval, *Registre des procès-verbaux de la Faculté de Théologie de Paris*, I, *1505–1523* (1917), 327–30, 337–8, notes 32, 33.
[2] AN x I A 1525, ff. 23, 113, 185, 238ᵛ.
[3] The Preamble is printed in the first gathering of the book, as part of the 'prelims' (which would be printed last), the main text beginning further on; but this is not conclusive, as it could be regarded as part of the prefatory material.

they reported favourably on it. The Faculty, having seen Chevallon's *requête* and the Parlement's reply, and also received the report of Beda and De Quercu, then formally gave its consent to the book being printed and put on sale, adding the commendation that it was useful to scholars and preachers in the church ('tanquam utilem ecclesie studiosis et predicatoribus et predicare volentibus'). The procedure was however soon preferred of obtaining the *visa* first, and presenting it to the Parlement when applying for the privilege.

Thereafter it is fairly common for the Parlement to record that it had seen a certificate from the Faculty of Theology before granting a privilege for a book on a religious subject, as in the formula 'Veu par la court ledict livre, la certification de la faculté de theologie, et tout consideré' (PA 1524, 14). The court accepted an application from Galliot Du Pré for a French version of the *Catalogus sanctorum* of Petrus Natalibus 'visité et corrigé par ung maistre docteur en Theologie' (PA 1524, 5) but normally the court expected a formal certificate, even when the author was himself a member of the Faculty of Theology (PA 1524, 14) or a member of the much-respected Carthusian order (PA 1525, 5). The Parlement did not, however, automatically grant a privilege on being shown a favourable report from the Faculty. Thus it considered a report from one of its own number, a *conseiller*, as well as the certificate from the Faculty of Theology, in the case of a 'Propositio contra Lutherum et sequaces eius' (PA 1524, 12). And before granting a privilege for the *Propugnaculum ecclesiae adversus lutheranos* of Josse Clichtoue, himself a member of the Faculty, the court examined the book itself, and consulted the *procureur général*, as well as seeing the report of the Faculty ('Veu par la Court ladicte requeste, la conclusion de la faculté de theologie prinse sur ledict volume, icelluy examiné, et ouy sur ce le procureur general du Roy, et tout consideré', PA 1525, 8). Even when relieved of the obligation to use its own discretion about summoning expert theological advice, it remained vigilant about safeguarding the interests of the Crown and watchful too for anything with political implications.

The certificate from the Faculty of Theology sometimes recorded positive approval and not merely a declaration of orthodoxy, anticipating in some measure the practice of the seventeenth and eighteenth centuries when the censor's *visa* might embody a full testimonial to the quality and interest of the work. Occasionally the Parlement, in recording the grant of a privilege, took note of these expressions of approval. Thus in the case of the Sermons of Robert Messier, the court had before it the certificate of the Faculty 'par laquelle elle certifie avoir visité certain opuscule de sermons du temps de quaresme compilé par ledict Robert Messier suppliant qu'elle a trouvé assez tolerable et utile' (PA 1525, 1). And it observed, concerning Clichtoue's *Antilutherus*, 'la declaration faicte par la faculté de theologie de ladicte université, que lesdictz livres sont utiles et povoyent estre imprimez et exposez en vente' (PA 1524, 10).

The Parlement itself never expressed any opinion on the merits of the books for which it granted privileges.

On occasion, the Parlement might authorise the publication of one contentious work and forbid another. Thus on 18 March 1517 it allowed a petition by Bonaventura Nepveu for permission to publish his *Tractatulus dictus deffensorium Fratrum Minorum de Observantia* (Paris, Regnault Chaudière, 1517, 8°)[1] and forbade the publication of Boniface de Ceva's pamphlet on the other side, in the long-running dispute before the Parlement between the rival groups of Franciscans. This was not a privilege: reprints of Nepveu's work were not forbidden.

THE PRÉVÔT OF PARIS AND ROYAL OFFICERS IN THE PROVINCES

In the court of the Prévôt at the Châtelet of Paris publications of a very slight and ephemeral nature were sometimes granted privileges, though for a short period of time. But there are also instances of publishers obtaining a simple *congé* or permission for small books and pamphlets on affairs of current public interest. A flurry of such publications reflected public interest in Louis XII's campaigns in Italy and the concern of royal publicists that the king's actions should be supported by his people.[2] The firm in Lyon or Paris which was first with news of events and with informed discussion of them might well hope to sell a large number of copies quickly. Among them was *L'Armée du roy qu'il avoit contre les Vénitiens*, an account of the battle of Agnadello, printed by Martin Alexandre in Paris 'sous le congié de monseigneur le prevost ou son lieutenant' (PR 1509, 4*), and the *Œuvre nouvellement translatée de Italienne rime* celebrating the king's spectacular entry into Milan, printed with 'congé et licence' by Noel Abraham in Lyon (PR 1509, 5*). Apparently this was something less than a privilege, since no mention is made of forbidding other members of the book-trade to print or sell these items. What good, then, was a *congé* to the applicant? Was it likely to give him at least some initial advantage, and to that extent deter possible competitors from immediately copying it? Certainly prospective purchasers might opt for an edition which advertised a *congé*. It was evidence of official approval, and guaranteed that the contents were neither subversive nor wildly inaccurate. Its main use on the other hand may have been to secure the position of the publisher, who, in dealing in such 'hot' news, may sometimes himself have feared to disseminate material which might prove to be unwelcome to the authorities. Another possibility is that the

---

[1] Sainte-Geneviève D.8°.11.066 Rés. (pièce 2). The *arrêt*, in the form of Letters Patent in Latin issued as by the king in Parlement, is printed at the end, on ff. xxx verso and xxxi.

[2] See J. P. Seguin, *L'information en France de Louis XII à Henri II*, Travaux d'Humanisme et Renaissance, 44 (Geneva, 1961), pp. 29–30; Bernard Quilliet, *Louis XII, père du peuple* (1986), p. 393.

congé represented a failed application for a privilege, a sort of consolation prize. The only case which would support such an interpretation is much later, in 1527 (PR 1527, 4): then, the *Lieutenant Civil* of Paris refused an application for a privilege but granted a *permission* and *congé*, *Congés* without privileges were never issued by the Parlement or the royal chancery, only by the local courts, and they are few in number, though more may have been given than have survived. The holders had thought them worth paying for, and that is all that can be said for certain.

There are traces of such *congés* being granted by royal officials other than the Prévôt of Paris. The news sheet entitled *La coppie des lettres que Monsieur le mareschal de Trevoul a envoiées au Roy*, dated on internal evidence May 1511, bears the words at the foot of the title-page, 'Fait par le congié de justice' (PR 1511, 1). The printing of this pamphlet has been assigned tentatively to Rouen;[1] if that is correct the authorisation probably came from the Bailli of Rouen. The *Style* of the court of the Bailli of the duchy of Berry and of the court of the Prévôt of Bourges, published in 1512 'par l'auctorité, congié et licence' of the Bailli himself (PR 1512, 1), may be an example. Another is an account of the state entry into Paris of Louis XII's bride, princess Mary of England (6 November 1514), of which some copies display a permission granted by the Prévôt de l'Hôtel, in the following terms:

> De par monsieur le prevost de l'hostel.
> Nous avons permis et donné congé à Guillaume Varin suppliant de faire imprimer l'entrée de la Royne Et la vendre et distribuer. Fait à Paris le Roy y estant le .x. jour de Novembre. Mil cinq cens et .xiiii. Par nous Jehan de Fontaine / seigneur d'Aulhac / conseillier chambellain du roy nostre sire / et prevost de l'hostel dudit seigneur. (PR 1514, 4*)

The jurisdiction of the Prévôt de l'Hôtel extended to the whole royal household and all persons following the court, and to all cases and all crimes arising within it, up to ten leagues round the royal residence.[2] He may not have regarded it as within his competence to forbid anyone except Guillaume Varin to print an account of the new queen's entry into Paris, but his authorisation must have given Varin's edition the status of an official one and been good publicity. It is possible that Varin had some connection with the royal household: he is not known to have been a publisher or printer in Paris.

The first grant by the Prévôt of Paris to be printed verbatim by the beneficiary gives both permission and privilege, the publication in question being the text of the treaty of Saint-Germain-en-Laye which had just been signed between the kings of France and England. It reads,

> ¶ De par le prevost de Paris
> ou son lieutenant criminel.
> ¶ Il est permis à Guillaume Sanxon libraire povoir faire imprimer la copie des lettres

---

[1] Seguin, *L'information en France de Louis XII à Henri II*, no. 42, p. 68.
[2] R. Doucet, *Les institutions de la France au xvie siècle* (1948), I, pp. 117–18.

missives du roy nostre sire et le cry fait par vertu d'icelles cy dessus transcriptz. Et est deffendu à tous libraires et imprimeurs de la ville de Paris de non imprimer ou faire imprimer aucuns jusques à en huyt jours prochainement venant. Sur peine de confiscation desdites impressions et d'amende arbitraire. De ce faire a luy donne povoir.
Fait soubz nostre signet le jeudi .xvii. jour d'aoust. Mil cinq cens et xiiii. Ainsi signé. G. Maillart.   Almaury. (PR 1514, 2)

The text of the treaty was already known to the Prévôt and his officers, since the formal proclamation of it had been made by Normandy Herald in the Prévôt's court the previous day, 16 August 1514, in their presence, and recorded by the *greffier*, as is clear from the printed pamphlet itself (f. 3^v).

When they were confronted by a proposed publication of which they had no such previous knowledge, they examined it with some care; they might require the deletion of part of it.

How many applications were refused altogether, because the contents of the book were not approved, cannot be known. Normally such refusals have left no trace. But there is certainly a case of refusal for *part* of a book: an order of December 1515 expressly excludes, from the grant of the Prévôt's permission and privilege, *one* item of the copy submitted (PR 1515, 2):

¶ De par le prevost de Paris
¶ Il est permis à Guillaume le Normant et Pierre Martin imprimeurs de povoir imprimer et faire imprimer ung petit livre intitulé L'epistre qu'a voulu mander France à la mere du roy pour aliance *fors et excepté la chanson de la victoire contre les Suisses estant à la fin d'iceluy* et iceluy vendre et distribuer à qui bon leur semblera et est deffendu à tous aultres imprimeurs de non imprimer ledit livre du jourduy jusques à trois moys sur paine de confiscation desdits livres et d'amende arbitraire. Fait soubz nostre signet le mescredi [*sic*] .v. jour de decembre l'an .M. cinq cens et quinze. Signé   Amaury. (italics mine)

This anonymous pamphlet, as printed, consists of a eulogy in ten-syllable couplets of poor literary quality but unexceptionable patriotism, supposed to be spoken by the land of France to Louise of Savoy and her son the king. The *Chanson*, which in the copy submitted to the Prévôt followed the eulogy, presumably celebrated the king's victory at Marignano. What the Prévôt found to be objectionable about it can only be guessed. Perhaps it was too violently anti-Swiss. The French authorities must have been well aware that the next turn of international events might make the king seek Swiss aid.

The next privilege granted by the Prévôt of Paris of which we have the details (PR 1516, 1) expressly gives both permission and privilege as two separate clauses:

¶ Veu ce livre et la requeste faicte par Clement Longis et ouy sur ce les gens du roy a esté permis audit Longis imprimer ou faire imprimer cedit livre / et sont deffences faictes à tous autres imprimeurs de ne imprimer ou faire imprimer / vendre ne faire vendre ledit livre d'autres que ceulx qui auront esté imprimez ou fait imprimer par ledit suppliant jusques à deux ans prochainement venans sur peine de confiscation des ditz livres et d'amende arbitraire. Fiat le .xix.ᵉ de septembre mil cinq cens et seize. Ruzé.

It is clear from this text that the Prévôt, like the *conseillers* of the Parlement, gave careful consideration to the contents of a book submitted for a privilege before deciding to grant an application, particularly consulting the 'gens du roy' – here probably the king's *procureur* in the court of the *prévôté* at the Châtelet – over any text which might however remotely affect the interests of the Crown. This book, *La vie et les miracles de Saint Eusice*, sounds innocent enough, but, the saint's chief claim to fame being that he had supported King Childebert with his prayers against the Arians, an account of his doings might be thought of concern to the dynasty. There is on the other hand no question of consulting any theologians.

The 'permission' element implied in the grant of a privilege was not always made explicit even by the Prévôt of Paris. The Letters Patent obtained from the Prévôt the same year by Guillaume Michel (PR 1516, 2) refer only to his request to have a privilege in his book and to the decision to grant him the privilege for two years. On the other hand, a request from François Regnault which asked only for a privilege was granted with the addition of an explicit permission to print it (PR 1517, 7).

The Prévôt gave Galliot Du Pré a privilege for the modernised version of *Le Roman de la Rose* (PR 1526, 2) only after hearing the opinion of the *procureur du roi* in his court ('oy sur ce le procureur du Roy nostre sire audit Chastellet pour et au nom dudit seigneur'). Galliot may have had to make out a special case for his edition, for reasons which had nothing to do with the acceptability of the contents: was there a reason for granting a privilege in it at all, seeing that the *Roman de la Rose* had been in circulation both in manuscript and in print for many years? But there may have been other grounds for the Prévôt to consult the *procureur du roi* as to the contents. The second part of the *Roman*, by Jean de Meung, contains some very radical criticism of established institutions, ranging from marriage to the origins of kingship. The poem's antiquity and immense popularity gave it, in these matters, a sort of licence. A modernised version of it, in altering some of the wording of the traditional text, might be a means of introducing ideas which were downright subversive. This did not prove to be the case when Galliot's 'up-dated' version was examined.

In 1527 there was to be a case which clearly illustrated the distinction currently made in the *Prévôté* between permission and privilege. Jacques Nyverd sought permission to print the Treaty of Amiens, which had just been proclaimed in Paris, and asked for a privilege in it for eight days. The new *Lieutenant Civil*, Antoine Du Bourg, readily gave permission but expressly refused the grant of a privilege ('sans aucune prohibition aux autres imprimeurs de povoir ce faire', PR 1527, 4). The Lieutenant may have considered that he had shown Nyverd sufficient favour in agreeing to provide him with an authenticated copy of the text, enabling him to be the first person to print it, and that it was not in the public interest to prevent any other edition appearing for a week.

The Prévôt of Paris, and senior officers of the Crown in the provinces, had another occasion to inspect new books proposed for publication under privilege if the successful applicant to the chancery brought his Letters Patent to the local court for *entérinement* or registration. This meant that the authenticity of the document was checked. It seems also that in some cases an independent report on the book itself was called for. The elaborate *lettres d'attache* obtained by Lemaire de Belges for his royal privilege (CH 1509, 2), from the Lieutenant General of the *sénéchaussée* of Lyon were given without any such formality. But the privilege granted by the chancery to Guillaume Eustace for two books (CH 1521, 1) was recorded, signed and sealed by the Prévôt of Paris only after he had sought the opinion of certain *conseillers* in his court and also of the *procureur du roi*. ('Et ouy sur ce l'oppinion d'aucuns conseillers du Roy nostre sire ou chastellet de Paris estans en la chambre du conseil dudit chastellet. Ouy aussi sur icelles le procureur du Roy.') Why such precautions were taken before authorising the registration of the Letters Patent of Eustace is not clear. One of the books was a devotional work by Guillaume Alexis, a much-respected writer of the late fifteenth century, the other selected letters of St Jerome in translation. Both were on religious subjects, and both were in the vernacular, and the time was very close when such works could no longer be published without the *imprimatur* of the Faculty of Theology.

At first sight, there appears to be an omission in all these arrangements for checking the contents of books before the grant of a privilege: what was there to prevent the privilege-holder from adding or altering things between obtaining the grant and putting the book on sale? That the case of Geoffroy Boussard before the Parlement (already noted)[1] is the only one of its kind suggests that most authors and publishers were too afraid of the consequences of being found out, to do so. Not only would they instantly have forfeited the privilege itself, but they could be proceeded against for contempt of court and severely fined.

The only formal requirement that I have found, that the book, when completed or in proof, should be brought to the court to be checked before being sold is in the privilege given by the Parlement of Toulouse for the *Consuetudines Tholose* with which the city authorities as well as the Parlement were concerned: 'pourveu que avant que ledict suppliant puisse vendre ledict livre ou faire vendre, qu'il sera tenu nous monstrer la premiere impression d'icelluy pour icelle communiquer ausdits cappitols affin que l'on le puisse corriger et emender si besoing est et veoir s'il est bien' (PA 1523, 2). This is clearly aimed at ensuring complete accuracy. There was, however, to be a

---

[1] See above, pp. 109–10.

clause in a privilege granted by the *prévôté* on 12 January 1527: 'à la charge toutesvoyes de ne l'exposer en vente jusques à ce qu'il ait esté collationné à celluy sur lequel avons decerné ceste presente permission'. This occurs in the privilege, printed on the verso of the title, granted to Nicole Volcyr de Sérouville, secretary and historian of the duke of Lorraine, for the *Histoire et recueil de la victoire obtenue contre les lutheriens* (Paris, 1526; PR 1527, 1). There were several other special precautions about the grant of this privilege. The king's advocate in the court of the Prévôt, the veteran François Goyet, was commissioned to examine the book. It was only when he reported that he had found nothing in it which was 'prejudiciable ne dommageable à la chose publicque' that the certificate from the Faculty of Theology was taken into consideration, to show that 'ce qui concernoit ladicte theologie n'estoit pernicieux ne digne de reprehension'. Jean de La Barre, *garde de la prévôté de Paris*, on whose authority the privilege was issued, had only held office since April 1526, the appointment being one of the rewards granted him by Francis I, whose captivity he had shared. He was clearly taking no chances, with a book describing such recent and controversial events, by an author whose allegiance was to a foreign prince.

At this period, application for a book-privilege was a request for a favour, not compliance with a law. In submitting the book for which he was seeking a privilege, author or publisher knew that it would probably be inspected and might be refused a privilege if found to be unacceptable. To most applicants the likelihood that the book would be subjected to scrutiny must have seemed the natural condition of getting the privilege. In many cases the approval implied by the grant of the privilege was of no particular value to him. Would more people, for example, buy *La forest de conscience* (PR 1516, 2) because it had been granted a privilege by the Prévôt of Paris? On the other hand, the desire to obtain written official approval in some form was probably sometimes one of the motives for seeking a privilege. Doubts and fears may have been very real over publishing new books or pamphlets on certain subjects, as we have seen. To secure a privilege was then a sort of insurance against needlessly offending the government or powerful institutions and individuals. The 'permission' element was always present in a privilege, but it did not amount to a system of censorship. The chancery, the lawcourts and the royal officers between them probably saw a good proportion of the works being published for the first time, and thus had the opportunity to scrutinise them. But they only saw books which were submitted to them voluntarily by their authors or publishers.

6 · DATING AND DURATION OF PRIVILEGES

DURATION OF PRIVILEGES

During the period up to 1526 inclusive, the royal government in France, its courts and its officers gave no book-privileges for an unlimited period, and only two for as much as ten years, both of these to authors with highly original projects (CH 1522, 4 and CH 1526, 2). Occasionally there were loopholes in the terms of the grant which enabled the beneficiary to practise considerable delay in making use of his privilege.[1] The reckless giving of far-reaching monopolies, which in Venice had produced a situation of chaos in the book-trade by 1517,[2] and was to be the curse of Elizabethan England, was, however, avoided. Whether by luck or good management, whether by study of foreign precedents or consultation with well-informed opinion in France, the granting of these favours was conducted with restraint and care. A certain consistency can also be observed in the duration for which they were given. A privilege might indeed be given, as has been noted, for as much as ten years, and it might be given for as little as eight days (e.g. PR 1514, 2), but normal practice was far from being so variable as this might lead one to suppose.

The first French book-privilege of all (CH 1498, 1) was granted for a period of five years. The book in question, a huge undertaking, was printed at Lyon, where Italian practice in the matter of privileges would be familiar to the leading members of the book-trade, and the preface was composed, to incorporate a summary of the privilege, by the humanist Janus Lascaris, who had recently come to the French court from Italy. No other French five-year privilege is known until 1519.

This remained an isolated instance. When Louis XII began to grant book-privileges to his subjects in France with any frequency, it was not earlier than 1507, and then for periods of two or three years. In his capacity as duke of Milan, he granted somewhat longer periods, continuing in this respect the policy of the Sforza dukes of Milan. Thus he granted a four-year privilege to Janus Parrhasius for his edition of Sedulius' *Carmen paschale* (Milan, 1 July 1501),[3] and a ten-year privilege to the Da Legnano brothers for the more

---

[1] See below, pp. 135–6.   [2] See above, pp. 6–7.   [3] See above, p. 6.

substantial *Commentaria in secundam partem Digesti* by Giasone Dal Maino in 1502.[1] This had no influence on his grants of privileges in France itself. When Louis XII granted a personal privilege to the veteran Paris book-seller Antoine Vérard, first referred to in January 1508 (CH 1507, 1), it was for three years, apparently in any item which Vérard should be the first to publish. Soon afterwards he granted a similar personal privilege to Guillaume Eustace, bookseller to the king (CH 1508, 2): this was for two years. Thereafter no such personal privileges were granted in the period up to 1526. Grants were made only for specific books, or, occasionally, for pairs or groups of books, which are named. These too, under Louis XII, were limited to two or three years.

The earliest applications by authors to the royal chancery evidently left it to the king to determine the duration of the privilege. Eloi d'Amerval set out his case and then simply requested the king's 'grace et liberalité' (CH 1508, 1). Nicole Bohier asked for his publisher, Simon Vincent of Lyon, to have the exclusive right in four works 'jusques à tel temps qu'il nous plaira', in the words of the Letters Patent (CH 1509, 1). Both were given two years. The choice of this term of years was thus arrived at by the chancellor or his officials. Whatever their reasons, the decision was certainly not haphazard. It may have taken account of the grant made to Guillaume Eustace. It may have resulted from informal consultations with the applicants and their publishers, and with responsible members of the book-trade such as the *libraires jurés* of Paris University, who could be trusted to advise on the length of time that it would probably take for the publisher to sell his edition or a reasonable proportion of it before others were permitted to reprint it.

Within two months of Bohier's privilege, an application was presented which specifically asked for three years. This came from Jean Lemaire de Belges, a professional man of letters, and concerned his historical fantasy, *Les Illustrations de Gaule et singularitz de Troye*, which he evidently, and rightly, expected to be a best-seller. The three-year term of duration was duly granted. Lemaire clearly regarded this as a generous concession, for he had the words 'Cum priuilegio regio amplissimo' printed on the title-page (CH 1509, 2). It was in fact to become almost standard practice for the rest of Louis XII's reign. It was, however, only under Francis I that grants for *over* three years were given, and then only occasionally, before 1526.

The exact duration of the chancery privilege is known in ninety-four cases for the period 1498–1526 (treating the personal privilege granted to Antoine Vérard and to Guillaume Eustace each as one grant) and they are distributed as follows:

---

[1] Milan, 1502, fol. Lucca, Bibl. Capitolare, 379/6, quoted by L. Balsamo, *Giovann' Angelo Scinzenzeler: tipografo in Milano 1500–1526* (Florence, 1959), p. 66, Annali no. 23; the privilege is summarised in the colophon of the *commentaria*.

1 year	3
2 years	20
3 years	55
4 years	10
5 years	3
6 years	1
10 years	2
	94

The six-year grant, and one of the ten-year grants, were obtained by Geofroy Tory (CH 1524, 1 and CH 1526, 2), for work which was certainly original in the highest degree. The other ten-year grant went to Oronce Finé (CH 1522, 4), who did not complete and publish the work for which he had obtained the privilege until 1532. The terms of the privilege are known only from the Latin summary which he included in the printed book. It seems likely that they took account of the importance of the mathematical projects on which he was engaged already in 1522, and the great skill and expense which would be required to print and illustrate them. He had in the interval been appointed the first royal professor of mathematics, a post which he held from 1530 to 1555.

The form in which the royal chancery usually issued book-privileges does not normally state whether there is any discrepancy between the term of years granted and the term of years requested by the applicant. There is, however, one exception before 1526, which shows that the chancery did not automatically give the duration desired by the petitioner. Enguilbert de Marnef in Poitiers published the first printed edition of a famous early book on coastal navigation, *Le grant routtier* of Pierre Garcie dit Ferrande. He was granted a two-year privilege for it (CH 1520, 4), but the privilege states that de Marnef had asked for 3 years. The secretary who signed it, Mareschal, who appears never to have drawn up any other book-privilege, may have preserved a feature, namely the term of years originally asked for, which it was the custom of his colleagues to omit. The slip in a book of Galliot Du Pré, which prints at the end 'Avec le privilege du Roy nostre sire jusques à trois ans', when the privilege is correctly stated on the title-page to be for two years (CH 1517, 1(3)), may also reflect the difference between what Galliot had hoped or expected to receive and what he got.

The Parlement of Paris during this period virtually standardised on two years as the duration of a privilege. Its earliest grants, it is true, were for one year (PA 1507, 1, and PA 1508, 1), but it gave a one-year privilege only once subsequently, when the object of the grant was a Papal Bull (PA 1520, 1). On nine occasions it issued a privilege for three years. The remaining privileges are all for two years.

As in the case of requests to the royal chancery, some applicants did not ask for any specific term of years. Time is not mentioned at all (e.g. PA 1514, 9), or a formula is used such as 'jusques à tel temps qu'il plairoit à ladite cour' (PA 1521, 2) or 'jusqu'à certain temps' (PA 1524, 14). On such occasions the Parlement normally gave two years. The few applicants who asked for two years seem to have been allowed that duration, except in the case of PA 1520, 1, when the book that was the main subject of the request was refused a privilege.

Of the eighty-eight known to have been granted two years by the Parlement of Paris, at least sixty applications had requested three or four years, and one (PA 1526, 2) had requested six. The court, even when it had decided in principle to grant a privilege, evidently looked critically at the term asked for, and allowed no more than two years unless it saw very good reason to allow three, which was its upper limit.

The *Grands Jours*, sessions held in certain provincial capitals under the presidency of two commissioners from the Parlement of Paris, rarely gave privileges. When they did, they followed the example of the Parlement itself in the matter of duration. The *Grands Jours de Berry*, sitting at Bourges, issued a privilege in favour of a Bourges bookseller for the charter which had set up the court: he had asked for four years, and was granted two (PA 1518, 5).

The provincial Parlements also tended to be sparing in the duration of the grants they made. The most independent of them, the Parlement of Toulouse, made an exceptional grant of five years in 1523. This was for the *Consuetudines Tholose* (PA 1523, 2). Otherwise its practice, as far as can be judged from the small number of grants of which full details are known, was in line with that of Paris. Thus it twice granted two years as the applicants had requested (PA 1517, 3, and PA 1522, 7), both to booksellers, and once three years, as requested (PA 1517, 5), this time to an author, a local doctor, for a substantial medical work of his own composition. The Echiquier or Parlement of Rouen is known to have given one two-year privilege, for the *Style* of the court itself: this was in response to a request for four years (PA 1516, 3). Such other privileges as the Echiquier granted up to 1527 seem to have been for much shorter periods. Thus in 1519 an applicant seeking a privilege for certain *Ordonnances* issued by the court asked only for a grant until the coming Easter 'ou tel temps qu'il plaira a ladicte court limiter', and duly received his privilege up to Easter, which was only about eight months, the grant being made on 4 August 1519 and Easter falling in 1520 on 8 April (PA 1519, 3). An earlier privilege granted by the Echiquier for some of its *Ordonnances* ran from 12 September to the following 1 March, less than six months (PA 1513, 3). The earliest privilege known to have been granted by the Parlement of Brittany was for its own *Ordonnances* and was for two years: this was not until 1535.[1]

It would appear, then, that three years was regarded by the sovereign courts as a maximum, which was only exceeded once, in the case of the

---

[1] See above, p. 48.

Toulouse privilege already mentioned (PA 1523, 2). The Parlement of Paris gave this maximum of three years only nine times during the period up to 1526 inclusive. Were the books, which thus received the maximum duration, exceptional in their size and character?

The first (PA 1509, 1) was an exposition of the Pauline Epistles, attributed to St Bruno, edited by certain doctors of the Sorbonne; it was printed in style, and was the first work of scholarship ever to be submitted to the Parlement for a privilege. It was 1514 before the Parlement granted any more three-year privileges. In that year there were two. A new translation into French of Petrarch's *Trionfi*, sumptuously printed and illustrated, was an obvious candidate (PA 1514, 7); the pair of new works on scholastic philosophy published by Jean Granjon was evidently considered so (PA 1514, 9). In 1515 the only three-year grant went to an elaborate guide-book to Italy, which boasted a map which is specially mentioned in the privilege (PA 1515, 4). By 1516 one of the books covered by PA 1514, 9 had sold so well that Granjon obtained a further three-year grant for a revised edition of it (PA 1516, 9). A three-year grant for the romance *La conqueste de Trebisonde* (PA 1518, 2), dedicated to the queen, was given both by the Parlement and by the Prévôt. The next three-year privilege occurs in 1520, obtained by an author, Claude Perron, for his *Compendium philosophiae naturalis* (PA 1520, 3), a modest original contribution to the study of physics and astronomy, which had an ambitious diagram of the celestial spheres inserted in it. It is obscure why Simon Vincent of Lyon was allowed a three-year period for a standard legal work (PA 1521, 1), though it may have been the first French edition of it: no surviving copy has been traced, and it is in doubt whether Vincent ever actually published it. The only other three-year privilege given by the Paris Parlement during this period is more easily accounted for. It covered a monumental work of scholarship, the records of the early Councils of the Church edited by Jacques Merlin, the basis of all later editions (PA 1524, 13). On the available evidence, the choice of books granted the longer duration shows signs of being rational rather than capricious.

Book-privileges granted by the lawcourts (Parlements, Cour des Aides and *Grands Jours*) so far traced total 119. Of these the duration is known for 113, and it is distributed as follows:

Less than 1 year	3
1 year	4
2 years	95
3 years	10
4 years	0
5 years	1 (PA 1523, 2)
Over 5 years	0
	113

In the case of privileges granted by the Prévôt of Paris, the Bailli of Rouen, or simply 'par justice', the duration is known for sixty-seven. It is distributed as follows:

Less than 1 year	11
1 year	12
2 years	15
3 years	26
4 years	3
5 years or more	0
	67

Privileges for less than a year, some even for a few days, are the most noticeable feature of the Prévôt's grants, particularly for the first years of his privilege-giving. They had never been given for such short periods by the royal chancery or by the Paris Parlement. They may even have been more numerous than the surviving evidence suggests, for they were sought to protect ephemeral publications, some of which, in the nature of things, may have perished altogether.

Privileges for two and three years granted by the Prévôt appear for the first time in 1516. They reflect a change of policy, apparently due to the new Prévôt, Gabriel d'Allegre, in welcoming literary and academic works of more than passing interest. What purpose had the previous very short privileges served?

The profits to be expected from the sale of printed newsletters depended on the publisher being ahead of possible competitors. By 1514 there are two fully authenticated cases of privileges in such publications being obtained for a period of eight days. Guillaume Sanxon was granted such a privilege for the text of the newly concluded treaty of Saint-Germain-en-Laye, which had only just been proclaimed in the court of the Prévôt of Paris (PR 1514, 2), and Guillaume Mart for an account of the very recent arrival of the English princess, Mary Tudor, and her marriage to Louis XII at Abbeville (PR 1514, 3). Another eight-day privilege, which I presume to have been likewise granted by the Prévôt, was to appear in one of the accounts of the Field of the Cloth of Gold (PR 1520, 7). Fifteen days were thought adequate for a description of the coronation of Francis I at Reims (PR 1515, 1). Six weeks was the term given for the Entry into Paris of the queen (PR 1517, 4), by the Prévôt of Paris, and for the king's Entry into Rouen (PR 1517, 6), by the Bailli of Rouen. Literary works which were closely linked with events of the moment also tended to receive fairly short-term privileges. Pierre Gringore, always topical, advertised privileges for under a year (PR 1509, 3; PR 1510, 2). Laurent Desmoulins had about four months for a *Déploration* on the death of Anne of Brittany (PR 1514, 1), and an anonymous author's eulogy on the mother of the new king, Louise of Savoy, three months (PR 1515, 2). Where every week, or in some cases every day, that passed might matter to the person bearing the expenses of having such things printed, it was natural to apply to a lower court; the appeal of them to the public might have waned before an application had been considered by the Parlement (let alone the royal chancery), whereas almost immediate action might be hoped for from the Prévôt.

Privileges for one full year are also much more numerous among those granted by the Prévôt than in those by the royal chancery or by the Parlement. Some were given for literary works apparently judged too slight to warrant a longer term, such as Gringore's *Les folles entreprises* (PR 1505, 1) and *Les Abuz du Monde* (PR 1509, 6), or *Le Cymetiere des Malheureux* by Desmoulins (PR 1511, 2). Likewise one year was granted by the Lieutenant General of the Bailli of Rouen to Pierre Fabri's *Le defensore de la concepcion de la glorieuse vierge Marie* (PR 1514, 5). Others represented a reduction in the term requested by an applicant: for instance, three years were asked for in at least two instances (PR 1517, 7 and PR 1522, 1) when only one year was allowed. The very few one-year privileges granted by the royal chancery or by the Parlement concern publications of mainly topical interest. The two earliest Parlement privileges were for one year only and relate to current events (PA 1507, 1 and PA 1508, 1). Thereafter up to 1527 the one known single-year grant by the Parlement of Paris was for a papal Bull (PA 1520, 1). The only known one-year grants issued by the royal chancery, both to Galliot Du Pré, were for an account by Montjoie, King of Arms, of the tournament held in Paris to celebrate the state entry into Paris of Mary Tudor as queen of France (CH 1514, 5), and for an anonymous pamphlet by a royal apologist denouncing the treaty of Madrid (CH 1526, 1).

Even at the *prévôté* of Paris, a tendency can be observed from about 1520 onwards to give somewhat longer privileges. After that date I have found no privilege given by the Prévôt for less than a year, and only one for one year. If he kept in line with the practice of the Parlement, he was more generous in the issue of three-year privileges: he gave nine three-year grants in 1520 where the Parlement appears only to have given nine in the course of the whole period. In 1521 the Prévôt even began to give privileges for four years, a concession hitherto given only by the royal chancery. He had, however, given no more than four of these by 1526, and then for substantial books (PR 1521, 2; 1521, 4; 1524, 2; 1525, 1). And on two occasions about this time he granted only three years where four had been requested (PR 1521, 4 and PR 1523, 5). Moreover, he granted three years on the only occasion before 1526 when the choice of the term of years was left entirely to him and was not specified in the application (PR 1523, 3), the occasion being a Greek-Latin dictionary.

From 1517 onwards, books printed 'Cum priuilegio', without stating which authority had issued the privilege, sometimes provide information on the duration of it. There are twenty-six such books. Ten advertise a privilege for two years, and sixteen for three years.

To sum up: the practice of the royal chancery, beginning with privileges of two years, soon stabilised at three years (over 58 per cent), though by 1526 some shorter and some longer grants had been made; the sovereign courts treated three years as a maximum, and two years as a norm; the Prévôt of Paris and other royal officers usually granted two or three years for books, and sometimes much less for pamphlets and newsletters. It appears therefore that two or three years, depending on the estimated cost of producing the book, was regarded by the authorities in France up to 1526 as the standard duration for a book of any consequence.

Five years after the end of the period under consideration here, the city of Basle decided, instead of issuing endless individual privileges, to make a general rule for its own printers. Henceforth no Basle printer should reprint another Basle printer's copy until three years from the date of publication. The city was one of the greatest international centres of the European printing and publishing industry, and the authorities must have taken careful advice before making such a decree, as it was to be strictly enforced. The duration was evidently calculated, it has been remarked, to allow an edition of a successful book to be sold.[1] In the light of this rule, French practice in the period up to 1526 in determining the duration of privileges may be considered reasonable.

HOW RECKONED (DATE OF GRANT, DATE OF PUBLICATION, ETC.)

Whatever the duration of the privilege, its useful life from the point of view of the beneficiary depended on the date from which it was reckoned. At the opening of the period with which we are here concerned there could be no doubt about the reckoning. Letters Patent issued in the name of the king or by his officers took effect from the date when they were sealed, and judgements of the courts took effect as soon as they had been given. Authors and publishers, seeking a new kind of favour from a long-established system, at first took this for granted. And indeed, if the work, whether book or pamphlet, which they sought to protect was ready or almost ready to put on sale, they had no reason to wish for anything else. It was not, however, always to the applicant's advantage that the concession should be reckoned from the date when it was obtained. The most convenient moment for him to apply to the royal chancery, to the Parlement, or the Prévôt or Bailli of his area, or the moment when his application succeeded, might be well ahead of the date when he

---

[1] Basel St. A. Ratsbücher A 6, 22ᵛ, 18 October 1531, quoted by Martin Steinmann, *Johannes Oporinus* (Basle/Stuttgart, 1966), p. 56. Dr Steinmann comments, 'Die Frist war offenbar so berechnet, dass die Auflage eines erfolgreichen Buches abgesetzt werden konnte', and he adds, 'Die Bestimmung wurde streng befolgt.' Three years was stated by Willem Vorsterman of Antwerp in 1514 to have been the recognised though unofficial time which printers in Brabant allowed a colleague to sell a new book. See above, pp. 15–16.

could expect to complete the printing and publishing of the book. Every day's delay in bringing out the book then shortened the period of usefulness of his privilege. It soon dawned on applicants that in these circumstances, they should try to obtain an additional concession, namely that the duration of the privilege should run from the date when the book was published, whenever that was. The courts did not prove very cooperative in allowing these delays. The royal chancery was more obliging.

The five earliest book-privileges to be issued from the French royal chancery all state or imply that the duration of the favour should be reckoned from the date of the grant. Three specify 'à compter du jour et dacte de la presentacion de cesdictes presentes' (CH 1508, 1; 1509, 1; 1511, 2); one says simply 'jusques à trois ans' (CH 1509, 2) and one 'jusques à troys ans prochainement venans' (CH 1511, 3). Of these five, one (CH 1509, 2) illustrates the risks to which this limitation might expose the beneficiary. The holder of it, Jean Lemaire de Belges, had obtained it at Lyon, 30 July 1509, for the first book of *Les illustrations de Gaule et singularitez de Troye*, but his publisher, Etienne Baland, did not bring out the first edition until May 1511, when two-thirds of the period of validity of the privilege had already expired.[1] The first privilege expressly granted to run from the date when the book or books should be completed is the important 'package' privilege obtained in 1512 by Jean Petit (CH 1512, 1), valid – in the words of Petit's Latin summary – 'ab impressione dictorum operum'.[2] Following this, Michel Le Noir obtained a privilege for the romance *Huon de Bordeaux*, 'à compter du jour et dacte que ledit livre sera achevé de imprimer' (CH 1513, 3). Le Noir not only printed the text of the privilege in full but called attention in the colophon to the fact that it was to run 'jusques à deux ans finitz et acomplys à prendre du jour que ledict livre sera imprimé qui est le .xxvi. jour de novembre mil .v. cens et treize' (f. 188). He was thus able to claim the full duration of his privilege, granted on 9 June 1513, though the book did not come out until 26 November. But the chancery on other occasions might revert to the reckoning from the issue of the grant, e.g. 'a date presentium ad triennium' (CH 1519, 7).

The Parlement of Paris almost always reckoned the duration of the privilege from the date when it was granted. The earliest Parlement privilege of which the text is extant (PR 1509, 1) was to take effect 'de huy [modern French *d'aujourd'hui*] jusques à deux ans'. Thereafter these words or similar ones are used, or else a formula like 'jusques à deux ans prochainement venans' (e.g. PA 1512, 2), which amounts to the same thing. The *conseillers* were evidently reluctant to encourage 'dog-in-the-manger' publishers who kept the public waiting indefinitely for the privileged book or books to appear. In any case, their policy of inspecting every book submitted to them before deciding whether to grant a privilege at all virtually ruled out publications for

---

[1] J. Abélard, *Les illustrations de Gaule*, pp. 59–60.   [2] See below, pp. 131–4.

which there were only vague plans. The Parlement made an exception for a small number of serious new works on scholastic philosophy of which Jean Granjon, one of the university's *libraires jurés*, was in each case joint or sole publisher: it specified that the first (PA 1509, 3) should run 'depuys le jour qu'il sera achevé de imprimer', the second, for two books (PA 1516, 8), 'à commencer au jour qu'ilz seront parachevez de imprimer', and later (PA 1517, 6) directing that the grant should be reckoned 'à commencer du jour que lesdicts livres seront parachevés de imprimer'. The 1517 publication was a massive work, nothing less than the *Reportata* or lectures of Duns Scotus on the four books of the *Sentences*, edited by three leading philosophers of the Paris Faculty of Theology. Each of the four parts constituted a large folio volume, separately dated, and it was well into the following year before Granjon had completed the whole undertaking. The Parlement was probably able to inspect the edited manuscript from which Granjon proposed to print, and perhaps specimens of the printed pages of the first volume. It is understandable that the Parlement should make a special concession for a publication of such importance to all students of scholastic philosophy, which would be slow and costly to produce.

Another exceptional case was the privilege granted by the Parlement to Constantin Fradin of Lyon (PA 1520, 2). This was obtained by Fradin on 20 December 1520, and it specified that his term of two years should run from the year 1521 ('jusques au terme de deux ans commençant à l'an mille cinq cens .xxi.'). Fradin could well have pleaded that, as he had to travel back to Lyon in mid-winter, and would not be able to begin printing until the Christmas holidays were over, it would be a serious diminution of his grant to insist on reckoning it from 20 December, especially as two books were included in the privilege. The Parlement probably meant 1521 o.s. which would give him until Easter (20 April 1521). And in fact one of them, the *Arismethique* of Etienne de La Roche, was not completed until 2 June. The 'package' privilege obtained by Claude Chevallon (PA 1519, 4) was to run 'jusques à deux ans finiz et accompliz, à commencer du jour que ledit livre sera achevé de imprimer' in the case of each book. But for this provision, the privilege would have expired before all the books had been published, for the last did not come out until 1523, though Chevallon may well have been able to show them all in manuscript to the Parlement in 1519. The Parlement also allowed Badius and Petit to reckon their privilege for the works of Hugh of St Victor from the date when the book should be completed ('jusques à deux ans à compter du jour qu'ilz seront parachevez'), which to some extent made up for the reduction of its duration from the six years requested by the publishers to two years (PA 1526, 2). These concessions did not signal a change of policy on the part of the Parlement. Simon de Colines asked in an application in 1524 for a privilege to run 'jusques à deux ans apres ladicte impression parachevée' (PA 1524, 10), and again in 1525 (PA 1525, 8): on both occasions the

Parlement gave him his two years simply 'jusques à deux ans prochainement venans', thus tacitly rejecting the request for the deferred privilege.

The practice of the provincial Parlements seems to have been to reckon the duration of the privilege from the date of the grant, to judge by the few examples of book-privileges given by them of which the text is printed in the books in question. The only specimen available for the Echiquier or Parlement of Rouen specifies 'deux ans du jour et date de ces presentes' (PA 1516, 3). The Parlement of Toulouse gave privileges 'durant le terme de deux ans prochains venant' (PA 1517, 3), 'D'huy à trois ans' (PA 1517, 5), 'à compter du jour de la date de ces presentes' (PA 1522, 7), 'durant le terme de cinq ans prochainement venant' (PA 1523, 2), and – just after the period here under consideration – 'Troys ans à compter de la date de ces presentes' (PA 1527, 1).

The courts of the Prévôt of Paris, and of the Baillis in the provinces, were also wary of granting deferred privileges. A grant issued on behalf of the Bailli of Rouen in 1514 was to run for one year, from the date of the grant ('d'un an du jour d'uy', PR 1514, 5). Twelve grants issued by the Prévôt of Paris in 1516–20 inclusive, of which the terms are known, all specify that they are to be reckoned from the date on which they were given. In 1520 an application to the Prévôt by Pierre Le Brodeur requested three years 'à compter du jour que ledit livre sera achevé de imprimer' but he received 'trois ans prochainement venans' (PR 1520, 12). Thereafter, of the privileges issued by the Prévôt which are known in detail, up to 1526, only four were to be reckoned from the date of completion (PR 1521, 2; 1521, 5; 1524, 1; 1525, 1).

A deferred privilege, valid from whenever the book in question should be printed and published, was not subject to any restriction during this period in France. The authorities could have stipulated that publication should take place by some particular date, as Charles V's Privy Council did in 1517 in giving a four-year privilege for the 'Divisiekronieck'.[1] They did not do so.

PRIVILEGES FOR TWO OR MORE BOOKS, AND 'PACKAGE' PRIVILEGES

Most of the privileges in the period up to 1526 inclusive were given for one particular book. An author or publisher who had two books ready or nearly ready at the same time was free to ask that both should be included in the same privilege. This was evidently regarded as a reasonable request. The royal chancery gave at least thirteen such privileges, and even the Parlement of Paris gave eight.

Requests for the privilege to include *more* than two books were probably rare. Few publishers had three or more first editions ready at the same time.

[1] See above, pp. 18–19.

The 'deferred' privilege, giving the holder the right to reckon the duration from the date when the book should be published, did however open the way for a publisher with an important series of first editions in prospect to secure a privilege for all of them in advance. Only very well-organised and very substantial publishers could be in this position. Most publishers lived a much more hand-to-mouth existence. But grants for a veritable 'package' of new books *were* sought and granted occasionally within the royal chancery. There were at least some Italian precedents: five or six items were included in a Milan privilege of 1498.[1] The beneficiary must have found the proceeding more saving of time and money than seeking a fresh privilege for each book as he brought it out, even if the fees and the gratuities demanded were larger at the time.

The royal chancery

The chancery never granted, any more than did the Parlement, a privilege for a whole category of books, such as Bibles. On several occasions, however, it granted a privilege for a considerable number of individual books to the same author or publisher. These were enumerated, so the concession differed from the 'personal' privileges granted by Louis XII to Anthoine Vérard and to Guillaume Eustace, which evidently gave them 'carte blanche' to claim automatically, from then onwards, a privilege in any book which they should be the first to publish.

Thus a privilege was obtained by Nicole Bohier for four different works composed or edited by him, all of which he planned to entrust to the Lyon publisher Simon Vincent (CII 1509, 1). They were a treatise on the powers of the Papal Legate in France, an edition of the *Coutumes* of the realm, an edition of Gulielmus Mandagotus' *Tractatus de electione* and of 'les reigles de droit'. The relevant passage of the Letters Patent reads:

certains livres l'ung desquels livres est la puissance et faculté de nostre trescher et feal cousin le cardinal d'Amboyse legat en France. L'aultre les coustumes de nostre royaulme de France additionnees en l'onneur faveur et contemplation de nostre amé et feal chancelier Jehan de Ganay chevalier; le tiers Mandagot ès honneurs et faveur de noz amez et feaulx conseillers les evesques de Roddes et d'Angolesme et l'aultre dygne des reigles de droit ... lesquelz livres de faculté coustumier Mandagot et Reigles ledit Boyer a intention faire faire imprimer par un nommé Symon Vincent.

The extract from the text of the privilege is here quoted from the Mandagotus where it is printed in full, enumerating all four works. Bohier's editing of the *Coutumes* was in fact confined to the *Coutume* of Bourges. At least the first three of the works mentioned were duly published in the course of 1509.

Another royal privilege granted to an author for several different books was that obtained by Jean Lode, 'licencié en loix et tenant tutelle en l'université

---

[1] See above, p. 5.

d'Orleans'. Lode had composed two little dialogues in Latin hexametres, one entitled 'Tymon adversus ingratos' and the other 'De iustitia et pietate Celeucri Locrorum regis'; he had edited Plutarch's *De praeceptis coniugalibus* (itself translated from Greek into Latin) and translated it into French; and he had translated the treatise of Francesco Filelfo, *De educatione liberorum*, from Latin into French, under the title *Le guidon des parents en l'instruction et direction de leurs enfans*. (His publisher, Gilles de Gourmont, had printed the Latin original of this in 1508.) The Filelfo, an attractive little book, came out in 1513, the Plutarch about the same time, undated; both give the privilege in full (CH 1513, 2), complete with the titles of all the books covered by it.

Publishers might make a case for a 'package' covering a whole group of books, unconnected by the tie of common authorship, and linked only by the fact that they all formed part of the applicant's publishing programme over the next few months or years.

A privilege of this kind, printed in full in each of the four books it covered, was obtained by Michel Le Noir in 1517 (CH 1517, 6). The project was indeed a notable one, comprising the first editions of *L'instruction d'ung jeune prince* (by Ghillebert de Lannoy), of a modern version of the romance *Guerin de Montglane*, of the famous story *Le petit Jean de Saintré* by Antoine de La Sale, and of an edition of *Les passaiges d'oultremer faitz par les françoys*, an account of the crusades by Sebastien Mamerot enlarged and brought up to date with the Spanish conquest of Granada, all very well printed. The text of the privilege leaves no doubt that it was granted for all four books on the same occasion, and that it was to run in each case for three years from the date when the book was completed ('qu'il puisse et luy soit loysible imprimer ou faire imprimer lesdictz livres dessusdictz mentionez jusques à trois ans prochainement venant, à compter du jour et dacte que lesdictz livres seront imprimez, sans que durant ledict temps aulcuns libraires, imprimeurs ne autres puissent iceulx livres imprimer ou faire imprimer ne vendre'). Accordingly Le Noir was able to space out the four editions at his leisure and still get the full benefit of his three-year privilege, granted on 12 August 1517, for each. According to the colophons, *L'instruction d'ung jeune prince* was completed on 26 January 1517 (1518 n.s.), *Le petit Jehan de Saintré* on 15 March 1517 (1518 n.s.), and *Les passaiges d'Oultremer* on 27 November 1518.

Another fully documented 'package' privilege obtained from the royal chancery by a publisher was that granted to Durand Gerlier in 1519 (CH 1519, 2). Gerlier was the holder of the royal privilege for the text of the Concordat concluded between Francis I and the Papacy. When he received further material relevant to the Concordat (additional papal bulls etc.) to print with it, he applied for a new privilege. At the same time, he took the opportunity of including in his application two other books which he planned to print. One was a translation into French of the Georgics of Virgil, which he had commissioned from Guillaume Michel de Tours: the other was the

Protocol formulary or *stille* in use by the notaries of the court of the Prévôt of Paris, the Châtelet. Accordingly the privilege was granted to him for 'lesditz concordatz avecques icelles bulles et nos lettres ainsi à luy baillees que dict est pour y adjouter, ensemble les dessusdictz Georgicques et formulaire'.

Durand Gerlier had good reason to wish to advertise his privilege for the Concordat, and it is not surprising to find him printing the whole privilege word for word, all four pages of it, in the translation of the Georgics when he published it. It must none the less have seemed mainly irrelevant to readers of the Georgics. And not all publishers attached this amount of importance to printing the whole text of a privilege, including details of books other than the one in hand.

The 'package' privileges already described are authenticated by the full text of the original Letters Patent printed in one or more of the books in question. There are however three other and more far-reaching 'package' privileges, two granted to Jean Petit and one to Regnault Chaudière, which are not overtly advertised in this way by the beneficiaries: Petit alludes to them only in printed summaries. The existence of these three 'package' privileges becomes apparent only after comparing with each other the privileges referred to in several individual books issued by the same publisher. Nothing at first sight suggests that the privilege, summarised in one of these books, included any other publications than the one at which the reader is looking. Only scrutiny of the details shows that several different books refer to exactly the same Letters Patent, identified by the same place and date, the same secretary's signature, the same duration of the privilege and the same concession that the duration should be reckoned from the eventual date of publication of the book. There was no possible motive for concealing the 'package': the decision in Petit's case to omit the full text of the Letters Patent, and to suppress the titles of the other books enumerated in them, seems to have been dictated by considerations of saving work and saving space, which must have outweighed whatever advantage there might have been in advertising the other books in this way as available or forthcoming or in preparation. Chaudière prints the whole document except for the titles of other books covered by the same privilege.

The first clue to the existence of his first and largest 'package' privilege is provided by Jean Petit in a publication of 1512, the Lent sermons of Jean Raulin, one of the most popular and respected preachers in Paris at the time (CH 1512, 1(1)). Petit had obtained a Parlement privilege for this volume of Raulin's sermons on 5 March (PA 1512, 1), for two years where he had requested three. Only a few days later, at Blois on 12 March, he succeeded in getting a grant from the royal chancery which not only gave him the desired three years but covered other books as well (CH 1512, 1). He did not publish the royal privilege in its entirety in the Raulin Lent sermons, but he had the following summary printed there immediately after the text of his Parlement privilege:

Et oultre ledict Jehan Petit a obtenu du Roy nostre sire lettres patentes datees du .xij. jour de Mars, L'an mil cinqcentz et unze [1512 n.s.] par lesquelles est permis à icelluy Petit imprimer / et faire imprimer ce present livre et autres livres nommez esdictes lettres / et d'iceulx faire son profict ainsi que font et ont acoustumé faire les autres imprimeurs. Et est defendu à tous autres de ne imprimer ce present livre durant le temps de trois ans apres que ledict Petit l'aura imprimé / ou fait imprimer / ne eulx en mesler en maniere que ce soit / non obstans quelzonques ordonnances / inhibitions / ou defenses à ce contraires.
Donné à Bloys l'an et jour desusditz. Par le Roy. Et signé Geuffroy.

What were the 'other books named in the said Letters Patent'?

At least seven other books have come to light, each published by a partnership of which Jean Petit was one and each summarising the same three-year privilege granted to Jean Petit and his partners at Blois on 12 March 1512 (n.s.), signed by the secretary Geuffroy, reckoning the duration of the privilege from the date of publication of the book, which is duly inserted.

The first of these seven books to come out was a classic of scholastic philosophy, the commentary by Adam Godham or Woodham (d. 1358), pupil and defender of Ockham, on the *Sentences*. It was published jointly by Jean Petit, Jean Granjon and Poncet Le Preux, printed for them by Jean Barbier (CH 1512, 1(2)). It carries the following statement on the verso of the title-page:

¶ Le Roy nostre sire a donné privilege troys ans à Jehan Petit et à Jehan Granjon et à Poncet le Preux / Libraires juréz de l'université de Paris. pour ce present livre Adam Super Sententiis de imprimer ce dit livre. Et defent à tous aultres imprimeurs et libraires de ce Royaulme de non imprimer ne faire imprimer vendre / ne distribuer aultres que ceulx que lesditz libraires auront fait imprimer de ce jourdhuy .xij. jour d'avril. M.ccccc. et xij. sur peine de confiscacion desditz livres et d'amande arbitraire. Donné à Bletz le. xij. jour de Mars. M.ccccc. et xj. avant pasques. Par le Roy ainsy syné Geffroy.

Following this publication, with the privilege reckoned from 12 April 1512, came the *Summa in questionibus Armenorum* of Richard FitzRalph, archbishop of Armagh (d. 1360). The *Summa* was edited by Jean le Sueur, and the summary of its privilege names Jean Petit and Poncet Le Preux as the publishers and gives 15 July 1512 as the date from which the three years are to be counted (CH 1512, 1(2)). The text of the summary may be compared with that printed in the commentary of Godham:

Le roy nostre sire a donné privilayge Troys ans à Jehan Petit librayre juré de l'université de Paris Et Ponset le Preux asosié avec ledit Petit pour ce present livre *Armacanus de questionibus Hermenie* de imprimer ce dit livre. Et defent à tous autres Imprimeurs et libraytes de ce Royaume de non imprimer ne fayre imprimer vendre ne distribuer autres que ceulx que lesdis libraytes desus nommés auront fayt imprimer de ce jourduy quinsieme jour de Juillet mil cinq cens et douze jusques à troys ans inclus sur paynne de confiscation desdis livres et de amende arbitrayre. Donné à Blays le douzieme jour de mars l'an mil cinq cens et unze avant pasques. Par le Roy. Ainsi signé Geuffroy

Despite small differences of spelling (*Bletz* and *Blays* are both phonetic spellings for Blois, the 'oi' being so pronounced at this period), and the omission of Jean Granjon as a co-partner in the second, it is evident that these two summaries are invoking the same privilege.

A work of canon law, *Lectura in quinque Decretalium Gregorianarum libros*, by Cardinal Henricus Hostiensis, came out two months later, summarising the privilege given at Blois on 12 March 1512, in this instance to reckon the three-year period from 12 September 1512. It was published jointly by Jean Petit and Thielman Kerver (CH 1512, 1(4)). This time the summary of the terms of the privilege has been re-drafted, and read as follows:

¶ Le Roy nostre sire a donné et octroyé à Jehan Petit libraire juré de l'université de Paris. Et Thielman Kerver Imprimeur et libraire juré en ladicte université Privilege de troys ans pour ce present livre intitulé *La lecture d'Hostiense sur les decretales* de imprimer et faire imprimer. Et a defendu et defend à tous autres de ce royaulme de non imprimer ne faire imprimer: vendre: ne distribuer autres que ceulx que lesditz libraires dessus nommez auront faict imprimer: ne eulx en mesler en maniere que ce soit du jour dhuy xij. de semptembre mil cinq centz et douze jusques à troys ans revolus et acomplis. Non obstant quelsconques ordonnances / inhibicions / ou defenses à ce contraires sur certaines grandes peines à plain et bien au long declarees ès lettres du dessusdict privilege. Donné à Bloys le douziesme jour de Mars L'an Mil cinq centz et unze. Par le Roy. Et signé Geuffroy.

This statement, as printed in the Hostiensis, is repeated word for word in four subsequent books, the only alterations being (1) the names of Petit's collaborators, (2) the title of the book, and (3) the date from which the three-year privilege was to be reckoned. These four books are, in order of publication,

Origen, *Opera* ed. J. Merlin, 1512, fol. 4 vols. Jean Petit and Josse Badius, Badius being the printer of it. Privilege to run from 13 October 1512.

(CH 1512, 1(5))

Gregory of Tours, *Historia Francorum*, '1522' [*sic* for 1512], fol. Jean Petit and Josse Badius, Badius being the printer of it. Privilege to run from 3 November 1512.

(CH 1512, 1(6))

Sigebert of Gembloux, *Chronicon*, 1513, 4°. Jean Petit and Henri Estienne, Estienne being the printer of it. Privilege to run from 7 June 1513.

(CH 1512, 1(7))

Aimoinus, *De regum procerumque Francorum origine*, 1514, fol. Jean Petit and Josse Badius, Badius being the printer of it. Privilege to run from 12 August 1514.

(CH 1512, 1(8))

The Origen in addition displays, at the end of Volume IV, in a column parallel with the French statement of the privilege, a statement in Latin by

Jean Petit and Josse Badius which describes the work itself and goes on to say, 'Our Most Christian King of France Louis XII, looking at all these things with a favourable eye and weighing them in a just balance, has granted privilege to the bookseller and printer, that no one in his aforesaid kingdom should be so bold as to reprint or cause to be reprinted the said works during the next three years after the printing of the said works, or to sell any printed elsewhere, on pain of the severe penalty contained in the document drawn up on this matter...' and then introduces the French summary 'lest someone should allege ignorance as an excuse'.[1]

The original Letters Patent alluded to in all eight books, granted at Blois on 12 March 1512 (n.s.), must then have been granted to Jean Petit for all these books, some ready for publication, others in preparation, for a period of three years, to be reckoned in each case from the date of their completion whatever that might be. The programme was large and costly even by Petit's standards, and after the Raulin sermons each of these publications was issued in partnership with another leading Paris publisher. Indeed the terms of the Letters Patent were evidently drawn up so as to include his partners in the enterprise whoever they might be, as did, for instance, the privilege alluded to in a later publication of Petit (CH 1521, 3) which expressly forbade the sale of copies 'autres que ceulx que ledit libraire et sesdits compaignons font imprimer', the book in question being in fact published by Petit in partnership with François Regnault. This is how the summary of the 1512 privilege printed by Henri Estienne in the *editio princeps* of Sigebert of Gembloux (CH 1512, 1(7)), published jointly by Petit and Estienne, could quite legitimately refer to the privilege as having been granted to Petit and Estienne, though this makes it appear at first sight as if it were a different grant from that invoked by, for example, Petit and Badius in another book, such as the Origen (CH 1512, 1(5)). The advantage presumably was, that any copies of the edition bearing the name and mark of the partner rather than that of Petit could be clearly seen as protected by Petit's privilege. The reluctance of Petit and his partners and printers to reproduce the full text of the Letters Patent does not have anything suspicious about it. The document must have been very long, and to print summaries was quite a common practice.[2]

Before the privilege had expired on the Aimoinus, Jean Petit had secured another 'package' privilege from the royal chancery. This was obtained from the new king, Francis I, at Lyon on 24 July 1515, and was signed by the

---

[1] Quae omnia christianissimus Francorum Rex noster Ludouicus duodecimus equissimo oculo perspiciens et iusta lance pensitans; priuilegium bibliopolæ et impressori concessit: ne quis in dicto regno suo audeat eadem opera intra triennium proximum ab impressione dictorum operum rursus imprimere: aut imprimendi curare: aut alibi impressa venundare sub graui poena in instrumento super ea facto contenta: cuius ne quis ignorantiæ velum sibi prætendat: etiam gallicis verbis tenorem adiunximus extractum.

[2] See below, p. 144.

secretary J. Bartélemy (CH 1515, 5), again for three years, to be reckoned from the date of publication of each of the books included in it. The text of this privilege, like that granted to Petit by Louis XII at Blois 12 March 1512, was never published by Petit in its entirety, but it is referred to in a number of books brought out by Petit in the course of the following few years, which have so far been identified as follows, in order of their publication:

11 Sept.	1515	Jérôme de Hangest, *De causis*	(CH 1515, 5(1))
8 Nov.	1515	Jean Raulin, *Sermones in aduentu*	(CH 1515, 5(2))
31 April	1518	Jean Raulin, *Doctrinale mortis*	(CH 1515, 5(3))
13 June	1519	Jérôme de Hangest, *Moralia*	(CH 1515, 5(4))
15 Oct.	1519	Peter of Blois, *Opera*, ed. J. Merlin	(CH 1515, 5(5))
23 March	1520	Jean Raulin, *Sermones de Eucharistia*	(CH 1515, 5(6))
27 Aug.	1528	Jérôme de Hangest, *De possibili praeceptorum diuinorum impletione in Lutherum*	(CH 1515, 5(7))
17 Aug.	1529	Jérôme de Hangest, *Aduersus antimarianos propugnaculum*	(CH 1515, 5(8))

In the last-mentioned of these books, the summary provided by Jean Petit reads as follows:

Le Privilege
Le Roy nostre Sire a donné privilege trois ans à Jehan Petit Libraire juré de l'université de Paris pour tous les livres composés de nouveau par nostre maistre de Hangest dont ce present livre en est intitulé *Propugnaculum Mariae in Antimarianos* et deffend à tous aultres imprimeurs et libraires de ce royaulme imprimer ou faire imprimer vendre ou distribuer autres que ceulx que ledict libraire faict imprimer de ce jourdhuy xviie jour d'aoust Mil cinq cens xxix que ledit livre a esté achevé de imprimer jusques à trois ans finis et accomplis sur peine de confiscation desdicts livres et de amende arbitrairc. Et fut ce privilege donné audit libraire à Lion, le xxiiiie jour de Julliet L'an Mil cinq cens et quinze.
Par le Roy   Ainsi signé   Bartelmy [sic]

There are recognisable links between some of these items and the contents of Petit's earlier 'package' privilege (CH 1512, 1). Sermons of Jean Raulin had featured in the previous privilege. Jacques Merlin, editor of the 1519 Peter of Blois, had edited Origen for Petit's earlier series (CH 1512, 1(5)). The provision in the 1515 'package' privilege for the works of Jérôme de Hangest, on the other hand, represents the most extraordinary extension to be found in this period of the effects of a 'package' privilege, providing as it does for cover of works which were not published until fourteen or fifteen years later and which, being aimed at Luther, cannot by their very nature even have been planned at the time when the 'package' was obtained. The last work by Hangest in the list, the *Propugnaculum*, is the only one where Petit's summary of the privilege includes the vital clause, namely, that the privilege was for all new works composed by Hangest ('pour tous les livres composés de nouveau par nostre maistre de Hangest, dont ce present livre en est'). Whether the chancery fully realised the implications of this concession or not, it meant that, as long as Petit and Hangest were both alive, they could go on invoking the privilege of 24 July 1515 for Hangest's new publications. Petit was a powerful figure in the French book-trade; Hangest was wealthy and aristocratic and could wield considerable influence. Even so, such a grant created a remarkable precedent and it was not until many years later that it was in fact matched by any 'package' privilege. It may, incidentally, serve as a warning that if a privilege sometimes seems to be wrongly dated because it covers a book dealing with events which had not yet taken place when the privilege was granted, the possibility that it formed part of a generously worded 'package' privilege should not be forgotten.

Another substantial three-year 'package' privilege, though not on the scale of the two obtained by Jean Petit, was the one granted to Regnault Chaudière at Saint-Germain-en-Laye on 3 May 1519 (CH 1519, 6). Chaudière had been to the court at Saint-Germain exactly a month before to get a privilege for two separate works of Claude de Seyssel (CH 1519, 4, 3 April 1519), but this time he had secured the *magnum opus* of Seyssel, *La grant monarchie de France*, and had lined up in addition at least four other new books. The privilege of 3 May 1519, signed 'Par le roy, l'evesque de Troyes, confesseur, et aultres presens, Gedoyn', is printed in its entirety in each of these five books, except that only the book in question is named, the other titles being omitted. Thus, as in the two Jean Petit 'package' privileges already described, it is only comparison of the books with each other which reveals that it is the same privilege which is invoked by all of them. (Gedoyn's signature, which was evidently very hard to decipher, was misread as Hedoyn by four of them and as Godoyn by one: this is the only variation between them.) Chaudière's was a more restricted publishing 'package' than those of Jean Petit: even so, it was 1521 before he had brought out all five books covered by his privilege of 3 May 1519. Seyssel's *La grant monarchie de France* was completed on 21 July 1519; *Le Livre de la discipline d'amour divine* on 28 November 1519; Ravisius Textor's *Officina* on 27 November 1520; Le Cirier's *Tractatus de iure primogeniturae* on 1 February 1521 (Chaudière specifies that this is *calculo romano*, i.e. new style); while *Quatre voyes spirituelles pour aller à Dieu* is undated.

Lesser 'package' privileges obtained from the royal chancery which have come to light, relating to a group of *three* different books, often similarly omit any mention of other books covered by the same privilege when printed or summarised by the beneficiary. (CH 1514, 3; 1515, 7; 1517, 1; and 1519, 3 if we treat Patricius' *De regno*, and the French translation of it as two separate items.) None of them show any notable delay, on the privilege-holder's part, in using the privilege.

The Parlement and the Prévôt of Paris

In the case of the Parlement of Paris, an early example of a two-book privilege is provided by the registers of the court, which show that on 13 July 1512 Henry Estienne obtained a privilege for the first edition of the Antonine Itinerary and for the *Oratio de laude Ludouici regis* of Christophe de Longueil or Longolius (PA 1512, 7). Two years later, Jean de Gourmont was granted a privilege for works of Sabellicus on the history of Venice and also for an *Elucidarius carminum poetarum* (PA 1514, 1). Unlike Henri Estienne, who had not judged it necessary to print the text of his privilege in the books, Gourmont printed an 'Extraict des registres de Parlement' in each of the two publications, specifying 'deux petitz livres, l'un appellé Magnus Elucidarius carminum poetarum et l'autre appellé parva opera Sabellici.' Some publishers however, even when otherwise giving the full text of the 'Extraict des registres de Parlement' in a book, included only the title of the book in question, and omitted the other book or books covered by the same privilege. It may have seemed to them or to their printers irrelevant and even confusing to include them, and obviously to leave them out saved time and space. Thus Constantin Fradin published the *Arismethique* of Etienne de La Roche, with 'Cum priuilegio' on the title-page and the 'Extraict des registres de Parlement' on the verso, and the 'Extraict' as there printed begins:

Sur la requeste ce jour d'uy baillée à la court par Constantin Fradin imprimeur et librayre en la ville de Lyon par la quelle il requeroit luy estre permis de imprimer ou fayre imprimer ung livre d'arismethique et geometrie novellement composé par maistre Estienne de La Roche dict Villefranche: Et defenses estre faictes à tous Imprimeurs et librayres ne imprimer ne faire imprimer ledit livre . . .

and records the court's grant of the privilege for 'ledit livre'. But we know, from the original of the entry in the Parlement register, that Fradin had in fact sought and obtained a privilege for this and another book, *Le Guidon en françoys* by Jean Falcon (PA 1520, 2). And when we turn to *Le Guidon en francoys*, as published by Fradin the same year as the *Arismethique*, we find exactly the same privilege printed in it but without any mention of the *Arismethique*. Clearly Fradin thought it a waste of time and space to mention the other book. The more books covered by a privilege, the greater the printer's reluctance to include all the titles when he reproduced it.

Normally the Parlement did not grant privileges to the same applicant on the same date for more than two books. It was clearly its policy to see any book for which a privilege was sought, before reaching a decision. This tended to exclude privileges for a larger group of books. The applicant would presumably have to produce the copy from which he proposed to have them printed, and this presupposed an exceptionally well-organised programme. Furthermore, the Parlement was reluctant to allow its privileges to be reckoned from the date of publication.

There are however two instances, neither of them recorded in the extant registers of the Parlement, where a privilege had evidently been granted for a whole group of books on the same occasion, one for four books and the other for five. Comparison between books all claiming a privilege given by the Parlement to the same publisher on the same date, and authenticated by the same signatory, makes this clear. The first of them was granted to Guillaume Eustace on 6 September 1512 (PA 1512, 9(1–4)). It is printed in full by Eustace in the *Stilus parlamenti curie*, drawn up originally by Guillermus de Brolio, and edited by Antoine Robert, the *greffier criminel* of the court.[1] The text of the privilege, as printed in the book itself, speaks only of this particular book, 'ne imprimerent seu imprimere facerent Stilum dicte nostre curie in latino per se nuper impressum'. But we find exactly the same privilege issued on 6 September 1512 and signed by Robert, in a translation into Latin of the Farce of Pathelin, *Comedia noua que Veterator inscribitur, alias Pathelinus*, also published by Guillaume Eustace, this time mentioning only the *Comedia noua* and making no reference to the *Stilus*. And it is claimed in two other publications of Guillaume Eustace, an *Ordinatio seu declaratio facta super xiii punctis stili*, and the *Ordonnances de parlement touchant tous especialement les parties qui y ont à plaidier* (1512). One can only conclude that the original privilege of 6 September 1512 covered all four publications, and that Guillaume Eustace, seeing no reason to mention all four in reprinting the text of the privilege, omitted the three other titles. At least the 'package' sought by Eustace had a certain coherence: all the items included in it were directly connected with the Parlement itself, even the Farce of Pathelin, since the play probably originated in the *Basoche* or social club of the Paris law students and included scenes in court, with the presiding magistrate ending the case by inviting the 'rogue' advocate Pathelin to dinner. A privilege of three books can also be detected among the Parlement grants for 1517 (PA 1517, 9). These were three separate works on Aristotle by the Spanish Paris theologian Juan de Celaya, one published with the date 1517 and two with the date 1518; the publisher, Hémon Le Fèvre, displayed in each of the three books a privilege granted by the Parlement on 31 December 1517, the *Extraict des registres* signed by Antoine Robert. Finally, there appears in several books published between 1519 and 1523 by Claude Chevallon a two-year Parlement privilege dated 29 August 1519 and authenticated by Robert (in one of them misprinted Robertet, the name of an important royal secretary of state, the compositor having perhaps heard of him and taken the paraph after Robert's signature for 'et'). The latest book to show it is a collection of Sunday sermons, *Sermones dominicales*, by the Dominican theologian Guillaume Pepin, a popular preacher, which was completed by Chevallon on 18 June 1523. On the verso of the title-page is printed the 'Extraict des registres de Parlement': the only book there

---

[1] See above, p. 70.

mentioned is the *Sermones dominicales*. Two earlier works by Guillaume Pepin however display the same privilege granted to Chevallon on 29 August 1519; the *Super confiteor* (24 September 1519) and the *Rosarium aureum mysicum* (18 January 1520 n.s.), with very small variations easily accounted for by the compositor's haste or carelessness, e.g. *Super confiteor* omits the words 'vendre ne faire vendre' the first time. The same privilege appears in Chevallon's edition of Michel Menot's *De federe et pace inuenda* (1519), and in the copies (of which only one survives) issued in Chevallon's name of Armand de Bellevue's *Sermones ex Psalterio*, a joint publication by Chevallon, Josse Badius and Jean Le Messier (the printer of it) in 1519, both these books probably dating from the months following the grant of the privilege which would according to Old Style dating still be 1519 until Easter. The inclusion of five books in the same privilege is thus evident. This and a clause 'à commencer du jour que ledit livre sera achevé de imprimer', allowing Chevallon to reckon the duration from the publication-date of each book, enabled him to spread out the use of the privilege over almost four years (PA 1519, 4), making this the nearest approach to a 'package' privilege to be granted by the Parlement.

No 'package' privileges are known to have been granted during this period by the Prévôt of Paris. Possibly the officials of the *prévôté* thought them a favour which only the royal chancery could confer. Possibly applicants feared to rely on the Prévôt for such a long-term commitment, knowing that the holder of the office and his lieutenants could be removed at any time by the king and replaced by someone else who might take a different view of such grants. There is indeed only one certain instance of the Prévôt granting a privilege for even two separate works (PR 1526, 2) and a possible instance of a privilege for three works (PR 1523, 1).

7 · DISPLAY AND ADVERTISEMENT OF PRIVILEGES

CHOICE OF POSITION IN BOOKS: PRINTING IN FULL OR SUMMARY

Throughout the period 1498–1526 printers, publishers and authors enjoyed complete freedom to advertise possession of a privilege as they thought best.

The first French-printed book to obtain a privilege (CH 1498, 1) was the *Canon* of Avicenna with the commentary of Jacques Despars. This great book was undertaken by Johann Trechsel, a German printer who had settled in Lyon. In his favour, or that of his heirs, a royal privilege was obtained for five years. This privilege is known through a summary of it incorporated in the prefatory letter by Janus Lascaris, under the heading 'Operis huius magistri Jacobi de Partibus in Auicennam nuncupatio ac priuilegii ne alibi imprimatur aut aliunde aduehatur manifestatio.'[1] In the latter part of this letter, beginning 'Quod ut sine preiudicio aut damno impressorum in lucem edatur', we recognise behind the Latin paraphrase the terms of Letters Patent issued by the royal chancery, but there is nothing to say where or when it was granted, or by whom it is signed.

This is a very literary way of notifying the privilege. The same procedure was followed by Conrad Celtes, when he edited the works of Hroswitha in 1501:[2] the imperial privilege, one of the first if not the first to be granted for a book, is paraphrased in his preface, in terms which leave no doubt about its scope, but there is no mention of it on the title-page and no details as to where, when and by whom it was signed. It was clearly only appropriate as long as the privilege of the king of France or of the emperor was a quite exceptional favour. It did not serve as a precedent.

In any case, the end of the book, rather than the beginning, was the position in which most readers at the close of the fifteenth century would expect to find if anywhere details of the place, date and circumstances of publication. Such was the tradition in manuscripts, and many of the books in circulation were still manuscripts or early printed books which took manuscripts as their models. The title-page of a printed book was not at once developed for general

---

[1] Reproduced in A. Claudin, *Histoire de l'imprimerie en France au xv* siècle* (1900), IV, p. 88. Cf. ibid. p. 51.
[2] See above, pp. 13–14.

use by the early printers. We know it as the natural place to look not only for the author and title, but the place and date of publication, and the publisher's name – with or without his trade-mark – with notice of copyright tending in a present-day book to be printed overleaf. At the beginning of the sixteenth century in France it was still something of a novelty. Accordingly, when privileges first began (and indeed occasionally afterwards), notice that a book is published under privilege is often given only at the end, or at some other point within the volume, and with no mention on the title-page. Pierre Gringore, the earliest French author to obtain privileges for his works, began by advertising them in the colophon at the end of the book *Les folles entreprises* (PR 1505, 1) with the following statement on the verso of the last leaf:

¶ Il est dit par l'ordonnance de justice que l'acteur de cedict liure nommé Pierre Gringoire a privilege de le vendre et distribuer du jourduy jusques à ung an / sans que autre le puisse faire imprimer ne vendre fors ceulx à qui il en ballera et distribuera / et ce sur peine de confiscation des livres et d'amende arbitraire. Imprimé à Paris par maistre Pierre le Dru imprimeur pour icelluy Gringoire le .xxiii. jour de decembre. L'an mil cinq cens et cinq.

There is no other notification of the privilege, and no other particulars of it. This is certainly not an oversight. Gringore at this period was an important figure in the Paris entertainment world, as well as being a trusted supporter of government policies. He employed Le Dru to print his works, but kept the publication and sale of them in his own hands, at his house at the Sign of 'Mère Sotte' on the Pont Notre-Dame. He knew quite well what he was doing. And in 1509 he was still notifying the book-trade and the public of his privilege exclusively at the end of his books (PR 1509, 2 and 3). By 1516 on the other hand, in *Les fantasies de mère Sotte*, he had the words 'Cum priuilegio regis' printed on the title-page, and his Letters Patent printed in full on a following page, with no reference to the privilege at the end (CH 1516, 3).

Antoine Vérard first advertised in the *Epistres Sainct Pol glosées*, of which the colophon is dated 7 January 1507, that is, 1508 n.s., a privilege for three years granted to him by the king, which evidently applied to any work which he should be the first person to publish (CH 1507, 1). There is, however, no mention of this concession on the title-page. It is summarised, following the colophon, on the verso of the last leaf. By this time Vérard had been in business for over thirty years and had published eighty-three books. He too began by ignoring the title-page as a place to draw attention to his privilege. It was only after four more publications that he or the printers employed by him thought of it. He seems to have had the words 'Cum priuilegio' printed on the title-page first in *L'homme juste et l'homme mondain* (19 July 1508), and the words 'Cum priuilegio regis' for the first time in the *Dialogue monseigneur S. Grégoire* (20 March 1510 n.s.). But he continued up to the last book printed for him, in August 1512, to summarise his privilege at the end of the volume as well.

Guillaume Eustace had a new printer's mark engraved for himself on obtaining, soon after Vérard, a personal or standing privilege from the king. This incorporates the words 'Cum gratia et priuilegio regis', and was used in the books to which the privilege applied. But it was not always on the title-page that he placed it. And a summary of his privilege is almost always provided at the end of the book.

Early privileges granted by the Parlement of Paris and by the Prévôt of Paris likewise tend often to be advertised at the end of the book with no mention of them on the title-page (e.g. PA 1507, 1; PA 1508, 1; PR 1508, 1). The first printer to reproduce the text of a Parlement privilege in full, Berthold Rembolt (PA 1509, 1), placed it prominently on the verso of the title-page but did not think it necessary to mention it at all on the title-page itself. Examples can be found for a considerable time after this of privileges being well shown off in the book without any 'Cum priuilegio' formula being displayed on the title-page (e.g. PA 1511, 2; 1514, 7; 1516, 6).

An extraordinary use of the title-page to advertise a privilege was made on the other hand by the first French author to obtain Letters Patent from the royal chancery, Eloi d'Amerval (CH 1508, 1). In his *Deablerie*, the full text of the grant is printed at the end of the table of contents. But a versified summary of it, half jocular, half portentous, in the same jog-trot couplets as the *Deablerie* itself, fourteen lines of it, appears, on the title-page, immediately below a woodcut depicting the mouth of hell with devils. The idea of the versified privilege had been anticipated by an Italian man of letters, Bettin da Trezzo, in his *Letilogia*, published in 1488 at Milan.[1] It is not inconceivable that d'Amerval had seen this book. But in France at least that way of displaying the privilege, and on the title-page, was not imitated afterwards. It might well have seemed suitable only to a humourist, as d'Amerval evidently was, and to a humourist certain that the joke would be taken in good part by the prince who had granted the favour.

No printer gave the complete text of the privilege on the title page. There are, however, a few instances of very detailed summaries of the terms of the grant being given here. In the first edition (January 1515, n.s.) of *L'hystoire du sainct greeal* we see printed immediately below the mark of Michel Le Noir, who printed it, and published it with Jean Petit and Galliot Du Pré:

Avec le privilege du roy nostre sire jusques à trois ans lequel s'ensuyt. Le roy nostre sire a donné et ottroyé lettres de grace et privilege à Galiot Du Pré marchant libraire demourant à Paris de faire imprimer le livre du sainct greaal. Et deffend ledict seigneur à tous marchans libraires et aultre quelconques du royaulme de France qu'ilz ne impriment ne facent imprimer ledict livre jusques à troys ans apres ensuyvans finis et acomplis en cas de debat lesdictes inhibitions et deffences tenans nonobstant autres lettres subreptices et à ce contraires.
Donné à Paris le xxviij jour de Janvier
Mil cinq cens et quatorze.
Par le roy / et syné Bucelly   (CH 1515, 1)

---

[1] See above, p. 4.

On the title-page of the *Summula* of Raymundus de Peñaforte, a classic of canon law, with the *lucubratio* of Jean Chappuys, Thielman Kerver printed a Latin summary for the latter, beginning 'Cum priuilegio ne quis...' and explaining that it was for two years, setting out the penalties for infringement, and boasting of possession of Letters Patent to this effect bearing the royal seal (CH 1516, 4). Nearly as long is the Latin summary on the title-page of a work printed by Jean (II) Du Pré for Amédée Meigret (CH 1519, 11). It can only be supposed that these were cases in which the risk of unauthorised copying was particularly serious or considered to be so by the privilege-holder, and accordingly the one place was chosen in which it could not possibly be overlooked.

Michel Le Noir, who since 1504 had indeed good reason to be wary,[1] and who had printed the *Deablerie* of Eloi d'Amerval with the versified privilege on the title-page, was careful to ensure whenever he had a First Edition to launch that no member of the public or the trade could miss the privilege. In *Huon de Bordeaux* (CH 1513, 3) the title-page shows immediately after the full title of the romance the words 'imprimé par le congié et previlege du Roy nostre sire comme il appert à fin de la table de ce present livre': the full text of his Letters Patent is indeed printed, with a whole page to itself, at the end of the table of contents (See Plate 4, p. 86). And for good measure Le Noir works into the colophon a summary of the grant: 'lequel a previllege du Roy nostre sire que nul autre que luy ne le peult imprimer, ne faire imprimer autre que luy et ses commys, jusques à deux ans finitz et accomplys à prendre du jour que ledit livre sera imprimé qui est le xxvi jour de novembre mil v cens et treize'. Four years later he had a 'package' privilege covering Antoine de La Sale, *Le petit Jean de Saintré*, and three other books (CH 1517, 6). On the title-page of this novel he printed the words 'Cum priuilegio', and the verso of the title-page the complete text of the Letters Patent; and, at the end of the book, he again called attention to his privilege, specifying the page on which it was to be found. ('Et a previlege de trois ans que nul libraire ne autre ne le peut faire imprimer ne vendre que ceulx que ledit Noir a imprimez comme il appert plus à plain à la seconde paige de ce present livre'.)

The way in which possession of a privilege was advertised in the book which it protected was at the discretion of the printer or the publisher or author who employed him.

One of the earliest privileges issued by the royal chancery under Francis I directed that the Letters Patent should be 'written' in each copy of the book so that no one should be able to plead ignorance as an excuse for disregarding the privilege (CH 1515, 2), 'et affin que nulz ne pretendent cause de ignorance voulons que à chacun desditz livres ces presentes soient escriptes'. This provision, in the patent granted to Antoine Bonnemère for Symphorien

---

[1] See above, p. 36.

Champier's *Periarchon*, is exceptional. It may have been suggested by Bonnemère or his *procureur*, or introduced by the secretary who drew it up in the chancery, De Rillac, or Reilhac, who is not known to have signed any book-rivilege but this one.

There were, however, many beneficiaries who saw for themselves the advantage of printing the entire text of the privilege, omitting (if they omitted anything from it) only the title or titles of any other books covered by the same privilege. Among these were, in addition to Bonnemère, Michel Le Noir, Jean Petit, Galliot Du Pré, the de Marnef brothers, Regnault Chaudière, Jean de La Garde, and, in Lyon, Constantin Fradin. On the only previous occasion when Bonnemère is known to have obtained a royal privilege (CH 1514, 4) he had certainly printed the whole privilege in the book. Although summaries were preferred by some publishers and printers, and a few contented themselves with 'Cum regio priuilegio' or 'Cum priuilegio regis' on the title-page, the majority of them displayed their Letters Patent.

To print the original document conferring the privilege raised certain practical problems. Privileges issued by the royal chancery were always in the form of Letters Patent; so, occasionally, were those issued by the Prévôt of Paris. These were lengthy pieces of copy which were not part of the text. Even the 'Extraict des registres de Parlement', or the applicant's *requête* with the Prévôt's reply appended, took up a good deal of space. Where were they to be put?

Dedications, prefaces, complimentary verses and the like, which in a new book might, like privileges, reach the printer last, were traditionally placed at the beginning of the book, where they could be included in a gathering of 'prelims'. Many printers found it natural to treat privileges thus. Others still associated the end rather than the beginning of the book with providing information of a commercial kind, and associated the privilege with the colophon. A few experimented with showing it at the very end of the 'prelims', facing the first page of the book. Readers, at least, could hardly fail to notice it there, though it was less likely to catch the attention of another publisher or bookseller. The end of the book had on the other hand one obvious disadvantage: it was liable, especially if the privilege was printed on a page by itself, to become detached from the rest of the book.

The verso of the title-page was the favourite place to put the text of royal Letters Patent conferring the privilege. Out of seventy-nine books examined for this purpose, forty-seven show the text printed in this position; a further eleven are, though not on the verso of the title-page, as soon after it as other material (such as a dedication) would allow. In six cases the printer used a page not otherwise occupied at the end of the table of contents (which in French books of this period is normally at the beginning of the book), facing the first page of the book itself. In fifteen cases he printed the privilege at the end of the book. Of these fifteen cases ten are books printed in places other than Paris.

Even the practice of one and the same firm may however vary. Regnault Chaudière, an important Paris publisher who did all his own printing, provides an illustration of this variety. In two separate treatises of Claude de Seyssel, he printed his Letters Patent at the end of one, and on the verso of the title of another (CH 1519, 4 (1 and 2). On another occasion, within a group of five books covered by the same privilege (CH 1519, 6), he printed the privilege on the verso of the title in three of them and at the end of the other two.

Privileges obtained from the Parlement of Paris were generally reproduced in full in the books to which they referred. They consisted of a few lines, an authenticated transcript of the actual decision of the court, usually with the name of the clerk who had signed the transcript. The favourite place for showing them was the verso of the title-page. There are at least sixty cases of this, and another thirteen are near the beginning of the book. Only eleven appear at the end. They are rarely summarised. The earliest experiments in advertising a privilege from the Prévôt of Paris, or from some local court, usually took the form of a summary incorporated in the colophon (e.g. PR 1509, 4). When publishers began to print them *in extenso*, which was not until about 1514–16, they still at first placed them at the end of the book. This was soon abandoned in favour of the verso of the title-page. As against five at the end of the book, all before 1517, there are twenty-three on the verso of the title-page between 1516 and 1526.

Although there was an increasing tendency to standardise on the verso of the title-page, the exigencies of the moment, such as an author who insisted on his dedication or complimentary verses appearing in that position of advantage, evidently sometimes caused the privilege to be placed later in the book.

PRESENTATION

In addition to determining where to print the privilege, and whether to print it in full or not, the compositor or his employer had to decide how to print it.

At the beginning of the sixteenth century in France most books were printed in gothic (black letter) type, whether in *lettres bâtardes*, especially if in French, or in *lettres de forme* (textura) or in *lettres de somme* (rotunda). The first press in France, set up in 1470, printed in roman type, but it was a private enterprise sponsored by two Fellows of the Sorbonne with humanist tastes and was in advance of its time.[1] The principal printer employed at it soon abandoned

---

[1] A. Claudin, *The first Paris press: an account of the books printed for G. Fichet and J. Heynlin 1470–1472*, Illustrated Monographs issued by the Bibliographical Society, no. vi (1898); Jeanne Veyrin-Forrer, 'Aux origines de l'imprimerie française: l'atelier de la Sorbonne et ses mécènes, 1470–1473', *L'art du livre à l'Imprimerie nationale* (1973), pp. 32–53; reprinted in the volume of her

roman type, even for Latin, when left on his own to make a living in the Paris book-trade. None the less the tradition thus begun was not wholly forgotten. And some of the leading Paris university printer-publishers, notably Henri (I) Estienne and Josse Badius, when they began to do business in the early years of the sixteenth century, adopted roman type when printing classical or humanist Latin, and led a movement, which was eventually to prevail, towards extending its use to all academic and educational printing.

The privilege being a document drawn up in French, most printers set it up in *lettres bâtardes*. If the rest of the book was also in French, the printer might continue with the same type. Thus in the case of *Huon de Bordeaux* (CH 1513, 3) the only extra prominence he gave to the privilege was to space it out with more ceremony. In a theological or philosophical work, printed in *lettres de forme* or *lettres de somme*, with numerous abbreviations well understood by the readers of such books, the display of the privilege in *lettres bâtardes* served to emphasise that this was something different and to draw attention to it (e.g. PA 1509, 1). What was to be done, though, if the book itself was to be set up in roman type, and not in gothic at all?

In the early years of the book-privilege system in France, the decision seemed obvious. Letters Patent or 'Extraicts des registres de Parlement', if printed in full, were set up in gothic, whatever the choice of type for the rest of the book. A good example is Symphorien Champier's *Periarchon* (CH 1515, 2), which Antoine Bonnemère printed entirely in roman, except for the words 'Cum priuilegio regis' on the title-page and the text of the privilege itself at the end. Examples of this practice can be found right up to the end of the period (e.g. PA 1524, 10). If a French summary of the privilege is given, there is less reluctance to use roman, but the heading or opening words may be in gothic. Thus Henry Estienne provided a summary of the privilege for the 1513 edition of Sigebert of Gembloux in which he was partner to Jean Petit the privilege holder: this summary, like the book itself, is printed in roman, but it is preceded by the words 'Privilege pour ce present livre', displayed in a large *lettre de forme* (CH 1512, 1 (7)) which also features on the title-page to print the words 'Cum priuilegio' where everything else is in roman (see Plate 6).

Nicolas des Prés, printing for Claude Chevallon and Gilles de Gourmont the *Aurea opuscula* of Jacques Almain, set the whole of the Letters Patent in roman, like the text of the book, except for the closing formula and the secretary's signature, 'Par le Roy à la relation du conseil. Ainsi siné Guiot.' which are in a much larger gothic type (CH 1518, 3). Printing the following year for Conrad Resch. the *Tractatus noticiarum* of Gervase Waim, des Prés made his concession to tradition in a different way: the whole of the first line, 'Francoys par la grace de dieu roy de Fran /', is printed in large gothic type, all the rest of the document in roman (CH 1519, 1).

collected articles under the title *La lettre et le texte*, Collection de l'Ecole Normale Supérieure de Jeunes Filles, no. 34 (1987), pp. 161–87.

Priuilege pour ce psnt liure

⸿Le Roy noſtre ſire a dŏne & octroye a Iehan Petit libraire iure de luniuerſite de Paris;& a Henri Eſtiéne imprimeur
en ladicte vniuerſite Priuilege de troys ans pour ce preſent liure intitule les Chroniques de Sigebert:de imprimer & faire
imprimer.& a defendu & defend a to⁹ aultres de ce Royaulme de non imprimer ne faire imprimer / vendre ne diſtribuer
aultre que ceulx que leſdicts libraires deſſus nŏmes aurŏt fait.
imprimer/ ne eulx en meſler en maniere que ce ſoit du iour-
duy.vij.iour de Iuin lan mil cinq cens & treze:iuſques a troys
ans reuolus & accomplis. Non obſtāt quelconques ordŏnā-
ces/inhibitions ou defenſes a ce contraires ſur certaines grandes peines/a plain & bien au long declarees es lettres du deſ-
ſuſdit priuilege. Done a bloys le douzieme iour de Mars lan
mil cinq cens & vnze Par le Roy.Et ſigne Geuffroy.

⸿Alphabeticus index hiſtoriarum in hoc opere cŏtentarū:
per foliorū numerū ſignatus,cui quidem numero prepoſitus
punctus/primū folij latus indicat:poſtpoſitus aute/ſecundū.

Plate 6   Heading in gothic (textura) to a summary of a privilege by Henri (I) Estienne (1512)

147

It seems however to have been Pierre Vidoue who first wholly abandoned gothic for the privilege, when he was printing a book in roman. He printed in full, entirely in roman type, for Jacques Kerver's edition of a work against Luther by Johannes Eck, the royal privilege (obtained by Conrad Resch), making a very fine page of it, the first line beginning with a handsome ornamental F for François and completed in capital letters (CH 1521, 4). He printed also wholly in roman the *Extraict des registres de Parlement* in the *De tralatione Bibliae* of Pierre Sutor, published by Jean Petit (PA 1524, 14), only the large ornamental capital S which begins the first line belonging to a more fanciful style of design.

Hesitation about abandoning the traditional gothic type for printing the text of the privilege may have haunted even Geofroy Tory, who probably did more than anyone else in France to promote the advance of roman type, the improvement of its design, and decoration in keeping with it. In his *Horae*, printed for him by Simon de Colines in 1525, he revolutionised the presentation of Books of Hours, replacing the gothic type, and the styles of illustration which were the time-honoured way of producing them, by roman type and elegant line-drawings and decorations in the classical taste. Yet in the first issue of the *Horae*, dated 16 January 1525 (CH 1524, 2) he or Colines decided to print the privilege on two pages, each facing a page of roman, in gothic. In copies dated Tuesday 17 January 1525 the 'prelims' have been re-arranged, and one of the results is that the privilege is now on the verso of the title-page and the facing page and is printed in roman. If, as appears to be the case, these alterations were made within a day or two of the first copies being completed, it shows that Tory or Colines or both of them found the juxtaposition of the gothic privilege with pages of roman type incongruous, and at once set about rectifying it. In the *Champ fleury*, for which the privilege was granted in 1526 but which did not appear until 1529, the text of the privilege is printed in roman (CH 1526, 2).

To print the words 'Cum priuilegio' or 'Cum priuilegio regis' on the title-page in gothic, even when the rest of the page and the whole book was set in roman, remained a common custom for a long time. Here again there are signs of change towards the end of the period. Simon de Colines began by following the practice of his predecessor Henri Estienne. One of the last books to appear under Henri Estienne's name, for which Colines obtained the priuilege, the *Promptuarium* of Jean de Montholon (CH 1520, 7), uses gothic for the opening word of the title and then for the words 'Cum gratia et privilegio' which are printed across the bottom of the page, though everything also on the page is in roman. In 1522, however, Colines printed the *Commentarii initiatorii in quatuor Euangelia* of Jacques Lefèvre d'Etaples, displaying the words 'CVM PRIVILEGIO REGIS', in capitals, on the title-page, in roman type like everything else in the book (CH 1522, 2).

To print the words in red was another possibility (e.g. CH 1513, 5;

CH 1514, 4). The device of splitting the words, placing 'Cum pri-' on one side of the printer's mark and '-vilegio' on the other was used by Antoine Du Ry printing for Simon Vincent at Lyon (CH 1515, 7 (1)), by a printer working for Jean Petit (CH 1520, 5 (2)), and Damien Higman (PR 1522, 2), among others.

Printers who made no attempt to reproduce the original French document conferring the privilege, and substituted a summary of it in Latin, naturally had no hesitation in printing the Latin summary in roman type. Here any attempts to put on a typographical display took a different form. The Latin summary could be set up in a large roman type, wholly or partly in capitals. Well shown off, it could thus be made to look distinctly classical, suggesting the appearance of an inscription (e.g. CH 1520, 10).

Josse Badius Ascensius, the main exponent of the Latin summary of the privilege, rarely indulged in much typographical display for it. In the *Summae quaestionum* of Henry of Ghent a relatively full Latin summary is printed on the last page, in nineteen lines of diminishing length tapering to a single word at the bottom, to which is appended the name of the royal secretary who signed the original (CH 1518, 5 (2)). When publishing a book in partnership with other members of the trade, he occasionally printed the text of the document, perhaps in deference to the wishes of colleagues who attached more importance to this than he did. Thus having obtained a Parlement privilege for a book on scholastic philosophy which he himself printed, and which he published jointly with Simon Vincent and Michel Conrad of Lyon, he adopted the following procedure. On the title-page and in the colophon he advertised, in Latin, his possession of a privilege, and stated that it could be found on the verso of the title-page, in Volume II. Here he gave first a Latin summary of the privilege, with an explanation, not to say apology, for the document being issued in French ('Ut sequens instrumentum pro more curiae supradictae gallice scriptum latius declarat'). Only then comes, printed in a small gothic type, the 'Extraict des registres de Parlement' conferring the privilege (PA 1518, 3).

Most of the printers who reproduced the complete text of their privilege showed it off as conspicuously as their resources permitted. Berthold Rembolt displayed his first privilege (PA 1509, 1) on the verso of the title-page within a frame formed by units of ornamental border, as he had done with the title-page. Many printers took pains to present it on a page by itself, or, in the case of a small format, where necessary on several successive pages. The first letter was often the occasion to use a large ornamental capital, whether the L for Louis (e.g. CH 1513, 3) or the F for François (e.g. CH 1518, 3) or the L for Louise when the king's mother was Regent (e.g. CH 1525, 4), in royal Letters Patent; the A for 'A tous ...' in Letters Patent from the Prévôt of Paris (e.g. PR 1516, 2); the S for 'Supplie humblement' for the opening phrase of petitions (e.g. PR 1520, 5); and the V for the initial formula 'Veue par la

Court' (e.g. PA 1514, 7) in privileges granted by the Parlement. The remaining letters of the first word, or the whole first line, may be printed in larger type than the remainder of the privilege.

Letters Patent, fair-copied in traditional style by skilled clerks in the royal chancery, or in the office of the Prévôt of Paris, were imposing documents, and some printers visibly tried to imitate the lay-out and general appearance of the original. A good example is provided by Michel Le Noir in his edition of *Huon de Bordeaux* (CH 1513, 3). The privilege granted to him by Louis XII, announced on the title-page, is given a page to itself after the table of contents, facing the beginning of the text. First comes a heading, *S'ensuyt le previlege* in a large gothic type. Then the opening words *Loys par la grace de dieu* are given special treatment: the initial L is taken from a set of ornamental capitals used in the rest of the book at the beginning of each chapter; the rest of the phrase is set up in the same large type as the one used for the heading, apart from the O which is a capital from a still larger fount. The rest of the privilege is set up in the same type as the romance itself. Below, carefully indented, and preceded by a paragraph sign, is the authority for the sealing of the document, 'Par le roy, Maistre Pierre de la Vernade, maistre des requestes ordinaires present', and the word 'Signé' to show that the name which follows was an autograph signature in the original Letters Patent. Below again, centred at the foot of the page, is the name of the signatory, 'J. Morelet' (see Plate 4, p. 86).

Other forms of privilege are also sometimes presented in a way intended to recall the look of the original document. In the case of the 'Extraict des registres de Parlement' the possibilities for display were limited, but some printers did their best to show it off. Thus Galliot Du Pré had the privilege in Jean de Selve's *Tractatus beneficialis* (PA 1514, 4) carefully spaced, and the opening phrase 'Veue par la court la requeste . . .' is printed in gothic type, an ornamental initial being used for the capital V, which takes up five lines of the text. Berthold Rembolt printed in larger type the judgement of the court actually conferring the privilege ('La dicte court a defendu . . .'), in his edition of Boniface de Ceva, *Sermones quadragesimales* (PA 1517, 1). The form characteristic of the *prévôté* of Paris, which shows the petition exactly as presented by the applicant followed by the order given in response, could be set up with more variety. A nice example is the French translation of Polydore Virgil, *De inuentoribus rerum* (PR 1520, 12). Here the printer, Pierre Le Brodeur, began with his own *requête*, headed 'A Monseigneur le prevost de Paris' introduced by a paragraph sign. The classic opening phrase, 'Supplye humblement . . .', gave him the opportunity to use an amusing initial letter, an elaborate calligraphic S from which the pen had made the profile of a man's face to look out. After the ritual conclusion, 'Et vous ferez bien', Le Brodeur left a space, and then printed the Prévôt's answer, the words 'Ainsi signé Alegre' set out below in the position the signature would occupy in the original (see Plate 7).

¶ A Monseigneur le preuost de Paris.

Supplye humblement Pierre le Brodeur Marchant Libraire de mourant en ceste ville de Paris: Comme ledit supplyant puis aucun temps enca ait fait translater de latin en langaige vulgai re le liure de Polidorus de inuentoribus rerum/auql sont conte nues quasi infinies belles sentences et choses dignes de memoi re/pour laquelle chose faire ledit supplyant a expose partie de ses deniers Ce considere et quil puisse estre aucunement recompese de sesoitz deniers Il vous plaise luy octroyer conge et licence de iceluy liure ainsi translate faire im primer et exposer en vente/et que deffences soyent faictes a tous autres libraires et imprimeurs de ne imprimer ne faire imprimer ou exposer en vete ledit liure dau tre impression que celle dudit supplyant iusques a trois ans a compter du iour que ledit liure sera acheue De imprimer/et sur grosses peines et amende arbitraire et vous ferez bien.

¶ Il est permis audit supplyant dimprimer ou faire imprimer ledit liure Et def fences faictes a tous autres libraires et imprimeurs de ne imprimer ou vendre le dit liure dautre impression que celle dudit supplyant De trois ans prochainemet Vends Sur peine de perdicion des liures par eulx imprimez et damende arbitrai re. fait soubz nostre seing manuel le.xx viie.de nouembre Mil cinq cens vingt. Ainsi signe Alegre.

Plate 7   Polydore Virgil's *De inuentoribus rerum* in French: application for privilege for the translation, and the Prévôt's reply (1520) (*reduced*)

The signature of the secretary, clerk or other authorised signatory was normally extended or followed by his paraph, a calligraphic flourish which, being quite elaborate, was hard to imitate exactly and was an additional precaution against forgery. These could not be reproduced in print. A Rouen printer privileged to print the *Stille* of the Parlement of Normandy was indeed so anxious to give the precise text of the certificate or 'Extraict des registres' which he had obtained that he printed the words 'ung paraffe' immediately after the name of the *greffier* Surreau who had signed it (PA 1516, 3). And Antoine Bonnemère, in the privilege for the *Periarchon* (CH 1515, 2) follows the name of the secretary, De Rillac, with some symbols which may be intended to stand for De Rillac's paraph.

On Letters Patent, whether issued by the royal chancery or by the court of the Prévôt, the seal affixed below the secretary's signature was a conspicuous feature as well as essential to the validity of the document. No printer attempted to reproduce it, but particulars of the sealing in the chancery were given with great care in a few books (CH 1516, 2; 1518, 1; 1520, 2; 1520, 8 and

9; 1525, 3), even including in at least one case, the method by which *entérinement* of the royal Letters Patent was sealed at the *prévôté* (CH 1524, 2). The way Letters Patent issued by the *prévoté* itself were sealed was occasionally described (e.g. PR 1520, 9). The presence of the royal seal is sometimes specifically mentioned in the Latin paraphrases or summaries of privileges given by Badius and others (e.g; 'sub poena contenta in diplomate authentico super ea re legitime consignato', CH 1524, 1; 'ut patentibus litteris sigillo regiae curiae rite munitis liquere protestamur', CH 1511, 1). More often its presence seems to be taken for granted.

The privilege being an official document, issued on royal authority, whether by the chancery, by one of the Parlements, or by the Prévôt of Paris and other officials of the Crown, printers who possessed a nice woodcut of the Arms of France with its three lilies were ready to use it in their display of the privilege. This custom is in no way confined to books of which the content is of an official or patriotic nature (such as Claude de Seyssel's *La grant monarchie de France*, printed and published by Regnault Chaudière, CH 1519, 6(1)), but is attested from 1509 onwards in books of purely academic or popular interest. Berthold Rembolt featured the crowned *écu de France* over his Parlement privilege (PA 1509, 1) in the commentaries on St Paul attributed to St Bruno; Philippe Pigouchet, printing for Jean Granjon the *Quartus sententiarum* of the philosopher John Mair or Major, showed off the Parlement privilege (PA 1509, 3) adorned with the *écu de France* within the collar of the royal order of Saint-Michel, with Louis XII's personal emblem of the porcupine added for good measure. At Lyon, Jean de Vingle printed in 1511 for Jean Robion and Jean de Clauso the treatise *De viribus iuramenti* of Antonius de Petrutia, displaying the Arms of France on the title-page above the words 'cum priuilegio regis', while the Letters Patent are printed on the verso (CH 1511, 2). Other users of the Arms of France in connection with the display of privileges were Jean de La Garde (e.g. PA 1516, 4: PR 1516, 5), Francois Regnault (e.g. PA 1516, 5), Enguilbert de Marnef (e.g. CH 1520, 3), and – very frequently – Galliot Du Pré (see Plate 8). An allusion to the lilies of France must be seen too in the fine woodcut of a lily used in conjunction with the text of a privilege by Jean Granjon (e.g. PA 1514, 9(1)). Guillaume Eustace had a printer's mark cut for him for use in some of the books which he published under his personal privilege (e.g. CH 1508, 2(4)), incorporating the Arms of France and the words 'Cum gratia et priuilegio regis' (see Plate 1, p. 23).

PRIVILEGES PARAPHRASED OR ANNOUNCED IN LATIN, AND SOME SPECIAL CASES

In 1520, Conrad Resch advertised a three-year privilege on the title of Q. Asconius Paedianus, *Enarrationes* on Cicero's orations, and provided a Latin summary on the verso of f. 3 which in fact gave no further details except the

Cᵒ priuilege pour le present liure.

Tous ceulx qui ces presentes lettres Berrõt Gabriel baron et seigñr daleigre/sainct iust/millau/torzet/sainct dier ꝗ de puis sol/conseiller chambellam du Roy nostre sire ꝗ garde de la preuoste de Paris salut. Scauoir faisons que ouye la requeste le iourduy a nous faicte par honnorable homme Galiot du pre marchant libraire iure en luniuersite de paris a ce ꝗ luy Voulsissions permettre reffaire imprimer et Bendre ce present liure Intitule le rommant de la rose/lequel auroit puis nagueres faict rescripre reueoir et corriger/et pour ce faire auroit fraye grans sommes de deniers. Et ordõner deffences estre faictes a tous imprimeurs et aultres quil appar tiendra de ne imprimer ne faire imprimer ledit liure sur la coppie dudit suppliãt ne en son preiudice en quelque maniere que ce soit ne icelluy Bendre ne distribuer ius ques a trois ans ensuyuans sur peine de confiscation desditz liures et damende ar bitraire a ce quil se puisse rembourser des fraitz et mises quil luy a conuenu et con uiendra faire tant a la correction que impression dudit liure. Considere lequel le requeste et oy sur ce le procureur du Roy nostre sire audit Chastellet pour ꝗ au nom dudit seigneur et tout considere nous audit Galiot du pre auons permis et permet tons de faire imprimer et Bendre les liure/et auons faict et faisons deffences a tous imprimeurs libraires ꝗ autres ꝗl appartiendra de ne imprimer ne faire iprimer les li ure sur la coppie dudit Galiot ne en son preiudice en quelque maniere que ce soit ne icelluy Bendre iusques a deux ans ensuyuans. Et ce sur peine de confiscation desd li ures et damende arbitraire a ce que ledit du pre se puisse rembourser des fraitz ꝗ mi ses quil luy a conuenu faire a la correction et impression dudit liure. En tesmoing de ce nous auons faict mettre a ces presentes le seel de ladicte preuoste de Paris ce fut faict le ieudy dixneufiesme iour dapuril Mil cinq cẽs Bingtsix apres pasques. Et signe.

Plate 8 Arms of France above the heading of the Prévôt's privilege for a modernised version of the *Roman de la Rose* (1526) (*reduced*)

penalties for infringement. On the other hand, the summary declared his willingness to show the document whenever need arose and good reason was shown ('cuius exemplum apud se Conradus habet idipsum deprompturus atque exhibiturus quoties opus fuerit et iure petetur', CH 1520, 11). In 1521 he advertised a privilege similarly in a philosophical work of Gabriel Biel, and inserted at the end of the book an address to the reader, 'De priuilegio et gratia huius operis emissoribus concessis', again offering to show the 'instrumentum publicum' to any legitimate enquirer (PR 1521, 1). This time, however, he gave it as a reason for omitting to print the text that it was written in French and that ignorance of French might be made an excuse for disregarding it ('quia gallice scriptum, ne quis sermonis ignorationem excuset, his non est insertum'), all this appearing rather oddly over the signature of Louis Ruzé, the Lieutenant Civil who had issued the privilege.

A few other university publishers similarly printed a summary of their privilege couched in classical Latin, sometimes meeting possible objections by stating that they withheld the text of the document because it was by ancient custom written in French, but were willing to show the original to any enquirer with reasonable cause to ask for it, e.g. Damien Higman at the end of his edition of the works of Peter the Venerable, 1522 'Cuius rei testimonium fidele habet instrumentum, sed gallice pro veteri more scriptum: eiusque videndi potestatem omnibus rite exacturis est facturus', PR 1522, 2). What justification was there for this reticence about printing a document in French?

Paris academic publishers might expect to sell many copies of their editions in foreign countries. The appearance of a document in French in such books, otherwise wholly in Latin, might appear strange or even incomprehensible abroad. For French, although spoken in territories well beyond the eastern frontiers of the kingdom of France, and familiar to polite society in Britain and the Low Countries (for instance), was not the international language which it was later to become. Scholars in Spain, or in the southern half of Italy, or in parts of Germany – not to mention eastern Europe – might not know it at all. Nor, if they did, would they be interested in the privilege. Outside France, advertisement of the privilege served one purpose only, namely to warn foreign members of the book-trade that, if they reprinted the book, they would not be able to sell their copies legally in France. Still, the majority of French publishers who catered for an international market *did* print their privilege. Badius, who set the example of Latin summaries, may have been actuated by an unusually acute sense of incongruity about printing something in the vernacular within a Latin book, possibly originating in some kind of intellectual snobbery on the part of an ex-schoolmaster who was touchy about his claims to be a humanist.

Latin summaries seem often devised as much to impress by the elegance of their language as to provide precise information about the terms of the grant and the authority on which it had been issued. Badius in particular is at pains to use terms which might have been understood by Cicero. The consent of the *Lieutenant Civil* of the Prévôt of Paris becomes 'suffragio literarum bonarum doctissimi et dulcissimi praesidii' (PR 1520, 10). The Parlement of Paris becomes the Senate ('Cauitque Senatus Parlamentæus ne quis alius biennio proximo imprimat', PA 1522, 2). However, in Merlin's edition of the Councils of the Church, published in 1524 by Galliot Du Pré, there is a reasonably accurate Latin translation of the original Letters Patent (issued on 25 August 1520); of the *entérinement* of them by the Prévôt of Paris ('in curia magnifici domini Prefecti urbis lutetiane') on 18 September; and of the privilege confirming it which Galliot obtained from the Parlement ('Priuilegium prefectorum pretorio incorruptissimi Parisiorum senatus') on 7 September 1524 (CH 1520, 3(2) and PA 1524, 13). Galliot's publication of Pierre Cottereau on the magistratures of France even translates into an attempt at acceptable Latin prose an ordinary 'Extraict des registres de Parlement' on the verso of the title-page ('Copia ex actuario sacri consistorii Parisiensis. – Centumuiralis senatus auctoritate pro illustri literarum amplitudine concessum est Galioto a prato', PA 1525, 7). This was probably the author's idea, as it is quite unlike Galliot's usual practice. The flattering identification of the Parlement with the Roman Senate admittedly was timely in August 1525.

The 'threatening' style of privilege summary affected by some Italian publishers[1] is rare in France. Jean Petit had a Latin *Admonitio* printed in Quinziano Stoa's *Christiana opera* (CH 1514, 2) which began, 'It is decreed by Letters of the king that no bookseller should be so insolent, and no printer so bold, as to dare to print this book or scheme to have it printed for the coming three years,' and continued by addressing anyone who might think of so doing, 'Ho there, you, whoever you are...' etc. A similar *Admonitio* appears the same year in Jean de Gourmont's edition of Quinziano Stoa's *Cleopolis* (PA 1514, 8), warning of a privilege granted by the Parlement. Quinziano had been used to publishing his works in Italy. His *Orpheos*, included by Gourmont with the new work *Cleopolis* by Gourmont, was first printed 'cum gratia et priuilegio' in 1510 in Milan. It seems likely therefore that it was he who dictated this form of words to both his Paris publishers, rather than Petit and Gourmont each deciding in this particular case to use a formula which neither had hitherto adopted. Jean de Gourmont did however employ a much milder version of this warning later, when he printed at the end of Enzinas, *Exponibilia* (CH 1521, 6(2)): 'Cauetur ne quis impune attentet hunc librum imprimere, ut amplissimo patet Priuilegio a Regia maiestate nobis condonato M.d.xxi.'

A milder form of this device occurs in 1520, when Claude Perroneus, author of a *Compendium philosophiae naturalis*, incorporated a eulogy of his publisher

---

[1] See above, p. 5.

Damien Higman and some details of his privilege in an address 'Ad archetypos nostros amicos' at the end of the book. Only the words 'Cum priuilegio' appear on the title-page, but in this address the author alludes to the Parlement ('maiores senatus') having shown their appreciation of Higman and their concern for the public good by prohibiting the printing of this book by anyone else for three years. 'Cauete igitur obsecro – et Claudium vestrum semper amate', concludes the author appealingly (PA 1520, 3).

Pierre Gromors and Pierre Gaudoul adopted a formula somewhat similar when they published Augerius' grammatical work: having printed 'Cum priuilegio ad biennium' on the title-page, they added at the end the words 'Cauetur priuilegio nostro, ne quis habeat imprimere hoc opus ante biennium, sub poena confiscationis librorum et emenda arbitraria', and the date, still however omitting to say which authority had issued the privilege (CP 1522, 2). Prigent Calvarin used wording of this 'warning' nature in his edition of a work by Manderston, saying at the end, 'Cauetur ne quis impune attentet hunc librum imprimere, ut amplissimo patet priuilegio a regia maiestate nobis condonato', with the date, adding conspicuously 'Cum priuilegio Regis', leaving the beholder in no doubt who had given the privilege but omitting to state for how long (CH 1522, 7).

If the practice of Badius was relatively standardised, it is at first sight surprising to find a Latin work of which he was the co-publisher, the well-known devotional work *Speculum ecclesiae* by St Edmund of Abingdon, printed throughout in gothic type, showing no mention at all of a privilege on the title-page, and displaying a summary in French at the end: 'Imprimé de privilege jusques à deux ans de par monsieur le prevost de Paris le .vii. de Avril Mil cinq cens .xix.' (PR 1520, 2). The explanation is perhaps that his partner Jean Du Pré may have obtained the privilege and determined how it should be advertised – may, indeed, have been the printer of the book. A divergence between Badius and another of his partners is apparent in an edition of Armand de Bellevue's *Sermones ex Psalterio* which he shared in 1519 with Jacques Le Messier (who printed it) and Claude Chevallon (who obtained the privilege for it): the surviving copy in the name of Chevallon advertises a two-year privilege on the title-page, inviting the reader to look for the document on the next page, where it duly appears (PA 1519, 4(1)); whereas the privilege is not given in the copies printed to be sold by Badius.

The Latin formula 'Cum priuilegio' soon became so well known that it is frequently to be found on the title-page of works wholly in French, for example in *Le siècle doré* of Guillaume Michel (PR 1522, 1) or *La déploration de l'église militante* of Jean Bouchet (PA 1512, 5) or *Les excellentes cronicques du prince Judas Machabeus* of Charles de Saint-Gelais (CH 1514, 4). French versions of the formula are on the other hand freely used on the title-page of books printed in French, e.g. 'Avec le privilege de messieurs de Parlement' (PA 1513, 2) or simply 'Avec privilege' (PR 1520, 5, see Plate 5a, p. 89) the vernacular form 'previllege' being sometimes found, e.g. 'Avec previllege du roy nostre sire' (CH 1513, 4(1)). Sometimes they are supplemented by being repeated in Latin at the end of the book, as in the case of the last two examples quoted.

Individual variants on the formula occasionally appear. Galliot Du Pré's edition of Jean de Selve, *Tractatus beneficialis* (PA 1514, 4), carries on the title-page the words 'Cum gratia et auxilio regio inuictissimo', which might lead one to assume that the privilege was issued by the royal chancery, though it was in fact granted by the Parlement of Paris, of which the author was a prominent member.

Galliot Du Pré, one of the most consistent supporters of the privilege system, was careful to give maximum publicity to his privileges in his books, but had no standard practice about the form of announcement. Thus in three books published under the same privilege, all printed for him by Pierre Vidoue, and all of them in French, we find the following variations in treatment:

CH 1517, 1(1) 'Cum priuilegio regis' on title-page.
Text of privilege on verso.
'Avec le privillege du Roy nostre sire, comme il appert par ses lettres patentes', after the colophon.

CH 1517, 1(2) 'Cum priuilegio regis' on title-page.
Text of privilege on verso, continued on facing page.
'Cum priuilegio regis' at the end.

CH 1517, 1(3) 'Avec le privilege du Roy nostre sire jusques à deux ans / comme il apert par ses lettres patentes' on title-page.
'S'ensuyt le privilege de ce present livre' on verso.
Text of privilege on the two following pages.
'Avec le privilege du Roy nostre sire jusques à trois ans' [*sic*] at the end.

There are cases where the printer has been at pains to direct attention to the exact place in the book where the privilege is given in full or at least in a detailed summary. Badius pioneered this practice (which he did not always follow) when he printed on the title-page of his edition of Cicero (CH 1511, 1) the words, 'Gratia & priuilegio ab Regia munificentia concessis: de quibus ad calcem operis.' At the end of the text and the commentary, incorporated in the colophon, Badius indeed prints a summary (in Latin) of a three-year royal privilege granting him exclusive rights in his *explanatio* – not, of course, in the Cicero text itself. Similarly, when a mention of the privilege is printed at the end of the book and *not* on the title-page, a reference may be given to the earlier page where the privilege is to be found: 'comme il appert par le double dudit privilege inseré au premier cayer de ce present livre' when the text appears on f. 4 of the 'prelims', facing the first page of the text (PA 1511, 1). Some publishers advertised the duration of the privilege on the title-page even when they intended to print the text in full elsewhere in the book, and said so. Thus Claude Chevallon printed on the title-page 'Cum gratia et priuilegio biennii ut proxima patebit pagella', referring to what was on the verso (PA 1519, 4(1, 2, 3, 5)), though he omitted to mention the privilege at all on the title-page in another book in the same series (PA 1519, 4(4)). And Gaspard Philippe of Bordeaux printed 'Cum priuilegio ad triennium ut in fine sequentis tabule', referring to the position at the end of the table of contents which he had chosen to display the text of his Letters Patent (CH 1520, 10). Conrad Resch even printed a full summary of his privilege on the title-page of a book by Gervase Waim, directing attention to its contents and explaining exactly where it was to be found – 'in instrumento e facie libri impresso' – when the document is indeed printed verbatim facing the first page of the text of the book (CH 1519, 1(1).

Not all privilege-holders thought it necessary to provide *any* particulars. From 1507 onwards, books are to be found, printed and published in France, which bear only the words 'Cum priuilegio' or 'Cum gratia et priuilegio' or 'Avec privilege'. In the course of making the present study, I have found seventy-three, and there are probably more. (This formula is distinct from 'Cum priuilegio regis', which at least shows that the authority which issued the grant was the royal chancery.) A further twenty-two add to this formula the *duration* of the privilege, the earliest example of this variant coming from Durand Gerlier (*CP* 1517, 2). The first use of the 'Cum priuilegio' formula, with no further particulars, seems to be at Lyon (*CP* 1509, 2). The largest number found for any one year is twenty-two, in 1520. It appears to decline in popularity after this, for the remaining years up to 1526. There is no reason to doubt that an authentic privilege lay behind these uninformative announcements. Henri Estienne, being the holder of valid Parlement privileges, put only 'Cum priuilegio ne quis temere hoc ab hinc duos annos imprimat' (PA 1512, 7), and 'Cum priuilegio' (PA 1518, 7) in the books in question. It would have been a grave offence to claim a privilege where there was none, and an offence easily exposed.

Publishers and printers who put only 'cum priuilegio' on the title-page presumably relied upon being asked for details by any fellow-members of the booktrade who desired to reprint that book when it was no longer protected by privilege. Sometimes requests to be shown the privilege are indeed anticipated. Badius said on the title-page of his own edition of Quintilian, 'Vaenundantur cum gratia et priuilegio', and then 'Priuilegii forma, cuius prolixior est explicatio, apud Badium est, qui omnibus iure petentibus eius vidende faciet potestatem.' It was in fact a Parlement privilege, for two years, granted on 16 January 1516, as we know from the entry in the Parlement register (PA 1516, 2). On another occasion, Badius made a longer statement to the same effect on the last page of a book (*CP* 1519, 2):

Cautum est auctoritate principali vt auctentico liquet instrumento nequis hoc opusculum biennio proximo in regno Franciae imprimat praeter Badium aut aliubi impressum vaenundet, sub poena contenta in eodem instrumento quod iustis rationibus expetentibus communicabitur...

It was no part of his practice to provide consistently in his books the sort of details which would authenticate the privilege. In the last-mentioned case, for instance, he does not state which French authority had given the privilege – it might be the chancery, the Parlement or the Prévôt, though I think the latter is the most likely – nor the place and date of the issue of the document, nor the name of the official who signed it. The reason given by Badius in the first example for not printing the privilege, namely its length ('cuius prolixior est explicatio'), can hardly have been the main one in the case of a Parlement privilege, which was only a few lines transcribing the entry in the Parlement register, though it would be applicable to Letters Patent.

There are a few cases where some copies of an edition display a privilege and others do not. In certain presentation copies, the privilege has been deliberately replaced or excised.[1] But this is not always the explanation. There are two copies of the commentary by Dionysius Cisterciensis on the Fourth Book of the Sentences, published by Poncet Le Preux (PA 1511, 2) in the Bibliothèque Nationale. Neither advertises possession of a privilege on the title-page. One copy (Rés. D. 74) prints a Parlement privilege at the end of the table of contents, the other (Rés. D. 72.1) shows no such privilege. Possibly the first few copies of the preliminary gathering had already been printed before the result of an application for privilege was known. Possibly the omission was an oversight which was noticed and rectified after a few copies had been printed. Belated arrival of a privilege is probably reflected in the copy I have consulted of Le Roy's *Mirouer de penitence* (PA 1512, 3), where a strip of paper, with a Parlement grant printed on it, is pasted on to a page at the end of the book. Sometimes the publisher anticipated the grant: thus in the *Practica judiciaria* (CH 1515, 8) he had the Letters Patent printed, in the form he hoped to receive them, with blanks left for the place, day and month of the grant, which are filled in by hand. A yet more last-minute attempt to record the grant of a privilege is possibly to be found in the first edition of Guillaume Le Rouillé's *Justiciae et injusticiae descriptionum compendium*, 1520, fol., published by Claude Chevallon: in both the copies of this very rare edition which I have been able to see (BN Rés. F. 1236 and BL 1602/147), between the last lines of the text and the colophon, a sixteenth-century hand has inserted the inscription 'Cum preuilegio biēnio'. The book, a handsome illustrated volume dedicated to Charles, duke of Alençon, might well have qualified for a privilege, but the evidence seems inconclusive.

A singular case of failure to provide adequate information about a privilege occurs in a Latin poem, *Concordia Galliae et Britanniae*, published without date

[1] See below, pp. 160–3.

or place of issue, and without the name of a publisher or printer, giving only the formula 'Cum gratia et privilegio' on the title-page (*CP* 1518, 7). The author was Stephanus Templerius Aurelius, that is, Etienne Templier of Orleans, who dedicated it to Michel Boudet, bishop of Langres, and on the verso of the title-page there are commendatory verses to the reader by Io. Mottanus Briocensis, Almoner to the King. It may be conjectured that it was printed at the author's expense for presentation to his friends and patrons, under a privilege which he himself had obtained. Perhaps in haste to get it out while the subject was topical, referring to the position in Anglo-French relations either in 1518 (as supposed by the BN catalogue) or in 1520 (as guessed by the BL catalogue), he may have omitted to give details of the privilege to the printer, who, not himself dealing in the sale of the book, did not trouble to put his name to it. Thus a law-abiding member of the book-trade who wished to reprint it would have had considerable difficulty in contacting the owner of the rights in it, unless he could get in touch with the author. It does not appear that the poem was in fact pirated. One of the descriptions of the Field of the Cloth of Gold (PR 1520, 7) was still more uninformative about the privilege-holder: 'Cum priuilegio / Pour huyt jours' was clearly stated in the pamphlet, but it has neither author, publisher, place, nor date.

DELETION OF PRIVILEGE IN CERTAIN COPIES

The privilege was to most authors, and to most members of the book-trade, an asset to be displayed with pride or at least advertised with care. Some hesitation in this matter can, however, be detected when a special copy was ordered for presentation to a great patron or for inclusion in a bibliophile's collection. For many years after the general adoption of printing such copies were often required to look as far as possible like an illuminated manuscript, that is, the text of the book was printed like the ordinary copies for sale to the general public but decorated by hand and sometimes modified to leave space for original miniatures, the owner's arms frequently appearing in the scheme of decoration. The object being to produce a unique copy, for that particular person, might it not seem incongruous to include the privilege, which drew attention to the fact that the book formed part of an edition available in commerce?

From the beginning, there were differing responses to this question. *Les folles entreprises*, by Pierre Gringore, was printed for the author under his privilege (PR 1505, 1) 'par l'ordonnance de justice' which was summarised in the colophon. Several copies were printed on vellum. Two of these are in the Bibliothèque Nationale. Both were prepared for important customers, the illustrations being illuminated by hand. One, Vélins 2244, retains the colophon advertising the privilege, which is indeed ruled in red and distinguished by the hand-coloured initial capital letter. In the other, Vélins 2245, the reference to the privilege has been very carefully erased, though traces of the printed characters are visible.

If divergencies like this can occur between two vellum copies, they are naturally also to be found between a specially prepared vellum copy of a book and the ordinary copies printed on paper. An early instance is *La louenge des roys de France*, by André de La Vigne. The privilege obtained for it by Eustace de Brie, from the Parlement of Paris and the *procureur du roi* in the Parlement (PA 1507, 1), is summarised in the colophon, beginning with the words 'Cy fine la louenge des roys de France imprimée à Paris de par Eustace de Brie demourant au Sabot derriere la Magdaleine. Et luy a donné la court de Parlement . . .' in the copies put on sale in the ordinary way, of which several examples survive. But a hand-decorated vellum copy in the Bibliothèque Nationale, Vélins 2243, retains of this colophon only the words 'Cy fine la louenge des roys de France imprimée à Paris', everything that follows being erased.

Certain vellum copies intended for presentation to the king or to some other royal or princely personage show still greater modifications, resulting in the suppression of a privilege displayed in the ordinary paper copies.

Charles de Saint-Gelais, canon and bishop elect of Angoulême, completed in 1514 *Les excellentes chronicques du prince Judas Machabeus*. It was printed by Antoine Bonnemère, who obtained for it a privilege from Louis XII, dated 19 September 1514 (CH 1514, 4). The copies sold to the general public show on the title-page the words 'cum priuilegio regis amplissimo' and the complete text of the Letters Patent on the verso of it. But Saint-Gelais intended (as the privilege makes it clear) to dedicate the work to François, Duc de Valois, the heir presumptive to the throne of France, and he had a special vellum copy prepared, to present to him (BN Vélins 1128). Such individually prepared copies of a printed book were still presented to grand patrons or ordered by them fairly frequently at this period: Antoine Vérard had specialised in supplying them to royalty and to other wealthy customers.[1] This one was duly supplied with miniatures and with initial letters gilded and painted. But furthermore, the first two leaves of the printed edition were removed and replaced by two leaves entirely in manuscript: instead of the printed title-page there is a calligraphic title embellished with the Arms of France, while the verso shows a miniature of the king enthroned in state, thus eliminating all mention of the privilege. Louis XII may have been despaired of by the time the presentation copy was being completed, for the style of the person addressed in the prologue was left blank by the printer and the description of

---

[1] See *Manuscripts in the fifty years after the invention of printing*, ed. J. B. Trapp (London, Warburg Institute, 1983), esp. E. P. Spencer, 'Antoine Vérard's illuminated vellum incunables' (pp. 62–5) and M. B. Winn, 'Antoine Vérard's presentation manuscripts and printed books' (pp. 66–74).

the king as 'trespuissant et treschrestien prince Françoys de Valloys par la grace de dieu Roy de France premier de ce nom' was filled in by hand. I think the decision to omit Louis XII's privilege from the presentation copy must have been taken to the belief that he would no longer be alive by the time the book was presented.

Symphorien Champier had his *Grans croniques des gestes des princes des pays de Savoye* published in 1516 and dedicated it to Louise of Savoy, mother of the new king Francis I. Jean de La Garde, who was the publisher and printer of it, obtained a privilege for it from the Parlement of Paris (PA 1516, 4), and he printed the privilege on the verso of the title-page, with the Arms of France, as well as putting 'Cum priuilegio' on the title-page itself. In the vellum copy prepared for presentation to Louise herself, however (BN Vélins 1173), all reference to the privilege has been eliminated. The title-page has been re-set by the printer without the words 'Cum priuilegio', and the verso retains only the Arms of France, the rest of the page being left blank. Indeed everything relating to the commercial production of the book has been removed. The last leaf, bearing the long colophon which gives details of the publisher and the date, has been removed, and, on the title-page, the words 'nouvellement imprimees à Paris pour Jehan de la garde. Champier.', which follow the title of the book, have been carefully erased by hand. Instead, the Arms of Savoy on the title-page and the Arms of France on the verso have been gilded and coloured. Where the first page of the text, in the ordinary copies, has a woodcut showing a scholar at work, the presentation copy has a miniature showing Louise receiving the book, enthroned beside her son the king, and all the illustrations and the initials are embellished with gold and colours.

In the copy of Paulus Aemilius, *De rebus gestis Francorum*, presumed to have been prepared for the king himself (BN Vélins 734) the first printed leaf has been removed, and the recto of the second leaf, carrying the beginning of the preface, is decorated by hand in gold and colours with a border incorporating the king's personal emblem of the salamander and the arms of France. In eliminating the ordinary title-page, the person who prepared this copy suppressed the summary of the privilege (CH 1517, 7), which, as we know from paper copies of the book (e.g. BN Rés.L^{35} 22), was printed there.

From the printer's point of view, any modifications required to produce a unique copy for presentation might be costly, but they were not particularly difficult. All printing on vellum demanded great skill and had to be specially done, whether a whole book or a few pages in a book, such as the Canon of the Mass which, receiving much harder wear than the rest of the Missal as it was in daily use, was often printed on vellum even when the edition was in other respects on paper. To re-set a page, omitting certain features of the paper copies, was a relatively simple matter, if the customer wanted it so and was ready to pay extra for it.

There were, however, customers who saw no need at all to omit mention of the printer or of the privilege when they ordered a special copy.

A sumptuous vellum copy exists in the Bibliothèque Nationale of the *Quodlibeta* of Henry of Ghent (Vélins 343–4) in which the privilege (CH 1518, 5(1)) is advertised on the title-page and summarised on the verso of the last leaf exactly as in the ordinary paper copies. To Josse Badius Ascensius, the printer and publisher of the book, it had been a work of piety to produce the first edition of his illustrious compatriot's philosophical writings, and he inserted a dedication of his own to Louis de Flandres, a magistrate of Ghent. But the editor was Friar Alfonso de Villa Sancta, a Spanish Franciscan resident at the Recollect convent in Paris, using a manuscript lent by the Paris Carmelites, and his dedication aimed higher, to the Archduke Charles who had recently become king of Spain, the future Emperor Charles V: was not Charles count of Flanders, and was not Ghent his birthplace? And so in this special copy, facing the dedication, there is a miniature of Charles, crowned and enthroned as king, holding sword and orb. The miniature is not a presentation scene, and Van Praet may have gone too far[1] in assuming that this was the copy actually presented to Charles, but it must at least have been made for someone closely connected with his court. Though relations between him and Francis I were still amicable in 1518, it would not have been surprising if reference to the king of France's privilege had been deleted as incongruous or irrelevant in such a copy as this.

The vellum presentation copy of Petrus de Biaxio's *Opus conficiundarum electionum directorium* (PA 1511, 3) was certainly prepared to the instructions of the author, a councillor of the king of Navarre, who dedicated it to Cardinal d'Albret (d. 1520). It is ruled throughout in red, with the initials decorated in gold and colour, and a miniature (on f. 20ᵛ) of the cardinal receiving the book from the author. But no attempt was made to remove mention of the privilege. On the contrary, the privilege is decorated by hand in the same manner as the rest of the book. Another very grand vellum copy treating the privilege (PA 1524, 3) with ceremony is that of the first edition of Commynes now in the Bibliothèque Nationale (Vélins 754). The owner of this copy, or the person who presented it to him, had it decorated by hand and embellished with his coat of arms, a trotting white horse: the Parlement privilege printed on the verso of the title-page shows the Arms of France and the initial V coloured or gilded, and all the capital letters in the text of the privilege are touched up with yellow in the same way as the text of Commynes. Other examples of fine vellum copies in which the privilege is left intact are

Chastellain, *Le Temple de Jean Boccace* (CH 1517, 1(2))　　BN Vélins 775
Fichet, *Consolatio luctus et mortis* (PA 1521, 4)　　　　　　BN Vélins 1920
Patricius, *De regno* (CH 1519, 3(1))　　　　　　　　　　　　BN Vélins 408–9

[1] J. B. B. Van Praet, *Catalogue des livres imprimés sur vélin de la bibliothèque du roi*, 6 vols. (1822–8), I, no. 411.

Le Cirier, *De iure primogeniturae* (CH 1519, 6(4)) BN Vélins 419
and another Commynes, the second 1524 edition BN Vélins 755

A decision *not* to advertise the privilege in a special vellum copy may sometimes have been dictated by fear of incompatibility between it and the destined recipient. Louise of Savoy, the king's mother, might be less than pleased to turn over the first page of the Chronicles of the dukes and princes of Savoy to find an extract from the registers of the Parlement of Paris. Francis I himself, just after his accession, might think it inappropriate to see prominently displayed the Letters Patent granted for the book by his predecessor, which indeed, in the view of some experts, would have been no longer valid unless confirmed by the new sovereign.

Where the text or the mention of a privilege is suppressed for no such obvious possible reason, especially where details of the place and date of printing are also sacrificed, it is likely that both were deemed to smack too much of mass production to feature in a copy lavishly treated for a particular patron. To that extent, these suppressions may therefore serve as a reminder that the privilege was essentially a commercial monopoly at this period, a characteristic of its nature which might on occasion outweigh any prestige value it possessed.

8 · THE RANGE OF INTERESTS REFLECTED IN PRIVILEGED BOOKS: ANALYSIS BY SUBJECT

At least 463 books are known to have been published under privilege in France up to 1526 inclusive. What were they?

Analysis of our Register shows that religion, with 113 items, is the largest category, closely followed by law, with 105 items. History and current events account for 78 items, philosophy for 48, education and commentaries on classical texts for 48, literature of entertainment (poetry, fiction, drama etc.), chiefly in French, for 45, medicine and surgery for 14, geography and travel for 8 and mathematics for 4.

RELIGION

A known 113 books, almost 24 per cent of all books published under privilege in France up to 1526 inclusive, can be classed under the heading Religion.

This is the more remarkable because no privileges were granted for editions of the Bible. The principle, that the Bible had been and should remain free to all to print, was indeed explicitly recognised by 1528. In that year a privilege was granted by Francis I to Robert Estienne for his pioneer critical edition of the Vulgate, but *only* for his textual apparatus, improved glossary of proper names, tables and indices, which he could reasonably claim to be his own work: 'N'entendons toutesfoys que la Bible ne puisse estre imprimée par les libraires et ainsi qu'il a esté par cy devant, sans toutesfoys la dicte table, conferance [collation] et interpretation par ledict suppliant pretenduz avoir faict rediger et mettre en ordre' (CH 1528, 1). Books of Hours required by the pious laity, and liturgical books needed by the clergy, also lay outside the privilege system, with very few exceptions. Antoine Vérard, fresh from obtaining a personal privilege which seems to have applied to any book which he should be the first person to publish, invoked this privilege in his 1508 *Les Heures Nostre Dame à l'usaige de Romme nouvellement translatées* (CH 1507, 1 (5)), but in none of his subsequent editions of the Hours. No other Book of Hours, among the scores published in France during the ensuing years, appears to have received a privilege until that of Geofroy Tory, which offered a completely novel design in typography, decoration and illustration (CH 1524, 2). Of the innumerable liturgical books required in cathedrals and parish churches, monastic houses and colleges, royal, episcopal and private chapels, there appear to be, up to 1526, only five editions laying claim to a privilege, and those within a restricted area. These are, in order of publication: a revised breviary of the diocese of Saint-Pol-de-Léon in Brittany, printed 'cum priuilegio' (*CP* 1516, 6); a breviary printed by Thielman Kerver for the royal abbey of Fontevrault (CH 1518, 7); a breviary for the Carthusians, also by Kerver (*CP* 1522, 4); a missal of Clermont and Saint-Flour (CH 1522, 3 (1)), for which the privilege was obtained by Jacques Mareschal dit Roland at Lyon; and a missal of Poitiers 'cum priuilegio' (*CP* 1524, 3).

Devotional literature in the vernacular, for which there was an inexhaustible market at this period, was the object of privileges in some cases. The *Contemplations historiées sur la passion*, attributed to Gerson, came out under the personal privilege held by Antoine Vérard (CH 1507, 1 (4)). Simon Vostre obtained a privilege for *Le mirouer de penitence*, by François Le Roy or Regius, of Evreux, of the reformed order of Fontevrault An additional item concluded this work, 'Le devot trespas de venerable et religieuse personne Frere Jacques Daniel, docteur en chacun droit, et confesseur des filles Dieu de Paris ... nouvellement descript jouxte la reale verité par le confesseur de la Magdalene d'Orleans, assistant à la dormition dudit frere Jacques Daniel.' It may have been the inclusion of this account, perhaps almost amounting to a newsletter and probably of considerable interest to pious circles in Paris, which decided Simon Vostre to seek a privilege for it (PA 1512, 3). Martin Morin of Rouen obtained a grant from the Bailli for a work in French on the Immaculate Conception by Pierre Le Fevre or Fabri (PR 1514, 5). Pasquier Le Moine, in quest of a privilege from the royal chancery for his account of Francis I's coronation and campaigns, took advantage of the opportunity to include another work of his composition, *L'ardant miroir de grace* (CH 1519, 9). This is an allegory of his journey through life, in which, after falling a victim to several false guides, he is presented to Faith, Fortitude and Law, 'femmes de grant et excellent estat', who are melting precious metals in a crucible to produce the Burning Mirror of Grace. Guillaume Michel de Tours had a privilege from the Prévôt for his book *La forest de conscience*, another devout allegorical tale (PR 1516, 2). Two anonymous sets of spiritual exercises, forerunners of St Ignatius of Loyola, were included in a privilege granted the same year to Regnault Chaudière: *Le livre de la discipline d'amour divine* and *Cy commencent quatre voyes spirituelles pour aller à dieu* (CH 1519, 6 (2 and 5)). Guillaume Eustace published an edition of *Le dialogue du crucifx et du pélerin* written in 1486 by Guillaume Alexis,[1] prior of Bussy, on a pilgrimage to the Holy Land where he died (CH 1521, 1 (1)). Under the same privilege,

---

[1] *Œuvres poétiques de Guillaume Alexis*, ed. A. Piaget and E. Picot, 3 vols, SATF (1896–1908). The Dialogue is printed in vol. III, pp. 15–123. Eustace's edition had been preceded by an edition printed by Jean Trepperel, s.d. (1501 or 1502), 4°. BN Rés.D.5022(3), both illustrated in the SATF edition. Trepperel's edition may have been out of print by 1521, or Eustace may genuinely not have known of its existence.

Eustace brought out an imposing volume of the letters of St Jerome in French (CH 1521, 1 (2)). A small selection of the letters, translated for Anne of Brittany, had appeared in the name of Jean de La Garde, under privilege (PR 1519, 1): the two year privilege for the earlier edition had by then expired, and that of Eustace was of a nature to supersede it. Otherwise, translations into French of such works are rarely to be found among books qualifying for privileges. *Les epistres Sainct Pol glosées* was the first book to appear under the personal privilege of Antoine Vérard (CH 1507, 1 (1)) and St Augustine's *Exposition sur le Psautier* appeared 'cum priuilegio' (*CP* 1520, 1). On the other hand a simple broadsheet of devotions in verse, arranged within and around the outline of a shield, under the title of *Le blason des armes du pouvre pescheur*, devised by a journeyman bookseller named Pierre Aubry, was granted a privilege by the Parlement (PA 1524, 4).

For the lives of saints, popular as these were with the general public, few book-privileges were obtained. It may often have been hard for the applicant to establish that a particular life, or translation of it into French, had never been printed before. Antoine Vérard and Guillaume Eustace each brought out one saint's life under their respective personal royal privileges. Vérard published *La vie monseigneur Sainct Germain* (CH 1507, 1 (11)). St Germanus (c. 378–448), bishop of Auxerre, played a commanding part in the history of Gaul in his time; his cult was closely associated with the French monarchy and is commemorated in innumerable dedications of churches in France. Vérard's may well have been the first printed translation into French of the *Vita*. Eustace published a volume incorporating a life of St Clare of Assisi, *La perfection des filles religieuses avec la vie et miracles de ma dame saincte Clare* (CH 1508, 2 (14)). Clément Longis produced under privilege *La vie et les miracles de Saint Eusice* (PR 1516, 1), a saint venerated in only a few places in France but who had supported king Childebert against the Arians. Nicolas de La Barre obtained a privilege for the Papal Bull canonising St Francis of Paola, (PA 1520, 1) who had prophesied that Francis of Angoulême would one day become king of France, and so did Galliot Du Pré for a French translation of Petrus de Natalibus' Catalogue of Saints (PA 1524, 5).

By contrast, privileges were frequently sought and frequently given for what might appear a somewhat forbidding category, namely sermons. There was keen interest at this period, both among the clergy and among devout laymen, in the courses of sermons delivered by eminent preachers of the time or of the past. This does not only reflect interest in religion: the pulpit was one of the principal places from which uninhibited comment on public affairs and social problems could be heard, not excluding denunciation of abuses in church and state. In their published form, printed, as they were, in Latin, or Latin with some explanations in French, they reached only an educated public, but it was evidently a large one. From the beginning of the privilege system onwards, the first publisher to secure the text of such a collection of sermons usually armed himself with a privilege, and reprints soon after the expiry of the privilege bear witness to the prudence of this measure.

Among the privileges in this category the most numerous are those obtained, both before and after his death in 1515, for the sermons of Jean Raulin, the monastic reformer, well known in Paris (having been head of the Collège de Navarre), and greatly respected. These included Raulin's sermons for Lent (CH 1512, 1 (1)), on Penance, under the title *Itinerarium Paradisi* (*CP* 1514, 3), for Advent, on Death, on the Eucharist (CH 1515, 5 (2, 3 and 6)), and on Saints' Days (PA 1524, 8), not to mention his letters (CH 1520, 5 (1)). Guillaume Pepin, from the Dominican priory of Evreux, was a particularly popular preacher in Paris: his sermons published under privilege included those for the Gospels and Epistles on Sundays and those on the *Confiteor* (PA 1519, 4 (4 and 5)), and those on the Destruction of Niniveh – by Niniveh meaning Vice (*CP* 1525, 4). Among other sermon collections to receive privilege were those preached in Lent by Jean Clérée (*CP* 1520, 18), Michel Menot (PA 1525, 3) and Robert Messier (PA 1525, 1), and in Lent and in Advent by Boniface de Ceva (PA 1517, 1 and PA 1518, 6); on the Psalms by Armand de Bellevue (PA 1519, 4 (1)); for the Sundays of the winter and of the summer months, and by the Spanish Dominican Sancho de Porta (*CP* 1513, 3 and 4); the sermons of Pierre Richard of Coutances (*CP* 1518, 3A); and the sermons of Bertrand de La Tour or De Turre edited by Pierre de Neufve, Principal of the Collège de Dainville (PA 1521, 7).

If some of the doctors of theology in the Paris Faculty were thus active in preaching and provided their publishers with very saleable books in so doing, others cultivated the field of ecclesiastical history and unearthed or edited texts which also were of interest to a large educated public. Guillaume Petit, or Parvi, bishop of Troyes, Inquisitor General in France, confessor to Louis XII and Francis I and, under the latter, librarian of the royal collection of Blois, used his great position and the funds put at his disposal to seek out manuscripts of value from the past which were hitherto unpublished and to arrange for them to be edited and printed. He was also well placed to facilitate the grant of a privilege where this was appropriate (e.g. CH 1519, 6). A somewhat younger theologian who shared his interests and was inspired by him, Jacques Merlin, had originally come to Paris to study philosophy under Pierre Tartaret, but branched out into the study of the early church, of the Fathers and of the classics of medieval piety. He edited Origen: not in Greek,[1] to which the resources of French scholarship and French printing were unequal at so early a date, but in reputable Latin translations, some by Origen's opponent St Jerome. He included Origen's *Contra Celsum* (enumerating and answering a Jewish attack on the divinity of Christ) in the version of the Italian humanist Cristoforo Persona. He added an *Apologia* of his own for

[1] The Greek text was first edited by Erasmus with a Latin translation of his own (Basle, Froben, 1536).

Origen. Thus set up, his edition obtained a privilege in a group of publications, of which some were sponsored by Guillaume Petit, published by his kinsman Jean Petit (CH 1512, 1). For a work this nature it proved to be something of a best-seller. Petit and Badius, the original publishers, issued it again in 1519, 1522 and 1530, and there was a Lyon reprint in 1536. A good deal of curiosity was felt about Origen, as well as some suspicion. He, or at least some of his opinions, had been condemned by an early Council of the Church, and Merlin's edition was the object of a bitter and prolonged quarrel within the Paris Faculty of Theology between Merlin himself and Noël Beda, who wished it to be prohibited. This battle of giants was no doubt good publicity for the book. Otherwise patristic studies were scantily represented at this period in France. Nicolas Berauld or Beraldus, a layman, was responsible for an edition of the works of St Athanasius which earned a privilege (CH 1518, 4 (1)). What he did was to bring together and edit the best available Latin translations, by various hands, which had already been printed in various places and at various times. One of the translators, Cristoforo de Persona, had in 1477 attributed to St Athanasius some commentaries on St Paul's Epistles which were really by Theophylact, an eleventh-century Byzantine theologian; Berauld was misled by this into including these commentaries in his edition, though he corrected the mistake in the 1534 reprint. The enterprise was none the less to some extent original, and Berauld threw in for good measure the *Paraclesis to the Reader* which Erasmus had written two years before, in 1516, for the first edition of his Greek Testament. Josse Badius similarly edited and himself published Latin translations of works by St Basil which had been collected and brought home from Italy by Lefèvre d'Etaples (PR 1520, 11). It has been said of this edition, 'The letters on reading the pagan classics and on the solitary life were well known, but Badius' is the first printing of so important a collection of Basil's works.'[1]

The Latin Fathers of the Church had already been widely printed by the early years of the sixteenth century. It would have been hard to make out a case for a privilege for an edition of their works unless it had some novel feature, or could be shown to contain hitherto unpublished material, or displayed such learning that it renewed the study of the author in question as the editions prepared by Erasmus of St Ambrose (1527) and St Augustine (1529), printed by Froben at Basle with imperial privilege, were destined to do. An edited selection of St Gregory's works on the New Testament by Alulphus Tornacensis, dedicated to Geofroy Boussard, Dean of the Paris Faculty of Theology, obtained a privilege (*CP* 1516, 1): a reputable but unoriginal edition of St Gregory's complete works published by Jean Petit in 1518 did not. A truly pioneer enterprise, on the other hand, was Jacques

[1] E. F. Rice, *The prefatory epistles of Jacques Lefèvre d'Etaples and related texts* (New York and London, 1972), pp. 419–21.

Merlin's edition of the acts of the first four General Councils of the Church (PA 1524, 13). It was reprinted at Cologne in 1530 and became the basis of all subsequent editions.

Important texts of religious writers of the preceding four centuries or even earlier, which had still never been printed, were to hand in college, cathedral and monastery libraries in France. Usually the institutions which owned the manuscripts, the scholars who had the interest and competence to edit them, and the publishers who foresaw a good sale for them, all took a share in various degrees in promoting the first editions, as far as one can see. In many cases the authors had studied or taught in France at some period, whether they were French or not. Among the first editions thus to appear and duly obtain privileges were (in order of the grant of the privilege): an *Expositio* on the Epistles of St Paul, attributed to St Bruno (PA 1509, 1); the *Summa in quaestionibus Armenorum* and other works by Richard FitzRalph, archbishop of Armagh (Armacensis), famous for a dialogue with representatives of the Armenian Church and for his defence of the secular clergy against the friars (CH 1512, 1 (3)); the works of Peter of Blois (CH 1515, 5 (5)), and of Richard of Saint-Victor (CH 1518, 4 (2)) of whom the Venice edition of 1516 was incomplete, both these writers edited by Jacques Merlin; the treatise *De altaris mysterio* of Innocent III under the title *De officio missae*, printed for the Prior of the Paris Carthusians (PA 1518, 1); the *Contemplationes Idiotae* of Raymond Jordanus (*CP* 1519, 6); the *Speculum ecclesiae* of St Edmund of Abingdon (PR 1520, 2); the Sermons of St Antony of Padua (PR 1520, 10); commentaries on books of the Bible by the Venerable Bede (PR 1521, 3); works of Nicolas Clamenge (*CP* 1521, 3), and of Peter the Venerable, abbot of Cluny (PR 1522, 2); sermons on the Psalms by Philippe de Grève (PR 1522, 4); works of St Lawrence Giustiniani, patriarch of Venice (CH 1524, 1); the *Expositio* of Psalm 118 (119) attributed to St Bonaventura (PA 1524, 6); the complete works of St Bruno (PR 1524, 2), published by Badius for the Carthusian Order; and the works of Hugh of St Victor (PA 1526, 2). Among more recent religious books to be published under privilege was the *Consolatio luctus et mortis* of Guillaume Fichet, who, with Peter Heynlin, had in 1470 brought the first printing press to France (PA 1521, 4). Living theologians rarely applied for privileges. An exception was Alfonso Ricz or Ricius, author of *Eruditiones christiane religionis*, a treatise on the virtues and vices (CH 1512, 4); he was well placed to seek a privilege from Louis XII, being 'confesseur du commun de l'hostel dudict seigneur'.

John Mair or Major, a Paris Doctor of Theology but better known as a philosopher, published in 1518 'cum priuilegio' the Gospel of St Matthew with an 'ad literam' Exposition dealing with 308 doubts and difficulties; in his absence in Scotland the book was edited by one of his pupils, Jacques Godequin (*CP* 1518, 4). In the same year Jacques Lefèvre d'Etaples brought out 'cum priuilegio' his critical study of the tradition which identified St Mary

Magdalen with the woman who anointed Christ's feet in the house of Simon and with Mary the sister of Martha and Lazarus (*CP* 1518, 2). Replies to Lefèvre's arguments by John Fisher, printed like Lefèvre's book by Henri Estienne, also advertised the possession of privileges (*CP* 1519, 1, and *CP* 1519, 8). Lefèvre's *Commentarii initiatorii* on the four gospels had a privilege (CH 1522, 2) and so did his translation of the four gospels into French (*CP* 1523, 2). The first French editions of new books by biblical scholars in neighbouring countries also obtained privileges in a few cases: Petrus Gillius of Albi edited the *Tertia quinquagena* or discussion of fifty points of interpretation in the Bible by Antonius Nebrissensis (*CP* 1520, 14), of which the first edition had appeared at Alcalá in Spain in 1516, four years before. Conrad Resch, who had close connections with Basle, published Erasmus' *Paraphrasis in euangelium Matthei* (CH 1523, 4) and his work on the Lord's Prayer (PA 1524, 1), within months of the first editions, printed at Basle by Froben.

From 1517 onwards the utterances of Luther began to cause alarm in orthodox circles in France. The *Moralia* of Jérôme de Hangest, a prominent Paris theologian, dealt with the doctrine of free will, evidently with this in mind, though Luther was not mentioned by name; this came out in 1519, under a 'package' privilege covering Hangest's works obtained earlier by Jean Petit (CH 1515, 5 (4)). Conrad Resch, always in close touch with new publications in the German-speaking countries, printed the treatise *De primatu Petri* by Luther's principal opponent Johannes Eck, displaying a privilege from the royal chancery as well as the papal privilege granted to the author (CH 1521, 4). Two books by another Paris theologian, Josse Clichtoue or Clichtove, *Antilutherus* and *Propugnaculum ecclesiae*, came out with privileges (PA 1524, 10 and PA 1525, 8). One of his colleagues in the Faculty of Theology, Pierre Cousturier or Sutor, in his *De tralatione Bibliae*, opposed all new translations of the Bible and especially translations into the vernacular (PA 1524, 14). The same year, the astute Jean Petit judged it opportune to publish an enlarged edition of the *Catalogus haereticorum* of Bernardus Lutzenburgensis (PA 1524, 7). The increase in religious controversy does not appear, however, to have made much difference to the proportion of new books in the 'religion' category which were granted privileges.

LAW AND POLITICAL THEORY

Canon and Civil Law, with political theory (usually the domain of lawyers at this period) account for fifty-seven books published under privilege. If privileged editions of *Coutumes*, *Ordonnances* and *Styles* are added, numbering forty-eight in all, the total is 105, the largest category after Religion.

The texts required for the study of Civil Law, and the standard commentaries on them, were in print before any general use of the privilege-system grew up. The *Corpus juris civilis*, like the Bible, could be printed by anyone, though in practice the scale of the task demanded resources which only the larger firms could command. Paris publishers were not at any special advantage in this field. There was no Faculty of Civil Law in Paris University, though the presence of the Parlement brought to the capital as residents or visitors a large number of lawyers, and leading booksellers plied their trade within the premises of the Parlement itself. It was in the south of France that the tradition of Roman Law was strongest, and where it continued to shape the laws actually in force. And as an academic subject it was particularly cultivated at the University of Toulouse. One of the 'finds' made by publishers was the *Lectura super I. librum Institutionum* of Pierre de Belleperche or De Bella Pertica (d. 1308), a former chancellor of France, who had taught at Toulouse and at Orleans (PA 1514, 3). In other cases privileges might be obtained for works which had indeed been printed before but might well be difficult to get in France, or appear in improved editions. Thus a volume of *Regule e toto iure delecte* by Bartholomeus Socinus (1436–1507) and other legal works appeared with a privilege (PA 1513, 1). The rate at which privileges were given for Roman Law studies seems to have increased slightly towards the end of the period (e.g. PA 1520, 4; PA 1522, 1; *CP* 1525, 1: PA 1526, 1).

Canon Law, or the law of the Church, was studied as generally at this period as Civil Law. The two indeed interacted at so many points with each other, and with the current law of the land, that many ambitious lawyers made it their business to obtain a degree in both, and a licentiate, or still better a doctorate, *utriusque juris* was a qualification much respected. Here the Paris book-trade was on its own ground, for the Faculty of Canon Law in Paris University was an important centre of studies in the subject. The fundamental texts required by students were, as in the case of the *Corpus juris civilis*, already in print. At most, Guillaume Eustace used his personal privilege of 1508 from the king for editions, prepared by Claudius de Niceyo, of three volumes of the *Corpus juris canonici* published in 1509 and 1510 (CH 1508, 2) (3, 5 and 7). Standard works long since in print, like those of Durandus, might be given a privilege if newly edited by a competent French lawyer (e.g. PA 1513, 4). Problems raised by the relations between the royal power and the papacy, especially the Concordat of 1516, and the elections to benefices in the French church, were on the other hand burning topical issues. Texts of the Pragmatic Sanction and of the Concordat, officially approved, received privileges and were sometimes accompanied by commentaries or by relevant treatises revived from the past (e.g. PA 1508, 1; CH 1518, 2; CH 1519, 2 (1). Works like those of Petrus de Biaxio on the conduct of elections (PA 1511, 3) or the *Tractatus beneficialis* of Jean de Selve (PA 1514, 4) would be received by the general public of the day as of immediate interest.

Coutumes qualified for a privilege if they were being printed for the first time after official codification and royal approval, or after a revision. An edition with a commentary and indices drawn up by a lawyer with specialist knowledge might also qualify, even though the *Coutume* itself was already well established and in print. Thus we find, to take them in order of the dates of the privileges, the *Coutume* of Touraine (CH 1507, 1 (3)), Chartres (PA 1509, 2), Maine (PA 1509, 4), Anjou (PA 1510, 1), Orleans (PA 1510, 2), Auvergne (PA 1511, 1), Chaumont en Bassigny (PA 1511, 4), Paris (PA 1513, 2), Anjou with tables etc. by Jean Bodin (PA 1514, 6), Sens (CH 1514, 3 (3)), Burgundy with the commentary of Barthélemy de Chasseneuz (CH 1515, 7 (2)) and of Hugues Descousu (CH 1516, 1 (1)), Vitry en Partois (PA 1516, 1), Troyes (PA 1516, 7), Poitou (CH 1517, 5), Bourbonnais (PA 1522, 6), Toulouse (PA 1523, 2), Blois (PA 1524, 11), and Bourbonnais again (PA 1525, 4). An early attempt at a complete collection of them, *Les grandes coustumes generalles et particulieres du royaume de France*, also obtained a privilege (CH 1517, 3). It is possible that other separate editions of particular *Coutumes* obtained privileges, in addition to those listed above. Such booklets would tend to be discarded when they were superseded, quite apart from the wear and tear of constant use, and in some cases (e.g. Chaumont en Bassigny, 1511) only one copy survives, the sole testimony to the existence of the privilege.

Le grant coustumier de France et instructions de practicque of Jacques d'Ableiges, which obtained a privilege from Louis XII confirmed by Francis I (CH 1514, 1 (2), cf. CH 1515, 3), was on the other hand not a collection of *Coutumes*, though it is of great importance for the study of their history, especially that of the *Coutume* of Paris. The author, who completed it by 1389 when he was Bailli of Evreux, made a compilation which included the *Style* or procedure of the Chambre des Enquêtes of the Parlement and another *Style* of the *commissaires* of the Parlement, the *Stylus curiae Parlementi* of Guillaume Du Breuil, the *Constitutions du Châtelet de Paris*, and other legal documents. The work of Du Breuil, edited by Antoine Robert, had already come out in 1512 under a privilege for two years obtained by Guillaume Eustace (PA 1512, 9 (1)), and in 1511 Eustace had also issued, under probably his personal royal privilege, the first printed edition of another standard fourteenth-century authority on the procedure of the Parlement, that of Jean Masuer (CH 1508, 2 (9)). Privileges for the current *Style* of any particular lawcourt were normally sought from the court concerned: that of the *Echiquier* or Parlement of Rouen was given by the *Echiquier* itself (PA 1516, 3), that of the court of the *Grands Jours* of Berry by the court at Bourges (PA 1518, 5). That of the lawcourts of Brittany was, however, obtained from the chancery of the duchy, issued by the Council in the king's name (CH 1525, 3). The *Prothocolle des notaires du chastellet de Paris* was covered by a grant obtained for this and other official publications, including the Concordat, from the royal chancery (CH 1519, 2 (3)), while the Prévôt of Paris at the Châtelet gave a privilege for the *Style* of the court of the *bailliage* of Sens (PR 1520, 9).

In 1510 Guillaume Eustace published *Les Ordonnances royaulx*, 'avec les stilles de Parlement et de Chastellet', with an improved Latin text of the

Pragmatic Sanction, using (it may be assumed) the personal privilege which he had recently obtained for his new publications (CH 1508, 2 (6)). Other collections of *Ordonnances* subsequently came out under privilege (PA 1512, 4 and PA 1512, 6; PA 1515, 1; CH 1522, (2)). Particular *ordonnances* such as those 'sur le faict des chasses' by the king (CH 1517, 4), or those issued to deal with specific problems by the Parlement of Rouen (PA 1513, 3, and PA 1519, 3), were also the object of privileges. Later in the century the French crown attempted to invest the office of Printer to the King with the monopoly in such publications, particularly in the case of Robert (II) Estienne.[1] In the period with which we are dealing, the field was wholly open to private enterprise, though privileges were evidently in practice given for such items only to well-known and responsible publishers.

The learning of contemporary French lawyers is quite well represented in the legal works which obtained privileges. Among them may be noted Barthélemy de Chasseneuz, king's advocate at Autun, and author of the *Commentaria in consuetudines ducatus Burgundie* (CH 1515, 7 (2)); Etienne Malleret, *docteur ès droictz*, and author of *De electionibus et beneficiis ecclesiasticis* (CH 1515, 9); Vincent Cigauld, *licencié en loix*, judge of Brivadois, who himself obtained a grant for a group of his legal studies (CH 1516, 2); Jean Le Cirier, advocate in the Parlement of Paris and a lecturer in the Faculty of Canon Law, whose *Tractatus de iure primogeniturae* came out in 1521 (CH 1519, 6 (4)), and Jean de Montholon, whose *Promptuarium* was a kind of encyclopaedia of Canon and Civil Law (CH 1520, 7).

The earliest and most active in writing and sponsoring publications of legal interest was, however, Nicole Bohier, or Boerius, whose distinguished career culminated in his appointment as president of the Parlement of Bordeaux. And the list of these publications gives a good idea of the range of subjects for which a public could be found, and for which therefore it was worthwhile for an author or publisher to seek privileges, within the field of law. His first grant (CH 1509, 1) covered his *Tractatus* on the powers of Cardinal Georges d'Amboise, as papal legate, his Latin glosses on the *Coutume* of the duchy of Berry, and his edition (with commentary) of Cardinal Gulielmus Mandagotus, *Tractatus de electione*. His second grant (CH 1512, 3) covered at least two works. One was a study of the powers of the royal Council and of the Parlement, by Jean Montaigne, with a dedication by the author in which he refers eulogistically to Bohier. Another was the *Leges Longobardorum* or *Libri feudorum*, always to be found at this period at the end of the *Corpus juris civilis*, published with a preface and annotations by Bohier himself. Bohier's third privilege, obtained from the chancery in August 1515 (CH 1515, 7), extended to three different books, and seems to show him more in the role of a promoter

---

[1] See my article, 'The publication of the royal edicts and ordinances under Charles IX: the destiny of Robert (II) Estienne as King's Printer', *Proceedings of the Huguenot Society of London*, XIX (1954), pp. 41–59.

Oyſe mere du Roy ducheſſe Dan//
goulmois z Daniou:conteſſe du adaine z de Bien:
Regente en France Aux bailly z pzeuoſt de Paris:ſe=
nechal de Lyon:bailly de adaſcon:bailly de Rouen:z a
tous les aultres inſticiers z officies du Roy noſtre treſ=
cher ſeigneur z filz:ou a leurs lieuxtenans Salut.
Lumble ſupplication de noſtre bien ayme Conſtantin
Fradin:libzaire:cytoien de Lyon : auons receu : conte=
nant Que puis aucun temps en ca il a recouuert certain
liure z traictier intitule Joannes de Terra rubea contra rebelles Francie:lequel
liure enſemble vng petit traictier appelle Panegyzicus ad Franciam Francieqz
regem:compoſe par maiſtre Jaques Bonandi lincencie en chaſcu dzoit:leſquelz
liure z traictier nont point encoures eſtez impzimez:ledict ſuppliant a faict veoir
cozriger z gloſer par ledict maiſtre Jaques Bonandi:fozt vtiles z pzouffitables
a la choſe publicque:il feroit voulentiers impzimer z publier. mais il doubte que
ſi toſt quil les auroit faict impzimer z publier aucuns autres libzaires ou impzi=
meurs les feiſſent impzimer.et pourtant ne pourroit recouurer ſes fraiz z miſes
qui ſont ia grans pour auoir recouuert leſdictz liures z traictier z iceulx faict coz=
riger z gloſer:z luy conuiédra encoures faire pluſieurs autres grans fraiz z miſes
pour impzimer leſdictz liure z traictier:leſquelz il feroit en dangier de perdre ſi lon
impzimoit leſdictz liures apzes luy:qui feroit a ſon grant dommaige:ſi par nous
ne luy eſtoit ſur ce pourueu de remede connenable humblemét requerant icelluy.
Pource eſt il:que nous ce conſidere:en vertu de noſtredict pouoir:auctozite:z re=
gence auons pezmis z octroye:permettons z octroyons audit ſuppliant de grace
eſpecial par ces pzeſentes:z donnons pouoir:conge z licence dimpzimer:ou faire
impzimer leſdictz liure z traictier:iceulx publier z vendre a ſon pzouffit pour re=
couurer ſeſo.couſtz:fraiz z miſes pour le temps z eſpace de troys ans pzouchains
venás a compter du iour la fin de limpzeſſion deſdictz liure z traictier:ſans ce que
durant ledict temps de troys ans aucun autre que ledict ſuppliát de quelque eſtat
ou condition quil ſoit puiſſe impzimer ne faire impzimer:vendre ne faire vendre
leſdictz liure z traictier:ne aucuns deulx en ce royaulme:pais z ſeigneuries de no
ſtredict ſeigneur z filz ſur poyne de confiſcation deſdictz linres z daméde arbitrai=
re.Si vous mandons:commandons:z treſexpzeſſement enioignons en vertu de
noſtredict pounoir:regence z auctozite que en enſuyuant noſdictz conge:licence z
octroy vous faictes ou faictes faire expzeſſes inhibitions z deffences de par le roy
noſtredict ſeigneur z filz z nous:a tous libzaires:impzimeurs z autres quil appar
tiendra de non impzimer:ne faire impzimer:z vendre ne faire vendre leſdictz liure
z traictier en ce royaulme pays z ſeignourie de noſtredict ſeigneur z filz ſur les pei
nes que deſſus.Et en cas doppoſition:ou debat leſdictes inhibitions z deffences
tenans.Non obſtant oppoſitions ou appellations quelzconques z ſans pzeiudi=
ce dicelles faictes au ſurplus aux parties oyes raiſon et inſtice.Car ainſi nous
plaiſt eſtre faict.Nonobſtant comme deſſus quelzconques lettres ſubzeptices im
petrees ou a impetrer a ce contraires.Et pource que lon pourra auoir a faire de
ces pzeſentes en pluſieurs lieux voulons que au vidimus dicelles faict ſoubz ſeel
royal foy ſoit adiouſtee comme a loziginal. Donne a ſainct Juſt ſur Lyon
le.xvij.iour de Nouembze lan adil cinq cens vingt cinq.
Par madame regente en France a la relation du conſeil.
Jnuyneau.

Plate 9   Joannes de Terra Rubea, *Contra rebelles*, with privilege granted by Louise of Savoy,
the king's mother, as Regent (1525)

of legal publications, a role which his close association with Simon Vincent of Lyon helped him to play. The books were the *Quaestiones aureae* and *Tractatus de Feudis* of Pierre de Belleperche, edited by Jean Thierry of Langres, doctor of laws; the commentary on the *coutume* of Burgundy by Chasseneuz, already mentioned; and the *Tractatus* and *Singularia* of Guido Papa, a famous luminary of the Parlement of Dauphiné, edited again by Jean Thierry, though a dedication by Vincent to Bohier shows that the latter was closely involved in the project. The last privilege obtained by Bohier so far noticed is for a work on canon law by Petrus de Ancharano of Bologna (CH 1519, 5). Quite unlike any of these publications, and the only one for which his publishers and not he himself obtained the privilege (CH 1515, 4), is Bohier's own treatise *De seditiosis*. This was prompted by the trial at Agen, in which he had taken part as one of the commissioners sent by Louis XII, of the inhabitants who had staged an alarming riot there in 1513. Following his treatise, he printed in the original French the text of the judgement given at the end of the trial itself, and provided an illustration, which must have been prepared under his instructions, of the scene in court, showing the judges (himself among them) and officials, and the defendants, each labelled with his name. This had been a sensational case. The rioters had seized control of the town for several days, and imprisoned the consuls in the town hall, directly defying the royal authority. All those convicted received exemplary punishment. Two of the ringleaders were hanged. Most of the others were heavily fined, or banished, or both. Bohier's decision to publish the full judgement, including the whole account of the proceedings, as a sort of *pièce justificative* to his essay on sedition, is therefore quite understandable.

Works which can be classified as political theory were sometimes published under privilege. The *Somnium viridarii*, probably written by Philippe de Mézières in 1376, had lost nothing of its relevance to the situation when it was printed for the first time in 1516 (PA 1516, 6); the French version, *Le songe du vergier*, was long since in print. The topical interest of the treatise *Contra rebelles suorum regum* was still more immediate when it was first printed in 1525 (CH 1524, 4); the author, Jean (Joannes) de Terre Vermeille or De Terra Rubea, one of Charles VII's publicists, was an extreme advocate of the divine right of kings, writing in a time of national crisis, and it was a timely move to have it printed when the treason of the Connétable and the king's defeat at Pavia made loyalty more imperative than ever. The editor, Jacques Bonaud, *in utroque jure licentiatus*, added a panegyric of France of his own composition, and dedicated the book to the chancellor, who, as the chief supporter of Francis I's absolutism, may well have prompted the publication, and expedited the grant of the privilege. Of contemporary French writers, Claude de Seyssel was perhaps the most important political theorist, though his conception of the French constitution was very different from that of the apologists of absolute monarchy: the *Grant monarchie de France* was included in a privilege obtained by Regnault Chaudière (CH 1519, 6). Among foreign works in this field to receive privileges in France were More's *Utopia* with commentary by Erasmus (*CP* 1517, 6) and the treatise *De regno et regis institutione* by Francesco Patrizzi (CH 1519, 3 (1)). And the first edition of the *Polycraticus* of the twelfth-century scholar John of Salisbury since the *editio princeps* printed by the Brothers of the Common Life at Brussels about 1480 appeared with privilege at Lyon in 1513 (*CP* 1513, 1).

HISTORY AND CURRENT EVENTS

In this field, at least seventy-eight items were published with a privilege, some composed by recent or contemporary writers, others dating from the past but hitherto not printed (or not printed in French). The oldest were those included in a 'package' privilege obtained by Jean Petit from the royal chancery (CH 1512, 1) to cover a group of books to be published by himself and various partners. They were the *Chronicon* of Sigebert of Gembloux, the *De regum Francorum origine* of Aimoinus of Fleury, and the *Historia Francorum* of Gregory of Tours. This promising start to publishing the *monumenta* of the national history of France had no immediate sequel, unless we count the works of Peter of Blois (CH 1515, 5 (5)), which are of historical as well as religious interest: it was evidently inspired by Guillaume Petit or Parvi, bishop of Troyes, the king's confessor, who actively promoted antiquarian studies. The chronicles kept at the royal abbey of Saint-Denis, the *Grandes chroniques de France*, were widely known by this time both in manuscript copies and in print, but the first edition to take the story beyond the reign of Louis XI obtained a royal privilege when published by Guillaume Eustace (CH 1514, 3 (2)). The *Compendium de origine et gestis Francorum* of Robert Gaguin had been printed several times by 1501, when he died, but Galliot Du Pré obtained a privilege for a French translation of it (CH 1513, 4 (1)), under the title somewhat confusingly of *Les grandes Cronicques*; and Pierre Viart obtained one for an edition equipped with a supplement to bring the work up to date in 1521 (PA 1521, 2).[1]

From the period before 1500 in France there were other historical works to be gleaned which had not yet appeared in print. The most momentous of these was the *Mémoires* of Philippe de Commynes (d. 1511), of which the part dealing with the reign of Louis XI was first published by Galliot Du Pré (PA 1524, 3). At the time there would have been almost equal interest in *Le rozier historial de France* (CH 1523, 2). For in this volume François Regnault printed a treatise on the education of a prince, *Le rosier des guerres*, which was generally attributed to Louis XI himself, though it is now known to have been written by Pierre Choysnet, a doctor and astrologer in his service. It was

[1] A. Molinier, *Sources de l'histoire de France des origines aux guerres d'Italie*, v–vi (1904), pp. 26–8; H. Hauser, *Sources de l'histoire de France, xvie siècle* (1909), I, pp. 18–19.

Regnault also who first printed *Le livre de la Toison d'Or*, by Guillaume Fillastre (d. 1473), chancellor of the Order of the Golden Fleece, hitherto available only in manuscripts owned by members of the Order (PA 1516, 5). Michel Le Noir produced *Les passaiges d'oultremer faitz par les Françoys*, by Sebastien Mamerot, a history of the part played by the French in the crusades from Charlemagne to 1462, adding later material to bring the story down to the conquest of Granada in 1492 (CH 1517, 6 (4)).

The official history of France was to have been written by the Veronese humanist Paulus Aemilius, brought in by Charles VIII and employed as 'orateur et chroniqueur du roi'. *De rebus gestis Francorum* never got further than Philip Augustus (CH 1517, 7); the author died in 1529, though continuations were later added by other hands. Tributes to great figures from the national past were attempted by several writers, ranging from Christophe de Longueil's eulogy of St Louis (PA 1512, 7 (2)) to Jean Bouchet's *L'histoire et cronicque de Clotaire* (CH 1518, 1). Such activity might extend to the contemporary era, as with Claude de Seyssel's *Les louanges du roy Louys xii* (CH 1507, 1 (7)). New histories of particular territories in France or on its borders were, on the other hand, produced in relatively large-scale works. Among those which came out under privilege were *Les grandes croniques de Bretaigne* of Alain Bouchard (CH 1514, 1 (1)); *Les grans croniques des gestes des princes de Savoye* of Symphorien Champier (PA 1516, 4); *Les gestes des Tholosains* of Nicolas Bertrand (PA 1517, 3); and *Les annales d'Acquitaine* of Jean Bouchet (PA 1524, 15). Enterprising publishers sponsored translations into French of ancient historians: Livy, *Le premier volume des grans decades* (CH 1514, 3 (1)); Suetonius, *Des faictz et gestes des douze Cesars* (CH 1520, 3 (1)); and Valerius Maximus, *Le floralier des histoires* (PR 1525, 1). Nor did they always shun romanticised history: *Le violier des histoires rommaines* (CH 1520, 8) is a version of the *Gesta Romanorum*. More workaday publications were French translations of the *Chronica chronicarum*, a long-established historical dictionary or repertory (CH 1521, 3), and of Sacchi de Platina's collection, containing genealogies of popes and reigning dynasties (CH 1519, 3 (2)). Occasionally recent Italian historians feature among works which obtained privileges in France. Such were Sabellicus, who had written in Latin the history of his native Venice (PA 1514, 1 (1)), and Polydore Virgil, whose *De inuentoribus rerum* was translated into French (PR 1520, 12).

The first contemporary events of which accounts appeared under privilege were episodes of Louis XII's campaigns in Italy, usually presented with a strong bias favouring the king's policies, such as *La chronique de Gennes* (PA 1507, 1 (2)), by an anonymous writer, and *L'entreprise de Venise* and *L'union des princes* (PR 1509, 2 and 3), by Pierre Gringore. Some accounts came out with a *congé*,[1] not specifically with privilege, such as *L'Armée du Roy qu'il avoit*

---

[1] See above, pp. 112–13.

contre les Vénitiens (PR 1509, 4*). The oration made before Pope Julius II by Cardinal Guillaume Briçonnet, described as an apologia for Louis XII, appeared 'cum priuilegio', however (*CP* 1507, 1), as did a French translation of the Pope's admonition against the Venetians (*CP* 1509, 2). Men of letters in the royal service made their contributions, such as Jean Danton's *Les espitres envoyées au Roy delà montz par les estatz de France*, for which his printer advertised possession of a privilege (*CP* 1509, 1). A naval engagement between English and Breton ships which took place on 10 August 1512 elicited a poem from Germain de Brie or Brixius, secretary to Anne of Brittany, *Chordigerae nauis conflagratio* (CH 1513, 1), praising the heroism of the commander of the Breton flagship which was destroyed. (The pugnacious tone of the poem much annoyed Brixius' English friends like Thomas More.)[1]

Obituaries too might qualify for privileges. An elegy by Antoine Forestier or Sylviolus, who described himself as 'a Parisian', commemorated the death (on 25 May 1510) of Georges d'Amboise, Cardinal Archbishop of Rouen and French Viceroy of Milan (PR 1510, 1). The death of Anne of Brittany (9 January 1514) was deplored not only by the faithful Germain de Brie but also by Laurent Desmoulins (PR 1514, 1), by Fausto Andrelini in a Latin panegyric (PA 1515, 3), and in a Latin lament put into the mouth of her daughter Claude by Arnaldus Avedelis called Sonis (*CP* 1514, 2). The ensuing treaty with England (PR 1514, 2), followed by Louis XII's marriage to Princess Mary of England as his third wife, brought festive occasions of which descriptions were much in demand: the new queen's arrival, and the wedding (PR 1514, 3), and her state entry into Paris (PR 1514, 4), with the customary jousts (CH 1514, 5). On the death of Louis XII and the accession of Francis I, the coronation at Reims (PR 1515, 1), and various congratulatory verses (e.g. PR 1515, 2), led up to many subsequent celebrations after the king's triumphant return from his campaign in Italy. Such were the state entry of Queen Claude into Paris (PR 1517, 4) and of the king into Rouen (PR 1517, 6), the reception of the English envoys on the engagement of the infant Dauphin Francis to the infant daughter of Henry VIII (CH 1518, 6 (1)), and the Field of the Cloth of Gold (PR 1520, 6). An anonymous account of the king's conquest of the duchy of Milan appeared in 1518 (PR 1518, 1). The only event outside France and the territories claimed by France of which the news appeared under privilege was the siege of Rhodes (PR 1525, 4). Naturally many such ephemeral publications appeared without a privilege in this period when application for a privilege was optional, for instance many of the other accounts of the Field of the Cloth of Gold.

[1] Erasmus, *Opus Epist.*, ed. Allen, I, pp. 447–8, and IV, pp. 218ff., 252 and 295 (note).

PHILOSOPHY

With forty-eight books, philosophy accounts for nearly 10 per cent of all published under privilege. This seems a high proportion, but it is not hard to explain. The centuries-old reputation of Paris University as a centre of the study of logic and philosophy was still attracting distinguished scholars and students. The first quarter of the sixteenth century indeed saw a revival of scholastic philosophy, mainly Nominalist. This was promoted, chiefly within the ranks of the Faculty of Theology, by masters from all over France and from some foreign countries as well. Certain Scottish, Spanish and Portuguese theologians were particularly prominent in this revival. Paris publishers, many of whom were in close touch with the university, eagerly sought new works by the most celebrated of these scholars as they were completed, or new editions revised by the authors, knowing that there would be a keen demand for them from an educated public which reached far beyond the confines of France, written as they were in Latin for an international clientele. Texts of the older scholastic philosophers whose works had not been printed before, many of whom had taught in Paris, were also forthcoming from the libraries of Paris colleges and religious houses.

There were texts which had been the staple of university teaching and research for so long that the fifteenth-century printers had put large numbers of copies into circulation already, in addition to the stocks of manuscript copies still in existence. Such were the *Sentences* of Peter Lombard, which in the twelfth century had contributed to founding the celebrity of the Paris school of philosophy. No privilege for his works could be expected by a French publisher of the early sixteenth century. But medieval and sixteenth-century philosophers, like some of their successors in our own time, often found it convenient to present the results of their inquiries in the form of a commentary on an existing text. The *Sentences*, or portions of them, were a favourite vehicle for such presentations. These commentaries, whether accompanied by the text to which they related or not, were themselves original works and eligible to receive privileges, and many examples are in fact found among privileged books on philosophy. Among the medieval masters, there appear in the privilege-lists Dionysius Cisterciensis (PA 1511, 2), Adam Godhamus or rather Woodham (CH 1512, 1 (2)), Joannes de Bassolis (*CP* 1517, 1), Petrus de Palude (PA 1517, 7 (1)), Henry of Ghent or Goethals (CH 1518, 5), Guillermus de Rubione (PA 1518, 3), Richard de Mediavilla or Middleton (*CP* 1519, 11), and Gabriel Biel (PR 1521, 1). John Duns Scotus came in for particular attention: privileges were obtained for his *Reportata super primum Sententiarum* edited by John Mair (PA 1517, 6), for his *Commentaria in duodecim libros Metaphysice Aristotelis* collected by Antonius Andreas (*CP* 1520, 15), and *Quaestiones quodlibetales* edited by Pierre Tartaret (PA 1519, 1).

The *Dux dubitantium* of Moses Maimonides, the twelfth-century Jewish philosopher, a learned attempt to reconcile faith and reason which had been known and studied through the Middle Ages, appeared with a privilege in 1520. It had been edited by Agostino Giustiniani, bishop of Nebbio, who was in Paris 1518–22 (PR 1520, 4A).

The contemporary philosopher for whose works privileges were most eagerly sought by publishers was John Mair or Major. Mair's reputation was already established, and his first works were already in print, before the privilege system was taken up by the academic publishers, but they made up for lost time once the system and its advantages were understood. Mair's *Quartus sententiarum*, brought out by Poncet le Preux and Jean Granjon, was the earliest book of this nature to receive a privilege in France (PA 1509, 3). Granjon followed it up with the *Summule* (PA 1514, 9 (2)), and an enlarged edition of the *Summule* two years later (PA 1516, 9), adding the *Insolubilia* (CP 1516, 3), a second edition of the commentary on the *Sentences*, Book II (CP 1519, 7), and the *Summaria in dyalecticen introductiones* (CP 1520, 13). Jean Petit and Gilles Gourmont had a privilege for a revised edition of Mair's *Octo libri physicorum* (PA 1526, 3). Jean Gourmont got a privilege for a book on dialectic by Mair's former student William Manderston (PA 1517, 7 (2)), and Prigent Calvarin for a revised edition of the book five years later (CH 1522, 7). Two works by Johannes Dullaert of Ghent, a famous logician of the Collège de Montaigu, another former pupil of Mair, came out under privilege (PR 1521, 4 and PR 1523, 5). Other well-known Paris scholars of the time for whose philosophical writings at least one privilege was granted were: Jérôme de Hangest (CH 1515, 5), Jacques Almain (PA 1516, 8), Antonio Coronel (PA 1514, 2), Ferdinand Enzinas (CH 1521, 6), Andreas de Novo Castro (PA 1514, 9 (2)), Gervase Waim (CH 1519, 1 (2)) and Juan de Celaya (PR 1516, 3 and 4; PR 1517, 3; PA 1517, 9; CP 1521, 4; CH 1523, 3).

It was in philosophical – or, for that matter, in juridical – works at first sight of no interest even in the sixteenth century except to specialists that writers sometimes expressed most freely their boldest speculations on matters of public interest. The first item of scholastic philosophy to gain a privilege, for instance, was the *Quartus sententiarum* of John Mair (PA 1509, 3). This was ostensibly a commentary on the Fourth Book of the *Sentences*. But Mair included in his work a discussion of the morality of usury – the practice of lending money at interest – and questioned the traditional teaching which condemned it as wrong in all circumstances, though this was the principle maintained officially by the Faculty of Theology.[1]

Ancient philosophy, on the other hand, called forth few books eligible for privileges. Modern Latin versions of Aristotle's *Physics*, some of them specially made by François Vatablus (PA 1518, 7), printed in parallel columns with the 'Antique tralatio', obtained a privilege. The Latin translation and

[1] R. de Roover, 'La pensée économique de Jean Mair', *Journal des Savants* (1970), fasc. 2, pp. 65–81, quoted by Farge, *Biographical Register*, p. 307.

commentary on the *Timaeus* of Plato, by Chalcidius, edited by Agostino Giustiniani, was published 'Cum priuilegio' (*CP* 1520, 21). Symphorien Champier published an exposition of Platonism, entitled *Periarchon*, for which his publisher obtained a grant (CH 1515, 2). Otherwise there is little reflection, among privileged books at this period, of the interest being shown by French men of letters in Platonism and Neoplatonism.

LITERATURE OF ENTERTAINMENT

The literature of entertainment, as one may call poetry, fiction and drama, chiefly in French, accounts for forty-seven items, or under 10 per cent of the total. Of living creative writers, those who obtained privileges were those best able, by the position in society which they occupied, official or unofficial, to defend their interests. Notable among these were Jean Lemaire de Belges, the most celebrated author of the period to write in French, but also historiographer to the queen (CH 1509, 2 and CH 1512, 2); and also, at a more popular level, Pierre Gringore, a successful satirist but also a committed defender of French royal policies (PR 1505, 1; PR 1509, 2; PR 1509, 3; PR 1509, 6; PR 1510, 2; CH 1516, 3; CH 1521, 5). Among the other authors of the time who were granted privileges were Eloi d'Amerval for his *Deablerie* (CH 1508, 1); Laurent Desmoulins for *Le cymetière des malheureux* (PR 1511, 2); Guillaume Michel de Tours for *Le siècle doré* (PR 1522, 1) as well as for *La forest de conscience* (PR 1516, 2), which has been considered under Religion; and Jean Bouchet (or rather his publishers) for *La déploration de l'église militante* (PA 1512, 5), *Le temple de bonne renommée* (CH 1517, 1 (3)) and *Le labirynth de Fortune* (CH 1522, 6), as well as for his historical works.

If publishers in the first quarter of the sixteenth century showed a relative lack of interest in procuring new literary works by contemporary authors, this was no doubt partly because there remained to be printed a considerable – though necessarily a dwindling – quantity of texts inherited from the past which could still be enjoyed, or which needed only adaptation for sixteenth-century readers to enjoy.

Outstanding among such texts was the poetry of Duke Charles of Orleans, who died in 1465. And indeed this poetry, or most of it, featured in one of the earliest books to be published by Antoine Vérard under his personal royal privilege (CH 1507, 1 (9)), which evidently covered any work which he should be the first to have printed. It was, however, a very strange publication. It was entitled *La chasse et le départ d'Amours*, and was published in 1509 under the name of Octavien de Saint-Gelais, bishop of Angoulême, a well-known man of letters recently dead, and of Blaise d'Auriol.[1] Not only was

---

[1] Charles d'Orléans, *Poésies*, ed. P. Champion, CFMA, 2 vols. (1923), Introduction, pp. viii–xxii. Octavien de Saint-Gelais (attrib.), *La Chasse d'Amours*, ed. M. B. Winn, TLF (1984), Introduction, pp. x–xi and xxxi.

there no mention of Duke Charles in this collection, but all the names of real people which could have connected any of the poetry with him were carefully replaced by allegorical figures, as if to throw the reader off the scent. As a result knowledge of his poetry remained confined to the royal family and their immediate circle, and the fact that he had been a poet at all was scarcely known to the general public. La Croix du Maine, who was most painstaking in his notices of fifteenth-century writers in his *Bibliothèque* of 1584, does not mention him. Yet his poetry survives in a dozen manuscripts, including his own copy. A selection of his poetry made from one of these manuscripts came out in his own name in 1740, and the first complete edition in 1803. What, then, was Antoine Vérard doing in 1509?

The poems which appear first in the collection are undoubtedly by Octavien de Saint-Gelais. They are followed by *La Chasse d'Amours*, a narrative poem of 8,828 lines, which is of uncertain but quite recent authorship. *La Chasse d'Amours* is based on *La Retenue d'Amours*, by Charles d'Orléans, in places textually. It is succeeded by a series of ballades and rondeaux, all presented as being the work of *L'Amant Parfait* (the hero of *La Chasse d'Amours*) and his lady, but really by identifiable authors of whom Charles d'Orléans is the most important. Further on in the collection there is another series of ballades and rondeaux, almost all by Charles d'Orléans, with all reference to him suppressed. Vérard had not always been scrupulous in his treatment of authors, dead or alive. His *Art de chevalerie selon Végèce* of 1488 was Christine de Pisan's *Le livre des fais d'armes et de chevalerie* of 1414: he omitted any mention of her name and even altered the text to make it appear that it was written by a man.[1] He published the earliest work of Jean Bouchet, *Les regnars traversans les perilleuses voyes*, some time between 1500 and 1503, under the name of Sebastian Brandt, the famous author of the *Ship of Fools*, and made changes in the text as well, a manoeuvre which Bouchet remembered with resentment over forty years later.[2] But to find Vérard taking such liberties with the duke of Orleans, who was the father of the reigning king, Louis XII, is another matter, especially as the publisher had close connections with the court. I do not know what the explanation is, and can only draw attention to the problem.

A minor classic of fifteenth-century poetry, *Les fortunes et adversitez de Jean Regnier*, came out under privilege in 1526 in quite different circumstances (PR 1524, 1). Regnier was a humbler contemporary of Charles d'Orléans. He had been the Bailli of Auxerre for the duke of Burgundy, and found his vocation for verse when in 1432, as he was returning from Rouen, he had the misfortune to be seized by brigands claiming allegiance to Charles VII and

---

[1] Marie-Josèphe Pinet, *Christine de Pisan 1364–1430* (1927), pp. 358–62. The standard work is now Charity C. Willard, *Christine de Pizan, her life and works* (New York, 1985).

[2] Jean Bouchet, *Epistres morales et familières* (Poitiers, 1545), Ep. xi. (fol. 47ᵛ). For another such case see M. B. Winn 'Publisher vs. author: Antoine Vérard, Jean Bouchet and l'Amoureux transy', *Bibliothèque d'Humanisme et Renaissance*, L (1988) pp. 39–55.

was held to ransom by them, suffering captivity in chains for almost two years until his wife and friends could raise the sum demanded and procure his release. During this time he consoled himself by writing poems in the stock forms of the day, poems which he subsequently added to and probably polished up. No manuscript of this work is known. It survives only in Jean de La Garde's printed edition. That edition is dedicated to one of Regnier's descendants, and it may have been published in agreement with the family or even perhaps at their instigation, from the author's own copy, probably preserved as an heirloom. It is printed with care, and equipped with numerous illustrations which were evidently made for the purpose, showing Regnier, his wife and other characters in the costume of their period. These woodcuts could have been based on sketches made for the author or even by him.[1]

A hitherto unpublished work of Georges Chastellain, *Le temple Jehan Boccace*,[2] was brought out under privilege by Galliot Du Pré (CH 1517, 1 (2)). This had been inspired by Boccaccio's works, *De casibus virorum illustrium* and *De claris mulieribus*, already well known in Chastellain's time both in the original and in the French version made by Laurent de Premierfait in 1409 (which was still being reprinted by Antoine Vérard in 1493). *Le temple Jehan Boccace* describes a vision in which the author beheld an immense cemetery commemorating famous people from antiquity onwards who had been remarkable for the greatness of their misfortunes. In the centre, full of inscriptions and epitaphs, stands a temple which enshrines the tomb of Boccaccio. To this gloomy scene the author gives considerable animation, picturing the recently dead hurrying in to stake out their claim to be immortalised in the temple. Margaret of Anjou, for whom the work was completed, finally enters to demand that her name should be admitted in her lifetime, arguing that her misfortunes are exceptional. Such is her vehemence that the shade of Boccaccio is aroused from the grave to confront her. He reminds her of the advantages she still enjoys: youth, health and offspring (this was written probably in 1463) and the possibility of a reversal of her ill fortune. An eloquent exhortation to patience, fortitude and submission to the will of God concludes the work. Though Chastellain's prose, always very individual, must have dated by 1517, there was still much here to appeal to an early sixteenth-century reader. The fascination of reading about great people, particularly when recalled by authors who had known them, was indeed as evident in the early sixteenth century as at the present day, even if the favoured literary forms have changed. *Le parement et triumphe des dames de*

---

[1] Modern edition by E. Droz, SATF (1923), with reproductions of the illustrations. Section on Regnier in Champion, *Histoire poétique du quinzième siècle* (1923), I, pp. 227–84.

[2] *Le temple Jehan Boccace* is printed, from MS sources, in the *Œuvres de Georges Chastellain*, ed. Kervyn de Lettenhove (Brussels, 1865), VII, pp. 75–143.

honneur, by Olivier de La Marche,[1] written in verse, devoting a stanza to each of the deceased ladies whom he wished to honour, must have been one of his last works, for it includes the death (which occurred in 1488) of Marie, wife of John of Calabria, daughter of Duke Charles I of Bourbon (stanza 167). However Jean Petit secured a copy of it, he clearly thought it would be of general interest, for it was the occasion of his first application for a privilege (PA 1510, 3). And as edited for him – not very faithfully – by Pierre Desrey it did indeed prove popular enough to be subsequently reprinted. (The most celebrated of La Marche's imaginative works, *Le chevalier délibéré*, had already been printed more than once before the end of the fifteenth century.)

Translations into French of the poets of antiquity occasionally appeared under privilege, probably when the publisher was able to show that he had specially commissioned a new translation. A French version of the *Remedia amoris*, and a translation of the *Æneid* of Virgil by Octavien de Saint-Gelais and Jean D'Ivry, were both published by Antoine Vérard under his personal privilege (CH 1507, 1, 12 and 14). The *Georgics* of Virgil, translated and 'moralised' by Guillaume Michel de Tours, were included in the 'package' privilege granted to Durand Gerlier for the Concordat (CH 1519, 2 (2)): here the terms of the privilege are known, and show that Gerlier had indeed commissioned the work ('il a puis naguieres à grans fraictz et despens faict translater de latin en francoys'). Translations of Italian poets appear in the privileged category still more rarely. The neo-Latin poet Baptista Spagnuoli, otherwise known as Mantuanus, was much appreciated in France for his elegance and his piety, and Jacques de Mortières, who translated into French one of his most important works, *La Parthenice*, obtained a privilege (CH 1522, 5). Barthélemy Vérard secured a privilege for a prose translation by Georges de La Forge of Petrarch's *Trionfi* (PA 1514, 7), with lavish illustrations, some taken from his father's stock, others, of high quality, specially made.[2] Among prose works from antiquity we find Plutarch, *Pour discerner ung vray amy d'aveques ung flateur* (PR 1520, 1), which the translator, François Sauvage, dedicated at Amboise on 1 May 1519 to John Poyntz, brother of the diplomat Sir Francis Poyntz.

The work of fifteenth-century prose fiction best known at the present day, *Le petit Jean de Saintré*, by Antoine de La Sale (d. 1460–1), was not printed until 1517, when Michel Le Noir obtained a privilege for it and for three other works (CH 1517, 6 (3)). It was also Le Noir who first printed La Sale's early work *La Salade*, famous for his account of his visit to 'Le paradis de la royne

---

[1] *Mémoires d'Olivier de La Marche*, ed. H. Beaune and J. D'Arbaumont, SHF (1888), IV, Notice bibliographique; *Œuvres poétiques*, pp. cxxx–cxxxviii, and J. Kalbfleisch, *Le triumphe des dames d'O. de La Marche*, Inaugural-Dissertation (Rostock, 1901).

[2] R. Brun, *Le livre illustré en France au XVIᵉ siècle* (1930), p. 283, attributes these with a query to the School of Perréal. One is illustrated by him as Planche IV.

Sibylle' (CH 1522, 1).[1] The most celebrated collection of short stories, *Les cent nouvelles nouvelles*, sometimes attributed mistakenly to Antoine de La Sale, had been published by Antoine Vérard in 1486.[2] The novel and the short story had not yet, however, become the literary forms most cultivated by ambitious authors. The prose romance, ancestor of the novel, was certainly very popular. So much of it had indeed been inherited from the past, in a state still useable or adaptable for early sixteenth-century readers to enjoy, that it was hardly realised until the success of Nicolas de Herberary with *Amadis de Gaule* in 1540 what a public there would be for a well-written story composed (it is virtually an original composition) purposely for contemporary taste.

And so from 1478 onwards a very large number of the most popular romances were printed, some of them, like *Les Quatre filz Aymon*, over and over again. At least three new ones were composed in the chivalrous manner, and all obtained privileges: *Les excellentes cronicques du prince Judas Machabeus*, by Charles de Saint-Gelais (CH 1514, 4), adapted from the biblical story; *La conqueste du trespuissant empire de Trebisonde*, a sequel to *Les quatre filz Aymon* arranged by an anonymous author who dedicated it to Queen Claude (PA 1518, 2); and *La conqueste de Grece faicte par Philippe de Madien* by Perrinet Dupin (PR 1525, 3 (2)). But nine prose romances of earlier origin[3] obtained privileges, evidently because they were wholly or partially hitherto unpublished. The prose version of *Huon de Bordeaux*, the famous thirteenth-century romance which introduced the character of Oberon the fairy king, was made in 1455: the printed edition of it in 1513 was the first publication of it, and it is known only in this form, no manuscript of it having survived (CH 1513, 3). *L'hystoire du sainct greaal* contains the *Estoire del Graal*, the *Perlesvaus* and the *Queste del Graal*: the first two of these, at least, had not been printed before (CH 1515, 1).[4] *Guérin de Montglane*, based on a thirteenth century original, was reworked in the fourteenth century: the 1517 edition seems to be the first edition of the prose romance (CH 1517, 6(2)). *Gérard de Nevers* is the first edition of the prose version, made for Charles de Clèves, comte de Nevers, who died in 1521, of the *Roman de la Violette*, by Gerbert de Montreuil (PR 1520, 3). *Jourdain de Blave* is a prose version of another thirteenth-century romance: it is known only from the printed edition (CH 1520, 1). *Berinus et Aygres* is a fourteenth-century prose romance, of which its modern editor assumes this edition to be the first (PR 1521, 5).[5] *Ysaïe le*

---

[1] Edition of *Le Petit Jean de Saintré* by P. Champion and F. Desonay (1926); edition of *La Salade* by F. Desonay in *Œuvres complètes d'Antoine de La Sale*, 1 (1935).

[2] J. Macfarlane, *Antoine Vérard* (1899), p. 2, n°. 4.

[3] See Georges Doutrepont, *Les mises en prose des épopées et des romans chevaleresques* (Brussels, 1939); Brian Woledge, *Bibliographie des romans et nouvelles en prose française antérieurs à 1500* (Geneva/Lille, 1954).

[4] C. E. Pickford, 'Les éditions imprimées des romans arthuriens en prose antérieurs à 1600', *Bulletin bibliographique de la Société Internationale Arthurienne*, XIII (1961), pp. 99–109.

[5] *Berinus, roman en prose du xive siècle*, ed. Robert Bossuet, SATF (1931), I, pp. xxxix–xl.

Triste is a late-medieval sequel to the Tristan and Iseut legend purporting to record the hitherto unpublished adventures of their son (PR 1522, 3). The *Histoire singulière* is a second sequel to the *Quatre filz Aymon*, carrying the story into the next generation, including the episode of Mabrian which had not until then been printed (PR 1525, 3 (1)). *Guy de Warwick*, originating in a thirteenth-century Anglo-Norman poem, was an adventure story which had been very popular both in France and England: this was the first printed edition of the French prose version (*CP* 1525, 2).

Privileges were rarely granted for plays. A political satire in the form of a morality, entitled *Le nouveau monde*, and a *Sotise à huit personnages* also of a topical nature, were published by Guillaume Eustace under his personal privilege (CH 1508, 2 (1 and 4)), perhaps being propaganda approved by the royal government. A translation into Latin of the well-known legal farce *Pathelin* was included in a privilege obtained by Eustace for a group of juridical works (PA 1512, 8). *Pathelin* in the original French had long since been printed, at Lyon in 1485 or 1496. It may have been considered, at this period, that performance in itself constituted publication, and that a play once performed was therefore usually ineligible for a privilege.

THE CLASSICS AND EDUCATION

The *editio princeps* of a work from classical antiquity had a strong claim to be granted a privilege. Such a windfall could normally hardly come the way of a French publisher in the first quarter of the sixteenth century. Henri (I) Estienne had, however, the honour of bringing out the first edition of the *Itinerarium Antonini Augusti*.[1] This was not a literary text, but an official guide to the Roman road system throughout the Empire, giving routes between the principal places, naming all the stages or stations between them and giving the distance between each stage in Roman miles. It is an important source for ancient history and topography. It was edited by Geofroy Tory from a manuscript, now lost, lent to him by Christophe de Longueil or Longolius (PA 1512, 7 (1)).

Classical texts already in print did not earn privileges. Certain features of a new edition, certain features of a new commentary, might have sufficient originality to do so. Thus the scholar-printer Josse Badius obtained privileges for his editions, with explanations and commentaries, of Plutarch's *Lives* (in Latin) and Seneca's *Tragedies* (CH 1514, 6); of Quintilian (PA 1516, 2), of Horace (*CP* 1519, 9) and of Aulus Gellius (*CP* 1519, 10). Sometimes a grant might be given for, say, a commentary on a single speech of Cicero such as that of Jean Vatel on *De lege Manilia* (*CP* 1520, 7). Such privileges did not make it illegal for other publishers in France to reprint the text itself. A new or

[1] The most modern edition of it is by O. Cuntz, *Itineraria Romana I* (Leipzig, 1929).

improved translation into Latin of a Greek text was also a possible candidate for a privilege. Thus an edition in Latin of the second-century historian Appian was published by Jean Petit in 1521 'cum priuilegio' (*CP* 1521, 2). At first sight there seems little justification for the grant of a privilege here. The Latin translation is that of Petrus Candidus, the Italian humanist, which had been printed many times, though admittedly it might have proved hard to obtain a copy of it in Paris in 1521. The dedication of Jean Petit's edition throws some light on the reasons for the privilege. It is by Nicolas Bérault (Beraldus), who claims in it that he had *revised* the translation. Bérault was a well-known teacher of Greek, a friend of Erasmus and of Budé, a protégé of Etienne Poncher, archbishop of Sens, and of François Poncher, bishop of Paris, to whom the edition of Appian is dedicated; he was also an advocate and eventually a *conseiller* in the Parlement of Paris. If his revision of the standard translation constituted a somewhat flimsy argument for seeking a privilege, he was well placed to plead his cause. Thirty years later, the Greek text itself of Appian was published by Charles Estienne, completing the work begun by his older brother Robert, under the privilege of the King's Printer in Greek. But in 1521 it would have been difficult to believe that a day would come when first editions of ancient Greek historians would be published in Paris.

Educational books, even taken in the widest sense, to include grammars and dictionaries, works on rhetoric, treatises on educational theory and repertories of classical myths and anecdotes, did not obtain privileges very frequently. They account for twenty-eight items, a little over 6 per cent of the total. Castellesi, *De sermone Latino* (*CP* 1517, 4), Despauterius, *De figuris* edited by Badius (*CP* 1519,. 2), Augerius, *Grammaticalium institutionum Liber* (*CP* 1522, 2), were among the offerings to the study of Latin. Gaza, *Grammatici institutiones libri IV*, with a Latin translation by Vatel (PA 1521, 5), Gulielmus Mainus and J. Cheradame, *Lexicon Graecum* (PR 1523, 3), and Chalcocondylas, *Grammaticae institutiones graecae*, edited by Melchior Wolmar (*CP* 1526, 1) reflect the growing interest in Greek. French had its exponents in the *Art de rhétorique* of Pierre Le Fèvre or Fabri (CH 1520, 6) and in the *Champ fleury* of Geofroy Tory (CH 1526, 2). Aids to the use of classical myth and story by poets and orators appear in forms ranging from the *Elucidarius carminum poetarum* of Conrad de Mure (PA 1514, 1 (2)) to the *Officina* of Ravisius Textor (CH 1519, 6 (3)). Jean Lode of Nantes, 'licencié en loix et tenant tutelle en l'université d'Orléans' as his privilege called him, translated into French the *De educatione liberorum* of Francesco Filelfo under the title *Le guidon des parents en l'instruction et direction de leurs enfans* (CH 1513, 2 (2)). Guillaume Houvetus of Chartres, teaching at the Collège de Narbonne in Paris, published 'cum priuilegio' a small collection of model letters, bilingual French and Latin, which he had dictated to his students, to enable them to write simple letters in correct Latin to their families and friends about their doings and their needs, his *Micropaedia epistolaris* (*CP* 1516, 2). Volcyr de Sérouville brought out a sort of courtesy book, suitably pious, for 'deux jeunes princes de renom' (CH 1523, 5), and Guillaume Eustace published the first edition of the medieval classic educational treatise of the Chevalier de La Tour Landry (CH 1508, 2 (15)).

MEDICINE AND SURGERY, GEOGRAPHY AND TRAVEL, MATHEMATICS

Medicine had inaugurated the granting of privileges in France. The 'Canon of Avicenna' with the commentary of Jacques Despars (d. 1458), who had been a leading light in the Paris Faculty of Medicine and a generous benefactor to the Faculty, was printed under privilege from his manuscript in 1498 (CH 1498, 1). While the Faculty was active in the sixteenth century in teaching and research, however, little new work in the subject was published. Medicine and surgery together make up only 3 per cent of all books published with privilege in this period. The Lyon physician and man of letters Symphorien Champier, among his numerous writings, contributed a preface to the medical works of Ishaq Israeli ben Salomon (CH 1515, 10) when they were printed for the first time, and edited a later edition of Avicenna (*CP* 1518, 5). A few well-known works by Italian physicians were published in France under privilege. Thus the *Tractatus de formatione corporis humani in utero* by Aegidius Colonna Romanus, edited by Johannes Benedictus Moncettus de Castellione Aretino, obtained a privilege (*CP* 1515, 1); the editor evidently had connections with England, for he dedicated the work to Henry VIII (9 February 1515) and addressed another preface to Henry Hornby, who had been secretary, chancellor and dean of the chapel to the Lady Margaret Beaufort.[1] Etienne Chenu of Toulouse (PA 1517, 5) and Gabriel Tarregua of Bordeaux (CH 1520, 10 and CH 1524, 3) were doctors who themselves were granted privileges for their medical works. Two studies were specially dedicated to the plague, those of Riva di San Nazzaro of Avignon (*CP* 1522, 3) and Lucena of Toulouse (PA 1523, 3), perhaps prompted by the epidemic of 1522.

The study of medicine could not be undertaken at this period without a knowledge of Latin. Such knowledge was not expected of surgeons. They required books in the vernacular. Dr Jean Falcon obtained a privilege for his commentaries in French on the *Guidon*, a standard work on surgery by Guido de Cauliaco (CH 1515, 1A, and revised edition PA 1520, 2 (2)). And a translation into French of Joannes de Vigo, under the title *La pratique de cirurgie* (CH 1525, 1) put another important work within the reach of surgeons who knew only their native language.

[1] On Hornby, see A. B. Emden, *Biographical register of the University of Cambridge to 1500* (Cambridge, 1963), pp. 313–14.

Doctors in the forefront of medical progress, on the other hand, looked to the writings of Hippocrates and Galen, which only a few qualified men could read in the original Greek. It was for this public that Thomas Linacre translated into Latin the treatise of Galen *De temperamentis*, published 'cum priuilegio' by Simon de Colines (*CP* 1523, 3).

In the field of natural science it is difficult to find, among books appearing under privilege, any titles beyond the *Compendium philosophiae naturalis* of Claude Perron (PA 1520, 3), the *De aequinoctiorum solsticiorumque inuentione* of Albertus Pighius (*CP* 1520, 17) and the *De naturae mirabilibus* (a collection of treatises, mostly Italian in origin, on physics and meteorology) of David Douglas (*CP* 1524, 4). In mathematics, only *L'arismethique nouvellement composée*, by Etienne de La Roche dit Ville Franche (PA 1520, 2 (1)), represents the subject in the privilege-lists until the *Protomathesis* of Oronce Finé (CH 1522, 4), which did not in fact appear until 1532. Geography too accounts for a very small number of privileges. This in turn reflects the relatively few new books of any consequence to appear on the subject during the period. Real curiosity about these matters on the part of the general public and critical appraisal of them seems to have been slow to develop. Jean de Gourmont reprinted in 1515 the *Orbis breviarium* of Zacharias Lilius, which had come out in Italy in 1493. This is entirely taken from ancient geographers, with no mention in the text, or the diagrams, of the New World which had been discovered since the author wrote it, but Gourmont seems to have had no difficulty in obtaining a privilege for his edition (PA 1515, 2). Travellers to Italy were catered for by the work of Jacques Signot (PA 1515, 4) and pilgrims to the Holy Land by *Le voyage de la saincte cité de Jérusalem* (PR 1517, 2) and by *Le grant voyage de Jherusalem* of Nicolas Le Huen (PR 1517, 7). The needs of shipping along the Atlantic and Channel coasts were met by the *Grant Routtier* of Pierre Garcie (CH 1520, 4, and *CP* 1525, 8). *Le nouveau monde et navigacions faictes par Emeric de Vespuce*, translated from the Italian[1] by Mathurin du Redouer, is the only book featuring in the privilege lists up to 1526 to report the new discoveries (CH 1517, 1 (1)).

---

[1] From Antonio Fracanzano da Montalboddo, *Paesi novamente retrovati*, according to Moreau, *Imprimeurs parisiens*, ii, p. 403.

9 · OWNERSHIP, ENFORCEMENT AND EFFICACY OF PRIVILEGES

OWNERSHIP AND TRANSFER OF PRIVILEGES

Within fifteen years of the end of the period under consideration, book-privileges were being made the object of a formal transfer of ownership before a notary. A contract between Nicolas de Herberay, seigneur des Essarts, author of *Amadis de Gaule*, and his publishers Jean Longis and Vincent Sertenas, dated 12 July 1540, provided that he would authorise them to publish and sell the book under the six-year privilege which he had obtained from the king at Paris on 2 July 1540. Under a further contract, dated 19 November 1540, he agreed to give them the copy of the three first books as soon as possible, and delivered to them, in the presence of the notaries, the Letters Patent from the king; in return, the publishers undertook to pay him, in instalments, the sum of eighty gold *écus*, and to give him twelve unbound copies of each volume, refraining from putting any on sale until the author had presented a copy to the king.[1] The lawyer Pierre de Rebuffi made a somewhat similar contract in 1545 with Galliot Du Pré, for a revised edition of his commentaries on the Concordat. That the author should hand over to the publisher the privilege, and the confirmation of it, which the king had given him, was part of his side of the bargain: in return, Galliot paid him twenty gold *écus* in cash, and promised to give him at the coming Whitsun five *écus* more with twelve bound copies of the book and a bound copy of Bohier's *Decisiones* and of the *Histoire ecclesiasticque*.[2] For a subsequent edition, Rebuffi in 1551 judged it unnecessary to go before a notary. Instead, he gave Galliot Du Pré a signed statement assigning to Du Pré the rights conferred on him by his privilege, dated 9 May 1549, which Du Pré carefully reproduced in the book:

Permisi ego subsignatus Galioto à Prato bibliopolae ut à Calend.Septemb. Anni M.D.LI in decennium superiore priuilegio concesso utatur.
    P.Rebuffus Iurium Doctor, & comes subscripsi.[3]

Where an author had not himself secured a privilege, but had a suitable book ready to be printed, it might be stated in the contract that his publisher should

---

[1] Annie Parent, *Les métiers du livre à Paris au xviᵉ siècle (1535–1560)* (Geneva, 1974), pp. 300–1, citing Minutier Central XIX 155, 12.7.1540 and 19.11.1540.
[2] Ibid. p. 311, citing M.C. VIII 71, 17.3.1545.
[3] BN 8°. Ld⁷ 24.c. Rebuffi's ten-year privilege is printed on the verso of the title-page.

obtain one. Thus, in 1547, Etienne Groulleau undertook to obtain a privilege at his own expense ('lequel privillege icellui Groulleau sera tenu obtenir à ses despens de la chancellerie') for *L'Epithome de la vraye astrologie et de la réprovée* of David Finarensis, a licenciate in medicine, of Orleans. The privilege was, on the other hand, to be wholly for Groulleau's benefit. He promised the author 100 unbound copies of the book, as well as paying for the printing entirely, but the author under the terms of the contract was not to dispose of any of these complimentary copies until the expiry of Groulleau's privilege.[1] Where the publisher was the owner of the privilege he might sell it to another publisher. Thus on 22 February 1546 Michel Fezandat made over to Oudin Petit a privilege which he and Jacques Kerver had obtained from the chancery on 6 January 1546: the transfer, for which Oudin paid the sum expended by Fezandat on getting the privilege, was made subject to the approval of the authority which had conferred the privilege.[2] In November 1559, Nicole Bacquenois, 'imprimeur juré en l'université de Reims', sold his six-year royal privilege (obtained by him on 28 July 1558) for two legal works by Claude Lyenard, advocate at Reims, to Sébastien Nivelle of Paris for fifteen *livres tournois*. The author was present, acting for Nivelle, and paid the money on his behalf.[3] Bacquenois had already published a first edition of the works (Reims, 1558, 8° BN F.39244), but the privilege was valid until 1564.

Another possibility was for the publisher who held the privilege to allow some other publisher to bring out the book under licence from him. Thus Jean Varice of Angers caused to be printed the *Ordonnances royaulx* (1539, 8°), 'auquel Galiot du Pré, Jean André et Yolande Bonhomme ont permis les faire imprimer selon leurs Privileges'.[4] A further variation was practised by Jean André of Paris. On 9 January 1540 he obtained from the Parlement of Paris a six-month privilege for the recent royal edict (published in the Parlement on 5 January 1540) on the reformation of royal offices, and within four days he published his edition, dated 13 January. But on 30 January he gave a procuration allowing Nicolas Petit, bookseller and printer of Lyon, to reprint his edition, according to the privilege obtained by him on 9 January, 'à la charge de tenir un loyal compte des gains'.[5] André did not relinquish the privilege, but he refrained from reprinting the edict in question himself until 25 February 1541. It seems therefore that André hired out his privilege to Nicolas Petit for use in the Lyon area on some sort of profit-sharing basis.

To what extent, if at all, had such practices been growing up during the period up to 1526?

---

[1] Parent, *Les métiers du livre*, p. 297, citing M.C. VIII 196, 22.8.47.

[2] Ibid. p. 121, n.1, citing M.C. LXXIII 7, 22.2.46.

[3] H. Jadart, *Les débuts de l'imprimerie à Reims 1550–1650* (1893), pp. 37–8, Documents inédits v.

[4] E. Pasquier and V. Dauphin, *Imprimeurs et libraires de l'Anjou* (Angers, 1932), p. 215. For the privileges in the *Ordonnances* held by these three Paris publishers, see Ph. Renouard, *Imprimeurs et libraires parisiens du xvie siècle*, 1 (1964), p. 49.

[5] Renouard, *Imprimeurs et libraires*, 1, p. 65, no. 136, and p. 67, no. 143.

In a number of cases an author or editor who sought a privilege had already agreed terms with a particular publisher, who is named in the privilege (CH 1498, 1; PR 1508, 1; CH 1509, 1; CH 1512, 4; CH 1516, 1). Where the author obtained the privilege and remained free to confer the benefit of it on any publisher he should choose, the formal assignment of the privilege is sometimes recorded with evident care.

Jean Lemaire de Belges thus placed on record in *Le second livre des illustrations de Gaule* (CH 1512, 2) the following statement, printed in the book:

L'acteur de ce present livre a communiqué son privilege royal en toute ample maniere comme il a obtenu du roy à Geufroy de Marnef Libraire juré de l'université de Paris: et à Hilaire Malican aussi libraire et marchant demourant à Bloys. Et est interdict à tous autres de non imprimer ce present livre: sur les peines contenues oudit privilege.

Jean Falcon provided his publisher with the privilege he had obtained for his commentary on the medical text known as *Le Guidon* (CH 1515, 1A), with the following declaration, which accompanies the printed text of the privilege:

Item veult ledict maistre Jehan Falcon docteur en medecine impetrant que le privilege soit communiqué pour vendre & distribuer ledict livre à honneste personne Constantin Fradin imprimeur & librayre demourant à Lyon sur le Rosne aupres de nostre dame de Confort.

The Italian humanist poet Publius Faustus Andrelinus (Fausto Andrelini), a client of the French court, obtained from the Parlement of Paris a privilege for his eulogy on the late queen, *In Annam Francorum reginam Panegyricon* (PA 1515, 3). The publisher, who was Josse Badius Ascensius, set out the privilege on the verso of the title-page followed by the words:

Faustus autem transtulit priuilegium hoc in Badium.
Faustus.

Pierre Gringore had a privilege from Francis I for *Les fantasies de mère Sotte* (CH 1516, 1). Following his usual practice he had the book printed himself. There is however also an undated edition printed for Jean Petit, 'ayant par transport le privilège dudict Mere Sotte autrement dit Pierre Gringore'.[1] The privilege was for four years, and Gringore may have been offered favourable terms by Petit to part with his rights in it when demand for the book continued.

The Lyon publisher Gilbert de Villiers brought out in 1520 a *Traicté de exhortation de paix*, with the statement 'Lequel de Villiers a eu permission de celuy qui a le privilege pour cinq ans. Seelé du grant seel du Roy. Et signé. P. Grabot', dated 7 August (CH 1520, 2). The work was topical, and may have emanated from a royal publicist who had obtained a privilege but preferred

---

[1] Ch. Oulmont, *La poésie morale, politique et dramatique à la veille de la Renaissance: Pierre Gringore* (Paris, 1911), p. 46.

not to put his name to it: this would explain why Villiers does not say who the privilege-holder was.

Such transactions as these, in the period before the Edict of Villers-Cotterets (1539) required more acts to be registered by a notary, were probably recorded by the exchange of a signed statement: that between Fausto Andrelini and Badius is indeed clearly intended to reproduce a statement authenticated by the autograph signature 'Faustus'.

Publication by a provincial firm of a book under licence from the Paris publisher who held the privilege is also attested quite early. Jean Petit obtained a Parlement privilege for the *Ordonnances royaulx* of 27 April 1512 (PA 1512, 4). They were printed at Angers for the bookseller Léon Cailler (1512, 8°), with the statement 'et a ledict Cailler obtins congié de Jehan Petit de faire imprimer les ordonnances lequel Patit a privillege de messeigneurs de Parlement en la manière qui s'ensuyt ...' (the text of Petit's grant is then printed in full).[1] Durand Gerlier obtained the privilege for the text of the Concordat between Francis I and the Pope, which was finally registered by the Parlement of Paris on 22 March 1517. Enguilbert de Marnef, the leading publisher and bookseller in Poitiers, reached a business agreement with Gerlier, under which he reprinted at Poitiers the Paris edition of Gerlier and sold it locally on Gerlier's behalf 'cum priuilegio regis' (CH 1518, 2).

In none of these pre-1526 cases is it known what concessions the privilege-holder received in the way of cash payments or rewards in kind like free copies, in return for assigning or hiring out his privilege. The author who held a privilege was, however, evidently conferring a certain favour on the publisher of his choice. That the transfer was recorded in print, even in a very few books, suggests that the disposal of the rights conferred by the privilege was from 1512 onwards already an element of recognised importance in author-publisher agreements.

PENALTIES AND LAWSUITS

All privileges of which the terms are known provide for the confiscation of any copies printed within the specified period without the privilege-holder's permission. In addition, a fine is threatened.

In the case of Letters Patent from the royal chancery, the fine is usually 'arbitraire', that is, to be decided at the discretion of the court. 'Sur grans peines à nous à appliquer et d'amende arbitraire' (CH 1509, 1), or simply 'Sur certaines et grans peines à nous à applicquer' (CH 1509, 2) are typical formulae. But between 1518 and 1526 there are seven privileges which name a specific fine of 100 silver marks: 'Sur peine de confiscation de ce qui auroit esté

---

[1] Pasquier and Dauphin, *Imprimeurs et libraires de l'Anjou*, p. 104, with reproduction of the first page which bears these particulars, from the copy in the library of Le Plessis-Villoutreys.

faict au contraire: et de cent marcs d'argent à nous à applicquer'[1] (CH 1518, 2. Cf. CH 1519, 3; 1520, 4; 1520, 6; 1523, 1; 1525, 2 and 1526, 2), as well as one naming a fine of twenty-five silver marks (CH 1524, 2). In two cases where we know the terms of the *entérinement* by royal officers, it included a fixed fine: the Lieutenant General of the Sénéchal of Lyon named 500 *livres tournois* in these instances (CH 1509, 2 and CH 1512, 3).

The Parlement of Paris standardised on 'amende arbitraire', as indeed it did in all matters where statutory offences were not involved. Henri Estienne asked for a fine of 500 *livres parisis* (PA 1512, 7), Randin for 100 *livres* (PA 1512, 10), Jean Petit for 500 *livres parisis* (PA 1512, 4) and on another occasion for 100 silver marks (PA 1517, 8). The Parlement ignored this particular item in their requests. It ignored, too, a request from Berthold Rembolt and Pierre Gromors that the penalties for infringing the privilege should include prison (PA 1517, 1).

The Prévôt of Paris, or his *Lieutenant Civil*, appears to have named a fixed fine in only one case. This was the Paris University *compendium*, a sort of year book, to be printed by Toussaint Denys. The *Lieutenant Civil*, Ruzé, threatened a fine of 10 *livres* for infringement of the privilege for it (PR 1517, 1). A privilege granted in 1525, on the other hand, names as the penalties the loss of the books which should have been printed for sale in defiance of the privilege, 'amende arbitraire', and 'dommaiges et interestz dudit suppliant' (PR 1525, 2), that is, with costs. Otherwise all privileges issued on his authority of which the terms are known mention confiscation and 'amende arbitraire'.

The only provincial Parlement which names specific fines in this period is the Parlement of Toulouse. This threatened a fine of 100 gold marks in the case of Nicolas Bertrand's *Les gestes des Tholosains* (PA 1517, 3) and the *Consuetudines Tholose* (PA 1523, 2), and fifty silver marks in the case of the *Articles et confirmations des privileges du pays de Languedoc* (PA 1522, 7). Just after the end of the period it named 100 silver marks as the fine for infringing the privilege for Johannes Maurus' *Expositio* of the Adages of Erasmus (PA 1527, 1).

Pirating a privileged edition while the privilege was valid, within the kingdom of France, might thus lead to severe punishment: confiscation of the illegally printed copies, a fine which might be heavy if the fixed fines named are anything to go by, and perhaps the costs of the case.

What action would a privilege-holder expect to take if he discovered copies of the book being printed or sold other than his own? One of the royal privileges goes into some detail about this, though it is difficult to know whether the procedure there specified is typical. The privilege-holder or his legal representative was entitled to ask the *huissier* to seize the copies of the book printed in defiance of the patent, and to summon the people in whose

---

[1] The *marc* was a specific weight of silver or gold, not money, in France.

possession they were found to appear before the nearest royal judge, to see whether they had incurred the penalties laid down and other conclusions which the privilege-holder and the *procureur du roi* might see had to be done:

mandons au premier nostre huissier ou sergent sur ce requis que à la requeste dudict exposant ou de son procureur pour luy pregne<nt> arestent et saisissent tous et chascuns les livres qui ou content [*sic*] de cesdictz presentes auroient esté faiz et imprimez et adjournent ceulx en la possession desquelz il<s> seront trouvés par devant le prochain juge royal pour veoir avoir encouru les peines desusdictes et aultres conclusions que ledict exposant et nostre procureur verroit estre à faire ... (CH 1515, 2)

This is a privilege which contains several other legal details not usually mentioned, perhaps because the secretary who drew it up, De Rillac, had not been responsible for any other known book-privilege and was being especially careful – or pedantic. The wording is in fact almost the same as that obtained much later, on 30 September 1559, from Francis II by Guillaume Aubert, who was an advocate in the Parlement of Paris, and evidently a stickler for form.[1]

An apparent case of defiance of a privilege occurs when the system had only just started, in 1509. A grant, which covered, among other books, Nicole Bohier's *Tractatus* on the powers of the papal legate, Georges d'Amboise, archbishop of Rouen, was made by the royal chancery in favour of Simon Vincent of Lyon at Bohier's request (CH 1509, 1 (1)) on 1 June 1509. Vincent's edition came out on 17 June. But an edition of the same work was published by Jean Petit in Paris on 7 September 1509 (BN Rés.E.5201). It is possible that Petit obtained this text independently, through (for instance) someone in the household of Georges d'Amboise, since he had close connections with Rouen. He may not have known when he published it in Paris in the first week of September that an edition authorised by Bohier had been published under privilege by Vincent on 17 June. The privilege-holder may by September have sold most of his copies, since the *Tractatus* was of considerable topical interest. He may have thought it a waste of money to institute proceedings against Petit by that time. He may have reached a settlement with him. It may or may not be coincidence that Petit himself first applied for a privilege on 13 July the following year (PA 1510, 3). Thereafter he became one of the staunchest supporters of the privilege-system.

In 1516, an action was in fact brought by him before the Parlement of Paris for alleged infringement of a privilege. On 28 June 1516 Petit had obtained from the Parlement the privilege in the *Coutumes* of Troyes for two years (PA 1516, 7). On 2 July 1516 he submitted a *requête* to the Parlement,

---

[1] 'Voulons et nous plait que tout ce qui aura esté faict contre la teneur du present privilege fust incontinent ... saisy et mis en nostre main, par le premier nostre huissier ou sergent sur ce requis, et ceux, qui auront attenté contre les presentes, adjournez pardevant celuy de vous [the royal officers] auquel la cognoissance en apartiendra etc'. G. Aubert, *L'histoire des guerres* (Paris, Vincent Sertenas, 1559, 4°). BL 9134.dd.1.

complaining that Guillaume Eustace had none the less printed these *Coutumes*, and asking that Eustace should be fined and his edition confiscated according to the provisions of the grant. The Parlement appointed certain commissioners from among its number to report on a possible settlement between the parties. On 5 September 1516 it gave judgement, after considering the *requête* and the report of its commissioners. Eustace was to bring to the court within three days whatever he had so far printed of the *Coutumes* of Troyes, and was to be compelled to obey if necessary by seizure of his possessions and other due the reasonable means. And he was forbidden to print or to sell any of these *Coutumes* for the duration of Petit's privilege and until the court had otherwise determined.[1] The immediate reason no doubt prompted Petit to get the original privilege and to defend it so vigorously: the *bailliage* of Troyes covered a large and important area, stretching from Provins in the west to Bar-sur-Aube in the east. Within this territory, an up-to-date edition of the *Coutumes* stood a good chance of being bought by every lawyer, landowner and municipality. But there was more at stake than this particular market. Petit held privileges for other *Coutumes*, and could not risk the precedent being established that other publishers could thus defy him. Indeed he said of Guillaume Eustace in his *requête* that Eustace was 'coutumier de ce fait', that is, an habitual offender in this respect, and it appears therefore that he feared further outrages from Eustace if he did not make a stand.

Did Eustace incur the full rigour of the threatened penalties for infringing Petit's privilege? He was certainly compelled to bring all the copies that he had printed to the Parlement, and was forbidden to print or sell any until Petit's privilege had expired and until the court should decide otherwise. This was in itself a serious loss. Whether the copies were actually destroyed is not clear. It is possible that the agreement imposed on the parties by the Parlement, mentioned in the judgement, provided for them being held until the privilege had expired and then sold by Eustace on terms favourable to Petit. There are some later examples of such settlements. For example in 1547 the Paris University bookseller Jean Foucher, a former apprentice or journeyman of Jean Petit, printed an edition of Budé, *De l'institution du prince*, for which Nicolas Paris, a merchant printer of Troyes, had obtained a privilege; the dispute ended with an agreement between the two men, before a notary, to divide between them the 1,200 copies which Foucher had printed.[2] But there appears to be no trace of any copies of the *Coutumes* of Troyes printed by Eustace.

Jean Petit was also a party, with a Rouen bookseller called Louis Bouvet, in a later case, in 1527, concerning a privilege, before the Parlement of Rouen.[3] This time, it was the grant itself which was contested. For when Petit and

[1] AN x 1 A 1518, f. 307ᵛ. Cf. Maugis, *Histoire du Parlement*, II, p. 314.
[2] Parent, *Les métiers du livre*, p. 148, quoting M.C. LXXIII. 10, 22.9.1547.
[3] See above, p. 57.

Bouvet asked for a privilege for seven years in the Antiphoner of the archdiocese of Rouen, which had never been printed before and had been costly to print, their application was opposed by Pierre Lignant, another Rouen bookseller. Lignant represented that he was 'l'ung des plus antiens libraires de ceste ville', and that he had prepared 'ung exemple entier et parfaict desdits antiphoniers pour icelluy mectre en impression'. He requested permission to print and sell his edition, and urged that the monopoly should not be granted to Petit and Bouvet. But after hearing all the reports on the case, and in agreement with the 'gens du roy', the Parlement awarded the privilege to Petit and Bouvet, for six years, on condition that they should not sell copies printed on parchment for more than twenty-two *livres tournois* and on paper for more than four *livres tournois* (PA 1527, 3).

Conflicting or overlapping grants of privileges occur surprisingly seldom, considering the number given and the diversity of authorities competent to give them. There is apparently no instance up to 1526. There is, however, a case in 1527–8 which merits attention. The Parlement of Bordeaux was induced on 4 September 1527 to give a privilege to the local printer Jean Guyart for the *Coutumes* of the city of Bordeaux and of the Bordelais, together with those of the Landes, as revised by a royal commission going back to 1521, and as finally approved and registered in the Parlement (PA 1527, 2). Secure in possession of this privilege, which was to run for three years from the date when he should complete the printing, Guyart had still not brought out his edition in February 1528. Meanwhile no less a person than the *greffier* of the Parlement, Maître Jean de Pontac, applied to the royal chancery for a privilege for the *Coutumes* in his own name, and duly obtained Letters Patent dated Paris, the last day of February 1528, giving him for four years the sole rights in the *Coutumes*, which he proposed to have printed at his own expense (CH 1528, 2). While in Paris, Jean de Pontac duly placed an order for the printing with Durand Gerlier, a highly respectable *libraire juré* of the university, and a neat twenty-eight folio volume was soon ready, displaying eulogistic dedications to the president of the Parlement of Bordeaux François de Belcier and to other Bordeaux dignitaries, and the text of the royal privilege on the verso of the title and following page. Guyart, finding that this edition was being put on sale, brought an action before the Parlement of Bordeaux against Jean de Pontac.

The situation must have been embarrassing for the Parlement. Not only was Pontac in possession of a royal privilege, but he was the senior official of the Parlement itself. However, the grant made by the Parlement to Guyart was undeniably made first, and judgement was given in his favour, to the extent that Pontac was forbidden to sell his edition during the three years that Guyart's privilege was valid, on pain of a fine of a thousand *livres*. Guyart was not awarded costs, and there was no mention of Pontac's edition being confiscated. Having won his case, on 6 June 1528 Guyart brought out his own edition, dated 3 July 1528, printing his privilege of 4 September 1527 on the verso of the title-page and the terms of the Parlement *arrêt* of 6 June 1528, upholding his claim to it, on the facing page. The *arrêt* refers to Pontac's edition only as 'les coustumes de Bourdeaulx par luy faictes imprimer à Paris' and makes no mention of the royal privilege which Pontac had obtained for it. Pontac would have been free to sell his edition as soon as Guyart's privilege had expired. Why, knowing better than anyone what his Parlement had granted Guyart, did Pontac go to the lengths of obtaining a royal privilege and having an edition printed at his own expense? Guyart was evidently very dilatory in taking up his privilege and printing the *Coutumes*.[1] Pontac may have begun to think that he was not going to do so at all. Meanwhile the many people who needed a copy of the revised *Coutumes* may well have been complaining, and the *greffier* would be at the receiving end of the complaints. Whatever the reason for his initiative, the reason for the grant of a royal privilege to him is clear enough. There were plenty of precedents for the *greffiers* receiving a privilege in respect of *Coutumes* and Pontac's application to the royal chancery would have seemed perfectly normal in the absence of any statement from him that a privilege had already been granted to someone else by the Parlement of Bordeaux.

REPRINTS AFTER EXPIRY OF A PRIVILEGE

A certain number of cases have been noticed, in the course of preparing the present work, of reprints being brought out by other publishers soon after the lapse of a privilege, sometimes so soon after that it can hardly be coincidence, that is, that a colleague was only waiting for the privilege to run out before copying the book. Here are some examples.

The first edition of the *Coutumes* of Maine came out in Paris with a privilege dated 7 September 1509 (PA 1509, 4), granted to Martin Le Saige, the *greffier*. It was to run for two years, so it expired on 6 September 1511. By 7 May 1513, a reprint had been completed by Martin Morin at Rouen (BN Rés.F.2345). This reprint reproduces word for word the conclusion of the original edition, which recorded the transcribing of the *Coutume* by Martin Le Saige, and the permission given to him by the Parlement to have it printed and to take whatever profit there might be in so doing: only the formula at the end, which forbade other printers to copy it for two years, was omitted, Le Saige's exclusive right in the copy having by then expired.

---

[1] J. Delpit, *Origines de l'imprimerie en Guyenne* (Bordeaux, 1869), pp. 39–43, first drew attention to this case, followed by A. Claudin, *Les origines et les débuts de l'imprimerie à Bordeaux* (1897), pp. 45–6. Delpit seems to imply that he had seen the originals of the entries printed by Guyart in the registers of the Parlement of Bordeaux. At the present day the series of the registers, preserved in the Archives de la Gironde, is incomplete, and there is a gap between Vol. xix (which ends at 16 September 1524) and Vol. xx (which begins May 1528), and a gap in Vol. xx from 30 May to 4 September 1528.

Galliot Du Pré obtained a privilege on 4 September 1512 for Joannes Franciscus de Pavinis, *De officio et potestate capituli sede vacante*, and other works on Canon and Civil Law (PA 1512, 8). The grant was for two years. It thus expired on 3 September 1514. By 1516 an edition in the same format had come out, published by François Regnault (BL 497.d.5).

Barthélemy Vérard published the first edition of a French translation of Petrarch's *Trionfi* with a privilege for three years reckoned from 23 May 1514 (PA 1514, 7) and due therefore to expire 22 May 1517. By 9 June 1519 it had been reprinted, in the same format, by Jean de La Garde (BN Rés.Yd 80), followed in 1520 by an edition from Hémon Le Fèvre (BN Rés.Yd 82).

On 9 November 1514 Guillaume Eustace published works by Le Chevalier de la Tour Landry and others. This was covered by his personal privilege, which was for two years (CH 1508, 2 (15)) for every new book that he should publish. The rights in this book therefore lapsed on 8 November 1516. Michel Le Noir reprinted it, in a different format, on 4 February 1517 (BL G.10398).

Jean Granjon obtained a privilege for the revised edition of John Mair's *Summule* (PA 1516, 9). It ran for three years, reckoned from 24 October 1516. It thus expired on 23 October 1519. By 12 October 1520 it had been reprinted at Caen by Laurent Hostingue, for Jean Petit of Paris and Michel Angier of Caen.[1]

Michel Angier seems indeed to have been on the lookout for items of interest published in Paris to reprint as soon as the privilege expired. Occasionally he made additions which gave the reprint itself a claim to a privilege. Galliot Du Pré published Alain Bouchart, *Les grandes cronicques de Bretaigne*, under a privilege dated 6 May 1514 (CH 1514, 1). The grant was for three years, and therefore ran out on 5 May 1517. By 10 June 1518 Angier had completed a reprint of it, with additions from Charles VIII to the christening of the Dauphin at Amboise on 25 April 1518, apparently derived mainly from printed news-sheets. This reprint was published 'Cum priuilegio' (*CP* 1518, 3).

Le violier des histoires rommaines moralisées had a privilege, granted to Jean de La Garde (CH 1520, 8). As it was valid for three years, to be reckoned from the date of publication, which was 6 April 1521, the privilege expired on 5 April 1524. Another publisher, Philippe Le Noir, reprinted the book on 20 September 1525 (BL G.17697).

The first French translation of Vigo's recent work on surgery, published at Lyon in 1525, had a privilege granted to the publishers (CH 1525, 1). It was for four years, and was due to expire on 30 September 1529. The first reprint of the translation was done in Paris in 1530: the publisher was again Philippe Le Noir (BN Rés.Fol.Td 7339A).

The new *Ordinationes* or synodal statutes of the diocese of Orléans were

---

[1] L. Delisle, *Catalogue des livres imprimés ou publiés à Caen avant le milieu du 16ᵉ siècle* (Caen, 1903), I, pp. 219–21.

published by Claude Chevallon of Paris, under a privilege dated 30 May 1525 (PA 1525, 6). The grant was for two years, and thus expired on 29 May 1527. A local edition, produced by Jacques Martinet, appeared at Orleans in 1528 (BN B.27333).

The first edition of the *Mémoires* of Philippe de Commynes (the Louis XI part) was published by Galliot Du Pré with a Parlement privilege dated 3 February 1524: it was for two years, and so expired on 2 February 1526 (PA 1524, 3). Galliot got the book out 26 April, and reprinted it 'nouvellement reveue et corrigée' with an index on 7 September, so it was evidently (as one would expect) something of a best-seller. The first reprint by another publisher as far as I know, was that of Claude Nourry at Lyon in 1526 (Bodl.Douce c.subt. 15).

Jean Bouchet, author of the celebrated *Annales d'Acquitaine* (PA 1524, 15, cf. above p. 183), saw to it after his disagreeable experience with Antoine Vérard that first editions of his works came out with a privilege granted to his accredited publisher or to himself, throughout this period, and during the years beyond it in which he continued to write new works and to revise existing ones. The author of the most recent book on Bouchet says:

There is some evidence that the privileges were respected; it is noticeable that the *Triomphes* [*Les Triumphes de la noble et amoureuse dame*, privilege dated 20 February 1531], which appears to have been extremely popular among Paris printers, was not printed by any of them until the original four-year privilege had expired. The edition of the *Annales* that they copied and expanded was that of 1535, which had appeared without a privilege.[1]

Sometimes a new publication sold sufficiently well to warrant a reprint by the privilege-holder while the privilege was still valid. Thus the *Annales d'Acquitaine* came out under privilege in 1524, and again on 3 March 1526 (BL 596.h.11). A collection of Latin translations of works by St Basil published by Josse Badius had a three-year privilege (PR 1520, 11), publication date 13 November 1520; Badius reprinted the whole work on 15 May 1523, displaying the original privilege, which was of course still valid for several months more.

When a book was reprinted after the expiry of the privilege under which it originally appeared, the privilege was normally deleted, and the announcement of a privilege on the title-page suppressed, whether the reprint was published by the privilege-holder or not. The only exception known to me is the edition of Jean Lemaire de Belges, *Les illustrations de Gaule*, published by François Regnault in 1523, which reproduces the privilege granted by Louis XII to the author when the book first appeared, in 1509. Both Louis XII and the author were dead when Regnault's edition came out. Perhaps Regnault thought it enough of a curiosity to be worth perpetuating. Perhaps his compositor included it without thinking, when he set up the new

[1] Jennifer Britnell, *Jean Bouchet* (Edinburgh, 1986), p. 300.

edition from the old, as he did when copying the 'Cum priuilegio' on the title-page. Regnault can hardly have hoped to persuade anybody that the Louis XII privilege gave *him* any rights in the book.

PRIVILEGES NOT OBTAINED

There were a good many *libraires* at this period both in Paris and in the provinces who were simply booksellers, that is, dealers in books. Of those who at least occasionally ventured on financing an edition, alone or in partnership, many dealt in categories of books which did not qualify for privileges. Those who specialised in Books of Hours and liturgical books, like Simon Vostre, relied upon the quality of their products, and their ability to offer good value for money, in a competitive market. Many were able to make a living by reprints of books for which there was a steady demand, particularly those which tended to wear out by constant use, from schoolbooks to romances, from cookery books to saints' lives. Others were on the lookout, as we have seen, for suitable privileged books to copy when the privilege had expired and demand for the book had persisted or built up again.

Durand Gerlier, whose career began in 1489 and only ended in 1529, an eminent *libraire juré* and publisher, seems to have obtained a single privilege, an important one, for the *Concordat* between the king and the Pope, to which he added other works in a 'package' privilege (CH 1518, 2; CH 1519, 2), and otherwise to have ignored privileges. A study of his publications might reveal the reason for this abstention. Henri (I) Estienne's shorter career covered the main period of development of the privilege-system up to his death in 1520. His publications included outstanding works being printed for the first time. But he obtained only two privileges in his own name (PA 1512, 7 and PA 1518, 7), apart from a publication shared with Jean Petit who held the privilege (CH 1512, 1(7)). Yet he published first editions of Richard of St Victor, Berno of Reichenau, and Ruysbroeck among others, St Paul's Epistles with the commentaries of Jacques Lefèvre d'Etaples, as well as wholly new works like the *Liber de intellectu* of Charles de Bouelles or Bovillus.[1] It would appear that such publications fell into a category that would easily qualify for a privilege of two or three years. It is possible that Estienne relied upon other methods of forestalling possible competitors. Working for the circle of patrons, friends, colleagues and former pupils of Jacques Lefèvre d'Etaples, both in France and abroad, he may have been able to estimate fairly accurately the number of copies which would be required. He could then at a given moment put them on sale both in his shop in Paris and at key points in his sales network (he was a *messager-juré* of the university). The supporters of

---

[1] A. E. Tyler (Elizabeth Armstrong), 'Jacques Lefèvre d'Etaples and Henry Estienne the elder 1502–20', in *The French Mind: studies in honour of Gustave Rudler*, ed. Will Moore, Rhoda Sutherland and Enid Starkie (Oxford, 1952), pp. 17–33.

Lefèvre, with missionary zeal, positively welcomed the re-printing of his works in other countries.[1] They were produced there for the pupils of Lefèvre's former pupils, and doubtless in places and in quantities which posed no threat to Estienne's sales. Financially Estienne was probably fairly secure, the wealthy Guillaume Briçonnet, bishop of Meaux, being a protector of Lefèvre. He may have been unconvinced of the usefulness of privileges for the very specialised kind of book he was publishing, and thought them an unnecessary expense.

A publisher who, unlike Estienne, soon began to seek privileges regularly for his new undertaking, Josse Badius, left some gaps in his privilege-coverage which are at first sight puzzling. There is no privilege for the first edition of Geoffrey of Monmouth. This admittedly was in July 1508: it would have been early to think of obtaining a privilege. The 1517 reprint shows that there was a certain demand for the book, but in 1508 it may have appeared of more specialised interest, limited to Brittany and possibly to Great Britain: the arms of Brittany appear in both editions and the promoter of the edition, Ivo or Yves Cevallat, writing from the college of Quimper, was evidently Breton. Such considerations also perhaps made it seem unnecessary to seek a privilege, though the book would probably have qualified for one, in the case of Badius' Saxo Grammaticus, *Danorum regum heroumque Historiae* (1514), which was also the first edition. Edited and perhaps partly subsidised by Christiern Pedersen, there are 111 extant copies listed in the *Inventaire chronologique*;[2] of these only eleven are in French libraries, and if that bears any relation to Badius's sales, he may have been correct in thinking that a privilege which could only protect him in France was not worth the outlay. In fact in France at least the work of Saxo Grammaticus was not reprinted. In the case of Badius' edition of St Hilary, *Opera complura* (1510), he included some works of which his was the first edition: either the authorities did not think there was enough *inédit* material in the book to warrant the issue of a privilege, or he himself did not think so.

Gilles de Gourmont published the Praise of Folly of Erasmus on 9 June 1511. The second edition came out at Basle in August. Badius brought out another edition of it, based on Gourmont's, 'revised and enlarged by the author', on 27 July 1512. It was also printed by Schürer at Strasburg in 1511 and 1512. Subsequently it had numerous reprints. A privilege would have enabled Gourmont to prevent a French reprint for two or three years, and to prevent the import of copies printed abroad for the same time. It may be that the Gourmont brothers were not yet 'privilege-conscious': neither Jean nor

---

[1] E.g. Michael Hummelberg sent a copy of a book edited by Lefèvre, first published by Estienne on 20 November 1508, to Beatus Rhenanus in April 1509, 'ut tua diligentia Germanicae iuuentuti typicis formis quam faberrime cures excudi'. On 30 July 1509 Beatus wrote back to say that the book had duly been reprinted, at Strasbourg, and sent greetings to Lefèvre. Rice, *The prefatory epistles*, 201–3.

[2] Moreau, *Inventaire chronologique*, II, no. 365.

Gilles obtained a privilege until 1518 (CH 1518, 6 and PA 1518, 1). It may be that Gilles was prepared to let his edition take its chance, with the advantage of at least a short start over his competitors.

It is thus possible to find or at least guess at an explanation, in a few cases, of books which might well have obtained privileges but which have none. In most cases however we have no means of telling whether no application for a privilege was made, or whether an application was made and refused. No trace is normally left by unsuccessful *requêtes*. In one instance, it is revealed because a publisher applied to the Parlement for two items, of which one was allowed and the other evidently rejected.[1] That is a glimpse of a process which may have been relatively common.

It is improbable that any *author* who desired a privilege for a new work of his, and could afford to pay for the grant, was refused. We may note, however, that alongside of authors like Jean Lemaire de Belges and Pierre Gringore, who themselves initiated the printing of their works and the protection of them by privileges, there were still others who preferred their works to circulate exclusively in manuscript among a few patrons and friends. Guillaume Crétin, who could equally readily have paid for his poems to be printed, died in 1525 with almost all his poetry still unpublished. It was only after his death that Galliot Du Pré was able to secure a manuscript and to include some of the poems in a collection of poetry by older authors, to be published under privilege (PR 1526, 1), and the following year that both Galliot Du Pré and Jean Longis obtained privileges for more hitherto unpublished works (PR 1527, 2 and PR 1527, 3). Jean Marot, who died about the same time as Crétin, also published nothing in his lifetime. His works began to be printed only in 1532. Both poets were connected with the royal court, and would no doubt have easily been granted privileges had they applied. Authors who allowed some of their works to be printed without privilege sometimes learnt the hard way that this exposed them to being misprinted, or to having items attributed to them which it suited the interests of the publisher to add but not theirs. The son of Jean Marot, the more famous Clément Marot, spoke in the preface to the *Adolescence Clémentine* in 1532 of 'le desplaisir que j'ay eu d'en ouyr cryer et publier par les rues une grande partie, toute incorrecte, mal imprimée, et plus au proffit du Libraire qu'à l'honneur de l'Autheur': this was in fact the first edition of any of his works to have a privilege.[2]

EXTENSION OF THE PRIVILEGE-SYSTEM

After 1526, the practice of seeking protection by privilege in France is to be

[1] See above, p. 93. Just after this period, the Prévot allowed a licence to print but refused a privilege (PR 1527, 4).

[2] Clément Marot, *Les Epitres*, ed. C. A. Mayer (London, 1958), pp. 95–6. Cf. Preface to the *Œuvres* of 1538, 'Clément Marot à ceulx qui par cy devant ont imprimé ses oeuvres', ibid., pp. 91–4.

found in other fields connected with the book-trade. The grant of privileges for maps is foreshadowed in *La totale et vraie description des Gaules et Ytalies* of Jacques Signot (PA 1515, 4), where a pull-out map of Italy has the publisher's name and 'Cum priuilegio' printed at the bottom, and the Parlement expressly included the map as well as the book itself in the *arrêt* ('lesdictz livres & carte'). Later, a map by itself might qualify for a privilege, such as the *Vraye description de la ville et chasteau de Guines*, which prints the statement that it is 'Extraict du desseing de Nicolas de Nicolay, geographe du Roy, avec privilege de sa majesté' (BN Est. Va 148); this was published in Paris after the capture of Calais in January 1558. The privileges obtained by Geofroy Tory (CH 1524, 2 and 1526, 2), which were in part to protect the original designs contained in these books for illustrations and decorations, were followed in 1530 by a book entirely of designs and patterns which appeared 'Cum priuilegio regis'. This was *La fleur de la science de Portraicture. Patrons de broderie facon arabique et Ytalique*, by Francesco di Pellegrino, a Florentine artist who had come to France to work with Rosso at Fontainebleau.[1] The artists who, with their engravings, made the work of Rosso at Fontainebleau familiar to a wide public, were possibly the first in France to obtain privileges for their productions. Pierre Milan, for instance, was able to put 'Cum priuilegio regis' at the bottom of his engravings of the *Danse des Dryades* and *Les Parques masquées*, both after Rosso, in 1545 at the latest, of the famous *Nymphe de Fontainebleau*, and of table silver.[2] Pierre Attaignant won a six-year privilege in 1531 from Francis I for his improved method of printing music and for the music books he printed,[3] and Robert Granjon a ten-year privilege in 1557 from Henry II for a new type-design, the so-called Civilité type, imitating handwriting.[4] Pierre Hamon, the king's scribe, obtained Letters Patent in 1561 granting him the exclusive rights in an engraved collection of specimens of calligraphy, the *Alphabet de l'invention des lettres en diverses escritures*, and he also had a privilege for a second and different *Alphabet* in 1566.[5]

Privileges had never been confined to printed books, but their presence in books probably brought this way of seeking protection to the attention of artistic and technical craftsmen who might otherwise not have thought of it.

[1] The only copy is in the Arsenal, 4°. Sc.A.4544 Rés. Exhibited in Paris, 1972, at the *Ecole de Fontainebleau* exhibition, no. 685 in the catalogue, with an illustration.

[2] *Ecole de Fontainebleau*, catalogue nos. 419, 421, 423, 438.

[3] D. Haertz, *Pierre Attaignant, royal printer of music* (Berkeley/Los Angeles, 1969), p. 174.

[4] Harry Carter and H. D. L. Vervliet, *Civilité types* (Oxford, 1966), pp. 19–21.

[5] Elizabeth Armstrong, 'Deux notes sur Pierre Hamon: 1 Ses deux alphabets et son privilège', *Bibliothèque d'Humanisme et Renaissance*, xxv (1963), pp. 543–7.

CONCLUSION

THE SPEED WITH WHICH the privilege-system became familiar to the educated public in France was remarkable. The first privilege issued by the royal chancery (CH 1498, 1) remained indeed an isolated episode until 1507–9. The first privilege granted by an officer of the Crown (PR 1505, 1) also had no sequel until 1507. In 1507 too the Parlement of Paris granted its first privilege (PA 1507, 1). By 1509 the system was establishing itself in the form that it was to follow for many years to come. Over the next twenty years, privileges came to cover probably the majority of books being printed for the first time, whether newly composed or inherited from the past. Just after the period here studied, in 1528, it had become so much a commonplace that it was the subject of a parody: the lawyer Gilles d'Aurigny brought out his humorous *Le cinquante-deuxiesme arrest d'amours, avecques ses ordonnances des masques* 'Cum priuilegio amoris amplissimo.'[1]

All the initiative came from authors and publishers, faced with an increasingly competitive situation. Privileges were sought not only by prominent authors and wealthy publishers, but also by relatively humble writers and *libraires*. They must have been reasonably satisfied with the results since they were prepared to pay for the costs.

Book-privileges did not originate in France. But they had there a better chance of providing some effective protection than most other states could offer.[2] And the French royal authority, whether exercised by the chancery, by the Paris and provincial Parlements, or by officials – notably the Prévôt of Paris – responded by 'playing fair' as far as possible with authors and publishers, and with the reading public. There was no favouritism. Normally they issued privileges only for genuinely new publications.[3] They gave periods of time averaging three years[4] – and three years was known in the European book-trade as far apart as Brabant in 1514 and Basle in 1531[5] as a reasonable time within which to sell the first edition of a book. Exceptionally they gave as much as ten years. Permission might in rare cases be given to include up to eight new books in the same privilege, and this 'package', if

---

[1] S.l. 8º. BN Rés.Y² 932. It was of course intended as a sequel to Martial d'Auvergne, *Les cinquante et un arrests d'Amours*, dating from 1460–5 (modern edition by Jean Rychner, SATF, 1951).
[2] See above, pp. 21–2.   [3] See above, pp. 92–8.   [4] See above, pp. 118–25.
[5] See above, pp. 15–16 and p. 125.

coupled with leave to reckon the validity of the grant from the date of the publication, could result in a book coming out under a privilege granted months or even years earlier.[1]

The privilege was a favour granted by the king's grace, conferring a commercial concession. The books for which it was sought might be examined by the authorities, and it might be refused for the whole or part of the proposed publication.[2] Privileges however did not form part of any system of licensing or censorship, at this period: the choice lay with authors and publishers of new works whether to apply for them or not.[3]

Privileges in France at this time offered a considerable degree of protection for a limited period against unauthorised reprinting of a new book within the country, and against the importing of editions reprinted abroad. A privilege put the author who obtained one in a stronger position in dealing with publishers.[4] The concept of literary property as we understand it indeed finds no expression in the French documents of the period. Authors and publishers relied on virtually the same arguments in seeking privileges: they might quote such considerations as public usefulness, but their main plea was always the expenditure of time, skill and money involved in producing the new book and the need to recoup themselves before others were allowed to reprint it.[5] But the author's privilege was a step in the right direction. Later in the century the publishable material from the past available to be printed for the first time dwindled, and the role of living authors became correspondingly more important to the book-trade. The professional man of letters came into existence. An eminent author might receive a privilege for ten years from publication in all the works he had written or might write.[6] But even that was in the future.

---

[1] See above, pp. 130–6.   [2] See above, p. 93, pp. 113–15.
[3] See above, Chapter 5.
[4] See above, pp. 191–4.   [5] See above, pp. 79–84.   [6] See above, pp. 83–4.

REGISTER

CH: Known grants by the royal chancery to 1526, inclusive, and grants for 1527–8 referred to in the text (page 209)

List of books known to have been published by Antoine Vérard under his personal privilege (CH 1507, 1) (page 238)

List of books known to have been published by Guillaume Eustace under his personal privilege (CH 1508, 2) (page 239)

PA: Known grants by the Parlements and other sovereign courts to 1526 inclusive, and grants for 1527 referred to in the text (page 240)

PR: Known grants by the Prévôt of Paris and other royal officers to 1526 inclusive, and grants for 1527 referred to in the text. An asterisk marks grants which give permission but apparently not specifically a privilege (page 268)

APPENDIX TO REGISTER

CP: Known books printed 'Cum priuilegio' when it is not known on what authority the privilege was given. Those printed 'Cum priuilegio regis' imply a grant from the royal chancery and are shown under the CH heading (page 283)

THE ARRANGEMENT OF THE REGISTER

The left-hand column gives the code-number, the place (in the case of chancery grants) and date of the privilege, or, failing that, any evidence for an approximate date, such as the colophon of the book. (The date of colophons is not normally given.)

The central column gives the beneficiary, the duration of the privilege, the author and short title of the book or books covered by it, and the evidence for the privilege itself.

The right-hand column gives the publisher (place of publication is Paris unless otherwise stated), the date and format of the book as printed, and the shelf-mark of the copy or principal copy consulted by me personally, or, in a very few cases, in a xerox copy. A copy in the BL, the Bodleian, or the BN has been quoted wherever possible, for the convenience of readers: no survey of locations is intended. Some Paris libraries other than the BN, and some provincial libraries, e.g. Toulouse, are rich in sixteenth-century editions; I have cited them only when no other copy was accessible.

ROYAL CHANCERY

CH 1498, 1   To Johannes Trechsel, or his successor or
              nominee,
              5 years, for   Lyon, J. Trechsel
              Despars (Jacques) *Explanatio in Avicenne*   (completed on his
              canonem ed. Jacques Ponceau.   death by J. Clein)
              Latin paraphrase incorporated in the preface   1498 fol. 4 vols.
              addressed by Janus Lascaris to Ponceau,   (last vol.
              printed on the verso of title-page of Vol. 1 (see completed 24
              above, p. 140), with no indication of place or December 1498)
              date of grant.   Bodl.Auct.2.Q.1.5

CH 1507, 1   To Antoine Vérard,   A. Vérard
N⁰s. 1–19   3 years, for   1507 (o.s.) fol.
(See separate *Les Epistres Sainct-Pol glosées*,   BL c.51.d.5
list below,   and subsequent books which he was the first to
pp. 238–9)   publish.
              Summary incorporated in the colophon, dated
              17 January 1508 n.s., with no indication of
              place or date of grant, but the privilege had
              presumably been obtained before the end of
              1507 (see above, pp. 21–2)

CH 1508, 1   To Eloi d'Amerval, author,
Blois,   2 years, for
29 January   d'Amerval (E.) *Le livre de la deablerie*   M. Le Noir
              L.P. printed at end of table of contents (f. Aᵛ), 1508 fol.
              Signed: Par le conseil   De Sanzay   BL c.6.b.16

CH 1508, 2   To Guillaume Eustace,
N⁰s. 1–16   2 years, for
(See separate *Le nouveau monde avec l'estrif du pourveu et de* G. Eustace
list, below, *l'ellectif, de l'ordinaire et du nommé*   s.d. 8°
pp. 239–40)   (variously attributed to Pierre Gringore, André BN Rés.Yᶜ 2988
              de La Vigne and Jean Bouchet)
              and certain subsequent books which he was the
              first to publish.
              Summary printed at the end, with no indication
              of place or date of grant but with the signature
              of the secretary Des Landes.
              The morality play *Le nouveau monde* was
              performed in Paris 11 June 1508.
              (See above, pp. 22, 119.)

CH 1509, 1
Lyon,
1 June

To Nicole Bohier (Boerius), author, for Simon
Vincent,
2 years, for

1. Bohier (N.) *Tractatus celebris de officio et potestate* Lyon, S. Vincent
   Georgii de Ambasia s.d. 8° (17 June)
   BN Rés. E.4237

2. Bohier (N.) *Consuetudines Biturigum ... Glossate* Lyon, S. Vincent
   (pr. J. Myt)
   s.d. 8°
   BM Lyon
   Rés.B.489565

3. Bohier (N.) *Tractatus de electione*, comm. Lyon, S. Vincent
   Mandagotus 1509 8°
   BL c.66.a.29(1)

L.P. printed at end of 1 and 3
Signed: Par le Roy   à vostre relation
Rusé

CH 1509, 2
Lyon,
30 July

To Jean Lemaire de Belges, author,
3 years, for

Lemaire de Belges (J.) *Les Illustrations de Gaule et* Lyon, E. Baland
singularitez de Troye 1510 4°
L.P. printed on f. A 2ᵛ BL G.10248 (1 and
Signed: Par le Roy   à vostre relation 4)
         Ruzé
Followed by:
Lettres d'attache of the Lieutenant General of
Lyon, Claude le Charron, 20 August 1509

Reprinted in full by J. Abélard, *Les illustrations de
Gaule et singularitez de Troye: Etude des éditions;
Genèse de l'œuvre* (Geneva, 1976), pp. 70–1.

CH 1510, 1
Col.
29 April

To Josse Badius, J. Badius (pr.),
3 years, for J. Petit and
Valerius Maximus, comm. Badius J. Koberger,
Latin summary of privilege, 'ut regio constat 1510 fol.
mandato sigillo munito', printed on title-page, BN Rés.z.197
and in more detail on recto of last fol.

CH 1511, 1 Col. 28 June	To Josse Badius, 3 years, for *Epistolae familiares M. T. Ciceronis*, comm. Badius Latin summary of privilege, 'Gratia & Priuilegio ab Regia munificentia concessis: de quibus ad calcem operis', printed on title-page, and in more detail on f. 314^r.	J. Badius (pr.) and J. Petit 1511 4° BN Rés.z.682
CH 1511, 2 Lyon, 25 August	To Jean Robion, 3 years, for Petrutia (Antonius de) *Tractatus de viribus* *iuramenti* L.P. printed on verso of title-page. Signed: Par le Roy à vostre relation Thurin Text in Baudrier, x, pp. 411–13	Lyon, J. Robion, and Toulouse, J. de Clauso (pr. J. de Vingle) 1511 8° BL 228.b.43
CH 1511, 3 Lyon, 25 August	To Jacques de Bouys (bookseller to the University of Orleans), 3 years, for Belviso (Jacques de) ed. N. Beraldus, *Consuetudines et usus feudorum* L.P., printed on penultimate f. of the book, after the colophon and the table of contents. Text in Baudrier, xii, pp. 327–9. (Date of book wrongly given as 1500.)	Lyon, J. Bouys (pr. J. Sacon) 1511 fol. BM Avignon Fol. 1413
CH 1512, 1 Blois, 12 March	To Jean Petit and his partners, 3 years, from date of publication of each book, for	

	1. Raulin (Jean) *Opus sermonum quadragesimalium*
	   [with Parlement privilege dated 5 March
	   1512, see PA 1512, 1]
		J. Petit
		1511 (o.s.) 4° 2
		vols.
		BN D.9501

	2. Godhamus i.e. Woodham (Adam) *Super* *quattuor libros sententiarum* ed. J. Major	J. Petit, J. Granjon and P. le Preux (pr. J. Barbier) 1512 fol. (16 April) BN Rés.D.72(2)

3. FitzRalph (Richard), archbishop of Armagh
Summa in questionibus Armenorum etc.

J. Petit and P. Le
Preux
1512 fol. (15 July)
Bodl.Auct.l.ǫ.IV
(1)

4. Bartholomaeis (Henricus de), Hostiensis
Lectura in V Decretalium Gregorianarum libros

J. Petit and T.
Kerver
(pr. B. Rembolt)
1512 fol. (12
September)
BN Rés.E.1028

5. Origen *Opera* (Latin trans. by St Jerome and
others) with *Apologia* for Origen by Jacques
Merlin

J. Petit and J.
Badius
(pr. J. Badius)
1512 fol. (15
October) 4 vols.
BN Vélins 272–5

6. Gregory of Tours *Historia Francorum* [and
other works] ed. Guillaume Petit

J. Petit and J.
Badius
(pr. J. Badius)
'1522' (for 1512)
fol.
(3 November)
Bodl.c.9.22.Jur

7. Sigebert of Gembloux *Chronicon* ed. Guillaume
Petit

J. Petit and H.
Estienne
(pr. H. Estienne)
1513 4^P (7 June)
BL 580.g.1.

8. Aimoinus, monk of Fleury *De regum
procerumque Francorum origine*

J. Petit and J.
Badius
(pr. J. Badius)
1514 fol. (12
August)
BL 9150.h.9(2)

L.P., summary printed on verso of title-page in
numbers 2, 7 and 8, facing first page of text in
numbers 1, 3 and 4, and at the end in numbers
5 and 6.
Signed: Par le Roy   Geuffroy.

CH 1512, 2 Blois, 1 May	To Jean Lemaire de Belges, author, 3 years, for Lemaire de Belges (J.) *Le second livre des* *illustrations de Gaule* L.P. printed on f. 2. Signed: par le Roy à vostre relation Ruzé Reprinted by J. Abélard, *Les illustrations de Gaule*, pp. 94–5.	G. de Marnef and H Malican of Blois 1512 4° Bodl. Douce M 100

CH 1512, 3
Blois,
3 June
	To Nicole Bohier, editor,
	3 years, for
	
	1. Montaigne (J.) *Tractatus de auctatoritate magni*
	   concilii
	
	2. *Leges Longobardorum … cum annotationibus*
	
	L.P., printed in 1 on f. K4 and followed by the
	lettres d'atache of the Lieutenant General of the
	sénéchaussée of Lyon, signed Claude le
	Charron, and in 2 on recto of last fol.
	Signed: Par le Roy à la relation du conseil
	                        Deslandes
		[De Marnef]
		s.d. 8°
		BL 8050.b.1.
		[Simon Vincent,
		Lyon]
		s.d. 8°
		BM Lyon
		Rés.B.485665.

CH 1512, 4 Blois, 11 November	To Jean Petit at the request of the author, 3 years, for Ricz (Alfonso) *Eruditiones christiane religionis* L.P., summary printed on fol. d 10ᵛ. Signed: Par le Roy Gedoyn	[J. Petit] s.d. 4° BN D.5137
CH 1513, 1 Col. 13 January n.s. (dedicated to Queen Anne October 1512)	To (author?) 3 years, for Brixius (Germain) *Chordigerae nauis conflagratio* L.P., summary on title-page and in colophon.	J. Badius 1513 4° Bodl.Douce B.subt.262
CH 1513, 2 Paris, 6 June	To Jean Lode, author and translator, 3 years, for	

1. *Tymon aduersus ingratos* and *De justicia et pietate*   No copy traced
   Celeucri (described in the privilege as 'deux
   petitz dyalogues en langue latine et vers
   hexametres')

2. Filelfo (F.) *Le guidon des parents en l'instruction et*   G. Gourmont
   direction de leurs enfans tr. J. Lode.   1513 8°
   BN Rés.R.2160

3. Plutarch, Γαμικα παραγγελματα: *Nuptialia*   G. Gourmont
   praecepta ed. J. Lode (Latin only, though a   s.d. 8°
   version into French is provided for in the   BN Rés.p.R.903
   privilege)

L.P. printed on verso of title-page in 2 and 3.
Signed: Par le Roy à la relation du conseil.
                    Hillaire

CH 1513, 3   To Michel Le Noir,
Paris,   2 years, for
9 June   *Les Prouesses du noble Huon de Bordeaux*   M. Le Noir
                  L.P. printed at end of table of contents.   1513 fol. (26
                  Signed: Par le Roy, Maistre Pierre de La   November)
                  Vernade, maistre des requestes ordinaires,   BL c.97.c.1
                  present.
                        J. Morelet

CH 1513, 4   To Galliot Du Pré,
Paris,   3 years, for
18 November

                  1. Gaguin (Robert) *Les grandes cronicques* (preface   G. Du Pré and
                     by Pierre Desrey)   P. LePreux
                     1514 fol.
                     Bodl.Douce
                     G.293

                  2. Durandus (Gulielmus) *Breuiarium aureum iuris*   G. Du Pré
                     canonici (preface by Gilles d'Aurigny)   1513 8°
                     BN Rés.E.4074

                  L.P. printed on verso of title-page of 1, and
                  summarised on fol. E8 of 2.
                  Signed: Par le Roy à la relation du conseil
                               Des Landes
                  For CH 1513, 4(2) Galliot Du Pré also had a
                  Parlement privilege, PA 1513, 4.

CH 1513, 5 Place and date not known	To the publisher (presumably), for Vidal du Four (Joannes) *Speculum morale totius* *sacræ scripturæ* 'Cum regio priuilegio' printed in red on title-page.	Lyon, Jean Moylin dit de Cambray 1513 fol. BN Rés.A.1946(2)
CH 1514, 1 Paris, 6 May	To Galliot Du Pré, 3 years, for	
	1. Bouchard (Alain) *Les grandes cronicques de* *Bretaigne*	G. Du Pré (pr. J. de la Roche) 1514 fol. (25 November) BN Rés.Lk² 442
	2. Ableiges (Jacques d') *Le grant coustumier de* *France*	G. Du Pré 1515 4° BN Rés.F.940
	L.P. printed on verso of title-page of 1. Signed: Par le Roy, Maistre Pierre de La Vernade chevalier maistre des requestes ordinaires de l'ostel: et aultres presens Geuffroy For the privilege of 2 and its confirmation by Francis I see CH 1515, 3	
CH 1514, 2 Col. 21 May	To Quinziano Stoa, author, 3 years, for Stoa (Quinziano) *Christiana opera* 'Admonitio' referring to royal privilege, printed on fol. A 6ʳ after commendatory verses.	J. Petit (pr. J. Barbier) 1514 fol. BN Rés.gYC 592
CH 1514, 3 Paris, 26 August	To Guillaume Eustace, 2 years, for	
	1. Livy, *Le premier volume des grans decades*	G. Eustace (vol. 3 with F. Regnault) 1514–15 fol. 3 vols. BN Rés.J.245
	2. *Grans croniques de France*	G. Eustace 1514 fol. 3 vols. BN Vélins 731–3

3. *Le grant coustumier de Sens* — G. Eustace (pr. Guillaume Desplains) 1516 8°

L.P. printed on verso of title-page of 1 and at end of 2, summarised on verso of title-page of 3. Signed: Par le Roy à la relacion du conseil, Garbot, 'Et à l'enterinement desdictes lettres signé Almaury.' — Arsenal 8° J. 3732

CH 1514, 4
Paris,
19 September — To Antoine Bonnemère,
3 years, for
Saint-Gelais (Charles de) *Les excellentes cronicques du prince Judas Machabeus* — A. Bonnemère 1514, fol.
L.P. printed on verso of title-page. — BL 3022.h.5
Signed: Par le Roy Maistre Jehan Hurault maistre des requestes ordinaires de l'ostel Et autres presens   Par le conseil   Guyot.

CH 1514, 5
Paris,
22 December — To Galliot Du Pré,
1 year, for
Montjoie *Le pas d'armes tenu à l'entrée de la Royne à Paris* — G. Du Pré 1514 4°
L.P. printed on verso of title-page. — BN Rothschild
Signed: Par le Roy. De Mousins [*sic*] — IV.6.81

CH 1514, 6 — To Josse Badius,
3 years, for
Col.
13 November — 1. Plutarch *Vitae*, Latin translation by Lapo da Firenze and others, ed. Badius — J. Badius and J. Petit 1514 fol. Bodl. fol. Δ108

Col.
7 December — 2. Seneca *Tragoediae*, comm. Badius and others — J. Badius 1514 fol. BL 833.m.16

Latin summary of royal privilege, printed at the end of both books, referring to a document given under the royal seal and signed Guernadon (may be two separate privileges), no date given.

CH 1515, 1
Paris,
27 January — To Galliot Du Pré,
3 years, for
L'hystoire du sainct greaal — J. Petit, G. Du Pré, and M. Le Noir
Summary printed below the mark of Michel Le Noir on the title-page, ending with the words 'Par le Roy / et syne Bucelly'. — 1514–16 fol. 2 vols. BN Rés.Y².23–4

CH 1515, 1A Paris, 19 February	To Jehan Falcon, author, 2 years, for Falcon (J.) *Les notables declaratifs sur le Guidon* L.P. printed at the end. Signed: Par le roy. De Moulins.	Lyon, C. Fradin 1515 4° BN Rés.Td.73.18
CH 1515, 2 Paris, 12 April	To Antoine Bonnemère, 3 years, for Champier (Symphorien) *Periarchon* L.P. printed at the end. Signed: De Rillac.	A. Bonnemère s.d. 4° BN Rés.R.745
CH 1515, 3 Paris, 24 April	To Galliot Du Pré, confirmation by Francis I of 3-year privilege granted by Louis XII on 6 May 1514, for Ableiges (Jacques d') *Le grant coustumier de France* LP. printed below Louis XII's privilege, on verso of title-page. Signed: Par le roy à la relation du conseil. Bucelly.	See CH 1514, 1.
CH 1515, 4 Paris, 26 April	To Geoffroy de Marnef and Simon Vincent, 2 years, for Bohier (Nicole) *De seditiosis* L.P. printed on verso of title-page. Signed: Par le Roy à la relation du conseil. Longuet.	Paris, G. De Marnef, and Lyon, S. Vincent s.d. 8° BN Rés.F.2292
CH 1515, 5 Lyon, 24 July	To Jean Petit, 3 years, for all new works composed by Jérôme de Hangest, and for certain books by the late Jean Raulin and others, including the following (in order of publication): 1. Hangest (J. de) *De causis* 2. Raulin (J.) *Opus sermonum de aduentu* 3. Raulin (J.) *Doctrinale mortis*	 J. Petit (pr. B. Rembolt) s.d. fol. Bodl.AA 59 Art.(1) J. Petit (pr. B. Rembolt) 1516 4° BN Rés.D.9494 J. Petit (pr. B. Rembolt) 1518 4° BN D.5642.

4. Hangest (J. de) *Moralia*		J. Petit 1519 fol. Bodl.AA 59 Art.(5)
5. Peter of Blois *Opera* ed. Jacques Merlin		J. Petit (pr. A. Boucard) 1519 fol. BN Rés.c.2486
6. Raulin (J.) *Sermones de eucharistia*		J. Petit 1519 fol. Bodl.Douce R.158
7. Hangest (J. de) *De possibili praeceptorum* *diuinorum impletione in Lutherum*		J. Petit (pr. J. Badius) 1528 4° BL 3837.a.31(2)
8. Hangest (J. de) *Aduersus antimarianos* *propugnaculum*		J. Petit 1529 4° BN D.7442(2)

L.P., summarised at the end of 3, on the final
page of the first gathering in 8, and on the verso
of the title-page of the other six books,
Signed: Par le Roy   J. Bartelemy

CH 1515, 6 Grenoble, 8 August	To Louis Olivelli 2 years, for Du Rivail (Aymar) *De historia iuris ciuilis et* *pontificii* L.P. printed on verso of title-page. Signed: Par le Roy dauphin vous et aultres presens Portier	Valence, L. Olivelli s.d. 4° BN Rés.F.2046

CH 1515, 7 Lyon, 16 August	To Nicole Bohier, for Simon Vincent, 3 years, for	
	1. Belleperche (Pierre de) *Questiones aureae* and *Tractatus de Feudis*, ed. J. Thierry	Lyon, S. Vincent (pr. A. Du Ry) 1517 8° BN Soc. Géo.Rés.K.2
	2. Chasseneuz (Barthélemy de) *Commentaria in* *consuetudines ducatus Burgundie*	Lyon, S. Vincent 1517 4° (pr. J. Mareschal) BN Rés.F.1230

	3. Papa (Guido) *Tractatus* and *Singularia* ed. J. Thierry	Lyon, S. Vincent (pr. J. Jonelle dit Piston) s.d 4° BM Lyon A.486493
	L.P. printed on verso of title in each book. Signed: Par le Roy à la relation du conseil P. Maillard	

CH 1515, 8
Lyon,
21 August
To Pierre Balet,
2 years, for
Belviso (Jacques de) *Practica judiciaria in criminalibus* ed. H. Descousu
L.P. printed on fol. O⁷, place, day and month filled in by hand.
Signed: Par le Roy à la relation du conseil
    Deslandes

Lyon, P. Balet
(pr. J. Moylin)
1515 8°
BM Lyon
Rés.B.508868

CH 1515, 9
Amboise,
19 September
To Guillaume Bouchet,
2 years, for
Malleret (Etienne) *De electionibus et beneficiis ecclesiasticis*
L.P. printed at the end.
Signed: Par le Roy à la relacion du conseil
    Deveignolles

Poitiers,
G. Bouchet
1515 4°
BN E.1998

CH 1515, 10
Col.
mense
decembri
To the publisher (presumably),
duration not stated, for
Ishaq Israeli ben Salomon, *Omnia opera*, preface by Symphorien Champier
'Cum priuilegio Pontificis maximi Leonis decimi & Francisci christianissimi Francorum regis', printed at the top of the title-page.

Lyon. B. Trot
(pr. J. de Platea)
1515 fol.
BN Rés.T²⁴ 3

CH 1516, 1
Crémieu,
19 May
To Hugues Descousu, editor, for Pierre Balet,
3 years, for

    1. *Les coustumes du pays de Bourgogne*

Lyon, P. Balet
(pr. A. du Ry)
1516 8°
BL 706.a.17

    2. Monaldus (Joannes) *Summa perutilis in utroque iure fundata*

Lyon, P. Balet
s.d. 8°
BL 5107.b.25

L.P. printed at the end of both books.
Signed: Par le Roy à la relation du conseil
    Longuet

CH 1516, 2
Issoire,
20 July

To Vincent Cigauld, author
3 years, for
Cigauld (V.) *Opus facta principum determinans &*
Consilium super alienatione iusticie
L.P. printed on verso of title-page.
Signed: Par le Roy à vostre relation:
et sellé à cire jaune   Deslandes

Lyon, L. Martin
(pr. S. Bevilaqua)
1516 8° (2 parts)
BL 8005.bbb.13

CH 1516, 3
Paris,
27 October

To Pierre Gringore, author
4 years, for
Gringore (P.) *Les fantasies de mere Sotte*
L.P. printed on fol. 2 (a ii^r).
Signed: Par le Roy à vostre relation
            Deslandes
Reproduced in full in the edition of *Les Fantasies*
de mère Sotte by R. L. Frautschi (Chapel Hill,
1962), Appendix I, pp. 223–4.

[J. Petit]
s.d. 4°
BN Rés.ye 290

CH 1516, 4
Col.
23 December

To the publisher (?) or editor
2 years, for
Peñaforte (Raymundus de) *Summula* ed.
J. Chappuys
On title: 'Cum priuilegio ne quis biennio
proximo hanc summulam praesertim cum
lucubratione Joannis Chappuis denuo
imprimat: sub pena arbitraria et applicationis
librorum eiusmodi ad fiscum regium ut constat
litteris nostris regio sigillo munitis.'

Thielman Kerver
and C. Le Lièvre
1516, 8°
Bodl.8° A.63 Linc.

CH 1516, 5
Published
1516

To the publisher (presumably),
4 years, for
Spagnuoli Mantuanus (Battista) [*Opera*]
On title: 'Cum gratia et priuilegio apostolico et
victoriosissimi Francisci Francorum regis', and
at end 'Cum gratia et priuilegio usque ad
quattuor annos'.

Lyon, Stephanus
de Basignana
Gorgonius
(pr. Bernard
Lescuyer)
1516 8° 3 vols.
BL 11409.bb.35

CH 1517, 1
Paris,
10 January

To Galliot du Pré,
2 years, for
1. *Le nouveau monde et navigacions faictes par Emeric*
de Vespuce [by Fracanzano da Montalboddo]
tr. Mathurin Du Redouer

G. Du Pré (pr. P.
Vidoue)
1517 4°
BN Rés.P.9

2. Chastellain (Georges) *Le temple Jehan Boccace*   G. Du Pré (pr. P.
(and works by other authors, not all included   Vidoue)
in the privilege)   1517 fol.
   BN Rés.z.349

3. Bouchet (Jean) *Le temple de bonne renommée*   G. Du Pré (pr. P.
   Vidoue)
   1516 (o.s.) 4°
   BN ye.357

4. *Le mirouer historial de France*   G. Du Pré (pr. P.
   Vidoue)
   1516 (o.s.) fol.
   BL c.55.h.7.

L.P. printed on verso of title-page in 1, 3 and 4,
on verso of title-page and following page in 2.
Signed: Par le Roy à la relation du conseil
     Deslandes.

CH 1517, 2
Paris,
2 February

To Guillaume Eustace,
2 years, for
Colonna (Egidio) *Le mirouer exemplaire des roys*   G. Eustace
L.P. printed on verso of title-page and following   1517 fol.
page.   BL 721.i.3
Signed: Par le Roy   De neufville.

CH 1517, 3
Paris,
9 March

To Jean de La Garde,
3 years, for
Les grandes coustumes generalles et particulieres du   J de La Garde
royaume de France   1517 fol.
L.P. printed on verso of title-page.   BN Rés.F.714
Signed: Par le Roy à la relation du conseil
     Saugeon
'Lesdictes lettres de privillege enterinees par
monseigneur le prevost de Paris ainsi qu'il
appert par les lettres dattees du vendredy .xx.
jour de mars Mil cinq cens et seize signé Corbie
et seellee en cire verte.'

CH 1517, 4
Paris,
19 May

To Jean Petit,
3 years, for
Les ordonnances royaulx sur le faict des chasses   J. Petit
L.P. printed on verso of title-page.   1517 8°
Signed: Par le Roy.   Robertet.   BN Vélins 1860

CH 1517, 5
29 June

To Pierre Marchant, *greffier, fermier de la*
sénéchaussée et comté de Poictou,
2 years, for | Paris/Poitiers, E.
Le coustumier du pays de Poictou nouvellement réformé | de Marnef
Privilege described, with some extracts, by A. | s.d. 4°
de La Bouraliére, *Les débuts de l'imprimerie à* | No copy traced.
Poitiers 1479–1515, 2nd edn (Paris, 1893), p. 58,
from a copy in the possession of M. Arthur
Labbé of Châtellerault.
Cf. La Bouralière, *L'imprimerie et la librairie à*
Poitiers pendant le xvie siècle (Paris, 1900), p. 60.

CH 1517, 6
Rouen,
12 August

To Michel Le Noir,
3 years, for
1. *L'instruction d'ung jeune prince* [by Guillebert de | M. Le Noir
Lannoy] | 1518 (26 January)
8°
BN Rés.E. 659

2. *Les deux tresplaisantes hystoires de Guerin de* | M Le Noir
Montglane et de Maugist d'Aigremeont | 1518 fol.
BL c.7.b.8

3. La Sale (Antoine de) *L'hystoyre du petit Jehan de* | M. Le Noir
Saintré | 1517 (o.s.) (15
March) fol.
Bodl.Douce s. 277

4. *Les passaiges d'Oultremer faitz par les francoys* [by | M. Le Noir
Sebastien Mamerot, with additions] | 1518 (27
November) fol.
BN Rés.La⁹ 2.

L.P. printed on the verso of title-page of each
book.
Signed: Par le Roy   à la relacion du conseil
Maillart

CH 1517, 7
Place and
date not
known

To the publisher (presumably),
3 years, for
Aemilius (Paulus) *De rebus gestis Francorum* | J. Badius
lib.IV. | s.d. fol.
On title-page: Regio priuilegio cautum est | BN Rés.L³⁵ 22 A
nequis intra triennium in regno Franciae hoc
opus rursus imprimat: aut alibi impressum
vendat.
(For the assignment of this edition to 1517, see
Renouard, *Imprimeurs et libraires parisiens,* II,
n°. 749)

CH 1518, 1
Amboise,
27 January

To Enguilbert de Marnef,
2 years, for
Bouchet (Jean) *L'histoire et cronicque de Clotaire et*   Poitiers, E. de
sa tresillustre espouse madame saincte Radegonde   Marnef
L.P. printed on verso of title-page.   1500 [*sic*] 4°
Signed: Par le Roy à vostre relation   BN Rés.D.67949
        De mousins [*sic* for Moulins]
Et seelé en cere jaulne à simple quehe

CH 1518, 2
4 March

To Durand Gerlier,
2 years, for
Concordata super contenta in Pragmatica sanctione   D. Gerlier, and E.
'Cum priuilegio regis' on title-page, with arms   de Marnef,
of Pope and king of France.   Poitiers (pr.)
See also CH 1519, 2   1518 4°
  BN Rés.p.z.167
  Cf. *Actes de François*
  Ier, VIII, 3^3
  supplément,
  N°. 32302,
  pp. 583–4.

CH 1518, 3
Amboise,
9 March

To Vincent Doesmier, editor,
3 years, for
Almain (Jacques) *Aurea opuscula*   C. Chevallon and
L.P. printed after the *Tabula*, facing first page of   G. de Gourmont
text.   (pr. N. des Prez)
Signed: Par le Roy à la relation du conseil   1518 fol.
            Guiot   Bodl.c.18.13.Th

CH 1518, 4
Angers,
19 June

To Jean Petit,
3 years, for
1. St Athanasius *Opera* ed. N. Beraldus (Latin   J. Petit
   trans. by Cristofero Persona and others)   1520 fol.
  BL 3625.b.1

2. Richard of Saint Victor *Opera* ed. J. Merlin   J. Petit (pr. A.
  Bocard)
  1518 fol.
  BN Rés.c.1006

L.P. summary printed on verso of title-page of
each book.
Signed: Par le Roy.   Des Landes.

CH 1518, 5

To Josse Badius,
3 years, for

Col. 22 August	1. Henry of Ghent *Quodlibeta*, ed. A. de Villa Sancta	J. Badius 1518 fol. BN Vélins 343–4
Col. 5 July 1520	2. Henry of Ghent *Summae quaestionum*	J. Badius 1520 fol. 2 vols. Bodl.G.1.1. Th

L.P. Latin summary printed on verso of last fol. of each book, giving no place or date of grant, the second concluding 'ut constat per literas patentes Regio Sigillo obsignatas, & concessas praesente & annuente perreuerendo in Christo patre, tunc Parrhisiorum Antistite, nunc autem Senonum Archiepiscopo dignissimo, multisque aliis fide dignis, subsignante Pedoyn [*sic*, for Gedoyn].' (Etienne Poncher, whose presence at the sealing of the grant is recorded in the summary printed in the *Quodlibeta*, as bishop of Paris, had become archbishop of Sens in March 1519.)

CH 1518, 6	To Jean de Gourmont, for an unstated period, for	
Col. 16 December	1. Rincius (Bernardinus) *Epitalamion in nuptiis Francisci Galliarum Delphini* [betrothal of the Dauphin to Henry VIII's daughter Mary, 5 October 1518]	J. de Gourmont s.d. 4° BL 596.e.34
Col. 23 December	2. Rincius (B.) *Sylva* [celebration of tournament and banquet at the Bastille, 22 December 1518]	J. de Gourmont 1518 4° BL 596.f.32
	3. Rincius (B.) *Le livre et forest* [French translation of *Sylva*]	J. de Gourmont 1518 4° BL 811.d.31(1)
	4. Pace (Richard) *Oratio nuptialis*	J. de Gourmont s.d. 4° BN G.2822
	5. Pace (R.) *Oraison en la louenge de la paix* [also on marriage treaty between French and England]	J. de Gourmont s.d. 4° BL G.6119(2)

Statement 'Cauete ne quis impune attentet hunc libellum imprimere: ut amplissimo patet priuilegio a regia maiestate nobis condonato. M.D.XVIII', printed at the end of each book (probably a 'package' privilege covering these and other small items published in connection with the royal betrothal).

CH 1518, 7
Col.
14 July and
26 October

To Thielman Kerver (presumably),
for
Breuiarium Deo dicatarum virginum ordinis
Fontisebraldi
'Cum priuilegio' printed at the end of each part
(presumably referring to a royal privilege, since
the book was printed for the royal convent of
Fontevrault).

T. Kerver
1518 8° (2 parts)
Ste Geneviève
8° BB 881
Rés.Inv.1067

CH 1519, 1
Paris,
7 February

To Conrad Resch,
3 years, for
1. Waim (Gervase) *Tractatus noticiarum*

C. Resch (pr. N.
des Préz)
1519 fol.
BN Rés.R.678(1)

2. Erasmus *Familiarium colloquiorum formulae (et
alla opera)*

C. Resch
(pr. H. Estienne)
1518 (o.s.) 4°
Maz. Rés.10122

L.P. printed facing first page of text of 1 (fol.
+ 4ᵛ).
Signed: Par le Roy à vostre relation. Bordel.
Entérinement mentioned on title-page ('Cum
gratia et priuilegio Regio a praefecto
parrhisiensi scito & ratificato').
The Erasmus has only 'Cum priuilegio regis' on
the title-page, but the colophon is 'Mense
Februario' which suggests that the privilege
of 7 February covered both books.

CH 1519, 2
Paris,
4 March

To Durand Gerlier,
2 years, for
1. *Les Concordatz*

[D. Gerlier]
(pr. F. Regnault)
s.d. 8°
Maz.Rés.26819

2. *Les Georgicques de Virgille* (tr. G. Michel)

D. Gerlier (pr. F.
d'Egmont)
1519 4°
BL 237.l.20

3. *Le Prothocolle des notaires du chastellet de Paris*

D. Gerlier
s.d. 4°
Edinburgh UL
De.3.40

L.P. printed on ff. 2ʳ–3ᵛ of 2 and 1ᵛ–2ᵛ of 3.
Signed: Par le Roy à vostre relation.   Bordel.

CH 1519, 3
Paris,
21 March

To Galliot Du Pré,
4 years, for
1. Patrizzi (Francisco) *De regno et regis institutione*
   ed. Jo. Savigneus
2. Sacchi de Platina (Bartholomaeus),
   Genealogies, faits et gestes des saints peres papes

3. Patricius (F.) *De l'institution et administration de
   la chose publique*

G. Du Pré
(pr. P. Vidoue)
1518 (o.s.) fol.
BN Vélins 408–9
G. Du Pré
(pr. P. Vidoue)
1519 fol.
BN Vélins 686

G. Du Pré
(pr. P. Vidoue)
1520 fol.
BN Vélins 410

L.P. printed on verso of title-page in 1 and 2.
Signed: Par le Roy à la relation du conseil.
            Demoulins.
'Avec le privilege du roi nostre sire' on f. 201ᵛ,
in 3. (French translation of 1.)

CH 1519, 4
Saint-
Germain-
en-Laye,
3 April

To Regnault Chaudière,
3 years, for
1. Seyssel (Claude de] *De diuina prouidentia*

2. Seyssel (C. de) *Aduersus errores et sectam
   Valdensium*

R. Chaudière
s.d. 4°
BN Rés.D.3629

R. Chaudière
1520 4°
BN Vélins 1781

L.P. printed at the end of 1 and on verso of
title-page of 2.
Signed: Par le Roy, Maistre Jehan Hurault
maistre des requestes ordinaires de l'hostel, et
aultres presens.   Gedoyn.

CH 1519, 5
Carrières,
18 April

To Nicole Bohier, for Simon Vincent,
5 years, for
Ancharano (Petrus de) *Lectura aurea super primo
Decretalium*...
L.P. printed on verso of title of the *Repertorium*
bound with Vol. II.
Signed: Par le Roy à la relation du conseil.
            Geuffroy.

Lyon, S. Vincent
(Vols. I–II)
Jacques
Mareschal,
Vols. III–V pr.
Jean Jonvelle (dit
Piston)
1518–19 fol. (5
vols.)
BN Rés.E.66

CH 1519, 6 Saint- Germain-en- Laye, 3 May	To Regnault Chaudière, 3 years, from the date of publication of each book, for 1. Seyssel (Claude de) *La grant monarchie de* *France*	R. Chaudière 1519 4° 21 July BN Vélins 2809
	2. *Le livre de la discipline d'amour divine*	R. Chaudière 1519 8° 28 November BN D.42239
	3. Ravisius Textor (Joannes) *Officina*	R. Chaudière 1520 fol. 27 November BL 613.l.22
	4. Le Cirier (Jean) *Tractatus de iure primogeniturae*	R. Chaudière 1521 fol. 1 February BN Vélins 419
	5. *Cy commencent quatre voyes spirituelles pour aller à* *Dieu*	R. Chaudière s.d. 4° (no colophon) Arsenal T 4° 2094

L.P. printed on verso of title-page of 1, 4 and 5,
and at the end of 2 and 3, omitting mention in
each case of the other books.
Signed: Par le Roy,
      l'evesque de Troyes, confesseur, et aultres
      presens.   Godoyn (for Gedoyn) in 4
                 Hedoyn (for Gedoyn) in the
      others.

CH 1519, 7 Carrières, 22 July	To Jean d'Ivry, author, 3 years, for d'Ivry (J.) *Scrinium medicine* Latin summary, printed on verso of last fol., referring to 'regio priuilegio literis auctenticis'. Signed: Bourdelles.	pr. for the author by Jean Du Pré. s.d. 12° BN Rés.8° T³⁰ 2
CH 1519, 8 Paris, 29 July	To the publisher (presumably), 3 years, for Bechichemus (Marinus) *Elegans et docta in C.* *Plinium Praelectio* (introduction by Erasmus) Latin summary, printed on verso of title-page. Signed: ex regio mandato, Bordel.	C. Resch (pr. P. Vidoue) 1519 fol. BL 442.h.4

CH 1519, 9 Paris, 3 August	To Pasquier Le Moine, author, 4 years, for 1. Le Moine (P.) *Le couronnement du roy François premier; le voyage et conqueste de Millan*	G. Couteau s.d. 4° BL 85.d.23
	2. Le Moine (P.) *L'ardant miroir de grace*	G. Couteau s.d. 8° BN ye 1384
	L.P. printed on verso of title-page in both books. Signed: Par le Roy à vostre relation. R. Guiot.	
CH 1519, 10 Col. 7 October	To author or publisher (presumably) for Balgenciacensis (Johannes) *De tribus virtutibus* ed. Antonius Toledus 'Cum priuilegio regio' on title-page. (No particulars about beneficiary, duration, or date and place of grant.)	Lyon, J. Osmont (pr. C. Nourry) 1519 8° Arsenal 8° T.3786
CH 1519, 11	To the author or publisher (presumably), 3 years, for Meigret (Amédée) *Questiones in libros de generatione & corruptione Aristotelis* Statement printed on title-page: 'Cum gratia & priuilegio Regis ne quis triennio proximo alibi imprimat aut impressum in regnum francorum inferat: sub pena in instrumento authentico super hoc confecto declarata.' No other particulars.	Jean Du Pré 1519 fol. BN Rés.R.547(3)
CH 1519, 12	To the publisher (presumably), period of duration not stated, for *Miscellanea ex diuersis historiographis, oratoribus* etc. Statement printed at the end, after errata: 'Cauet ne quis impune attentet hunc libellum imprimere; ut amplissimo patet priuilegio a regia majestate nobis condonato. M.D.XIX.' No other particulars. Cf. CH 1518, 6.	Jean de Gourmont 1519 4° BN Rés.z.1070(3)

CH 1520, 1 Paris, 12 May	To Michel Le Noir 3 years, for *Les faitz et prouesses du noble et vaillant chevalier* *Jourdain de Blaves* L.P. printed on verso of title-page. Signed: Par le Roy à vostre relation Guiot	M. Le Noir 1520 fol BN Rés.y² 155
CH 1520, 2 7 August	To an unnamed beneficiary (possibly the anonymous author) who authorised Gilbert de Villiers to use it, 5 years, for *Traicté de exhortation de paix* Statement printed after colophon, 'Lequel de Villiers a eu permission de celuy qui a le privilege pour cinq ans. Seelé du grant seel du Roy. Et signé. P. Grabot. dès l'année mil cinq cens vingt. Le vii. jour d'aoust.'	Lyon, G. de Villiers 1520 4° BM Troyes K.11.6596

CH 1520, 3
25 August
	To Galliot Du Pré,
	3 years, for
	1. Suetonius, *Des faictz et gestes des douze Cesars*
	
	2. *Tomus primus (secundus) quatuor conciliorum*
	   generalium ed. Jacques Merlin
	
	L.P., summarised in French in 1 and
	paraphrased in Latin in 2, printed on verso of
	title-page.
	Signed: Deslandes,
	followed by *entérinement* by the Prévôt at the
	Châtelet, dated 18 September and signed:
	        Corbie.
	Cf. PA 1524, 13.
		G. Du Pré
		(pr. P. Vidoue)
		s.d. fol.
		BN Rés.j.682
		G. Du Pré (pr. J.
		Cornillau)
		1524 fol.
		BL c.37.l.8

CH 1520, 4 Paris, 27 August	To Enguilbert de Marnef 2 years, for Garcie dit Ferrande (Pierre) *Le grant routtier et les* *jugemens d'Olleron* L.P. printed at end. Signed: De par le Roy à la relation du conseil Mareschal	Poitiers, E. de Marnef s.d. 4° BM Niort Rés.p.161 E

CH 1520, 5   To Jean Petit
Paris,   3 years, for
31 August   1. Raulin (Jean) *Epistolae*   J. Petit
                                                                         1521 4°
                                                                         Bodl.Th.4° R.7

               2. *Cathena aurea super Psalmos* [by a Carthusian]   J. Petit
                                                                         1520 4°
                                                                         BN Rés.A.4276

               L.P. summarised on verso of title-page of both
               books.
               Signed: Par le Roy.   Deslandes

CH 1520, 6   To Simon Gruel,
Paris,   3 years, for
21 September   Le Fèvre dit Fabri (Pierre) *Le grant et vray art de*   Rouen, S. Gruel
               pleine rhetorique   (pr. Thomas
               L.P. printed on verso of title-page.   Rayer)
               Signed: Par le Roy à vostre relation. Bordel.   1521 4°
               Reprinted by G. Lepreux, *Gallia typographica*, III,   BN Rés.X.1252
               i, pp. 367–8.

CH 1520, 7   To Simon de Colines,
Paris,   3 years, for
2 October   Montholon (Jean de) *Promptuarium diuini iuris et*   Henri Estienne
               utriusque humani   1520 fol. 2 vols.
               L.P. printed at the end.   Bodl.C.9.1.Jur
               Signed: Par le Roy à vostre relation.
                                             Bordel.

CH 1520, 8   To Jean de La Garde,
Paris,   3 years, for
6 October   *Le violier des histoires rommaines moralisées*   J. de La Garde
               L.P. printed on verso of title-page, 'scellé de cire   1521 fol.
               jaulne', secretary's name not printed.   Arsenal 4° H.1149
               'Enterinés par monsieur le prevost de Paris, xiii
               jour dudit moys audit an   signé   Lormier.'

CH 1520, 9   To Jean de Gourmont (presumably),
Col.   for
12 October   Aristotle *Naturalis auscultationis libri*   J. de Gourmont
               Statement, 'Cauetur ne quis impune attentet   1520 fol.
               hunc librum imprimere ut amplissimo patet   Paris, Faculté de
               priuilegio a regia maiestate nobis condonato   Médicine, 1399
               M.D.XX. Cum priuilegio regis', printed on last
               page.

CH 1520, 10
Amboise,
10 November

To Gabriel de Tarregua, author
3 years, for
Tarregua (G. de) *Summe diuersarum quaestionum medicinalium*
L.P. printed on recto of last f. of prelims, at end of table of contents.
Signed: Par le Roy. Robertet. Et seillé du grant sel dudict seignieur en cire jaulne à simple queuhe.

Bordeaux,
Gaspard Philippe
1520 fol.
BN Rés.T^{25}.1

CH 1520, 11

To Conrad Resch,
3 years, for
Asconius Paedianus (Q.) *In Orationes Ciceronis Enarrationes, cum aliis adjectis*
Latin summary, headed 'Ex textu regii priuilegii', printed on fol. 3^v of prelims, 'sicut aperte in Regio Dyplomate continentur'. No details of place or date of grant.

C. Resch
(pr. P. Vidoue)
1520 fol.
BN Rés.x.424

CH 1521, 1
Paris,
2 February

To Guillaume Eustace,
2 years, for
1. Alexis (Guillaume) *Le dialogue du crucifix et du pélerin*

G. Eustace
1521 8°
BN Rés.D.23080

2. St Jerome *Les epistres en françois*

G. Eustace
1520 (o.s.) fol.
BN Rés.c.456

L.P., summarised at the end of 1 and printed in full on verso of title-page of 2.
Signed: Par le Roy   De neufville, and *entérinement* by the Prévôt of Paris, signed: J. de Calais.

CH 1521, 2
Col.
10 March

To Jean Petit,
3 years, for
Pepin (Guillaume) *Speculum aureum super septem psalmos penitentiales*
Latin summary of royal privilege printed as part of colophon on recto of last fol.

J. Petit
1520 (o.s.) 8°
BN D.47370

CH 1521, 3
Sancerre,
2 April

To Jean Petit 'et à ses compaignons',
4 years, for
Chronica chronicarum abbregé
Summary of royal privilege printed as part of colophon at the end.
Signed: Par le Roy.   De la Chenaye, 'Et sont interinees lesdites lettres par Monsieur le prevost de Paris. Ainsi signé Ruzé.'

J. Petit and F.
Regnault
(pr. J. Ferrebouc)
1521 fol.
BN Vélins 13

CH 1521, 4
Paris,
14 December

To Conrad Resch,
3 years, for
Eck (Johannes) *De primatu Petri aduersus Ludderum*
L.P. printed on verso of title-page.
Signed: Par le Roy à vostre relation. Heruoet.

C. Resch
(pr. P. Vidoue)
1521 fol.
Bodl. M.8.9.Jur.
(Copies also in J. Kerver's name, e.g. Bodl.fol. Θ 651(b))

CH 1521, 5
Paris,
23 December

To Pierre Gringore, author,
4 years, for
Gringore (Pierre) *Les menus propos*
L.P. printed on both sides of fol. 2.
Signed: Par le Roy à la relation du conseil.
                         Thiboust.

pr. Gilles Couteau
for the author
1521 8°
Bodl.Douce G.175

CH 1521, 6
Year given
but not place,
day and
month. (After
10 July)

To Jean de Gourmont,
(duration of grant not given), for
1. Fernando de Enzinas *Oppositionum Libri duo*

2. Fernando de Enzinas *Exponibilia*

'Cum gratia et priuilegio regis', 'Cum priuilegio regis' on title-pages. At end, after colophon, in both books, 'Cauetur ne quis impune attentet hunc librum imprimere, ut amplissimo patet Priuilegio a Regia maiestate nobis condonato M.D.XXI.'

J. de Gourmont
1520 fol. 2 parts,
one 31 December
1520, one 10 July
1521
BM Albi 69
J. de Gourmont
1522, fol. (15 January)
Maz.Rés.3600

CH 1522, 1
Paris,
20 January

To Michel Le Noir,
3 years, for
La Salade [by Antoine de La Salle]
L.P. printed on recto of fol. 2.
Signed: Par le Roy à vostre relation
                         Guiot

M. Le Noir
1522 fol.
BN Rés.z.355

CH 1522, 1A
1 March

To Guy de Fontenaye, author,
(duration of grant not given) for
Magnum collectorium historicum (revised edn)
'Cum priuilegio regis' on title-page, and summary after colophon.

Jean de Gourmont
s.d. 4°
BN Rés.z.1069(1)

CH 1522, 2
Col.
June

To Simon de Colines (presumably),
(duration of grant not given) for
Jacques Lefèvre d'Etaples *Commentarii initiatorii
in iv. Euangelia*
'Cum priuilegio regis' on title-page.

Meaux,
S. de Colines
1522 fol.
BL 1355.k.12

CH 1522, 3
Lyon,
18 June

To Jacques Mareschal dit Roland, of Lyon,
3 years, for
1. *Missale Claromontense atque sancti Flori*
2. *Ordonnances royaulx*

Baudrier, XI,
pp. 421–3
and XI, pp. 414
and 377. (Only
known from the
transcripts by
Baudrier.)

L.P., reprinted by Baudrier, XI, pp. 384–6.
Signed: Par le Roy à vostre relation. L. Heruoet.

CH 1522, 4
Lyon, June
(exact date
not known)

To Oronce Finé, author,
10 years, for
Fine (O.) *Protomathesis*
Latin summary of L.P., printed on verso of
f. AA 3.
Signed: Bordellus.

G. Morrhy and J.
Petrus
1532 fol.
Bodl. H.3.13.Art.

CH 1522, 5
Lyon,
4 July

To Jacques de Mortières, translator,
3 years, for
Spagnuoli Mantuanus (Baptista) *La Parthenice*
L.P. printed on verso of title-page.
Signed: Par le Roy à vostre relation. Heroet.

Lyon, Claude
Nourry and J.
Besson
1523 4°
BN Rés.mYc 692

CH 1522, 6
Saint-
Germain-en-
Laye,
6 November

To Enguilbert de Marnef,
3 years, for
Bouchet (Jean) *Le labirynth de fortune*
Summary of L.P. printed on verso of title-page.
Signed: Par le Roy. Robertet.

Paris/Poitiers
E. de Marnef (pr.
Jacques Bouchet)
1524 4°
BN Rés.pYe 361

CH 1522, 7
Col.
10 December

To Prigent Calvarin,
(duration not stated), for
Manderston (William) *Tripartitum epithoma*
doctrinale ... tertio revisum
Notice in Latin printed at end, f. xvi verso,
referring to a privilege granted by the king,
giving the year 1522 and 'the last day of
December' as the date.

Prigent Calvarin
1523 4° 2 vols.
BN Rés.R.1443–4

CH 1523, 1
18 March
(or this may
be the date of
publication)

To Josse Badius
3 years, for
Rossetus (Petrus) *Paulus*
Latin summary of L.P. printed at end after
colophon 'Cautumque est priuilegio regio...'

J. Badius
1522 (o.s.) 4°
BL 78.c.8

CH 1523, 2
Paris,
23 March

To François Regnault,
4 years, for
Le rozier historial de France [by P. Choysnet]
L.P. printed on verso of title-page.
Signed: Par le Roy [signatory not named]

F. Regnault
1522 o.s. fol.
Bodl. M.2/16(2)
Jur.Seld.

CH 1523, 3
Paris,
2 April

To Hémon Le Fèvre
3 years, for
Celaya (J. de) *Aurea expositio in decem libros*
Ethicorum
L.P. printed on verso of title-page.
Signed: Par le Roy à la relation du conseil.
                                        Saugeon

H. Le Févre and
P. Viart
1523 fol.
Bodl.AA.77.Art.

CH 1523, 4

To Conrad Resch
4 years, for
Erasmus, *Paraphrasis in euangelium Matthei*
Latin summary of L.P. printed at end after
colophon.

C. Resch
(pr. P. Vidoue)
1523 8°
Bodl.Buchanan
g.43

CH 1523, 5
2 August

To Nicole Volcyr de Serouville, author,
4 years, for
Collectaneorum Libellus. Le petit Recueil instructif et
moral ...
Order, printed on last leaf, after the
certificate of the Faculty of Theology,
signed: Robertet

(pr. Didier
Maheu)
s.d. 4°
BN Rés.D.67938

CH 1524, 1
Col.
1 June
Dedication
1 July

To Josse Badius,
4 years, for
St Lawrence Giustiniani *Opera et vita: cum duplici*
indice, castagatius reposita ed. Gicolamo Cavalli
Latin summary of L.P., printed at end after
colophon, 'adnuente sapientissimo Francorum
cancellario D. Antonio a pratis.'

J. Badius
1524 fol.
BL C.81.h.5

CH 1524, 2
Avignon,
23 September

To Geofroy Tory,
6 years, for
Horae in laudem beatiss. semper Virginis Mariae
(design of illustrations, borders etc.)
L.P. printed on fol. A2^{r-v}, headed Privilege du
Roy nostre sire.
Signed: Par le Roy. Heruoet. Et seellé de cire
jaune en simple queue. Et en l'enterinement
signé Lormier / seellé de cire verte en double
queue.

G. Tory
(pr. S. de Colines)
1525 4°
BL C.27.k.15

Part reprinted in
A. Bernard,
Geofroy Tory,
pp. 148–9.

CH 1524, 3
Col.
19 October

To Gabriel de Tarregua, author,
2 years (renewal), for
Compendi on the 'Tegni' of Galen and the
Aphorisms of Hippocrates, added to a reissue of
his previous book (see CH 1520, 10).
Cf. A. Claudin, *Les origines et les débuts de*
l'imprimerie à Bordeaux (1897), pp. 17–25 and
37–41.

Bordeaux, J.
Guyart
1524 fol.
BN Rés.T^{25}.2

CH 1525, 1
Lyon,
1 October

To Benoît Bounyn and Jean Planfoys,
4 years, for
Vigo (Joannes de) *La pratique de cirurgie* tr.
Nicolas Godin
L.P. printed facing verso of title-page.
Signed: Par madame Regente de France à
vostre relacion   Des Landes

Lyon, B. Bounyn
and J. Planfoys
1525 4°
BN Rés.Td^{73}.39

CH 1525, 2
Lyon,
10 October

To Pierre Gringore, author,
3 years, for
Heures de Nostre Dame translatées en Francoys
L.P. printed on fols. A3^{r}–A3^{v}.
Signed: Par le Roy à vostre relacion.
Loys Hernoet [*sic*]

J. Petit
1525 4°
Bodl.Douce M.655

CH 1525, 3
Rennes,
25 October

To Jean Baudouyn, *huissier* of the chancery and
Council of the duchy of Brittany,
1 year, for
'statutz, ordonnances et édit ... sur le fait de la   Rennes, J.
pledoyerie de ce nostre d. pays et duché'   Baudouyn
L.P. printed on f. 205ᵛ of the *Coutume* of Brittany in   1528 8°
1528.   BN Rés.F.1666
Signed: Par le Roy usufructuaire et administrateur   Reprinted in
surdict à la relation du Conseil. N. Du Val. Et   Lepreux, *Gallia*
séellé de cire jaulne à simple cueue.   *typographica*, IV,
Documenta, 946
(incorrectly
stated to be for
the *Coutumes*
themselves).

CH 1525, 4
Saint-Just-
sur-Lyon,
17 November

To Constantin Fradin,
3 years, for
Terra Rubea (Joannes de) *Contra rebelles suorum*   Lyon, C.
regum ed. Jacques Bonaud.   Fradin (pr. J.
L.P. printed on verso of title-page   Crespin)
Signed: Par madame Regente en France à la   1526 4°
relation du conseil. Juvyneau.   Bodl.Seld.4°
   T.4.Jur.

CH 1526, 1
Amboise,
31 July

To Galliot Du Pré,
1 year, for
Apologia Madriciae conuentionis dissuasoria   G. Du Pré (pr.
L.P. printed on verso of title-page.   P. Vidoue)
Signed: Par le Roy. Hervoet.   1526 4°
The same privilege covers a French translation of   BN
the treatise, also published by G. Du Pré, s.d. 4°.   Rés.Lb³⁰.42.
Moreau, *Inventaire*, III, 1106, citing a copy in the
Musée Conde, Chantilly

CH 1526, 2
Chenonceaux
5 September

To Geofroy Tory, author,
10 years, for
Champ fleury, auquel est contenu l'art et science de la deue   G. Tory and G.
proportion des lettres ...   Gourmont
L.P. printed on fol. Aij (facing verso of title-page).   1529 fol.
Signed: Par le Roy. Breton. Et seelé de cire jaune   BL 60.e.14
en simple queue. Et en l'interinement signé
Lormier / seellé de cire verte, en double queue.

Selected privileges of 1527 and 1528 referred to in the text

CH 1527, 1 Compiègne, 15 October See above, p. 66–7.	To Jacques Colin 4 years, for Thucydides *L'histoire de la guerre entre les* *Peloponnesiens et Atheniens* tr. Claude de Seyssel Signé, Par le Roy, Victon, et scellées du grant seel de cyre jaulne en simple queue. AN y 8 fols. 271ʳ–272ʳ Summary printed on verso of title-page. Cf. *Actes de François 1ᵉʳ*, 1, 2,776 (p. 527)	J. Badius 1527 fol. BL c.79.c.8
CH 1527, 2 Paris, 7 November See above, p. 56.	To Jean Petit 4 years (6 requested), for 1. *Missale ad consuetudinem insignis ecclesie Ebroicensis* L.P. printed on verso of title-page. Signed: Par le Roy à vostre relation Herouet On title-page: 'Cum priuilegio Regis et eiusdem diocesis episcopi ne quispiam usque ad quadrennium eiusmodi imprimat vel imprimi faciat: ut in sequenti pagina declaratur...'	J. Petit (pr. J. Kerbriant and D. Maheu), also to be sold by Louis Bouvet at Rouen and by Jean Foucher at Evreux. 1527 fol. Ste Geneviève Fol. BB 134 Rés.Inv.143.
Col. 8 October 1527	2. *Missale ad consuetudinem insignis ecclesie* *Rothomagensis* On title-page: 'Cum priuilegio regis'.	J. Petit (pr. N. Prevost) Rouen: Jacques Cousin, Louis Bouvet, Guillaume Bavent. 1527 fol. BN Vélins 203
CH 1527, 3 Paris, 15 November See above, pp. 104–5.	To Pierre Gringore, author, 4 years, for 1. Gringore (P.) *Heures de Nostre Dame ... additionnées* *de plusieurs Chants royaulx.* 2. Gringore (P.) *Notables enseignemens ... nouvellement* *reveus et corrigés avecques plusieurs aultres adjoustez* L.P. printed on verso of title-page. Signed: Hamelin.	J. Petit s.d. 4° Bodl.Douce BB 152 F. Regnault 1528 8° BL 241.d.26

CH 1528, 1	To Robert Estienne,	R. Estienne
Paris,	5 years, for	1527–8 fol.
5 February	*Biblia* [as printed by Estienne with his collations,	Bodl.Bib.
See above,	tables and *interpretationes*]	Lat.c.1
p. 165.	L.P. printed on f. ff8ᵛ.	
	Signed: Par le Roy à vostre relation. Des Landes.	

CH 1528, 2	To Jean de Pontac, *greffier* of the Parlement of	
Paris,	Bordeaux,	
29 February	4 years, for	
See above,	*Les coustumes generalles de la ville de Bordeaulx,*	pr. Durand
pp. 198–9.	*seneschaussée de Guienne et pays de Bourdeloys*	Gerlier for J.
	L.P. printed on verso of title-page and following	de Pontac
	pages.	1527 (o.s.) 8°
	Signed: Par le Roy à vostre relacion. Herouet.	BM Bordeaux
	Cf. PA 1527, 2, for the prior claim of Jean Guyart.	J.3010/1
		Rés.(coffre)

List of books known to have been published by Antoine Vérard under his personal privilege (CH 1507, 1); see above, pp. 21–2.

1 *Les epistres Sainct Pol glosées*
   Colophon 17 January 1507/8
   Macfarlane, *Antoine Vérard*, no. 84
2 *La nef de santé* [by Nicolas de La Chesnaye]
   Colophon 17 January 1507/8
   Macfarlane no. 85 (Some copies, apparently printed before the grant of the privilege, have no date and no privilege, cf. Macfarlane no. 177).
3 *Coutumier de Touraine*
   Colophon 11 March 1507/8
   Macfarlane no. 86
4 *Contemplations historiées sur la Passion* [by Gerson]
   Colophon 26 March 1507/8
   Macfarlane no. 87
5 *Les Heures Nostre Dame à l'usaige de Romme nouvellement translatées*
   Colophon 14 July 1508
   Macfarlane no. 240
6 *L'homme juste et l'homme mondain* [by Simon Bougouyn]
   Colophon 19 July 1508
   Macfarlane no. 88
7 *Les louenges du Roy Louis XII* [by Claude de Seyssel]
   Colophon 24 December 1508
   Macfarlane no. 89
8 *L'espinette du jeune prince* [by Simon Bougouyn]
   Colophon 12 February 1508/9
   Macfarlane no. 90
9 *La chasse et le départ d'amours* [here attributed to Octavien de Saint-Gelais]
   Colophon 14 April 1509
   Macfarlane no. 91

10 *Compendium hystorial* [by Henry Romain, canon of Tournay]
Colophon 19 August 1509
Macfarlane no. 93

11 *La vie monseigneur Sainct Germain*
Colophon 12 November 1509
Macfarlane no. 94

12 Ovide, *Du remede d'amours*
Colophon 4 February 1509/10
Macfarlane no. 95

13 *Dialogue monseigneur Sainct Grégoire*
Colophon 20 March 1509/10
Macfarlane no. 96

14 *Les Eneydes* [by Virgil], transl. O. de Saint-Gelais and J. D'Ivry
Colophon 6 April 1509/10
Macfarlane no. 98

15 *La victoire du roy contre les Veniciens* [by Claude de Seyssel]
Colophon 12 May 1510
Macfarlane no. 98

16 Guillaume Pepin, *Speculum aureum super septem psalmost penitentiales*
Colophon 16 July 1510
Not in Macfarlane. Moreau, *Inventaire*, I, 1510, p. 173.

17 *Les grandes postilles* [compiled by P. Desrey] 5 vols.
Colophons 1511–12, completed 12 August 1512.
Macfarlane no. 99

18 *Le pelerinage de l'homme* [by Guillaume de Deguileville]
Colophon 4 April 1511/12
Macfarlane no. 101

19 *Liber auctoritatum* [by Nicolas de Querquetu or De la Chesnaye]
Colophon 24 July 1512
Macfarlane no. 102

List of books known to have been published by Guillaume Eustace under his personal privilege
(CH 1508, 2); see above, p. 22.

1 *Le nouveau monde, avec l'estrif du pourveu et de l'ellectif ... ensuivant la forme auctentique ordonnee par la pragmatique.*
s.d. 8°   BN Rés. ye.2988

2 Hug (Johannes) of Sélestat *Quadriuium ecclesie quattuor prelatorum officium*
1509 4° (1 August)   BL 1412.g.15

3 [Corpus Juris canonici. Bonifacius VII] *Textus Decretalium libri ... nuperrime correcti.*
1509 8° (29 January 1510 n.s.)   BL 5051.a.4(1)

4 *Sotise à huit personnaiges*
s.d. 8°   BN Rés.yf 2934

5 [Corpus Juris canonici. Gregorius IX] *Extravagantes XX.* ed. Claudius de Niceyo.
1510 8° (30 March)   BN Rés.E.5337

6   *Les Ordonnances royaulx ... et avec ce les stilles de Parlement et de Chastellet. Textus*
    pragmaticae Sanctionis nuper correctus et emendatus ed. Cosme Guymier.
                    1510 8° 2 vols. (28 April)   Maz.26819
7   [Corpus Juris canonici. Gregorius IX] *Textus Decretalium ... emendatus* ed.
    Claudius de Niceyo.
                    1510 8° (23 August)   BN Rés.E.9956
8   Londris (Joannes de) *Breuiarium sanctorum canonum humanorumque legum.* ('Cum
    priuilegio Regio e supreme parlamenti curie gratia'.)
                    1510 4° (12 November)   See below, p.
                                                   243, PA 1510, 4
9   Masuer (Joannes) *Aureus extractus ... consuetudines curieque Parlamenti supreme*
    stilum continens ed. Stephanus de Stasso.
                    1510 8° (19 January 1511 n.s.) BN Vélins 1883
10 *Consecratio et coronatio Regis Francie*
                    1510 8° (20 March 1511 n.s.)   BN Rés.Li²⁵.1.
11 Bouchet (Jean) *La déploration de l'église militante*
                    1512 8°   See PA 1512, 5
12 *Le livre des ordonnances des chevaliers de l'ordre de Saint-Michel*
                    1512 8° (14 October)   BN Rés.LI¹³.1
13 *Le conseil de paix*
                    s.d. 8°   BN Rés.YE
                                                   1634(1) (bound
                                                   with Bouchet's
                                                   La déploration)
14 *La perfection des filles religieuses, avec la vie et miracles de ma dame saincte Clare*
                    s.d. 8°   BN Rés.D.47403
15 La Tour Landry (Geoffroy de) *Le chevalier de la tour et le guidon des guerres*
                    1514 fol. (9 November)   BN Rés.Y².22
16 Dardanus (Bernardinus) *Ad magnificum D. Senatus Mediol. Cancellarium*
    (J. Olivier) *Silva extemporalis*
                    s.d. 8°   BN Rés.G.2805

PARLEMENTS AND OTHER SOVEREIGN COURTS
(Parlement of Paris unless otherwise stated)

Note

Some grants from the Parlement of Paris are recorded in the extant registers of the
Parlement Civil, series AN x 1 A. (See above, p. 34.) In these cases, a reference is
given here to the relevant volume and folio of the register. A very few grants are
known only from this source.

Most grants are known only in the form of an official certified copy, the 'Extraict
des registres de Parlement', here abbreviated to E.R.P., printed in the books which
the privileges protected.

There are other cases where the grant is known both from the entry in the register
and from the printed E.R.P.

PA 1507, 1
17 June

To Eustace de Brie,
1 year, for
1. La Vigne (André de) *La louenge des roys de France*

E. de Brie
1507 8°
BL 240.l.34

2. *La chronique de Gennes* ... *avec l'ordonnance* [10 May 1507] *avec la totalle description de toute Ytalie*

E. de Brie
s.d. 8°
Ste Geneviève
κ.8° 143¹
Rés.inv. 994

Summary printed in colophon of Eustace de Brie, 'Et lui a donné la court de parlement et procureur du roy ung an de temps à vendre lesditz livres. Et ont esté faictes deffences et inhibitions à tous librayres et imprimeurs et à tous autres de non imprimer ledit livre jusques à ung an prochain venant...' in 1, and (with minor differences of wording) in 2.

PA 1508, 1

To Martin Alexandre,
1 year, for
Perault (Guillaume) *Le traité de la pluralité des benefices*, with *La pragmatique sanction en francoys*
Summary printed in colophon, dated 12 April.

M. Alexandre
(pr. G. Philippe)
1508 4°
Bodl.Arch.b.e. 26

PA 1509, 1
12 January

To Berthold Rembolt,
3 years (6 requested), for
Expositio ... *in omnes diui Pauli epistolas* [here attributed to St Bruno]
E.R.P. printed on verso of title-page.
'Collacion est faicte. Robert.'
Reprinted above, p. 39.

B. Rembolt
s.d. 4°
Bodl.b.Th.22. 6.Linc.

PA 1509, 2
28 February

To Michel La Troyne, *greffier* of the *baillage* of Chartres,
2 years, for
Le coustumier de Chartres
Summary incorporated in the colophon, which is dated 13 March 1508 (o.s.)

Chartres, pr. Robert Pincelou for M. La Troyne
1508 (o.s.)
BL 1128.a.35(1)

241

PA 1509, 3   To Poncet Le Preux and Jean Granjon,
8 May   2 years (4 requested), for
              Mair (John) *Quartus sententiarum*   J. Granjon (pr.
              E.R.P. printed on verso of title-page.   P. Pigouchet)
              'Collation est faicte. Robert.'   1509 fol.
                                                                        BN Rés.D.2030

PA 1509, 4   To Martin Le Saige, *greffier* of the *sénéchaussée* of
7 September   Maine,
              2 years, for   pr. Gilles
              Coutumes du Maine   Couteau for M.
              Summary incorporated in the colophon, which is   le Saige
              dated 1 October 1509.   1509 8°
                                                                        BN Rés.F.1777

PA 1509, 5   *By the Parlement of Toulouse* (presumably)   Toulouse, Jean
Col.   beneficiary and term not stated, for Rorgues (Marc   Faure
18 November   de) *Elegantissima oratio ad celebrem et inclytam*   1509 4°
              uniuersitatem Cathurcensem (replying to the   Maz.Rés.10287
              conferment on him of an honorary degree in law at
              Cahors, of which he was the Vicar General)

PA 1510, 1   To Jean Dabert, *greffier* of the *sénéchaussée* of Anjou,
23 March   2 years, for
              Les coustumes d'Anjou   Angers,
              After colophon, 'Defense de la court'.   Mathurin
                                                                        Amar, Clement
                                                                        Alexandre,
                                                                        Leon Cailler,
                                                                        Jean Le Roy,
                                                                        Jean Arnoul
                                                                        (pr. Charles de
                                                                        Bongne)
                                                                        s.d. 8°
                                                                        BL 1607/1408

PA 1510, 2   To Jean Choquart and Jean Popineau, *greffiers* of
17 June   the *bailliage* of Orleans,
              2 years, for   Reprinted from
              Les coustumes du bailliage d'Orleans   the register by
              AN X I A 1513, f. 145ᵛ   Maugis,
                                                                        Histoire du
                                                                        Parlement, II,
                                                                        311, n°. 3.
                                                                        No copy of the
                                                                        printed book
                                                                        found.

PA 1510, 3
13 July

To Jean Petit and Michel Le Noir,
2 years, for
La Marche (Olivier de) *Le parement et triumphe des dames de honneur*, ed. Pierre Desrey.
AN X 1 A 1513, f. 175ᵛ.
E.R.P. printed on verso of title-page.
'Collation est faicte. Beldon.' And summary on title-page and in colophon.

J. Petit and M. Le Noir
s.d. 8°
BN Rés.ʏᴇ 1253

PA 1510, 4
13 August

To Guillaume Eustace,
2 years (4 requested), for
Londris (Jean de) *Breuiarium sanctorum humanorumque legum*
E.R.P. printed on verso of title-page.
'Collation est faicte. Robert.'

G. Eustace (pr. G. Le Rouge)
1510 4° (col. 12 November)
BN Rés.ᴇ.1867

PA 1511, 1
30 April

To Jean Petit,
2 years (3 requested), for
Les coustumes du hault et bas pays d'Auvergne
E.R.P. printed on fol. 4 of prelims facing first page of text.
'Ainsi signé. Robert.'

J. Petit (sold also by Loys Maritain, bookseller of Clermont-Ferrand)
1511 8° (col. 8 May)
BN Rés.ꜰ.1787

PA 1511, 2
4 July

To Poncet Le Preux,
2 years (3 requested), for
Dionysius Cisterciensis *In quatuor sententiarum* ed. Jean Masières
E.R.P. printed at end of table of contents facing first page of text.
'Collation est faicte. Pichon.'

Poncet Le Preux
s.d. fol.
BN Rés.ᴅ.74

PA 1511, 3
21 July

To Jean Petit
2 years (3 requested), for
Biaxio (Petrus de) *Praeclarum ac insigne opus conficiundarum electionum directorium...*
E.R.P. printed at end of index preceding text.
'Ainsi signé. Parent.'

J. Petit
1511 8°
BN Vélins 1837

PA 1511, 4 10 October	To Jean Petit, 2 years, as requested, for *Les coustumes du bailliage de Chaulmont en Bassigny* E.R.P. printed beginning on verso of title with summary at end of colophon. 'Ainsi signé. Parent.'	J. Petit (sold also by Jean Gautier, bookseller of Troyes) 1511 8° (col. 28 October) BM Chaumont (H.-M.)
PA 1512, 1 5 March	To Jean Petit, 2 years (3 requested), for Raulin (Jean) *Opus sermonum quadragesimalium* E.R.P. printed facing first page of text, no signatory of E.R.P. named, followed by royal privilege identical with the 'package' privilege dated Blois, 12 March 1512, CH 1512, 1(6).	J. Petit 1511 4° 2 vols. BN D. 9501
PA 1512, 2 6 April	To Jean Petit, 2 years (3 requested), for Surgetus (Jean) *Militaris disciplinae enchiridion* AN X I A 1514, f. 116ᵛ. E.R.P. printed on fol. 87ᵛ	J. Petit and Galliot Du Pré s.d. 8° BN Rés.F.1603
PA 1512, 3 19 April	To Simon Vostre, 2 years (3 requested), for Le Roy (Françoys) *Le mirouer de penitence* E.R.P. printed in the same type as the rest of the book on a strip of paper pasted onto the penultimate page in a space left free after the end of the text. 'Collation est faicte. Ainsy signé. Pichon.'	S. Vostre s.d. 8° 2 parts. BN Rés.D.4804

PA 1512, 4
12 May

To Jean Petit,
2 years (4 requested), for
Les ordonnances royaulx nouvellement publiees en ladicte court [27 April 1512]
AN x 1 A 1514, f. 144ᵛ.
No mention of the privilege in this copy of the book.

J. Petit
s.d. 8°
BN Rés.F.2359
Angers, for
Leon Cailler
1512 8° under
Petit's privilege
and with his
leave. See
Pasquier and
Dauphin,
*Imprimeurs et
libraires de
l'Anjou*, p. 104,
with
reproduction of
first page
bearing these
particulars.

PA 1512, 5
15 May

To Guillaume Eustace,
2 years (3 requested), for
Bouchet (Jean) *La déploration de l'église militante*
E.R.P. printed on verso of colophon.

G. Eustace
1512 8°
BN Rés.ye
1635

PA 1512, 6
Col.
16 May

By the Parlement of Toulouse (presumably),
To Jean de Clauso,
2 years, for
Les ordonnances royaulx novellement publiees à Paris [27 April 1512]
Summary printed in colophon: '...Et inhibitions et deffences à tous imprimeurs de non imprimer les dessusdictes jusques à deux ans passez excepté Jhean de Clauso libraire: ut patet in mandato', and Arms of Toulouse on the verso.

Toulouse
J. de Clauso,
dit Mondi
s.d. 8°
BM Lyon
373.480

PA 1512, 7
13 July

To Henri Estienne,
2 years (4 requested), for
1. *Itinerarium Antonini Augusti*

H. Estienne
1512 16°
Bodl.Art.Seld.
8° A.27

2. Longolius (Christophe) *Oratio de laude Ludouici regis*

H. Estienne
s.d. 4°
BL IA 40033(2)

AN X I A 1514, f. 195ʳ.
Announcement 'Cum priuilegio / ne quis temere hoc ab hinc / duos annos imprimat' printed on title-page in 1, with no other details.

PA 1512, 8
6 September

To Galliot Du Pré,
2 years (4 requested), for
Pavinis (Joannes Franciscus de) *Tractatus de officio et potestate capituli sede vacante*, and other works by various writers on canon and civil law
AN X I A 1514, f. 264
E.R.P. printed on verso of title-page.
'Collacion est faicte. Pichon.'

G. du Pré
(pr. N. des Prez)
1512 4°
BN Rés.F.1077

PA 1512, 9
6 September

To Guillaume Eustace,
2 years, for

1. Brolio (Guillermus de) *Stilus parlamenti curie*, ed. Antoine Robert and printed 'ipsius supreme curie nutu'

G. Eustace
1512 8°
BN Rés.F.2281

2. *Ordinatio seu declaratio facta super xiii punctis stili*

G. Eustace
s.d. 8°
BN Rés.F.1701

3. *Ordonnances de parlement touchant tous especialement les parties qui y ont à plaidier.*

G. Eustace
1512
H. W. Davies,
Fairfax Murray Cat., 1, p. 409
(reproduction on p. 596)

4. *Comedia nova que Veterator inscribitur alias Pathelinus* tr. Alexander Connybertus and ed. Joannes Morellus

G. Eustace
1512 8°
BN Vélins
2329

L.P. in Latin, issued in the king's name 'in parlamento nostro', 'Ainsi signé Robert', printed at the end of 1 and 4.

PA 1512, 10 20 December	To Jacques Guillotoys and Jean Randin, author (mistakenly termed a bookseller in the grant), 2 years (4 requested), for Randin (Jean) *Casus in quibus episcopi ... possunt* *subditos dispensare* E.R.P. printed on verso of title-page. 'Et au dessoubs est escript / collation est faicte. Signé A. Robert.'	J. Guillotoys s.d. 4° BN Rés.e.2216
PA 1513, 1 21 March	To Galliot Du Pré, 2 years (4 requested), for Socinus (Bartholomeus) *Regule ... e toto iure delecte* and other works on law by various writers, ed. Benedictus de Fossombrone AN x 1 A 1515, ff. 126ᵛ–127 E.R.P. printed on verso of title-page.	G. Du Pré s.d. 8° Moreau, *Inventaire*, ii, n°. 456
PA 1513, 2 13 May	To the *greffiers* of the Châtelet, 2 years (3 requested), for *Les coustumes generalles de la prevosté et vicomté de Paris* AN x 1 A 1515, fols. 181ᵛ–182ᵛ On title: 'Avec le privilege de messieurs de Parlement', and E.R.P. on verso of title-page continued and completed on facing page, followed by E.R.P. fixing the price, 23 May 1513, both signed Pichon.	J. Petit and G. Eustace s.d. 4° BL c.29.b.26 Reprinted M. Félibien, *Histoire de la* *ville de Paris* (1725), vol. iv, p. 627.
PA 1513, 3 12 September	*By the Parlement of Rouen,* To Martin Morin, to 1 March 1514, for *Ordonnances contre la peste* etc. Summary printed on title-page.	Rouen, M. Morin s.d. 4° BM Rouen Inc. p. 54.
PA 1513, 4 23 November	To Galliot Du Pré, 2 years (3 requested), for Durandus (Gulielmus) *Breuiarium aureum iuris* *canonici* ed. Gilles D'Aurigny. E.R.P. printed on f. E 7ᵛ, 'Collation est faicte. Ainsi signé. Robert.' followed by privilege from the king dated 18 November (see CH 1513, 4(2))	G. du Pré 1513 8° BN Rés.e. 4074

PA 1514, 1 2 January	To Jean de Gourmont, 2 years (3 requested), for 1. Coccius (Marcus Antonius, *Sabellicus*) *Rerum Venetorum Panegyricus primus* etc.	J. de Gourmont s.d. 4° BN Rés.MYC 286
	2. *Elucidarius carminum poetarum* [by Conrad de Mure]	J. de Gourmont s.d. 4° BN Rés.x.1573
	E.R.P. printed on verso of title-page in 1, no signatory named.	
PA 1514, 2 21 February	To Denis Roce, 2 years (3 requested), for Coronnel (Antonio) *Super praedicamenta Aristotelis* AN x 1 A 1516, f. 75	No edition by Denis Roce has been traced but there is an edition by Bernard Aubry, his son-in-law and successor (Roce having died in 1517). 1518 fol., with 'Cum priuilegio' on the title. Bodl. s.3.8.Jur
PA 1514, 3 18 March	To Nicolas Vaultier and Charles du Dé, 2 years (3 requested), for Bella Pertica or Belleperche (Pierre de) *Lectura super I. librum Institutionum* AN x 1 A 1515, f. 103^v 'Cum gratia et priuilegio' on title-page, no other details printed.	N. Vaultier s.d. 8° BN Vélins 1847
PA 1514, 4 21 April	To Galliot du Pré, 2 years (3 requested), for Selve (Jean de) *Tractatus beneficialis*, corrected and provided with index E.R.P. printed on verso of title-page. 'Collacion est faicte. Robert.'	G. du Pré s.d. 8° BN e.1388

PA 1514, 5
4 May

To Jean de Gourmont,
2 years (3 or 4 requested), for
Quinziano Stoa (G. F. Conti) *Ingeniosa disticha*
E.R.P. printed on f. P 6ʳ (page facing end of text
and errata)
'Collation est faicte. Ainsi signé Robert.'

J. de
Gourmont
s.d. 4°
BN Rés.myc
832(2)

PA 1514, 6
6 May

To Charles Bougne,
2 years (4 requested), for
Bodin (Jean) *Coutumes du pays d'Anjou: Tables et
répertoires*
AN x 1 A 1516, f. 154
No mention of privilege printed in the copy
consulted.

Angers, C.
Bougne (pr. M.
Morin, Rouen)
BL 5405.a.8(2)

PA 1514, 7
23 May

To Barthélemy Vérard,
3 years (as requested), for
Les triumphes messire francoys petracque [*sic*] [tr.
Georges de La Forge]
E.R.P. printed on verso of title-page.
'Ainsi signé Robert.'

B. Vérard
s.d. fol.
Bodl.Douce
P.27

PA 1514, 8
Col.
3 August

To Jean de Gourmont,
2 years, for
Quinziano Stoa (G. F. Conti) *Cleapolis, et Orpheos
Admonitio* by Gourmont, referring to the privilege
granted 'senatoriis literis', printed between Errata
and colophon.
AN x 1 A 1516, f. 247

J. de
Gourmont
1514 4°
BN Rés.myc
832(1)
Reprinted in
full in Félibien,
*Hist. de la ville
de Paris*, vol. II,
p. 630.

PA 1514, 9
3 October

To Jean Granjon,
3 years (no special period requested), for
1. Novo Castro (Andreas de) *Primum scriptum
Sententiarum*

J. Granjon
s.d. fol.
BL 472.b.8(1)

2. Mair (John) *Summule*

J. Granjon
1514 fol.
Maz.3594bis.
Rés.

E.R.P. printed on verso of title-page.
'Ainsi signé A. Robert.'

PA 1514, 10   To Jean de La Garde,
27 October   2 years (3 requested), for
Perusio (Petrus de) *Compendium aureum* [and other   J. de La Garde
treatises on canon law]   1514 8°
E.R.P. printed at end of text (f. 81ᵛ–92ᵛ) before the   BN Rés.E.4433
Tabula Alphabetica. 'Ainsi signé
Robert   Collacion est faicte'

PA 1515, 1   To Galliot Du Pré,
21 April   2 years (3 requested), for
Les ordonnances et status royaulx des feuz roys   G. Du Pré
E.R.P. printed on verso of title-page.   s.d. 4°
'Ainsi signé   Robert   Collation est faicte'   BN F.863

PA 1515, 2   To Jean Gourmont,
6 September   2 years (3 requested), for
Lilius (Zacharias) *Orbis breviarium*   J. Gourmont
E.R.P. printed on verso of title-page   1515 4°
'Ainsi signé Robert.'   BL 566.f.36

PA 1515, 3   To Fausto Andrelini, author,
20 November   2 years (as requested), for
Andrelini (F.) *In Annam Francorum reginam*   J. Badius
panegyricon   1515 4°
AN x 1 A 1518, f. 6   BN
E.R.P. printed on verso of title-page.   Rés.G.2810(13)
'Collation est faicte. Pichon.'

PA 1515, 4   To Toussaint Denys,
10 December   3 years (as requested), for
Signot (Jacques) *La totale et vraie description des*   T. Denys
Gaules et Ytalies [with map]   1515 4°
AN x 1 A 1518, f. 18   BN
E.R.P. printed on verso of title-page.   Rés.G.1248(1)
'Ainsi signé   Beldon'

PA 1515, 5   *By the Parlement of Toulouse* (presumably),
Col.   no details of exact date, duration or beneficiary
14 July   given, for   Toulouse,
Bertrand (Nicole) *De Tholosanorum gestis*   Joh. Magni
'Cum gratia amplissimoque Priuilegio', and picture   Johannis or
of the Toulouse Parlement in session, on the   Grandjean
title-page.   1515 fol.
For the French edition, bearing a full privilege   BN Rés.Lk⁷
from the Toulouse Parlement, see PA 1517, 3.   9721

PA 1516, 1
5 January

To Jean Petit,
2 years (3 requested), for
Les coustumes du bailliage de Victry en Partoys   J. Petit
AN x 1 A 1518, f. 44ᵛ   s.d. 8°
F.R.P. printed on verso of title-page.   BN Rés.f.2365
'Ainsi signé Beldon'

PA 1516, 2
16 January

To Josse Badius,
2 years (3 requested), for
Quintilian, *Oratoriae institutiones* ed. Badius   J. Badius and
AN x 1 A 1518, f. 60ᵛ   J. Petit
'Vaenundantur cum gratia et priuilegio' on   1516 fol.
title-page, with no other details.   BL 837.m.38

PA 1516, 3
14 February

By the Parlement of Rouen
To Jean Richard,
2 years (4 requested), for   Caen, M.
Le stille et ordre de proceder de la court (printed after *Le* Angier, and
grand coustumier de Normandie)   Rouen, J.
E.R.P. printed at the end of *Le stille*.   Richard
Signed: 'Ita est   Bordel /   BL 1238.f.12
             Surreau   ung paraffe'

PA 1516, 4
10 March

To Jean de La Garde,
2 years (3 requested), for
Champier (Symphorien) *Les grans croniques des gestes* J. de La Garde
des princes de pays de Savoye   1516 fol.
AN x 1 A 1518, f. 116ᵛ   BN Rés.Lk²
E.R.P. printed on verso of title-page.   1536
Signed: Pichon

PA 1516, 5
10 March

To François Regnault,
2 years (3 requested), for
Fillastre (Guillaume) *Le premier livre de la Toison* F. Regnault
d'Or   1516 fol.
E.R.P. printed on verso of title-page.   BL 204.e.2
Signed: Pichon

PA 1516, 6
27 May

To Galliot Du Pré
2 years (3 requested), for
Somnium viridarii, ed. Gilles d'Aurigny   G. Du Pré
E.R.P. printed on verso of title-page.   s.d. 4°
'Ainsi signé A. Robert'   BN e.1875

PA 1516, 7
27 June

To Jean Petit,
2 years (3 requested), for
Les coustumes du bailliage de Troyes
AN x 1 a 1518, f. 227^v
E.R.P. printed on verso of title-page.
'Ainsi signé   Pichon'

Paris, J. Petit,
and Troyes, J.
Gaultier
s.d. 8°
BN Rés.f.2017

PA 1516, 8
23 September

To Jean Granjon,
2 years (4 requested), for
Almain (Jacques) *In tertium Sententiarum utilis editio*
E.R.P. printed on verso of title-page.
'Ainsi signé   Robert'

J. Granjon
1516 4°
BN Rés.d.6152

PA 1516, 9
24 October

To Jean Granjon,
3 years, for
Mair (John) *Summule quibus de nouo addidit Tractatus duos*
E.R.P. printed on verso of title-page.
'Ainsi signé   A. Robert'

J. Granjon
1516 fol.
Maz. 3595

PA 1517, 1
5 January

To Berthold Rembolt and Pierre Gromors,
2 years (4 requested), for
Ceva (Boniface de) *Sermones quadragesimales*
E.R.P. printed after the preface and the verse
tributes to the author, on f. 4^r of the first
unnumbered gathering.
'Ainsi signé   Robert'

B. Rembolt
1517 4°
BN Rés.d.6936

PA 1517, 2
17 April

To Jean Gourmont,
2 years (no special period requested), for
Fontenaye (Guy de)
1. *Magna Synonima*

J. Gourmont
1517 4°
BN Rés.z
1069(2)

2. *Collectorium historicum*

J. Gourmont
1517 4°
Ste Geneviève.
8° z.244
Rés.inv.245

E.R.P. printed at the end of both books.
'Ainsi signé   Robert.'

PA 1517, 3 21 April	*By the Parlement of Toulouse,* To Antoine Le Blanc, 2 years (as requested), for Bertrand (Nicole) *Les gestes des Tholosains* Order, given in response to Le Blanc's *requête,* printed on f. A 2. Signed: G. d'Olivieres	Toulouse, A. Le Blanc (pr. O. Arnoullet, Lyon) 1517 4° BN Rés.Lk⁷.9722
PA 1517, 4 27 July	*By the Cour des Aides,* To Galliot Du Pre, 1 year (as requested), for *Les ordonnances royaulx sur le faict des tailles, aydes et* *gabelles* Extraict des registres de la cour des aydes, printed on verso of title-page. 'Ainsi signé Brinon'	G. Du Pré 1517 4° BN Vélins 1861
PA 1517, 5 8 August	*By the Parlement of Toulouse,* To Etienne Chenu, author, 3 years (as requested), for Chenu (E.) *Regimen castitatis conseruatiuum* E.R.P. printed at the end. Signed: Michaelis	Toulouse, J. Faure s.d. fol. BN Rés.R.571
PA 1517, 6 24 September	To Jean Granjon, 2 years (4 requested), for J. Duns Scotus, *Reportata super primum Sententiarum* E.R.P. printed on verso of title-page. 'Ainsi signé Robert'	J. Granjon 1518 fol. 4 parts Arsenal fol.T.1283
PA 1517, 7 30 Sept.	To Claude Chevallon and to Jean Gourmont, respectively, under one privilege, 2 years (as requested), for 1. Palude (Pierre de) *Tertium scriptum* 2. Mandison [Manderston] (William) *Tripartitum* *Epythome*	C. Chevallon 1517 fol. BN Rés.D.63 J. Gourmont (pr. C. Chevallon) 1517 4° BN Rés.R.1169

E.R.P. printed on f. aa8^v of the *Tertium scriptum*.
'Ainsi signé Robert'

PA 1517, 8 17 December	To Jean Petit, 2 years (3 requested), for Cappel (Jacques) *Fragmenta* E.R.P. printed at the end. 'Collation est faicte.'	J. Petit 1517 4° BN Rés.Lk^7 5981
PA 1517, 9 31 December	To Hémon le Févre, 2 years (3 requested), for 1. Celaya (Juan de) *Expositio in octo libros phisicorum Aristotelis* 2. Celaya (Juan de) *Expositio in libros de generatione et corruptione* 3. Celaya (Juan de) *Expositio in quatuor libros de celo et mundo* E.R.P. printed on verso of title-page. 'Ainsi signé Robert'	H. Le Févre 1517 fol. BN Rés.R.137 H. Le Févre 1518 fol. BN Rés.R136(5) H. Le Févre 1518 fol. BL 8705.g.1(2)
PA 1518, 1 16 February	To Jean du Pré and Gilles Gourmont, 2 years (3 requested), for Innocent III *De officio missae* E.R.P. printed on verso of title-page. 'Ainsi signé Robert'	J. du Pré and G. Gourmont 1518 4° BL 3475.bb.36
PA 1518, 2 Col. 19 March	To Yves Gallois, 3 years (duration requested not stated), for *La conqueste du trespuissant empire de Trebisonde* Summary of privilege granted by the Parlement and the Prévôt of Paris, printed on verso of title-page.	Y. Gallois 1520 4° BN Rés.Y^2 580.
PA 1518, 3 30 March	To Josse Badius, 2 years (3 requested), for Rubione (Guillermus de) *Disputata super iv lib.* *Magistri sententiarum* ed. Alfonso de Villa Santa. AN X 1 A 1520, f. 140 E.R.P. printed on verso of title-page, in part 2. 'Collation est faicte. Pichon.'	Paris, J. Badius, and Lyon, S. Vincent and M. Conrad 1518 fol. 2 parts. Bodl.R.2.3.Th

PA 1518, 4
16 April

To Galliot Du Pré,
2 years (3 requested), for
Fregoso (Battista) *De dictis factisque memorabilibus* ed. G. Du Pré
J. Daniel (pr. P. Vidoue)
E.R.P printed facing first page of text. 1518 4°
'Ainsi signé Robert.' BL 1433.c.4

PA 1518, 5
12 July

By the Grands Jours de Berry,
To Pierre de Sartières,
2 years (4 requested), for
La Chartre de l'erection des grans jours de Berry Bourges, P. de
Extraict des registres de la court des grans jours de Sartières.
Berry, printed on verso of the title-page. s.d. 8°
'Ainsi signé Vaucheron.' BN Rés.f.2286

PA 1518, 6
31 July

To Berthold Rembolt,
2 years (4 requested), for
Ceva (Boniface de) *Sermones prenatalicii* B. Rembolt
E.R.P. printed facing first page of text. 1518 4°
'Ainsi signé Robert' BN Rés.d.6938

PA 1518, 7
7 September

To Henri Estienne,
2 years (3 requested), for
Aristotle *Phisica* tr. F. Vatablus and J. Lefèvre H. Estienne
AN x 1 a 1520, f. 375 1518 fol.
Only 'cum priuilegio' on title-page. BN
Rés.r.615(1)

PA 1519, 1
28 March

To Pierre Gromors,
2 years (4 requested), for
Tataretus (Pierre) *In Jo. Scoti Quaestiones* P. Gromors,
E.R.P. printed on verso of title-page. and widow B.
'Ainsi signé Robert.' Rembolt
1519 fol.
Bodl.b.1.20
Art.Seld.

PA 1519, 2
31 July

To Hémon Le Fèvre,
2 years (3 requested), for
Columelle (Gérard) *In Aristotelis textum Peri* Jean Du Pré
Hermenias accuratissima Expositio and Hémon Le
E.R.P. printed on verso of title-page. Fèvre
'Ainsi signé Robert' 1520 fol.
BM Bordeaux,
s.147/3 Rés.

PA 1519, 3 4 August	*By the Parlement of Rouen,* To Thomas Du Four, until Easter (8 April 1520), as requested, for *Ordonnances pronuncees en la court de Parlement sur le* *faict de la chose publicque, c'est assavoir peste / filles* *publicques / vagabondz* etc. E.R.P. printed on f. [6]ᵛ at the end. 'Signé Surreau'	Rouen, T. Du Four, s.d. 4° BN Vélins 1867(5)
PA 1519, 4 29 August	To Claude Chevallon, 2 years (3 requested), for 1. Bellevue (Armand de) *Sermones ex Psalterio* ed. Jean de Vray	J. Le Messier, J. Badius and C. Chevallon (pr. Le Messiér) 1519 4° BM Beaune
	2. Menot (Michel) *De federe et pace inuenda*	C. Chevallon 1519 8° BN Rés.D.15433
	3. Pepin (Guillaume) *Rosarium aureum mysticum*	C. Chevallon 1519 8° BN Rés.D.15439
	4. Pepin (G.) *Sermones dominicales*	C. Chevallon and J. Petit 1523 8° BN D.47364
	5. Pepin (G.) *Super confiteor*	C. Chevallon 1519 8° BN D.85574

E.R.P. printed on verso of title-page in each book.*
'Collation est faicte. Ainsi signé   Robert'

---

* The copies of 1. published in the name of Badius do not display the text of the privilege: only
the one extant copy in the name of Chevallon (at Beaune) has it. See Renouard, *Imprimeurs*
parisiens, II, p. 171, no. 395.

PA 1519, 5 Col. 19 Dec.	*By the Parlement of Toulouse* (presumably); beneficiary, duration and date of grant not known, for Costa (Stephanus de) *Tractatus de consanguinitate et affinitate* Only 'Cum priuilegio' on title-page.	Toulouse, Jean Faure and Pierre Bergier 1519 4° BN Rés.ғ.828(3) (this copy has the Arms of Toulouse on a contemporary vellum binding)
PA 1520, 1 12 May	To Nicolas de La Barre, 1 year (2 requested), for *Bulle de la canonisation de Saint Francoys de Paule* AN x 1 A 1522, f. 177^v (The *requête* referred also to 'ung petit livre intitulé *De Inuentoribus Rerum*' but this book is not included in the grant.)	Cf. E. Droz, 'Une plaque de reliure', *Humanisme et Renaissance*, 1 (1934), p. 54, and H. W. Davies, *Fairfax Murray catalogue*, n°. 71.
PA 1520, 2 20 December	To Constantin Fradin, 2 years (4 requested), for 1. La Roche (Etienne de) *L'arismethique nouvellement composee*	Lyon, C. Fradin (pr. G. Huyon) 1529 4° BL 8505.f.21
	2. Falcon (Jean) *Le Guidon en francoys*	Lyon, C. Fradin 1520 4° BN Rés.ᴛd.73.14ᴀ.

AN x 1 A 1523, f. 25^v
E.R.P. printed on verso of title-page in both books.
Signed: Du Tillet.

PA 1520, 3   To Claude Perron, author,
              3 years, for
              Perron (C.) *Compendium philosophiae naturalis*   D. Higman
              Notice addressed by the author 'Ad archetypos   1520 4°
              nostros amicos' announcing 'maiores senatus ...   BL 536.h.28(2)
              prohibuerunt ne quis ante triennium hoc recenter
              conditum philosophiae compendium typis
              committeret cudendum', printed on verso of last
              leaf.
              Date of privilege not stated, but the book contains
              verses dated 1 November.

PA 1520, 4   *By the Parlement of Toulouse* (presumably),
              beneficiary, duration and date of grant not known,
              for
              Galiaule (Lancelot) *In L. Gallus ti. de lib. et post*   Toulouse, Jean
              hu.ff. Lectura   Faure,
              Only 'Cum priuilegio' on the title-page.   1520 4°
                                                                        BN Rés.F.828,1

PA 1521, 1   To Simon Vincent,
8 March   3 years, for
              San Giorgio (Giovanni Antonio da) *Super Codice et*   No copy of
              Digestis Veteribus   such an edition
              AN X 1 A 1523, f. 112   traced.

PA 1521, 2   To Pierre Viart,
27 May   2 years, for
              Gaguin (Robert) *De Francorum gestis* [with   P. Viart (pr. J.
              continuation]   Cornillau)
              AN X 1 A 1523, f. 214   1521 8°
              E.R.P. printed on verso of title-page.   Bodl.Vet.E.1.
              'Collation est faicte. Ainsi signé. De Brugvolles' [*sic*,   e.61
              for De Veignolles]

PA 1521, 3   To Jean Kerver and Hémon Le Fèvre,
11 July   2 years (4 requested), for
              Le Jars (Laziardus, Jean) *Epitomata*   J. Kerver and
              E.R.P. printed on verso of title-page.   H. Le Fèvre
              'Collation est faicte [no signatory named]   (pr. J. Du Pré)
                                                                        1521 fol.
                                                                        BL C.75.d.4(2)

PA 1521, 4
13 August

To Pierre Gromors,
2 years (3 requested), for
Fichet (Guillaume) *Consolatio luctus et mortis*, ed. N.   P. Gromors
Beraldus   1521 4°
E.R.P. printed on verso of title-page.   BN Rés.R.1217
'Robert. Collation est faicte.'
(The grant includes Fichet's *Rhetorica*, but the
Rhetorica does not appear in Gromors's edition.)

PA 1521, 5
8 October

To Jean Vatel,
2 years, for
Gaza (Theodorus) *Grammatici institutiones lib.IV.*   J. Badius and
(Latin translation provided by Vatel)   J. Vatel
Summary printed at the end (sig. c 4ʳ)   s.d. 4°
                                                      BL 1560/1742

PA 1521, 6
Col.
30 October

By the Parlement of Rouen,
To Jean Burges,
duration not stated, for
Ordonnances royaulx publiees en la court de Parlement de   Rouen, J.
Rouen par ordonnance d'icelle (27 November 1520)   Burges
'Cum priuilegio' printed on title-page and,   1520 8°
immediately below, the signature of the *greffier*   BN Rés.F.2297
'Ainsi signé   Surreau', at the end.

PA 1521, 7
Preface dated
30 November

To editor or publishers,
no details of exact date, duration or beneficiary
given, for
Turre (Bertrand de) *Sermones* ed. Pierre de Neufve   E. and J. de
'Cum priuilegio curie parlamentee [*sic*], ne quis   Marnef
venum exponat alia ymagine pressum ut liquido   1521 4°
patet instrumento', printed on title-page.   BN Vélins
                                                       1743

PA 1522, 1
14 January

To Simon Vincent,
2 months [*sic*], for
Benedictus (feu Maître), 'Sur le chapitre Ranutius   No copy of
extra de testamentis'   such an edition
AN x 1 a 1524, f. 56.   traced.

An edition of this work, *Gulielmi Benedicti …*
Repetitio … super cap. Raynutius … extra de testamentis
(S. Gryphius, Lyon, 1526, fol.) is attested by the
Biblioteca Colombina, 1 (Seville, 1888), p. 223. Cf.
Baudrier, *Bibliographie lyonnaise*, VIII, 42.

PA 1522, 2
20 January
To Josse Badius,
2 years (2 or 3 requested), for
Bouchard (Amaury) Τῆς Γυναικείας φύτλης
AN x 1 A 1524, f. 61
Latin summary printed at end.

J. Badius
1522 4°
BL c.41.d.8

PA 1522, 3
18 March
To Claude Chevallon,
2 years, for
Bersuire (Pierre) Reductorii moralis lib. XIV
E.R.P. printed after table of contents.
'Collation est faicte. Ainsi signé Malon.'

C. Chevallon
(pr. B.
Rembolt)
1521 (o.s.) fol.
BN Rés.D.1226

PA 1522, 4
28 March
To Jean Olivier,
2 years (3 requested), for
Boussard (Gaufredus) Interpretationes in VII Psalmos
penitentiales
AN x 1 A 1524, fols. 176ᵛ–177ʳ
E.R.P. printed on f. a7ᵛ.
'Collacion est faicte. Deveignolles.'

J. Olivier
1521 (o.s.) 8°
BN A.8241

PA 1522, 5
29 March
To Galliot Du Pré,
2 years (3 requested), for
Dallier (Lubin) De mandatis quae apostolica vocantur
dissertatio
AN x 1 A 1524, f. 177
E.R.P. printed on verso of title-page.
'Collation faicte. Deveignolles.'

G. Du Pré
(pr. P. Vidoue)
s.d. 8°
BN Rés.F.1809

PA 1522, 6
5 April
To Galliot Du Pré,
2 years (3 requested), for
Les coutumes du pays et duché de Bourbonnoys
E.R.P. printed on verso of title-page.
'Collation est faicte. De Veignolles.'

G. Du Pré
(pr. P. Vidoue)
s.d. 4°
BN Rés.F.2346

PA 1522, 7
21 June

By the Parlement of Toulouse,
To Mathieu Du Monde,
2 years (as requested), for
Les articles et confirmations des priuileges du pays de
Languedoc
L.P. printed on ff. A1ᵛ–A2ʳ.
'Donné à Tholose en la sale du Palais yssue de
ladicte court de matin soubs nos seels et seings
manuels cy mis le xxj iour de Juing l'an Mil cinq
cens et vingt deux.
H. Reynier.   S. Reynier'

Toulouse, M.
Du Monde (pr.
Eustache
Mareschal,
Arnauld
Guilhem Du
Boys and
Jehan
Damoysel)
1522 8°
BM Toulouse
Rés.D.XVI.342

PA 1523, 1
Col.
15 March
1522 (o.s.)

By the Parlement of Rouen,
To Jean Burges le jeune,
no details of exact date of grant or of duration
given, for
Les Ordonnances royaulx publiees en la Court de Parlement
à Rouen par ordonnance d'icelle (28 February 1521 n.s.)

Rouen, J.
Burges
[1522] 8°
BN Rés.F.2298

PA 1523, 2

By the Parlement of Toulouse,
To Antoine Le Blanc,
5 years (as requested), for
Consuetudines Tholose
E.R.P. printed on f. A2.
'Donné à Tholose soubs nos seing manuel et seel
armoyé de nos armes, le premier jour du moys
d'avril L'an mil cinq cens et xxij avant
Pasques.   G. Dolmyeres.'

Toulouse, A.
Le Blanc and
E. Mareschal
1522 4°
BN Rés.F.2325

PA 1523, 3
Col.
18 August

By the Parlement of Toulouse (presumably),
beneficiary, duration and date of grant not known,
for
Lucena (Ludovicus) *De tuenda peste integra valitudine*
(dedicated to Jean Chavanhac, Juge-Mage of
Toulouse 1495–1535)
Only 'Cum priuilegio' on the title-page.

Toulouse,
Hugonin de
Turquis (pr.
Mondete
Guimbaude,
widow of Jean
Faure)
1523 4°
BN Rés.TE³⁰
246

PA 1524, 1
11 January

To Conrad Resch,
2 years, for
Erasmus, *Precatio Dominica in septem portiones distributa*
'Cum priuilegio a Suprema Curia dato Anno M.D. XXIII. Tertio Idus Ianua. ad Biennium usque', printed on title-page (1524 n.s., as the First Edition, from which this is reprinted, did not come out at Basle until October 1523.)

C. Resch (pr.
P. Vidoue)
1523 (o.s.) 8°
BN 8°
z.14879(2)

PA 1524, 2
12 January

To Conrad Resch,
2 years (as requested), for
Bedtsbrugghe (Gillis van) *De usura centesima*
AN x 1 A 1526, f. 53
'Cum authoritate supreme curie et priuilegio in biennium' after colophon.

C. Resch (pr.
P. Vidoue)
1524 4°
Bodl. 4°
L.6.Jur.

PA 1524, 3
3 February

To Galliot Du Pré,
2 years (3 requested), for
Commynes (Philippe de) *Cronique du roy Loys*
AN x 1 A 1526, f. 73
E.R.P. printed on verso of title-page.
'Collacion est faicte. Ainsi signé. S. Du Tillet.'

G. Du Pré
1524 4°
BN Vélins 754

PA 1524, 4
29 February

To Pierre Aubry, author,
2 years (no special period requested), for a broadsheet, described as
'quelque portraict d'un escu par luy faict en une feille de papier, blasonné et moralisé de dictons et rondeaux et autres rimes devotes à l'environ, qu'il appelle: le blason des armes du pouvre pescheur'.
AN x 1 A 1526, f. 120

No copy traced.

PA 1524, 5
3 March

To Galliot Du Pré,
2 years (no special period requested), for
Natalibus (Petrus de) *Le catalogue des Saints translaté de latin en françois*
AN x 1 A 1526, f. 122ᵛ
E.R.P. printed on verso of title-page.
'Collacion est faicte. Ainsi signé. C. Du Tillet.'

G. Du Pré
s.d. fol.
BN Rés.H.365

PA 1524, 6
9 April

To Claude Chevallon,
2 years (3 requested), for
Super psalmo c.decimo octavo expositio (attributed to St
Bonaventura), with certain *opuscula* of St
Bonaventura.
AN x 1 a 1526, f. 177ᵛ
E.R.P. printed on verso of title-page.
(No signature)

C. Chevallon
1524 8°
BN a.6833

PA 1524, 6(A)
23 April

To Pierre Le Fèvre,
2 years, for
Tributiis (Pierre de) 'une repetition de la loi quarte
de sacrosanctis ecclesiis'
AN x 1 a 1526, f. 188

No copy of
such an edition
traced.

PA 1524, 7
29 April

To Jean Petit,
2 years, for
Lutzenburg (Bernardus) *Catalogus haereticorum:
aeditio tertia*
AN x 1 a 1526, f. 201.
E.R.P. printed on verso of title-page.
'Collation est faicte. De Veignolles.'

J. Petit (pr. P.
Vidoue)
1524 4°
BL 1364.d.2

PA 1524, 8
28 May

To Damien Higman,
2 years (3 requested), for
Raulin (Jean) *Sermonum de festiuitatibus sanctorum
prima pars*
AN x 1 a 1526, f. 233ᵛ

D. Higman
(pr. A.
Bonnemère)
1524 4°
BN d.9499

PA 1524, 9
3 June

To Regnault Chaudière,
2 years (3 requested), for
Ravisius Textor (Joannes) *Epitheta*
AN x 1 a 1526, ff. 241ᵛ–242
Only 'Cum priuilegio' on title-page.

R. Chaudière
(pr. P. Vidoue)
1524 fol.
BN Rés.x.627

PA 1524, 10
3 June

To Simon De Colines,
2 years (as requested), for
Clichtoue (Jodocus) *Antilutherus*
AN x 1 a 1526, f. 242.
E.R.P. printed on verso of title-page.
'Ainsi signé De Veignolles.'

S. De Colines
1524 fol.
Bodl.r.4.21.th

PA 1524, 11
8 August

To the *Eschevins, manans et habitans de Blois,*
2 years (no special period requested), for
Coustumes generalles du pays et conté de Bloys
AN x 1 A 1526, f. 314
E.R.P. printed on verso of title-page.
Signed   Du Tillet

pr. A. and N.
Les Couteaux
1524 4°
BN Rés.F.2216

PA 1524, 12
16 August

To Josse Badius and Regnauld Chaudière,
2 years (3 requested), for
'Propositio contra Lutherum et sequaces eius'
AN x 1 A 1526, f. 332

No copy of
such an edition
traced.

PA 1524, 13
7 September
Cf. CH 1520,
3(2)

To Galliot Du Pré,
3 years (as requested), for
Tomus primus (secundus) quatuor conciliorum generalium
ed. Jacques Merlin
AN x 1 A 1526, f. 360
'Priuilegium' (Latin paraphrase), printed on verso
of title-page after chancery privilege,
'Sic signatum. Collatio facta est. Seraphim du
Tillet.'

G. Du Pré (pr.
J. Cornillau)
1524 fol. 2 vols.
BL c.37.1.8

PA 1524, 14
5 December

To Jean Petit,
2 years (no special period requested), for
Cousturier or Sutor (Pierre) *De tralatione Bibliae*
E.R.P. printed on verso of title-page.
'Collation est faicte. Burdelot.'

J. Petit (pr. P.
Vidoue)
1525 fol.
BL 699.l.22

PA 1524, 15

No details of exact date, duration or beneficiary
given, for
Bouchet (Jean) *Les annalles d'Acquitaine*
'Cum priuilegio supreme curie parlamenti, Et sont
à vendre à Paris' etc., printed on the title-page.
(Colophon gives year-date 1524 but leaves blanks
for day and month of completion, in this copy.)

Paris/Poitiers,
E. de Marnef
and Jacques
Bouchet
1524 fol.
BL G.6385

PA 1525, 1
10 February

To Robert Messier, author, for Claude Chevallon,
2 years (permanent privilege for all Messier's
works requested),
Messier (Robert) *Super epistolas et evangelia totius*
Quadragesime sermones
AN x 1 A 1527, f. 132
E.R.P. printed on fol. c4^v facing first page of text.
'Ainsi signé   Du Teillet.'

C. Chevallon
(pr. B.
Rembolt)
s.d. 8°
Bodl. Tanner
885

PA 1525, 2 23 March	To Galliot Du Pré, 2 years, for Petrarch, *Des remedes de l'une et l'autre fortune* Authenticated summary of privilege, printed on verso of title-page, referring to the original, and signed: C. Du Tillet.	G. Du Pré 1524 fol. BL 29.e.5 Colophon 15 March 1523 *avant Pasques*, perhaps a mistake for 1524 (o.s.)
PA 1525, 3 8 April	To Claude Chevallon, 2 years, for Menot (Michel) *Sermones quadragesimales* E.R.P. printed on verso of title-page. 'Ainsi signé Du Teillet.'	C. Chevallon 1525 8° BN Rés.D. 15436
PA 1525, 4 29 April	To Galliot Du Pré, 2 years (3 requested), for *Les coustumes du pays et duché de Bourbonnais* AN x 1 A 1528, f. 408ᵛ (Date on f. 407ᵛ).	G. Du Pré (pr. A. Couteau) 1524/5 (10 April) 4° acc. to *Actes de Francois Iᵉʳ*, 1, p. 220, n°. 1211. No copy traced
PA 1525, 5 3 May	To Pierre Ricouart, 2 years (3 requested), for *Ung petit traicté bien devot contenant premierement une petite eschelle pour faire confession* by a Paris Carthusian E.R.P. printed on verso of title-page. Signed: Devignolles.	P. Ricouart s.d. 4° Maz.35841
PA 1525, 6 30 May	To Claude Chevallon, 2 years (3 requested), for *Ordinationes synodales ciuitatis & diocesis Aurelianensis* AN x 1 A 1528, f. 501ᵛ E.R.P. printed at the end (recto of last fol.). Signed: Du Teillet	C. Chevallon 1525 4° Maz. Rés. 13343

PA 1525, 7   To Galliot Du Pré,
8 August   2 years, for
             Cottereau (Pierre) *Les offices magistraux de France*   G. Du Pré (pr.
             (name of author given in dedication)   P. Vidoue)
             AN x 1 a 1528, f. 706^v 1525 4°
             'Copia ex actuario sacri consistorii Parisiensis'   BN Rés.f.841
             (E.R.P. translated into Latin). No signature.
             Printed on verso of title-page.

PA 1525, 8   To Simon de Colines,
28 November   2 years (as requested), for
              Clichtoue (Josse) *Propugnaculum ecclesiae*   S. de Colines
              aduersus lutheranos   1526 fol.
              AN x 1 a 1529, f. 25   Bodl. 8°
              E.R.P. printed on verso of title-page.   z.12.th

PA 1526, 1   To Josse Badius,
19 July   2 years, for
              Budé (Guillaume) *Altera editio annotationum in*   J. Badius
              Pandectas (xxv)   s.d. fol.
              AN x 1 a 1529, f. 323^v Cambridge UL
              E.R.P. printed on verso of title-page.   s*.2.27^1 (c)

PA 1526, 2   To Josse Badius and Jean Petit,
24 September   2 years (6 requested), for
               Hugh of St Victor *Opera*, ed. J. Borderius.   J. Badius (pr.)
               E.R.P. printed on verso of title-page in vol. 1.   and J. Petit
               Signed: 'Collation est faicte. Malon.'   1526 fol. 3 vols.
                                                                     Oxford,
                                                                     Merton
                                                                     College,
                                                                     80.i.37.

PA 1526, 3   To Jean Petit and Gilles Gourmont,
18 December   2 years (4 requested), for
               Mair (John) *Octo libri physicorum*   J. Petit and G.
               E.R.P. printed on verso of title-page.   Gourmont
               'Ainsi signé. Dutillet.'   1526 fol.
                                                             BN Rés.r.640

Privileges of 1527 referred to in the text

PA 1527, 1
2 March
See above,
p. 46.

By the Parlement of Toulouse,
To Gilbert Grosset, bookseller of Montauban, 3
years (3 or 4 requested), for
Maurus (Johannes) In Chiliades Adagiorum D.Erasmi
... Expositio
Privilege printed on verso of title-page, and
continued on the following pages.
'Donné à Tholose en la Salle du Palays yssue de
ladicte Court: de matin soubz noz Seing manuel et
Seel cy mys le segond jour de Mars Lan Mil cinq
cens & vingt six. Ainsi signé Jaques Rivirie.'

Montauban, G.
Grosset, and
Toulouse,
A. Maurin (pr.
I.c. = Jacques
Colomiès,
Toulouse)
s.d. 8°
BM Toulouse
Rés.D.xvi.727

PA 1527, 2
4 September
See above,
pp. 198–9.

By the Parlement of Bordeaux
To Jean Guyart, bookseller of Bordeaux,
3 years (4 requested), for
Les coustumes generalles de la ville de Bourdeaulx,
seneschaucée de Guyenne ... approuvées par la Court de
Parlement
E.R.P. printed on verso of title-page.
'Ainsi signé Collation est faicte. Perier.'
Additional E.R.P. printed on facing page, dated 6
June 1528, forbidding the greffier Jean de Pontac to
sell the edition he had had printed at Paris until
the expiry of Guyart's privilege (cf. CII 1529, 2).

Bordeaux, J.
Guyart
1528 4°
BM Bordeaux
J.3011 Rés.
(coffre)

PA 1527, 3
September
See above,
pp. 197–8.

By the Parlement of Rouen,
To Jean Petit of Paris and Louis Bouvet of Rouen,
6 years (7 requested), for
Antiphoners of the diocese of Rouen
Requête (dated 6 September) granted after a
counter-claim by Pierre Lignant, bookseller of
Rouen, had been heard.
Archives Départementales, Seine Maritime.
Série B. Registres du parlement de Rouen.
Arrêts juillet–septembre 1527 (pages unnumbered)
Signed: Billy. Challenge.

No copy
traced.

[Transcribed by C. A. J. Armstrong.]

ROYAL OFFICERS
(Prévôt of Paris unless otherwise stated)

PR 1505, 1   To Pierre Gringore, author,
1 year, for
Les folles entreprises   Pr. Pierre le
Summary of privilege 'par l'ordonnance de justice'   Dru for the
in colophon, which is dated 23 December 1505, on   author.
last page.   s.d. 8°
Reprinted above, p. 49.   BN Vélins
                                                            2244

PR 1508, 1   To Jean d'Ivry, translator, in favour of Guillaume
Eustace,
1 year from forthcoming Easter, to expire in 1509,
for
1. *Les triumphes de France* (Latin by Charles Curre)   G. Eustace (pr.
2. *Les faictz et gestes de M. le Légat* (Latin by Fausto   J. Barbier)
   Andrelini)   1508 4° (4
Summary of privilege 'De par le prevost de Paris   parts)
en ensuyvant la requeste presentee en la court de   BN Vélins
parlement', on verso of last fol. of *Les triumphes de*   2255–6
France.
Colophon of *Les faictz et gestes* dated 20 May 1508.
Reprinted in Van Praet, *Catalogue*, IV, p. 192,
no. 261

PR 1509, 1   To Jean d'Ivry, translator
1 year, from forthcoming Easter, to expire at Easter
1510 (31 March 1510), for
Les Ditz de Salomon et de Marcolphus. Les ditz des sept   G. Eustace
sages de Grèce.   s.d. 8°
Summary of privilege on verso of last f. of the *Ditz*   BM
des sept sages de Grèce, beginning 'De par le prevost   Aix-en-
de Paris...'   Provence,
                                                            Bibliothèque
                                                            Méjanes c.2978

PR 1509, 2   To Pierre Gringore, author,
until after next Easter Day (31 March 1510), for
Gringore (P.) *L'entreprise de Venise, avec les villes, citez,*
chasteaulx, forteresses et places que usurpent et detiennent   s.d. 8°
lesditz Veniciens   BN Rés.ye
Summary of privilege 'par l'ordonnance de justice'   4108
on recto of last fol.

PR 1509, 3   To Pierre Gringore, author,
              until coming feast of St John Baptist (24 June), for
              Gringore (P.) *L'union des princes* (written before   pr. for the
              Louis XII's victory at Agnadello, 14 May 1509)   author by P.
              Summary of privilege 'par justice', on verso of   Le Dru
              title-page   s.d. 8°
                                                                      BN Rothschild
                                                                      2824 IV, 9.69

PR 1509, 4*   To Martin Alexandre,
              congié de monseigneur le prevost ou son lieutenant, for
              L'Armée du Roy qu'il avoit contre les Venitiens (battle of
              Agnadello, 14 May 1509)   M. Alexandre
              Congé mentioned in the colophon.   [1509] 4°
                                                                      BL 596.e.33

PR 1509, 5*   To Noel Abraham,
              congé et licence, for
              Evre nouvellement translatee de Italienne rime en rime   Lyon, N.
              francoyse contenant l'advenement du tres chrestien Roy de   Abraham
              france Loys XII de ce nom à Millan...   1509, 8°
              Congé et licence mentioned in the colophon, which is BM Lyon,
              dated 9 June 1509.   Rés.B.485488

PR 1509, 6   To Pierre Gringore, author,
Col.   1 year, for
10 October   Gringore (P.) *Les Abuz du monde*   pr. for the
              Summary of privilege, granted 'par justice',   author by P.
              incorporated in colophon.   Le Dru
                                                                      s.d. 8°
                                                                      BL 11474.a.24

PR 1510, 1   *By the Bailli of Rouen* (presumably),
(After 25   To Louis Bouvet,
May, date of an unspecified term, for
death of   Sylviolus (Antonius) *De Georgii Ambasiani obitu*   Rouen, L.
Georges   At end: 'cum priuilegio ne quis alius imprimere   Bouvet (pr.
d'Amboise)   audeat sine iudicis auctoritate.'   Martin Morin)
                                                                      s.d. 4°
                                                                      BN Rés.G.2807

PR 1510, 2   To Pierre Gringore, author,
Col.   1 month from the completion of the book, for
14 August   Gringore (P.) *La coqueluche*   pr. for the
              At end: summary of privilege, granted 'par   author by P.
              l'ordonnance de justice' (fol. 8ᵛ)   Le Dru
                                                                      s.d. 8°
                                                                      BN Rés.ye
                                                                      1428

PR 1511, 1*   *By the Bailli of Rouen* (possibly),
(May 1511,   *congé*, beneficiary and term not specified, for
on internal   *La coppie des lettres que Monsieur le mareschal de Trevoul*   (Rouen?)
evidence)   *a envoiees au Roy nostre sire. Touchant l'entree de Boulogne*   s.d. 4°
   la grasse faicte par les francois.   Seguin,
   On title-page: 'Faict par le congié de justice.'   *L'information*,
   n°. 42, p. 68,
   with facsimile
   of title-page,
   from BN MSS
   n.a.fr. 7647,
   fols. 231–2.

PR 1511, 2   To the author or publishers (not specified),
Col.   1 year, for
31 July   Desmoulins (Laurent) *Le cymetière des malheureux*   Jean Petit and
   Summary of privilege, granted 'par justice',   Michel Le Noir
   incorporated in colophon   (pr.)
   1511 8°
   BN Rés.ye
   1353

PR 1512, 1   *By the Bailli of Berry*,
Col.   To the publishers (probably)
16 January   term not specified, for
   Le stille des auditoires de messieurs le bailly de Berry et le   E. De Marnef
   prevost de Bourges   1511 8ᵉ
   At the end: 'Imprimé à Paris par l'auctorité, congié   BN
   et licence de monseigneur le bailly de Berry ou son   Rés.F.1848(1)
   lieutenant...'

PR 1512, 2   To Josse Badius,
col.   term not specified, for
1 April   Vio (Thomas de, *Cajetanus*) *Auctoritas papae et concilii*   J. Badius
   Summary of privilege 'auctoritate regia et dictae   1512 4°
   uniuersitatis [Paris]' printed after colophon   Ste Geneviève,
   D. 4° 1284
   Inv.1322

PR 1514, 1   To Laurent Desmoulins, author,
Col.   until the next St John the Baptist (24 June), for
11 February   his *Déploration de la royne de France*, printed in Brie   s.l., s.d.
1513 (o.s.)   (Germain de) *Les epitaphes de Anne de Bretaigne royne*   BN Rothschild
   de France tr. L.D.   IV.9.69
   Summary, printed at the end, of privilege 'ordonné
   par justice.'

PR 1514, 2
17 August

To Guillaume Sanxon,
8 days, for
S'ensuyt le traicté de la paix [Treaty of
Saint-Germain-en-Laye, 15 August 1514]
Order, printed on fol. 4ʳ, 'soubz nostre signet'.
Signed: G. Maillart. Almaury.

s.d. 4°
BN Rés.pʏ²
49⁷

PR 1514, 3
25 October

To Guillaume Mart,
8 days, for
L'entree de la royne à Ableville [*sic*]
(marriage at Abbeville of Louis XII and Mary,
daughter of Henry VII of England, 9 October
1514)
At the end: 'De par le prevost de Paris, Il est
permis à Guillaume Mart libraire ... et deffences à
tous autres ... jusques à huyt jours passé. Fait
soubs nostre signet ... Ainsi signé: Almaury.'

G. Mart
s.d. 8°
Maz.35476

PR 1514, 4*

By the Prévôt de l'Hôtel,
to Guillaume Varin,
licence and presumably privilege for
L'entree de Marie d'Angleterre à Paris (6 November
1514)

G. Varin
s.d. 8°
BN Rés.ʟb²⁹
45 ᴀ

PR 1514, 5
24 November

By the Lieutenant General of the Bailli of Rouen,
To Martin Morin,
1 year from date of grant, for
Fabri (Pierre) *Le defensore de la concepcion de la
glorieuse vierge Marie*
At the end: 'De par le lieutenant general de
monsieur le bailli de Rouen.' Order made at the
request of Morin, 'Ainsi signé: Maillart.'

M. Morin,
Rouen
s.d. 4°
BN Rés.ᴅ.7602

PR 1515, 1
29 January

To Jehan Jhannot,
15 days, for
L'ordre du sacre et couronnement du roy Francoys premier
At end, summary of privilege granted 'par justice'.

J. Jhannot
s.d. 8°
BN Rés.ʟb³⁰ 21

PR 1515, 2
5 December

To Guillaume Le Normand and Pierre Martin,
3 months, for
*C'est l'epistre qu'a voulu mander France à la mere du roy
pour aliance*
Order, printed on last page, 'Fait soubz nostre
signet'.
Signed: Amaury.

G. Le
Normand and
P. Martin
s.d. 8°
BN Rés.ʏe 3967

PR 1516, 1	To Clément Longis,	
19 September	2 years, for	
	La vie et les miracles de saint Eusice	C. Longis
	Order printed on verso of title-page.	s.d. 4°
	Signed: Ruzé	BN Rés.Ln²⁷
		7276

PR 1516, 1, 19 September: To Clément Longis, 2 years, for *La vie et les miracles de saint Eusice*. Order printed on verso of title-page. Signed: Ruzé — C. Longis s.d. $4°$ BN Rés.Ln^{27} 7276

PR 1516, 2, Col. 30 September: To Guillaume Michel, author, 2 years, for Michel (G.) *La forest de conscience*. E.R.P. printed at end, given under the seal of the *prévôté*. Signed: Amaury — Michel Le Noir 1516 $8°$ Bodl. Douce MM 319. See E. Armstrong, 'Notes on the works of Guillaume Michel, dit de Tours', *Bibliothèque d'Humanisme et Renaissance*, xxx (1969), p. 261.

PR 1516, 3, 10 October: To Juan de Celaya, author, 2 years, for Celaya (J. de) *Expositio in librum predicabilium Porphirii*. Order, printed on verso of title-page, 'soubz nostre signet'. Signed: J. de Calais. — Hémon Le Fèvre s.d. fol. BN Rés.R.136

PR 1516, 4, 11 November: To Juan de Celaya, author, 2 years, for Celaya (J. de) *Expositio in libros priorum Aristotelis*. Order, printed on verso of title-page, 'soubz nostre signet'. Signed: J. de Calais. — Hémon Le Fèvre 1516 fol. Bodl. AA 59 Art(5)

PR 1516, 5, 2 December: To Jean de La Garde, 3 years, for Virgil, *Les Bucoliques de Virgille*, tr. Guillaume Michel. Order printed on verso of title-page. Signed: Alegre. — J. de La Garde 1516 $4°$ Bodl.Douce v.175

PR 1517, 1
2 March

To Toussaint Denys,
3 years, for
Compendium de multiplici Parisiensis uniuersitatis
magnificentia
Order, printed on verso of title-page, beginning 'Il
est permis de par monseigneur le lieutenant civil',
referring to a fuller document ('comme plus
amplement est contenu audit privilege')
Signed: Ruzé.

T. Denis
1517 4°
Bodl.BB
18.Art.Seld. (5)

PR 1517, 2
16 April

To Jean de La Garde,
3 years, for
Le voyage de la saincte cité de Jerusalem
Order printed on verso of title-page.
Signed: Alegre.

J. de La Garde
1517 4°
BN
Rés.o.2.f.31

PR 1517, 3
5 May

To Juan de Celaya, author,
2 years, for
Celaya (J. de) *Expositio in libros posteriorum*
Order, printed on verso of title-page, 'soubz nostre
signet'.
Signed: J. de Calais.

Hémon Le
Fèvre
s.d. fol.
Bodl.CC 7
Art.(4)

PR 1517, 4

To Jean Boissier,
until after the forthcoming Feast of St John the
Baptist (24 June), for
L'entrée de la royne de France à Paris [12 May 1517]
Summary of privilege, printed at the end,
beginning 'De l'ordonnance de monseigneur le
prevost de Paris et par commission de la court de
Parlement...'

J. Boissier
s.d. 8°
BN Rés.Lb³⁰ 29

PR 1517, 5
25 June

To Juan de Celaya, author,
2 years, for
Celaya (J. de) *Insolubilia et obligationes*
Order 'Fait soubz nostre signet', printed on verso
of title-page.
Signed: J. de Calais.

H. Le Févre
s.d. fol.
BM Bordeaux
s.147/4 Rés.

PR 1517, 6   *By the Bailli of Rouen* (presumably),
              To Louis Bouvet,
              until 12 September, for
              L'entrée de Francoys premier en sa bonne ville de Rouen [2   Rouen, L.
              August 1517]   Bouvet
              Privilege incorporated in colophon, Bouvet being   (pr. P. Olivier)
              'auctorisé à ce faire par justice et deffendu à tous   s.d. 4°
              aultres icelle imprimer sans l'auctorité de   BN
              justice...'   Rés.Lb³⁰.291

PR 1517, 7   To François Regnault,
4 September   1 year (3 requested), for
              Le grant voyage de Jerusalem [by Nicolas Le Huen]   F. Regnault
              Order, printed on verso of title-page, preceded by   (pr. N.
              the *requête*, and by an order of the *procureur du roi* in   Higman
              the court of the Châtelet signed Bouchier.   1517 4°
              Signed: Corbie.   BL G.6780
              Reprinted above, pp. 72–3.

PR 1518, 1   To Jacques Nyverd,
17 June   1 year, for
              Les conqueste et recouvrance de la duché de Millan   J. Nyverd
              Order printed on verso of title-page.   s.d. 8°
              Signed: Alegre.   BL 9150.a.29

PR 1518, 2   To Jean de La Garde,
2 July   2 years, for
              Michel (Guillaume) *Le penser de royal memoire*   J. de La Garde
              Order, printed on verso of title-page.   and P. Le
              Signed: Alegre.   Brodeur
                                                                             s.d. 4°
                                                                             BN Ye 376

PR 1518, 3   To Galliot Du Pré,
5 July   3 years, for
              [Etats généraux. Tours, 1484] *C'est l'ordre tenu...*   G. Du Pré
              Order, printed on verso of title-page, under the seal   s.d. 4°
              of the Prévôt.   BN Rés.Le¹⁰ 2
              Signed: Alegre.

PR 1519, 1   To Jean de La Garde,
17 January   2 years, for
              St Jerome, *Les epistres*, tr. Antoine Du Four   J. de La Garde
              Order, printed on verso of title-page.   1518 4°
              Signed: Allegre   BN Rés.c.5984

PR 1519, 2
18 February

To Jean Petit,
1 year, for
Lyon (Olivier de) *Oratio pro exemptione decimae*   J. Petit
Summary of a privilege issued under the seal of the   s.d. 4°
prévôté, printed at the end.   BN Rés.H.1035
Signed: Corbie.

PR 1519, 3
Dedication
21 July

To Josse Badius,
2 years, for
Quintilian, *Oratoriae institutiones* (revision of text   J. Badius
and commentaries by Badius)   1519 fol.
'Cum gratia et priuilegio biennali, ut publico   BN Rés.G.X.31
constat instrumento', on title-page. The dedication,
printed on the verso of the title-page, is addressed
by Badius to Louis Ruzé, the *Lieutenant Civil*.

PR 1520, 1
Dedication
1 May 1519
Col.
28 January
1520

To Yves Galloys,
3 years, for
Plutarch *Pour discerner ung vray amy d'avecques ung*   Y. Gallois
flateur, tr. François Sauvage   1520 4°
Summary of privilege, 'par justice' printed on verso   BN Rés.R.1151
of title-page.

PR 1520, 2
Col.
7 April

To the publishers (presumably),
2 years, for
St Edmund of Abingdon *Speculum ecclesiae*   J. Badius and
'Imprimé de privilege jusques à deux ans de par   J. Du Pré
monsieur le prevost de Paris le .vii. de Avril Mil   s.d. 8°
cinq cens .xix.', printed on last page.   Bodl.Vet.E1.f.
   79

PR 1520, 3
11 May

To Hémon Le Fèvre,
3 years, for
L'histoire de ... Gérard de Nevers et Euriant de Savoye   H. Le Fèvre
Order, preceded by the *requête*, printed on verso of   1520 4°
title-page, 'soubz nostre seing manuel'.   BN Rés.Y² 683
Signed: Alegre.

PR 1520, 4
6 June

To Toussaint Denys,
3 years, for
Taxe Cancellarie apostolice   T. Denys
Order, printed on verso of title-page, beginning   1520 4°
'Veue la requeste faicte par Toussains Denis',   BN Rés.E.1777
summarising a fuller document ('ainsi qu'il est
contenu plus à plain audit privilege à luy donné')
Signed: Rusé.

PR 1520, 4A To Josse Badius,
Col.   3 years, for
7 July   Maimonides (Moses) *Dux seu Director dubitantium*   J. Badius
             ed. Aug. Giustiniani.   1520 fol.
             Colophon concludes with the words, 'cum gratia &   BL 519.i.15(1)
             priuilegio in triennium proximum, Annuente
             literatorum omnium Mecoenate L. Ruze.'

PR 1520, 5   To Galliot Du Pré,
24 July   3 years, for
             Erasmus, *De la declamation des louenges de folie*   G. Du Pré (pr.
             L.P. under the seal of the *prévôté*, printed on verso Pierre Vidoue)
             of title-page.   1520 4°
             Signed: J. Corbie.   Bodl.
                                                                   Douce E.250

PR 1520, 6   To Jean Lescaille,
             1 year, to be reckoned from 31 July 1520, for
             L'ordonnance et ordre du tournoy [Field of the Cloth of   J. Lescaille (pr.
             Gold, 7–20 June 1520]   P. Vidoue)
             Order, printed facing first page of text, unsigned,   s.d. 4°
             but the form appears to indicate that it emanated   BN Rés.Lb³⁰.35
             from the Prévôt.

PR 1520, 7   To the publisher (presumably)
             8 days, for
             La description et ordre du camp, festins et joustes [Field of   s.l. s.d. 4°
             the Cloth of Gold, 7–20 June 1520]   BL c.33.d.22
             Probably granted by the Prévôt.   (2)
             'Cum priuilegio / Pour huyt iours' on title-page.

PR 1520, 8   To Josse Badius,
Col.   3 years, for
20 August   Budé (Guillaume) *Epistolae*   J. Badius
             'Cum gratia et priuilegio in triennium', the repeat   1520 4°
             on the last page concludes with the words 'L. Ruzé'   BL
             (signature of the *Lieutenant Civil*).   10905.ccc.28

PR 1520, 9   To Galliot Du Pré,
27 September 1 year, for
             Le stille du bailliage de Sens ed. François Boucher.   G. Du Pré
             L.P. summarised on verso of title-page, 'scellees en s.d. 4°
             cire verte'.   BN Rés.p.F.18
             Signed: J. Corbie.

PR 1520, 10 To Josse Badius,
Col. 3 years, for
23 October St Antony of Padua *Sermones dominicales* J. Badius
  Latin summary printed at end after colophon, 1520 8°
  'suffragio literarum bonarum doctissimi et Bodl.
  dulcissimi praesidii L. Ruzei.' Douce A.644

PR 1520, 11 To Josse Badius,
Col. 3 years, for
13 Nov. St Basil, *Opera* (Latin translations by Johannes J. Badius
  Argyropoulos and others) 1520 fol.
  Latin summary printed at the end, 'Astipulante BL 3625.f.4
  insigni morum literarum Mecoenate L. Ruzeo.'

PR 1520, 12 To Pierre Le Brodeur,
27 November 3 years, for
  Vergilius (Polydorus) *De l'invencion des choses*, tr. P. Le Brodeur
  Guillaume Michel 1521, fol.
  Order, preceded by the *requête*, printed on verso of BL c.55.h.11
  title-page, 'soubz nostre seing manuel'.
  Signed: Alegre

PR 1521, 1 To Conrad Resch,
Col. 3 years, for
13 January Biel (Gabriel) *Supplementum in octo et viginti* C. Resch. (pr.
  distinctiones ultimas quarti Magistri Senten. J. Badius)
  Latin summary printed at the end, 'cuius rei 1521 fol.
  publicum habet instrumentum. ... L. Ruzee.' BN Rés.D.67

PR 1521, 2 To the 'suppliantz' (presumably the publishers),
6 February 4 years, for
  Antravanensis (Petrus) *Aurea summa de fuga vitiorum* Toulouse,
  ed. Jo. Vignerius Antoine
  Order, printed on verso of title-page, beginning Maurin and
  'Veue la requeste de monseigneur le prevost de Gaston
  Paris', no signature given. Recolene (pr.
    Paris, Jean Du
    Pré)
    1521 8°
    BN
    Rés.D.13556

PR 1521, 3 To Josse Badius and Jean Petit,
Col. 1 June 3 years, for
  Bede (the Ven.) *Secundus operum tomus* J. Badius
  Latin summary, headed PRIVILEGIVM, printed at 1521 fol.
  the end, referring to an 'instrumentum' signed L. BL 3914.k.2
  Ruzes.

PR 1521, 4 5 October	To Bernard Aubry, 3 years (4 requested), for Dullaert (Johannes) *Quaestiones in Praedicabilia* *Porphyrii (cum additionibus Joannis Drabbe)* L.P. printed on verso of title-page. Signed: J. Lormier	B. Aubry (pr. M. Lesclencher) 1521 fol. Maz. 3580(1) Rés.
PR 1521, 5 Col. 18 December	To Jean Janot, 2 years, for *Le livre de Berinus et Aygres* Order, printed on verso of title-page, beginning 'Il a esté permis à honnorable homme Jehan Janot', summarising a fuller document ('comme plus a plain est contenu en son privilege').	J. Janot s.d. 4° BN Rés. Y² 671
PR 1522, 1 19 February	To Hémon Le Fèvre, 1 year (3 requested), for Michel (Guillaume) *Le siècle doré* Order, preceded by the *requête*, printed on verso of title-page. Signed: Lormier.	H. Le Fèvre 1521 4° BL c.39.g.1
PR 1522, 2 Col. 26 April	To Damien Higman, 3 years, for Peter the Venerable *Opera* ed. Pierre de Montmartre. Latin summary, headed PRIVILEGIVM, printed at the end of the first gathering, referring to an 'instrumentum' signed L. Ruze.	D. Higman 1522 fol. BN Rés.c.756
PR 1522, 3 10 November	To Galliot Du Pré, 3 years (as requested), for *Ysaïe le Triste* L.P. printed on verso of title-page, under the seal of the *prévôté*, signed: Lormier.	G. Du Pré (pr. P. Vidoue) s.d. fol. BL c.7.b.6
PR 1522, 4 Col. 1 January 1523 (grant presumably obtained in 1522)	To Josse Badius, 3 years, for Grève (Philippe de) *In Psalterium CCXXX sermones* Latin summary, printed on unnumbered last page, referring to a 'iustum ac legitimum diploma'. Signed: L. Ruzee.	J. Badius 1523 8° BL 843.k.6

PR 1523, 1 27 January	To Galliot Du Pré, 3 years, for 1. Budé (Guillaume) *Summaire ou Epitome du livre de* *Asse*	G. Du Pré (pr. P. Vidoue) 1522 8° BN J.17030
	2. *Recollection et accumulation des ordonnances ...* *concernans le faict des aydes ... pour le faict de la guerre*	G. Du Pré (pr. P. Vidoue) s.d. 8° BN Rés.F.1818
	L.P., under the seal of the Prévôt, signed J. Lormier, printed on the verso of the title-page in both books, in full in 1 and summarised in 2.	
PR 1523, 2 Col. 'sub Pascha' [5 April]	To Josse Badius, 3 years, for Persius *Satyrae* with the commentaries of Badius and others Latin summary, printed at the end, referring to a 'diploma' signed L. Ruzeus. (May be the same privilege as PR 1522, 4.)	J. Badius 1523 fol. BL 641.M.21
PR 1523, 3 13 April	To Gilles de Gourmont, 3 years (no special period requested), for Mainus (Gulielmus) and Cheradame (Joannes) *Lexicon Graecum* Order, preceded by the *requête*, printed on fol. 71ʳ. Signed: Ruzé.	G. de Gourmont 1523 4° BL G.7610
PR 1523, 4 Col. 1 October	To Josse Badius, 3 years, for Cicero *Cato Major* comm. François Sylvius (Dubois) Latin summary, printed at the end, referring to a 'priuilegium' concluding 'Adscribente clarissimo prudentissimoque Parrhisiorum a ciuilibus suppraefecto L. Ruzaeo.'	J. Badius 1523 4° BN Rés.R.1329
PR 1523, 5 12 November	To Bernard Aubry, 3 years (4 requested), for Dullaert (Johannes) *Quaestiones in librum* *Praedicamentorum Aristotelis secundam viam nominalium* L.P. printed on verso of title-page. Signed: J. Lormier.	B. Aubry (pr. A. Bonnemère) s.d. fol. Maz.3580(2) Rés.

PR 1524, 1 10 May	To Jean de La Garde, 2 years, for Regnier (Jean) *Les fortunes et adversitez* Order, printed on verso of title-page, headed 'De par le prevost de Paris ou son lieutenant'. Signed: Ruze.	J. de La Garde 1526 8° BN Rés.ye 1400
PR 1524, 2 Col. 'sub Pascha' (27 March) Dedication 27 April	To Josse Badius, 4 years, for St Bruno *Opera* Latin summary, printed at the end (f. 520ª), referring to a 'diploma' signed L. Ruzee, followed by a summary of an order by the Prior of the Carthusians, forbidding any member of the Order to cause any other edition to be printed or to buy any other edition, for four years.	J. Badius 1524 fol. Bodl. B.15.7.Th
PR 1525, 1 1 March	To Pierre le Brodeur, 4 years, as requested, for Valerius Maximus *Le floralier des histoires* tr. Guillaume Michel (abridgement by Robert de Valle) Order, preceded by the *requête*, printed on verso of title-page. Signed: Ruze	P. Le Brodeur (pr. A. Couteau) 1525 4° BN Rés.z.938
PR 1525, 2 8 May	To Galliot Du Pré, 2 years, for *La prison d'amours laquelle traicte de l'amour de Leriano et Laureole* Summary printed on verso of title-page, referring to a fuller document ('ainsi qu'il appert bien amplement par le privilege octroyé audit suppliant'). Signed: L. Ruzé	G. Du Pré (pr. A. Couteau) 1526 8° BL C.33.f.1
PR 1525, 3 14 November	To Galliot Du Pré, 3 years, as requested, for 1. *Histoire singuliere contenant la reste des faitz et gestes des quatre filz Aymon: Mabrian* L.P., summarised, printed on verso of title-page. Signed: Allegre 2. *La conqueste de Grece faicte par Philippe de Madien* [by Perrinet Dupin, acc. to BL Catalogue]	G. Du Pré (pr. J. Nyverd) s.d. fol. BL C.34.l.21 G. Du Pré (pr. J. Nyverd) 1527 fol. BL C.34.l.20

L.P., printed on verso of title-page, granting
prorogation of a privilege dated 14 November 1525
which had included both *Mabrian* and *La conqueste
de Grece*, the publisher not having succeded in
publishing the latter until later; three further years
from the date of the new grant, 4 February 1528
Signed: P. Moifait.

PR 1525, 4 Col. December	To the publisher (presumably), 2 years, for Jacques, bastard de Bourbon, *L'oppugnation de la noble cité de Rhodes* 'Avec privilege du prevost de Paris: par commandement de la court, pour deux ans finiz et accompliz', on the title-page.	G. de Gourmont (pr. P. Vidoue) 1525 4° BN Rés.ĸ.672
PR 1526, 1 8 February	To Galliot Du Pré 2 years, for *Traictez singuliers* [works by Lemaire de Belges, Chastelain, Molinet and Crétin] Summary printed on verso of title-page, referring to a fuller document ('ainsi qu'il appert par le privilege dudit seigneur donné et octroyé audit suppliant'). Signed: Allegre.	G. Du Pré (pr. A. Couteau) s.d. 8° BN Rés.ʏᴇ1256(1)
PR 1526, 2 19 April	To Galliot Du Pré, 2 years (3 requested), for 1. *Le Roman de la Rose* (modernised)	G. Du Pré (pr. A. Couteau) 1526 fol. Bodl.Malone 12
	2. Chartier (Alain) *Les faictz et dictz*	G. du Pré (pr. A. Couteau) 1526 fol. BN Rés.ʏᴇ34

L.P. printed on verso of title-page in both books.
Signed: P. Moyfait.

Grants of 1527 referred to in the text

PR 1527, 1 12 January See above, p. 117	To Nicole Volcyr de Sérouville, author, 3 years, for Volcyr de Sérouville (N.) *L'histoire et recueil de la victoire obtenue contre les seduyctz et abusez lutheriens par Anthoine, duc de Calabre* L.P., printed on verso of title-page, issued by Jean de La Barre, *Garde de la prevosté de Paris*, under the seal of the *prévôté*. Signed: P. Moifait.	[Galliot Du Pré] 1526 (o.s.) fol. BN ʟᴋ² 960

PR 1527, 2 16 March See above, p. 204.	To Galliot Du Pré, 3 years, for Guillaume Crétin, *Chants royaulx, oraisons et aultres* *petitz traictez* Privilege printed on verso of title-page. Signed: P. Moifait	G. Du Pré (pr. Simon Dubois) 1527 8° BN Rés.ye1393
PR 1527, 3 29 March See above, p. 204.	To Jean Longis, until Easter 1528 (12 April), Guillaume Crétin, *Le debat de deux dames sur le* *passetemps de la chasse* Privilege printed on verso of title-page. Signed: P. Moifait.	J. Longis (pr. Anthoine Couteau) 1526 (o.s.) 8° BN Rés.ye1395
PR 1527, 4 29 August See above, p. 115.	To Jacques Nyverd, *licence* to print (8-day *privilege* requested), for *Le traité de paix* (Treaty of Amiens) [28 August 1527] AN y8 f. 228^v 'Permis est audit suppliant de pouvoir faire imprimer ladicte paix sans aucune prohibition aux autres imprimeurs de povoir ce faire, faict le xxixme aoust vc xxvij Ainsi signé du Bourg.'	No copy of such an edition traced.

APPENDIX TO REGISTER

Known books printed 'Cum priuilegio' when it is not known on what authority the privilege was given.

All these books display the formula 'Cum priuilegio' or, less often, 'Cum gratia et priuilegio', printed on the title-page, unless otherwise stated.

CP 1507, 1	Briçonnet (Guillaume) *Pro rege Ludovico XII appologia*	Lyon, Vincent de Portonariis 1507 4° BN Rés.Lg⁶ 13
CP 1509, 1	Danton (Jean) *Les espitres envoyees au Roy tres-chrestien delà montz par les estatz de France* On fol. f2ʳ, at the end, 'avec privilege à luy donné'.	Lyon, Noel Abraham (pr. Claude de Troys) s.d. 4° BN Rés.ye 313
CP 1509, 2	[Julius II] *Monitoire de par nostre sainct pere le pape contre les Venitiens* tr. Joannes De Gradibus	Lyon, Noel Abraham s.d. 4° BN Rés.k.713
CP 1510, 1 Col. 23 August	Durandus (Gulielmus) *Rationale diuinorum officiorum*	Lyon, J. Huguetan and others (pr. Jacques Sacon) BM Lyon 321822
CP 1512, 1	Almain (Jean) *De auctoritate ecclesie*	Paris, Jean Granjon 1512 4° BN Rés.e.1892
CP 1512, 2	Mamerot (Sebastien) and others *Les passages de oultre mer*	Paris, François Regnault s.d. 8° BL 1058.b.27

CP 1512, 3	Coquillart (Guillaume) *S'ensuyvent les droitz nouveaulx, avec le debat des dames et des armes*	Paris, Widow Trepperel. s.d. 4° BN Rés.ye 233
CP 1513, 1 Col. 15 April	John of Salisbury, *Polycraticus*	Lyon, C. Fradin 1513, 8° Bodl.70.c.58
CP 1513, 2 Col. 2 August	Desmoulins (L.) *Le catholicon des maladvisez autrement dit le cymetiere des malheureux* 'Cum priuilegio' after colophon (f. 04ʳ).	Paris, J. Petit and M. Le Noir 1513 8° BN Rés.ye 1355
CP 1513, 3	Porta (Sancho de) *Sermones hyemales*	Lyon, Jo. Clein
CP 1513, 4	Porta (Sancho de) *Sermones estivales*	1513–14 4° BN D.11500
CP 1514, 1 Dedication Blois 19 February	Stoa (Quinziano) *Ad Ludovicum XII paraclesis*	Paris, J. de Gourmont s.d. 4° BN Rés.myc 832(3)
CP 1514, 2 Col. 12 June	Avedelis Sonis (A.) *Filiales lachrimae Claudie* [on death of Anne of Brittany, 9 January 1514] 'Cum gratia et priuilegio' in colophon (J 8)	Limoges, Richard de la Novade s.d. 4° BN Rés.lb²⁹ 45
CP 1514, 3	Raulin (J.) *Itinerarium paradisi*	Paris, J. Petit (pr. Rembolt) 1514 4° Maz. 35878
CP 1514, 4 Col. 5 September	Ponte (Petrus de) *Prima grammaticae artis Isagoge*	Paris, Denis Roce (pr. N. des Prez) 1514 4° BL 3837.b.26(2)
CP 1515, 1 Dedication 9 February 1515 (n.s.?)	Aegidius Romanus, *Tractatus de formatione corporis humani in utero*, ed. Jo. Benedictus Moncettus de Castellione Aretino.	Paris, Poncet Le Preux 1515 4° BN Rés.tb 68/8

CP 1515, 2	Joannes de Blavasco, *Ordo judiciarius*	Lyon, Simon Vincent (pr. Jean Thomas) 1515 8° BN Rés.F 2301
CP 1516, 1 15 January	[Gregory I, Pope] *Gregoriana super novum Testamentum . . . ab Alulpho collectum Tornacensi*	Paris, Berthold Rembolt 1516 4° BL 1105.e.1
CP 1516, 2 Letter on f. 24ᵛ dated 28 January 1515 (o.s.)	Houvetus (Guillaume) *Micropaedia epistolaris*	Paris, Jean Gourmont [1516] 8° BN Rés.Z 2099
CP 1516, 3 Col. 18 September	Mair (John) *Insolubilia* (Cf. PA 1516, 8 or 9)	Paris, J. Granjon (pr. J. Du Pré and J. LeMessier) 1516 4° BN Rés.PR 317
CP 1516, 4 Col. 29 October	Gatinaria (M.), *De curis egritudinum particularium*	Lyon, Vincent de Portonariis (pr. Simon Bevilaqua) misdated '1506' for 1516 4° BN Rés.TD 15c
CP 1516, 5 Col. 16 November	Pliny *Naturalis historie Libri xxxvii* ed. N. Beraldus	Paris, R. Chaudière 1516 fol. BL 456.b.3
CP 1516, 6	[Saint-Pol-de-Léon] *Breuiarium insignis ecclesie Leonensis, nuper emaculatum, recognitum . . . emendatum . . . auctum . . .*	Paris, pr. D. Maheu, Yves Quilleveré, Landerneau, Alain Prigent 1516 8° BN Rés.Inc.B 4920

CP 1517, 1 Not before 22 March 1517 when Parlement registered the Concordat.	*Concordata*	Paris, Durand Gerlier (pr. F. Regnault) s.d. 8° Maz.Rés.26819
CP 1517, 2 Not before 22 March 1517.	Elias (Elie de Bourdeilles) Archbishop of Tours, *Defensorium concordatorum* or *Contra Pragmaticam* *Gallorum sanctionem* 'Cum priuilegio ad biennium'	Paris, Durand Gerlier (pr. F. Regnault) s.d. 8° Maz.Rés.26819
CP 1517, 3 Col. 5 September	Bassolis (Joannes de) *In quatuor Sententiarum* *libros* [I and II]	Paris, F. Regnault and J. Frellon (pr. N. des Prez) 1517 fol. Ste Geneviève D 169(1) Inv.152
CP 1517, 4 Col. 16 September	Castellesi (Hadrian) *De sermone Latino* ed. Remigius Rufus 'Cum priuilegio ad triennium'	Paris [Pierre Gromors] 1517 4° BN Rés.x.835
CP 1517, 5	*Benedictina* ed. Michael de Puteo	Paris, J. du Pré and Jacques Le Messier (pr. G. de Gourmont) 1517 4° BN Rés.H.1038
CP 1517, 6	More (Thomas) *Utopia*	Paris, G. de Gourmont s.d. 8° BL c.65.e.1
CP 1518, 1 Col. 26 March	Durandus (G.) *Rationale diuinorum officiorum* ed. B. de Locatellis	Caen, Michel Angier, with J. Petit (pr. L. Hostingue) 1518 4° BN Rés.B.27884

CP 1518, 2   Lefèvre d'Etaples (J.) *De Maria Magdalena*   H. Estienne
1517 (o.s.) 4°
BN Rés.H.1545

CP 1518, 3
Col.
10 June
   Bouchard (A.) *Les grandes croniques de Bretaigne*
[with additions]
   Caen, Michel
Angier
1518 fol.
BN Rés.Lk² 442 A

CP 1518, 3A
Col. pt 1 15
June, pt 2 12
August
   Richardus (Petrus) *Sermonum opus*
   Paris, J. Petit (pr.
B. Rembolt)
1518 4°
Bodl.4° E.1.Th

CP 1518, 4
Col.
25 October
Dedication
22 November
   Mair (John) *In Mattheum ad literam expositio* ed.
J. Godequin
   Paris, J. Granjon
(pr. G. Desplains)
1518 fol.
BN Rés.A.1188

CP 1518, 5
Col.
6 December
   Avicenna *Canon* ed. Symphorien Champier
   Lyon, V. de
Portonariis
1518 fol.
BN Rés.Td⁶⁰ 15

CP 1518, 6
   Adamus Praemonstratensis, *Liber Beatae Mariae et Sancti Ioannis Baptiste ecclesie Premonstratensis*
   Paris, G. de
Gourmont
1518 fol.
Maz.7070

CP 1518, 7
   Templier (Etienne) *Concordia Galliae et Britanniae* (poem)
(Assigned by BL cat. to ?1520, by BN cat. to 1518, more correctly in view of the subject-matter. Cf. Hauser, *Les sources*, VII, p. 123, no. 1033.)
   s.l. s.d. 4°
BL 1070.m.47

CP 1519, 1
Col.
24 February
   Fisher (John) *De unica Magdalena*
'Cum gratia et priuilegio ... in biennium proximum'...
   Paris, J. Badius
1519 4°
Bodl.4° N.26.Th

CP 1519, 2
Col.
7 May
   Despauterius *De figuris* ed. Badius
'Cautum est auctoritate principali ... ne quis hoc opusculum biennio proximo in regno Franciae imprimat praeter Badium...' on verso of last fol.
   Paris, J. Badius
1519 4°
Renouard, *Imp.Par.* II, 405, p. 175, and *Badius*, II, 400.

CP 1519, 3 Erasmus *Christiani hominis institutum* (poem) ed. Paris, Nicolas de
Dedication Joannes Vatellus La Barre
25 May [1519] 4°
  Maz. 10617

CP 1519, 4 Transferred to above, PR 1519, 3.

CP 1519, 5 Theodoret Cyrensis *De curatione graecarum* Paris, H. Estienne
Col. July *affectionum* tr. Z. Acciaiuoli 1519 fol.
  BN Rés.c.245

CP 1519, 6 Jordanus (R.) *Contemplationes Idiotae* Paris, H. Estienne
After July as 1519 fol.
preface refers BN Vélins 1757
to Theodoret
(*CP* 1519, 5)
as published
nuper

CP 1519, 7 Mair (J.) *Editio secunda ... in secundum librum* Paris, J. Granjon
Col. *Sententiarum* 1519 fol.
18 August BN Rés.d 78

CP 1519, 8 Fisher (John) *Confutatio secundae disceptationis* Paris, J. Badius
3 September *Jacobi Fabri* 1519 4°
 'Cum gratia et priuilegio ... intra biennium...' Bodl.
  4° N 26(2) Th

CP 1519, 9 Horace *Opera* ed. J. Badius Paris, J. Badius
Col. 'Cum gratia et priuilegio' 1519 fol.
28 September In colophon: 'Cum gratia et priuilegio ne quis Bodl.f. 2.8.
 triennio proximo' etc. Art.Seld.

CP 1519, 10 Aulus Gellius, *Noctium Atticarum libri* ed. J. Paris, J. Badius
October Badius & Gilles Maserius 1519 fol.
 'Sub priuilegio & cautione ne quis etc in BL 833.l.8
 triennium ... imprimat.'
 In colophon: 'Cum gratia et priuilegio ne quis
 triennio proximo cum hisce scholiis et lucernulis
 imprimat'

CP 1519, 11 Middleton (R.) *Quodlibeta* Paris, C.
Col. 'Cum gratia & priuilegio biennii' Chevallon
12 November Possibly the same privilege as PA 1519, 4. 1519 8°
  BN Rés.d.11720

CP 1519, 12	Vigo (Joannes de) *Chirurgia*	Lyon, V. de Portonariis (pr. J. Myt) 1519 4° BN Rés.Td⁷³ 34A.
CP 1520, 1 Col. 22 January 1519 (o.s.)	St Augustine, *Exposition sur la premiere quinquagene du Psautier*	Lille, Jean Mullet / Paris, J. de la Porte (pr. G. Couteau) 1519 (o.s.) fol. BM Lille 43820
CP 1520, 3 13 February *supputatione romana*	(J.) Badius (ed.) *Allegoriae moralesque sententiae* 'Cum gratia et privilegio amplissimo, nequis preter Badium triennio proximo imprimat'	Paris, J. Badius 1520 fol. Bodl.L.I.8.Th
CP 1520, 3 Col. 26 February	Beda (Noel) *Apologia pro filiabus et nepotibus beatae Annae* 'Cum gratia & privilegio in Biennium'	Paris, J. Badius 1520 4° BL 4806.d.4
CP 1520, 4 Col. 10 March	Dictys Cretensis, *De bello Troiano*	Lyon, R. Morin (pr. J. Marion) 1520 4° BL 832.f.43(1)
CP 1520, 5 Vol. I 20 March, vol. III April	Boich (Bouhic) Henricus, *Censure ... in primum et secundum libros decretalium...*	Lyon, V. de Portonariis (pr. J. Sacon) 1520 fol. 3 vols. BN Rés.E.609
CP 1520, 6 28 March	Albertinis (F. de) *Mirabilia Rome*	Lyon, R. Morin (pr. J. Marion) 1520 4° BN Rés.K.530
CP 1520, 7 Dedication 29 March	Cicero, *Pro lege Manilia* interpr. Hier. Calvus and Ant. Luschus, ed. Jo. Vatellus 'Cum priuilegio' (and on p. 60 note of privilege to N. Crespin 'ad proximum triennium')	Paris, N. Crespin 1519 (o.s.) 4° Maz. 10274
CP 1520, 8 Dedication 15 May	Tataretus (P.) *In quartum Sententiarum Scoti* ed. Jo. Champaigne 'Cum gratia et priuilegio ad biennium'	Paris, C. Chevallon and B. Rembolt (pr.) 1520 fol. BN Rés.D.2574(1)

CP 1520, 9 Col. 14 July	Porchetus (S.) *Victoria aduersus impios Hebraeos* 'Cum gratia et priuilegio' on title, colophon specifying 'in triennium'.	Paris, G. Gourmont and F. Regnault (pr. G. Desplains) 1520 fol. BN Rés.A.1427
CP 1520, 10	Corbelin (Pierre) *Adagiales flosculi*	Paris, C. Chevallon (pr. B. Rembolt) 1520 4° BN Rés.z.960
CP 1520, 11	Dares Phrygius, *De excidio Troie, Cum figuris*	Paris, P. Gaudoul (pr. N. Des Prez) 1520 4° BN Rés.J.1719
CP 1520, 12 Col. 7 August	Bracelli (G.) *Lucubrationes de bello Hispaniensi* 'Venundantur cum gratia et priuilegio in triennium'	Paris, J. Badius 1520 4° BL 661.b.6
CP 1520, 13 Dedication 15 October	Mair (J.) *Summaria in dyalecticen introductiones*	Paris, J. Granjon 1520 fol. Maz. A.11717 Rés.
CP 1520, 14 Col. 1 November	Nebrissensis or Lebrija (A.) *In quinquaginta* *Sacrae Scripturae locos . . .*	Paris, R. Chaudière (pr. J. Du Pré) 1520 4° BN A.5320
CP 1520, 15 Col. 5 November	Duns Scotus (J.) *Commentaria in duodecim libros* *Metaphysice Aristotelis* ed. Antonius Andrea	Paris, J. Frellon (pr. P. Vidoue) 1520 fol. Bodl.AA.138 Art.
CP 1520, 16	Budé (G.) *De contemptu rerum fortuitarum* 'Cum gratia et priuilegio in triennium'	Paris, J. Badius s.d. 4° Bodl.c.2.10 Linc (6)
CP 1520, 17	Pighius (A.) *De aequinoctiorum solsticiorumque* *inuentione* 'Cum priuilegio in triennium'	Paris, C. Resch 1520 fol. BL c.54.f.22

CP 1520, 18   Clerée (J.) *Sermones quadragesimales*   Paris, F.
Regnault
1520 4°
Maz. 12427

Additional Badius editions of 1520

CP 1520, 19   Nicolaus ab Aquaevilla, *Sermones dominicales*   Paris, J. Badius
Col.   'Venundantur cum gratia & priuilegio nequis   and J. de
December   preter Iodoci Badii assensum triennio proximo   Marnef
1519   imprimat'   1520 4°
Dedication   BL 1230.a.33
13 January

CP 1520, 20   Odo [of Cheriton] *Flores sermonum*   Paris, J. Badius
Dedication   'Cum gratia & priuilegio nequis triennio proximo   1520 4°
13 January   nisi e re eiusdem Badii rursus imprimat'   Cambridge UL
G*.5.4¹(D)

CP 1520, 21   Plato *Timaeus* tr. Chalcidius, ed. A. Giustiniani   Paris, J. Badius
Col.   'Cum gratia & priuilegio in triennium proximum'   1520 fol.
27 June   Bodl.Byw.F.3.
11

CP 1520, 22   Philo Judaeus *Questiones super Genesim*   Paris, J. Badius
Col.   'Vaenundantur in aedibus Ascensianis cum gratia   1520 fol.
5 August   & priuilegio in triennium'   Bodl.
GG18(4)Art.
Seld.

CP 1521, 1   *Edit et mandement de Charles cinquiesme ... contre frere*   Paris, 'P.G.'
After 8 May   *Martin Luther*   (Pierre
1521   Gromors)
1521 4°
Ste Geneviève,
C 8° 548
inv.113.Rés.

CP 1521, 2   Appian *De bellis ciuilibus Romanorum* etc. Tr. P.   Paris, J. Petit
Col.   Candidus, ed. N. Beraldus   (pr. P. Vidoue)
September   1521 fol.
BM Bordeaux
D. 10013

CP 1521, Pref. 31 October	Clamenge (Nicolas) *Libri quinque ... De filio prodigo,* etc.	Paris, N. de La Barre 1521 4° BN D.3590
CP 1521, 4 Col. 24 December	Celaya (J. de) *Expositio in libros posteriorum Aristotelis*	Paris, H. Le Fèvre 1521 fol. Maz.3598A
CP 1521, 5	*Le livre du roi Modus ... sur la chasse* 'Cum priuilegio' on title. Privilege dated 10 October 1521, according to *Vente Lignerolles* (1894), I, 641 ('seul exemplaire comportant le privilège daté au f. a 4 v°' – Moreau, *Inventaire*, III, no. 185).	Paris J. Jehannot s.d. e° BN Vélins 1975
CP 1522, 1 Col. May	*La légende des Flamens, Artisiens et Haynuyers*	Paris, [F. Regnault] 1522 4° BL G.6222
CP 1522, 2	Augerius (Joannes) *Grammaticalium institutionum ... Liber* 'Cum priuilegio ad biennium', and mention, at the end of the book, of a privilege for two years, given in 1522, dated 19 August.	Paris, Pierre Gromors and Pierre Gaudoul 1522 4° Maz. Recueil Inc. 475. Rés.
CP 1522, 3 After 17 September 1522 when J. de Channey obtained Avignon privilege for the first edition of this book.	Riva di San Nazzaro (G. F.) *De peste* 'Cum priuilegio' after colophon.	Lyon, V. de Portonariis (pr. J. Sacon) 1522 4° BN Rés.F.823

CP 1522, 4	*Breuiarium Cartusiense*	Paris, T. Kerver 1522 16° II. Bohatta, *Bibliographie der Breviere 1501–1850* (Stuttgart, 1963), no. 547.
CP 1522, 5	Varignana (G. da) *Secreta sublimia ad varios curandos morbos*	Lyon, Jo. de Cambrey 1522 8° BN Rés. 4° Te¹⁷ 30 B
CP 1523, 1 Col. March	Chasseneuz (B. de) *Commentaria in consuetudines ducatus Burgundie. Secunda editio.*	Lyon, S. Vincent (pr. J. de Jonvelle) 1523 4° BL 5685 f.1.
CP 1523, 2 Col. 8 June	Lefèvre d'Etaples (J.) *Une epistre exhortatoire ... La saint evangile selon S. Matthieu...*	Paris, S. de Colines 1523 8° BN Rés.A 6414
CP 1523, 3	Galen *De temperamentis: De inaequali intemperie* tr. Thomas Linacre	Paris, S. de Colines 1523 fol. Bodl. Vet.E.I.C.5 [1]
CP 1524, 1 15 March	Foix (Jean de), archbishop of Bordeaux, *Constitutiones in suo sancto Synodo ... editae*	Bordeaux, J. Guyart 1524 4° BM Bordeaux J 4586 Rés. (coffre)
CP 1524, 2 Dedication 20 April	Pliny *Naturalis Historia* ed. H. Barbarus [with indices]	Paris, Pierre Gaudoul (pr. P. Vidoue) 1524 fol. 2 vols. BN Rés.S.427

CP 1524, 3 Col. 2 September	Fulvius (Andreas) *Illustrium imagines* 'Cum priuilegio' in circle on v° of fol. HH4 (at the end).	Lyon, J. Mousnier and F. Juste (pr. A. Blanchard) 1524 8° BL c.40.b.27
CP 1524, 4	Douglas (David) *De naturae mirabilibus opusculum*	Paris, Prigent Calvarin 1524 4° BL 538.e.27(1)
CP 1524, 5	Nevisanis (J. de) *Silua nuptialis*	Lyon, V. de Portonariis (pr. J. Moylin dit de Cambray) 1524 4° BN Rés.F.2222
CP 1525, 1 Col. 1 March	Gaius (Titus) *Institutionum Iuliique Pauli Sententiarum* ... *Opus* ed. A. Bouchardus	Paris, Conrad Resch (pr. P. Vidoue) 1525 4° Maz. 13887(2) Rés.
CP 1525, 2 Col. 12 March	*Guy de Warwich*	Paris, R. Regnault (pr. A. Couteau) 1525 fol. BL c.20.d.22
CP 1525, 3 Col. 8 April	*Missale insignis ecclesie Pictauensis*	Paris, J. Petit and E. de Marnef / Poitiers, Jacques Bouchet / Angers, J. Varice (pr. J. Kerbriant) 1525 fol. BM Poitiers BR 3

CP 1525, 4 Col. September	Pepin (G.) *Sermones quadraginta de destructione Niniue* 'Cum gratia et priuilegio in biennium'	Paris, C. Chevallon (pr. B. Rembolt) 1525 8° Ste Geneviève 8° D.5362 Inv.6392Rés.
CP 1525, 5 22 September	*Le traicté de la paix perpetuelle du roy* ... *avec Henry viii* 'Avec Privilege', and C P (Reproduction of title-page in Cat. Rothschild, vol. III, 2662, p. 463).	[Lyon], Claude Nourry s.d. 4° BN Rothschild IV.4.168
CP 1525, 6	Champier (Symphorien) *Les gestes de preulx chevalier Bayard*	Lyon, Gilbert de Villiers 1525 4° BN Rés. 4° L2²⁷ 1198c
CP 1525, 7	Cicero, *Pro lege Manilia* ed. J. Vatellus Cf. *CP* 1520, 7	Paris, P. Gaudoul 1525 4° BN Rés. pz 351
CP 1525, 8	Garcie dit Ferrande (Pierre) *Le grant routier et pilotage* ... Cf. CH 1520, 4 (privilege for 1st edition)	Rouen, J. Burges le Jeune 1525 4° BN Smith-Lesouëf, Rés. 198
CP 1526, 1 Col. 18 February 1525 (o.s.)	Chalcocondylas (D.) *Grammaticae institutiones graecae* ed. Melchior Wolmar	Paris, G. Gourmont 1526 4° BN Rés. px 459

SELECT BIBLIOGRAPHY

MANUSCRIPT SOURCES

Paris

Archives Nationales
  x 1 a 1504–29   Parlement Civil
  y 8   Châtelet

Bibliothèque Nationale: Réserve des Imprimés
  Philippe Renouard, *Imprimeurs parisiens*, 23 vols. (the volume on Galliot Du Pré is by
  Paul Delalain)

PRINTED SOURCES

Primary

1. Books printed in France 1498–1527 which contain a privilege or the summary or
   mention of a privilege.
   See above, *Register*, pp. 208–95.

2. Other
   Catalogue des Actes de Francois Ier, Académie des Sciences Morales, 10 vols.
   (1887–1908).
   Coyecque, Ernest. *Recueil des actes notariés relatifs à l'histoire de Paris et de ses environs au
   xvie siècle*, I (1905), II (1923).
   Erasmus, Desiderius. *Opus Epistolarum*, ed. P. S. and H. M. Allen and H. W. Garrod,
   11 vols. (Oxford, 1906–47).

Secondary

Note: Books and articles which are referred to only once in footnotes, and then to
establish one particular point, are not included in the bibliography. Full details of
date of publication etc. will be found in the relevant footnote.
  Books in English are published in London, and books in French in Paris, unless
otherwise stated.

Abelard, Jacques. *Les Illustrations de Gaule et singularitez de Troye. Etude des éditions. Genèse
de l'œuvre* (Geneva, 1976).

SELECTED BIBLIOGRAPHY

Aubert, F. 'Mandements et arrêts du Parlement en faveur de plusieurs libraires, imprimeurs et relieurs de Paris au xvie siècle', *Bulletin de la Sociéte de l'Histoire de Paris et de l'Ile-de-France* (1894), pp. 137–40.

Baudrier, H.-L. *Bibliographie lyonnaise*, 12 vols. (Lyon, 1895–1921)

Bernard, A. *Geofroy Tory, peintre et graveur, premier imprimeur réformateur de l'orthographe et de la typographie sous François 1er*, 2nd edn (1865).

British Library. *Short-title catalogue of books printed in France and of French books printed in other countries from 1470 to 1600 now in the British Museum.* [By H. Thomas.] (1924); *Supplement* (1986).

Claudin, A. *Histoire de l'imprimerie en France au xve et au xvie siècle*, 4 vols. (1900–14).

Les origines et les débuts de l'imprimerie à Bordeaux (Extrait de la *Revue catholique de Bordeaux*) (1897).

Origines et débuts de l'imprimerie à Poitiers (1897).

Davies, H. W. *Catalogue of a collection of early French books in the library of C. Fairfax Murray* (1910).

Doucet, R. *Les institutions de la France au xvie siècle*, 2 vols. (1948).

Dupont-Ferrier, G. see *Gallia Regia*.

Farge, J. K. *Biographical register of Paris doctors of theology 1500–1536*. Pontifical Institute of Medieval Studies: *Subsidia Mediaevalia* 10 (Toronto, 1980).

Fulin, R. 'Primi privilegi di stampa in Venezia', *Archivio Veneto*, I (1871), pp. 160–4.

'Documenti per servire alla storia della typografia veneziana', *Archivio Veneto*, XXIII (1882), pp. 84–212.

Gallia Regia, ou état des officiers royaux des bailliages et des sénéchaussées de 1328 à 1515, ed. G. Dupont-Ferrier, 6 vols. (1942–61).

Gouron, A. and Terrin, O. *Bibliographie des coutumes de France: éditions antérieures à la Révolution* (Geneva, 1975).

Haebler, K. *Bibliografía ibérica del siglo xv* (The Hague/Leipzig, 1903).

Hauser, H. *Les sources de l'histoire de France: xvie siècle*, 2 vols. (1906–9).

Hoffmann, G. D. *Von denen ältesten Kayserlichen und Landesherrlichen Bücher- Druck- und Verlagprivilegien* (s.l., 1777).

Horawitz, A. *Analecten zur Geschichte des Humanismus in Schwaben 1512–1518*, Sitzungsberichte der phil.-hist. Classe der kais. Akademie der Wissenschaften, LXXXVI, May 1877 (Vienna, 1877).

Knecht, R. J. *Francis I* (Cambridge, 1982).

Kolb, A. *Bibliographie des französischen Buches im 16. Jahrhundert: Druck. Illustration. Einband. Papiergeschichte*, Beiträge zum Buch- und Bibliothekswesen, 14 (Wiesbaden, 1966).

Labarre. A. 'Editions et privilèges des héritiers d'André Wechel à Francfort et à Hanau 1582–1627', *Gutenberg-Jahrbuch*, 1970, pp. 238–250.

La Bouralière, A. de *Les débuts de l'imprimerie à Poitiers 1479–1515*, 2nd edn (1893).

L'imprimerie et la librairie à Poitiers pendant le xvie siècle (1900).

Lepreux, G. *Gallia typographica ou Répertoire biographique et chronologique de tous les imprimeurs de France depuis les origines de l'imprimerie jusqu'à la Révolution*, 9 vols (1911–13).

Macfarlane, J. *Antoine Vérard*, Bibliographical Society Illustrated Monographs n°. VII (1900).

297

Michaud, Hélène. *La grande chancellerie et les écritures royales au xvie siècle. (1515–1589)*, Collection Mémoires et Documents publiés par la Société de l'Ecole des Chartes, 17 (1967).

Maugis, E. *Histoire du Parlement de Paris*, 3 vols. (1913–16).

Moreau, Brigitte. *Inventaire chronologique des éditions parisiennes du xvie siècle*, Histoire générale de Paris, I, 1501–10 (1972); II, 1511–20 (1977); III, 1521–30 (1985).

Motta, E. 'Di Filippo di Lavagna e di alcuni altri tipografi-editori Milanesi del quattrocento', *Archivio storico Lombardo*, series 3, x (1898), pp. 28–72.

Nielsen, L. *Dansk Bibliografi 1482–1550* (Copenhagen, 1919).

Nijhoff, W. and Kronenberg, M. E. *Nederlandsche Bibliographie van 1500 tot 1540*, 2 vols. (The Hague, 1923–42).

Norton, F. J. *Italian printers 1501–1520*, Cambridge Bibliographical Society (1958).

Oulmont, C. *La poésie morale, politique et dramatique à la veille de la Renaissance: Pierre Gringore* (1911).

Parent, Annie. *Les métiers du livre à Paris au xvie siècle (1535–1560)* Centre de Recherches d'Histoire et de Philologie de la IVe Section de l'Ecole pratique des Hautes Etudes, vi, Histoire et civilisation du livre, 6 (Geneva, 1974).

Pasquier, E. and Dauphin, V. *Imprimeurs et libraires de l'Anjou* (Angers, 1932).

Peixoto, Jorge. 'Os privilégios de impressão dos livros em Portugal no século XVI', *Gutenberg-Jahrbuch* (1966), pp. 265–72.

Pelissier, L. G. *Les sources milanaises de l'histoire de Louis XII: Trois registres de lettres ducales de Louis XII aux Archives de Milan*, Extrait du *Bulletin d'Histoire et de Philologie* (1892).

Ptaśnik, Joannes (ed.) *Monumenta poloniae typographica XV et XVI saeculorum. I, Cracovia impressorum XV et XVI saeculorum* (Leopoli [Lvov], 1922).

Renaudet, A. *Préréforme et humanisme à Paris pendant les premières guerres d'Italie (1494–1517)*, Bibliothèque de l'Institut de Florence: Université de Grenoble, Ire Série, vi (1916).

Renouard, Ph. *Bibliographie des éditions de Simon de Colines 1520–1546, avec une notice biographique* (1894).

Bibliographie des impressions et des oeuvres de Josse Badius Ascensius, imprimeur et humaniste 1462–1535, 3 vols. (1908).

Répertoire des imprimeurs parisiens, libraires, fondeurs de caractères et correcteurs d'imprimerie, depuis l'introduction de l'imprimerie à Paris (1470) jusqu'à la fin du seizième siècle, ed. J. Veyrin-Forrer and B. Moreau (1965).

Imprimeurs et libraires parisiens du xvie siècle, ouvrage publié d'après les manuscrits de Philippe Renouard par le Service des Travaux historiques de la Ville de Paris avec le concours de la Bibliothèque Nationale; Histoire générale de Paris: I, ABADA–AVRIL (1964); II, BAALEU–BANVILLE (1969); III, BAQUELIER–BILLON (1979); Fascicule BREYER (1982); Fascicule BRUMEN (1984); Fascicule CAVELLAT & MARNEF et CAVELLAT (1986); IV, BINET–BLUMENSTOCK (1986)

Répertoire bibliographique des livres imprimés en France au seizième siècle [by Louis Desgraves and others] Bibliotheca Bibliographica Aureliana (Baden-Baden, 1968–).

Rice, E. F. *The prefatory epistles of Jacques Lefèvre d'Etaples and related texts* (New York/London, 1972).

Schottenloher, K. 'Die Druckprivilegien des sechzehnten Jahrhunderts', *Gutenberg-Jahrbuch* (1933), pp. 89–111.

Seguin. J. P. *L'information en France de Louis XII à Henri II*, Travaux d'Humanisme et Renaissance, 44 (Geneva, 1961).

Terrasse, Ch. *François Ier, le roi et le règne*, vol. I (1945); vol. II (1948).

Tschemerzine, A. *Bibliographie d'éditions originales ou rares des auteurs français des xve, xvie, xviie et xviiie siècles*, 10 vols. (1927-33).

Van Praet, J. B. B. *Catalogue des livres imprimés sur vélin de la bibliothèque du roi*, 6 vols. (1822–8).

Verheyden, P. 'Drukkersoctrooien in de 16e eeuw', *Tijdschrift voor Boek- en Bibliotheekswesen*, VIII (1910), pp. 203–26.

INDEX OF PUBLISHERS,
PRINTERS AND BOOKSELLERS

GENERAL INDEX

Proper names and main subjects not mentioned in the list of contents, and titles of anonymous works. Mentions of Paris are omitted except for particular localities and institutions.

ordonnances, 35, 42, 45, 47, 48, 55, 173, 174, 233, 240, 245, 246, 247, 250, 253, 256, 259, 261, 279
Ordre (L') du sacre et couronnement du roy Francoys premier, 271
Origen, 133, 134, 168–9, 212
Orleans (Loiret), 25, 29, 101, 160, 172, 188, 192
  Bailli of, 67
  Coutume of, 42, 74, 91, 173, 242
  Ordinationes synodales of, 57, 74, 200–1, 265
Orleans, Charles, duke of (father of Louis XII), 182–3
Ortiz de Villegas, Diogo, bishop of Ceuta, 8
Otto, bishop of Freising, 14
Ovid, *Remedia amoris* in French translation, 185, 239
Oxford, 10, 59

Pace, Richard, 224
Padua, university of, 6
Palude, *see* Petrus de Palude
Papa, Guy, 31, 176, 219
Parent, *greffier* in the Parlement, 243, 244
Paris
  Châtelet, 48, 69
  diocese of, 106
  Coutume of, 43, 74, 173, 247
  Palais (lawcourts), 33, 49
  Pont Notre Dame, 141
  Prévôt des Marchands of, 107
  sign of the *Sabot*, 37; of *Mère Sotte*, 141
  Tour Saint-Jacques, 48
Paris
  University of, 13, 58, 59, 60, 100, 105, 107, 119, 172, 180, 195
  Colleges: Dainville, 168; Montaigu, 58, 181; Narbonne, 188; Navarre, 110, 168; Saint Bernard, 107; Sorbonne, 145
  Faculty of Canon Law, 172, 174
  Faculty of Medicine, 35, 189
  Faculty of Theology, 39, 58, 59, 60, 100–1, 103, 104, 110, 111, 116, 117, 122, 169, 171, 180, 181, 234
Parrhasius, Janus, 6, 24, 118
Passiranus, Joannes, 5
Pathelin, Farce of, Latin translation of, 93, 138, 187, 246
Patrizzi (Patricius) Francesco, 88, 136, 163, 177, 226
Paul, saint, 38, 167, 170, 209
Pavia, 4, 11
  battle of, 33
Pavinis, Joannes Franciscus de, 200, 246
Pedersen, Christiern, 203
Pallegrino, Francesco di (Pellegrin), 205

Pepin, Guillaume, OP, Paris Doctor of Theology, 88, 138, 139, 168, 231, 239, 256, 295
Pérault (Peraldus), Guillaume, 38, 241
Perfection (La) des filles religieuses avec la vie et miracles de ma dame saincte Clare, 167, 240
Perier, clerk in the Parlement of Bordeaux, 267
Perron (Perroneus), Claude, 122, 155, 190, 258
Persius, 279
Persona, Cristoforo, 168, 169
Peter of Blois, 135, 170, 177, 218
Peter the Venerable, Abbot of Cluny, 170, 278
Petit (Parvy) Guillaume, OP, Paris Doctor of Theology, bishop of Troyes, then of Senlis, 64, 102, 168, 169, 177, 227
Petrarch, 122, 185, 200, 249, 265
Petrus de Palude, 180, 253
Petrus de Perusio, 250
Petrus Lombardus, bishop of Paris, 180
Petrus, Cristiernus, cleric of Lund, 10
Petrutia, Antonius de, 30, 68, 152, 211
Philip Augustus, king of France, 178
Philip IV, king of France, 44
Philip the Fair, son of Maximilian I, king of Spain, 109
Philo Judaeus, 291
Picardy, 31
Pichon, Nicolas, *greffier civil* of the Parlement, 243, 244, 246, 247, 250, 251, 252, 254
Pighius, Albertus, 190, 290
Pirckheimer, Willibald, 15
Pisa, Council of, 58
Pius, Joannes Baptista, 5
Platina, *see* Sacchi
Plato, 182, 291
Plautus, 5
Pliny the Elder, 285, 293
Plutarch, 94, 130, 185, 187, 214, 216, 275
Poitiers (Vienne), 31, 36, 43, 57, 67, 120, 194
  Grands Jours of, 43
  missal of, 55, 166, 294
Poitou
  Coutume of, 91, 173, 222
  Sénéchal of, 67
Polo, Marco, Portuguese translation of, 7
Polydore Vergilius, *see* Vergilius
Ponceau, Jacques (Dr), *premier médicin* of Charles VIII, 7, 209
Poncher, Etienne, bishop of Paris, later archbishop of Sens, 64, 76, 109–10, 188, 224
Poncher, François (nephew of Etienne), bishop of Paris, 109–10, 188

Traité (Le) de paix (Treaty of Amiens, 1527), 282
Tributiis, Pierre de, 263
Trolle, Gustav, archbishop of Uppsala, 10 n. 2
Troycs (Aube), 35, 197
  Coutume of, 173, 196–7, 252
Tunstall, Cuthbert, bishop of London, later of Durham, 10, 11
Turre, Bertrand de, 168, 259
types, privileges for, 2, 205

Ulvsson, Jacobus, archbishop of Uppsala, 10
Ung petit Traicté...Une petite Echelle pour faire bonne confession, see Echelle
Uppsala, 10
Urne, Lage, bishop of Roskilde, 10

Valence (Drôme), 30, 68
Valerius Maximus, 76, 178, 210, 280
Valle, Robert de, 280
Varignana, Gulielmus de, 293
Varnbüler, Ulrich, councillor of Maximilian I, protonotary in the Reichskammergericht, 15
Varro, 5
Vatablus, François, royal professor of Hebrew, 97, 181, 255
Vatel, Jean (Jo. Vatellus), 187, 188, 259, 288, 289, 295
Vaucheron, *greffier* of the *Grands Jours* of Berry, 43
Veignolles, or Vignolles, Jean de, royal secretary and notary in the Parlement, 219, 258, 260, 263, 265
Vendôme, Charles, duke of, 94
Venice, 2, 3, 6, 11, 12, 16, 60, 93, 97, 118, 137, 170, 178
  ambassadors of, 29
Vercellanus, G., 94 n. 2
Vergil, 85, 185, 225, 239, 272
Vergilius, Polydore, 93, 150, 178, 277
Vespucci, Amerigo, 190, 220
Victon, royal secretary, 237

Vidal du Four (Vitalis), Joannes, 96, 215
Vie (La) et les miracles de Saint Eusice, 52, 115, 167, 272
Vie (La) monseigneur Sainct Germain, 167
Vienna, 14
Vienne (Isère), breviary of 55
Vigevano, 5
Vignier (Vignerius), Jean, O.P., 46, 277
Vigo, Joannes de, 189, 200, 235, 289
Villandry, Jean Breton, seigneur de, royal *conseiller* and secretary, *secrétaire des finances*, 77
Villa Sancta, Alfonso, Franciscan friar, 163, 224, 254
Villers-Cotterêts (Aisne), Edict of, 81, 194
Vinzalius, Joannes, 5
Vio, Thomas de, *Cajetanus*, 12, 13, 58, 270
Violier des histoires rommaines moralisées, 89, 178, 200, 230
Virgilius, Marcellus, 12 n. 7
Vitalis, *see* Vidal
Vitry-en-Partois (Vitry-le-François, Marne), *Coutume* of, 74, 173, 251
Volcyr de Sérouville, Nicolas, 20, 83, 117, 189, 234, 281
Voyage (Le) de la saincte cité de Jérusalem, 190, 273
Vray, Jean de, 256

Waim or Wain, Gervase, Paris Doctor of Theology, 88, 146, 158, 181, 225
Warham, William, archbishop of Canterbury, 10
Wels, (Tyrol), 2 n. 1, 18
Westminster, 10
Wolmar, Melchior, 188, 295
Woodham (Godhamus), Adam, 132, 180, 211
Wroclaw, 8
Würzburg, diocese of, 3

Ysaie le Triste, 89, 186, 278

Zelen, Henricus, official of the diocese of Cologne, 58